Non dilexerunt animam suam usque ad mortem.
The Latin, *Non dilexerunt animam suam usque ad mortem*,
translates, "... they loved not their lives unto the death." Revelation 12:11

On The Cover: *Massacres at Salzburg* took place in 1528 when
Prince-Archbishop Cardinal Matthaus Lang of Salzburg issued
mandates sending police in search of Anabaptists. Many were
captured and killed. This engraving illustrates the sufferings and
sacrifices these Dissenters endured when their government, in
conjunction with established religion, attempted to coerce and
impose uniformity of religious belief. Hence, this picture is a
reminder of the cost of religious liberty and the ever-present need
to maintain the separation of church and state. We use this art to
represent our Dissent and Nonconformity Series.

LUTHERAN REFORMERS AGAINST ANABAPTISTS

"They [the Anabaptists] teach that a Christian should not use a sword, should not serve as a magistrate, should not swear or hold property ... These articles are seditious and holders of them may be punished with a sword ... If it be objected that the magistrate should not compel anyone to the faith the answer is that he punishes no one for his opinions in his heart, but only on account of the outward word and teaching ... What now would happen if children were not baptized, if not that our whole society would become openly heathen? It is a serious matter to cast children out of Christendom and to have two sets of people, the one baptized and the other unbaptized, because then the Anabaptists have some dreadful articles, we judge that in this case also the obstinate are to be put to death."

Martin Luther; Philip Melanchthon; John Brenz;
Luther's Works Weimar Edition. Vol. 50, Page 12.

———————

"From the point of view of freedom of thought, the Lutheran Reformation may easily be weighed in the balance and found wanting. It is to be regretted that its spirit was inclined to be so exclusively dogmatic ... so little inspired by a tolerant charity. It may indeed be described as a crusade in favor of liberty, but only as that age understood liberty. This, it may be said, was in natural order of things. Luther and his fellow-reformers, who only saw with the light of the sixteenth century, could not be expected to see with that of the twentieth. True, but we should all the more guard against applying the word 'liberty' to the Lutheran Reformation as if it meant what we today understand by it. This is a mistake into which many Protestant writers, who confuse the principle with the practice of the Reformation, have fallen."

Dr. James Mackinnon
A History of Modern Liberty (London: Longmans, Green & Co., 1906)
Vol. 2, Page 130.

LUTHERAN REFORMERS AGAINST ANABAPTISTS

LUTHER, MELANCHTHON
AND MENIUS AND THE ANABAPTISTS
OF CENTRAL GERMANY

by

JOHN S. OYER
Goshen College, Indiana

The Hague
Martinus Nijhoff
1964

The Baptist Standard Bearer, Inc.

NUMBER ONE IRON OAKS DRIVE • PARIS, ARKANSAS 72855

Thou hast given a *standard* to them that fear thee;
that it may be displayed because of the truth.
-- *Psalm 60:4*

Reprinted
by

THE BAPTIST STANDARD BEARER, INC.
No. 1 Iron Oaks Drive
Paris, Arkansas 72855
(501) 963-3831

THE WALDENSIAN EMBLEM
lux lucet in tenebris
"The Light Shineth in the Darkness"

ISBN #1-57978-833-5

ACKNOWLEDGEMENTS

This book was first written as a doctoral dissertation and submitted to the History Department of the University of Chicago in 1959. The sections on Anabaptism in Central Germany were published in the *Mennonite Quarterly Review*, Vols. XXXIV (October, 1960) and XXXV (January, 1961). I wish to thank the editors of the *MQR* for permission to reprint those chapters. I have altered the chapters on Anabaptism principally by the inclusion of more material on Rink, material based on several of his writings to which I did not have access when I first wrote the dissertation in 1959. I have made minor alterations at other places.

I owe my deepest thanks to each of the following persons: the late Dean Harold S. Bender of the Goshen College Biblical Seminary for his suggestion of the topic and his frequent helpful comments; Professor Wilhelm Pauck, earlier of the University of Chicago and now of Union Theological Seminary, for his initial encouragement and advice; Professors Jaroslav Pelikan and Donald Lach, both of the University of Chicago during my student days, for undertaking to guide the dissertation and for their numerous suggestions for its improvement; Professors Heinrich Bornkamm and Walter Peter Fuchs, both of Heidelberg University, for many critical comments given to one who was not their own *cand. phil.*; Nelson Springer, curator of the Mennonite Historical Library at Goshen College, for bibliographical advice of the highest order; Frl. Fehringer, Secretary of the *Historisches Seminar* at Heidelberg University, for help in locating a place in the *Kandidatenzimmer;* Mrs. Carol Oyer for frequent help in the tedious work of correcting copy, proofreading, and indexing; Professor John H. Yoder of the Goshen College Biblical Seminary for his helpful comments on the material of chapters II and III. To all of these mentors and friends I acknowledge my indebtedness. If they have given of themselves to make this book more meaningful and accurate, the obscurities and errors remaining are still my own.

TABLE OF CONTENTS

LIST OF ABBREVIATIONS

ARG   *Archiv für Reformationsgeschichte.*

CR   *Corpus Reformatorum*

DeWette   *Dr. Martin Luther's Briefe, Sendschreiben, und Bedenken.* Edited by Wilhelm M. de Wette. 6 vols. Berlin, 1825–56.

EA   *Dr. Martin Luther's sämmtliche Werke.* 67 vols. Erlangen, 1826 ff.

ME   *Mennonite Encyclopedia.* 4 vols.

ML   *Mennonitisches Lexikon.* 3 vols.

MQR   *Mennonite Quarterly Review.*

TA, Hesse   *Urkundliche Quellen zur hessischen Reformationsgeschichte,* Vol. IV. Edited by G. Franz, *et al.* Marburg, 1951.

WA   *D. Martin Luther's Werke. Kritische Gesamtausgabe.* Edited by Knaake, Kawerau, *et al.* 57 vols. Weimar, 1883–1914.

WB   *D. Martin Luther's Briefwechsel, D. Martin Luther's Werke, kritische Gesamtausgabe.* Edited by Konrad Burdach, *et al.* 11 vols. Weimar, 1930 ff.

WT   *Tischreden, D. Martin Luther's Werke, kritische Gesamtausgabe.* Edited by Karl Drescher. 6 vols. Weimar, 1912 ff.

r.   *recto.*

v.   *verso.*
      In the absence of pagination in the sixteenth century brochures, I have used the signatures with the added identification r. or v. for *recto* or *verso.*

LUTHERAN REFORMERS AGAINST ANABAPTISTS

INTRODUCTION

Until well into the nineteenth century scholars have repeated a traditional view of Anabaptism when they turn to Reformation history.
They have regarded the Zwickau Prophets and Thomas Müntzer as the
instigators of the movement. The radical disturbance caused by the
Prophets and Müntzer in Wittenberg and the Saxon lands spread to
Switzerland, there to plague Zwingli and his following. In both regions
a radical spiritualism was the dominating element of the movement.
Anabaptism reached its peak of development in the forceful establishment of the Kingdom of Münster. Most historians have devoted the
major part of their discourse on Anabaptism to this model of fanaticism. After the rebellion was suppressed a rather pious but nonetheless
harsh converted priest named Menno Simons collected the dispersed
elements and attempted to direct them into more peaceful channels.
Other leaders, like David Joris, continued the radical spiritualism if
not the civil disorder. In this picture of the movement historians have
insisted on regarding more highly the similarities rather than the
differences in religious ideas of men such as Müntzer, Storch, Carlstadt,
Grebel, Manz, Sattler, Denk, Marpeck, Matthys, Jan van Leyden, Joris,
and Menno Simons. Even a cursory perusal of the writings of the
Reformers -- particularly those of Luther, Melanchthon, Menius, and
Bullinger -- reveals the identity of this traditional picture with that of
the sixteenth-century polemicists.

Of the traditionalist view two examples may be cited here. Among
the Swiss Reformed Johann Jakob Hottinger,[1] and from the Lutherans,
Johann Kurtz [2] stand out as perpetrators of the Reformers' views, both

[1] *Historia der Reformation in der Eidgenosschafft...* (Zurich: Bodmerischen Truckerey,
1708), especially pp. 218 ff, 384 ff, 497 ff.
[2] *Lehrbuch der Kirchengeschichte für Studierende* (9th ed.; Leipzig: August Neumann, 1885),
III, 42–57; 148–156 (in the 1885 edition). Among the older church historians Gottfried Arnold
wrote a sympathetic account undoubtedly because of his pietist inclinations. *Gottfried*

in content and in hostility. Hottinger appealed to the authority of the
Zurich reformers for those of his readers who might be dissatisfied with
his own denunciation of Anabaptist poison. Kurtz, whose manual
became the standard text in church history for several generations of
students in Germany, styled the Anabaptist movement the "Defor-
mation" in contrast to the theologically correct Reformation.

Some of the more recent students of the movement have tended to
abandon the hostility, though generally not the insistence on measuring
Anabaptism by the standard of Lutheran or Reformed orthodoxy.
Karl Holl [1] and Heinrich Boehmer [2] reaffirmed the continuity from
Müntzer to the later Anabaptists, all of whom were spiritualists. Both
men did an impressive amount of scholarly research on the figure of
Müntzer and wrote creative, stimulating interpretations of him. Their
remarks on Anabaptism in its relation to Müntzer must be considered
as speculative because neither did any research on the movement itself.
But their remarks, however insubstantial, were taken as authoritative
pronouncements by the scholarly world.[3] Fritz Heyer [4] later attempted
to supply the documentation, from Anabaptist sources, for the spiritualist part of the assessment. But Heyer, whose work is strongly
apologetic in character, is unconvincing precisely at the crucial point:
the distinction between Anabaptist and *unparteiisch* Spiritualist views
on the church.[5] A full generation of scholars, with Holl, Boehmer, and
Heyer, have not seriously questioned the Anabaptist origin in the
person and work of Müntzer, and its essential spiritualist character.
These elements of the old picture remain, though much of the hostility
has vanished and in most instances an earnest desire to be fair and
accurate has appeared.[6]

Arnolds unpartheyische Kirchen und Ketzer-Historie (Schaffhausen: Emanuel und Benedict
Hurter, 1742). This was first published in 1699.
    [1] *Gesammelte Aufsätze zur Kirchengeschichte* (Tübingen: Paul Siebeck, 1923), I, chapter vii,
"Luther und die Schwärmer," especially pp. 422–24, 437, 447–50, 457–59.
    [2] "Thomas Müntzer und das jüngste Deutschland," *Gesammelte Aufsätze* (Gotha: Perthes,
1927), especially pp. 221–22.
    [3] See the exchange between Eberlein and Wiswedel on this point: *Mühlhäuser Geschichts-
blätter*, XXVII (1926–27), 210–13; *ibid.*, XXX (1929–30), 268–73. Against Wiswedel's protest
to Holl's interpretation Eberlein pitted the authority of Holl: whoever heard of Wiswedel
anyway? The stature of Holl as an interpreter of Luther is undeniably very great indeed. But
in this instance Wiswedel had read the Anabaptists and Holl had not.
    [4] *Der Kirchenbegriff der Schwärmer*, "Schriften des Vereins für Reformationsgeschichte,"
Nr. 166 (Leipzig: Heinsius Nachfolger, 1939).
    [5] *Ibid.*, pp. 33–49.
    [6] For example Reinhold Seeberg, *Lehrbuch der Dogmengeschichte* (2d ed.; Erlangen:
Deichert, 1917–1920), IV, 28; Karl Heussi, *Kompendium der Kirchengeschichte* (10th ed.;
Tübingen: Siebeck, 1949), pp. 333–35; H. H. Bagger, "Anabaptists – Extinction or Extension
of the Reformation," *Lutheran Quarterly*, IV (1952), 243–60.

The appearance of published Anabaptist source materials in recent decades has radically altered the necessity for relying on the polemics for information on Anabaptism. Those scholars who have taken advantage of Anabaptist sources have been willing to question most of the elements in the traditional picture.[1] The twin questions of Anabaptist origins, especially in relation to Müntzer, and spiritualism in Anabaptism are up for reassessment.[2] Most of the recent writers are open to the idea, in sharp contrast to the traditional picture deriving from the Reformers, that the Anabaptists may appear quite different when they are allowed to speak for themselves. But there still remains the opportunity to write a wild account and find acceptance for it in some quarters of the academic world.[3]

As a contribution to the reassessment of the nature and place of the Radical Reformation, this study will make a fresh examination of the writings against the Anabaptists by the Lutheran Reformers, and of the Anabaptist movement itself in Central Germany. An attempt will be made to fix more precisely the nature of Anabaptism as the Lutherans saw it. Their picture will be evaluated in the light of the study of the movement in the geographical region where they knew it best. Finally an attempt will be made to ascertain the essential conflict in religious ideas between Lutherans and Anabaptists, based on the accusations of both parties. The study will consider the writings of Luther, Melanchthon, and Menius. Rhegius could have been added in order to cover the major Lutheran writers on the topic. But Rhegius knew a different Anabaptism, that of Denk and the South Germans. There were similarities, of course, between his Anabaptism and that

---

[1] See Walther Peter Fuchs, "Die Täufer," *Gebhardts Handbuch der deutschen Geschichte*, ed. Herbert Grundmann (8th ed.; Stuttgart: Union, 1955), II, 75–78 for a German view. See also Franklin Littell, *The Anabaptist View of the Church* (Berne, Ind.: Amer. Soc. of Church History, 1952; 2d revised ed.; Boston: Star King Press, 1958).

[2] For spiritualism see the exchange between Meihuizen and Friedmann: H. W. Meihuizen, "Spiritualistic Tendencies and Movements among the Dutch Mennonites of the Sixteenth and Seventeenth Centuries," *MQR*, XXVII (1953), 259–304; Robert Friedmann, "A Critical Discussion of Meihuizen's Study of 'Spiritual Trends,'" *MQR*, XXVIII (1954), 148–54. For the question of origins and the relation to Müntzer see the articles of Bender and Friedmann, and the responses: Harold S. Bender, "The Zwickau Prophets, Thomas Müntzer, and the Anabaptists," *MQR*, XXVII (1953), 3–16; Robert Friedmann, "Thomas Müntzer's Relation to Anabaptism," *MQR*, XXXI (1957), 75–87; Grete Mecenseffy, "Die Herkunft des oberösterreichischen Täufertums," *ARG*, XLVII (1956), 252–59.

[3] For example the Erlangen dissertation of Friedrich Rödel, "Die anarchischen Tendenzen bei den Wiedertäufern des Reformationszeitalters" (MS, 1950). Rödel sets for himself the task of ascertaining Anabaptist attitudes toward government, but he accepts as Anabaptists only those who have radical and violent attitudes toward government. Those that might profess peaceful intentions are hypocritical. He visualizes Anabaptists as people with a message that is overwhelmingly political; he cannot see their religious motivation.

of the Saxon trio. Nevertheless his exclusion permits a more unified treatment of the Anabaptism in question, and consequently of the evaluation of the Lutherans' view of the movement.

It should be immediately evident that in this study the Reformers do not appear always in a favorable light. They were unremittingly hostile. The topic of Anabaptism aroused them to the heights of passion, as it did most of the religious figures of the sixteenth century. There is anger and scorn on the Anabaptist side against the Reformers, too; but their wrath is not as evident because the records with few exceptions show them on the defensive. There will be no balanced picture of the Reformers in this book. Its purpose is not biographical. It must be remembered that the Luther who spoke on rebaptism, or on punishment of the Anabaptists, is the Luther who could also write the Treatise on Christian Liberty or the delightful fantasy on Paradise to his four-year old son, Hans. Melanchthon, who was unreservedly harsh with the Anabaptists, could be irenic to the Catholics at Augsburg or to the Swiss and Strassburgers at Kassel.[1]

No attempt will be made in this study to assess the relative importance of the Anabaptist movement to each of the three Lutherans. But a general comment on each would be in order. Luther was too preoccupied with other things to give due consideration to the radicals. He said as much in 1528.[2] The fact that he wrote only one major pamphlet against them is another indication of the same. But the problem disturbed him immensely. He expressed himself in some manner or other on Anabaptism in at least fifty letters or sermons or table conversations that happened to be recorded and preserved. Melanchthon devoted more time to analysis, refutation, and publication against the group. One suspects that this relatively greater concern derived from his practical experience as a church visitor in Saxon lands where he encountered radicals of various sorts who brought conflicts into the church. For Menius the struggle with Anabaptism was a major task. Of the three he was the most deeply involved in the cure of souls. His geographical location brought him into frequent contact with the results of Anabaptist evangelism. Combatting the radicals

---

[1] Biographers of Luther generally give ample coverage to Luther's irascibility and expressions of wrath. The same is not true for those who write on Melanchthon. Clyde Manschreck's *Melanchthon, The Quiet Reformer* (New York: Abingdon Press, 1958) is a splendid piece of scholarly research and creative writing; but it lacks precisely that balance in Melanchthon's character that a fuller treatment of his relations with some of the radicals could well give.

[2] Martin Luther, *Von der Widertauffe an zwen Pfarherrn, ein Brief* (Wittenberg: Georg Wachter, 1528); printed in *WA*, XXVI, 173.

was a major necessity in the life of the Lutheran pastor and superintendent who worked in the Eisenach region of Thuringia.

At the outset it is necessary to make clear what the term "Anabaptist" will mean in this study. It was never a very useful word because of its lack of precision. In former centuries, especially the sixteenth, it was a term of contempt, coined probably to bring certain persons under the punishment prescribed in the Justinian Code for those who were baptized a second time. The term has lost most of the hostility previously attached to it, but it has not gained in precision. It was used in the sixteenth century for a motley array of radicals or left-wingers. Here it will mean any one who practices or advocates adult or believers' baptism. The definition is still too broad in that it includes types of religious belief that are almost too diverse to provide grounds for a common discussion of them. In a discussion of Lutheran attitudes toward the Anabaptists it becomes necessary to use the term approximately as they used it. Luther, Melanchthon, and Menius each used the word in a still broader sense. But they clearly singled out baptism as the most significant issue to discuss when they broached the subject of Anabaptism.

The study must begin with an account of the *Schwärmer* – the Zwickau Prophets, Carlstadt, and Müntzer – because this is where the Lutherans began. In order to develop and analyze the Lutheran concept of Anabaptism, it is necessary to see it in Central Germany against the background of their previous encounters with the radicals.

CHAPTER I

THE *SCHWÄRMER*, LUTHER, AND MELANCHTHON

Luther's preaching and reforming activities produced the greatest excitement in Central Germany. In their wake appeared a number of radical movements, both unwanted and unexpected by the Reformer himself. He was forced to take issue with the extremists in order to guide the Reformation into more conservative channels. The examination of these unruly elements, called the *Schwärmer* by Luther, must begin with the Prophets of Zwickau. They were the first to trouble the peaceful progress of reform in Wittenberg. We will begin with their development in Zwickau itself.

Zwickau, located near the southern extremity of the Electoral Saxon lands, was a town of economic stature at the turn of the sixteenth century. It possessed a flourishing commerce, particularly in grain, as well as a thriving industry in cloth manufacture. During the 1470's silver mines in the near-by Schneeberg were opened; these proved to be very rich in the early years of production. But the wealth of the town was confined principally to a few of the burghers. The large flow of silver tended to raise prices more rapidly than wages with consequent economic suffering for the wage earners in the weaving industry. Even the masters were affected. The disparity in economic means between the rich, who were invariably associated with the mines, and the poor widened to the point where Zwickau in the early sixteenth century was a city ripe for revolt.[1]

Economic dissatisfaction among the lower classes worked against a background of late Medieval heresy, which also tended to alienate the social classes from each other. The Waldensians were strong in the Zwickau region after 1390. Their cohorts were raised largely from the handworker class, especially from the weavers. The records of the

---

[1] Paul Wappler, *Thomas Müntzer in Zwickau und die "Zwickauer Propheten"* (Zwickau: Zückler, 1908), pp. 1-5.

second half of the fifteenth century show evidence of Taborite, Beghard and Lollard [1] influences in the region also. The wealthy influential burghers tended to support the church against heresies entrenched in the lower classes.[2]

The ideas of Luther were brought to Zwickau in 1518, preached first by the Franciscan monk, Friedrich Myconius. In this instance an attack on the church won adherents among the leading burghers; the mayor, Hermann Mühlpfort, himself gave warm support to the new teaching. Luther even dedicated his 1520 "The Liberty of a Christian Man" to Mühlpfort.[3] It was upon Luther's recommendation at the Leipzig Debate that the pastor of St. Mary's Church, Egranus, invited Thomas Müntzer, who had embraced Luther's teaching, to serve as his substitute beginning in May, 1520.[4]

Müntzer was a man of unusual gifts, especially in the elocutionary arts. He was exceptionally well-versed in Scripture. He combined ability with an aggressive and ambitious nature, enough to cause difficulty wherever he went. He immediately aroused a storm of protest in Zwickau because he injudiciously accused the Franciscans of avarice. The embarrassed town council reluctantly supported him. But the vigor of his speech eventually drove many of the wealthier burghers to oppose him. When Egranus returned from his vacation in October, 1520, Müntzer was moved to St. Catherine's Church. The rejected Müntzer felt embittered, and turned increasingly to consort with the lower classes where he won a strong following. Here among the weavers and other handlaborers he met Nicholas Storch and began a relationship which was fruitful for both.[5]

Storch was the descendant of an erstwhile patriarchal family in Zwickau, one engaged in the weaving industry. In the second half of the fifteenth century the family's economic and political fortunes were eclipsed by the inflationary spiral. Storch early turned to a serious exercise of religion. His mastery of the Bible overwhelmed even Müntzer. But he brought what are called Bohemian Nicholite ideas to his interpretation of the Scriptures with the result that he advocated

---

[1] The Taborites were the extreme party of the Hussites. They wanted no compromise with the Catholic Church. The Beghards were a lay-monastic group who held goods in common and practiced works of charity. The Lollards were the followers of Wycliff who exercised a significant influence on the later Hussites of Bohemia.

[2] Wappler, *op. cit.*, p. 6.

[3] James Mackinnon, *Luther and the Reformation* (4 vols.; London: Longmans, Green, and Co., 1930), II, 264.

[4] Wappler, *op. cit.*, p. 7.

[5] *Ibid.*, pp. 7-11.

a reliance for ultimate Truth, not only on Scripture, but also on special revelations from God. This idea was by no means anathema to Müntzer, who had read and appreciated Tauler's distinction between the Inner and the Outer Word. Müntzer began to say that one learns more from the Inner Word, by which he meant revelations in dreams, visions, and ecstatic experiences, than from the Scripture which becomes a dead letter without the life of the Spirit's interpretation. Müntzer began to draw away from his former admiration for Luther.[1]

Both men believed in a conventicle Christianity. Though Müntzer was a pastor in the town, he tended to rely more on worship services and Bible study in homes than on his harangues from the pulpit. To Storch, a layman, the pulpit was closed anyway. One suspects that Müntzer relied on a kind of gathered church because he was accepted by certain of the lower class laborers but was rejected by the propertied upper class burghers. The gathered church concept did not otherwise fit into the pattern of his religious development. Despite the ostensible – and often real – leadership of Müntzer, gossip at least attributed the conventicles to the layman Storch, for they were called *Sekta Storchi- tarum*. It is clear that the small group meeting in private houses was the best medium for Storch to communicate his ideas. His influence was very great, both on the other laymen and also on Müntzer.[2]

Criticism of Müntzer increased after he began to associate with the laymen. Hotheaded by temperament, Müntzer replied with bitter public denunciations of even his milder critics. The town divided into two factions and occasionally violence flared. The council could never come to terms with the conflict because it was divided; at least two members were warm supporters of the Storch-Müntzer faction, while the Burgermeister was a firm advocate of the Lutheran faction led by Egranus. The situation was further exacerbated by the hostility of the Catholics, led by the Franciscans, to both major factions. The council finally compromised by asking Müntzer on April 16, 1521, to take a leave of absence. He refused. But he fled the next night in fear for his life. For his supporters, without his prior knowledge or advice, rioted and threatened to kill all those who were in any way responsible for the request that he leave.[3]

The departure of Müntzer from the Zwickau scene did nothing to relieve tension. Accusations continued; nasty cartoons appeared. There

---

[1] *Ibid.*, p. 12.
[2] *Ibid.*, pp. 11, 13.
[3] *Ibid.*, p. 17.

was more rioting. Duke John, brother of the Elector, became alarmed at the situation. By December the stalemated council finally determined to act. The leaders of the radical party were summoned to appear on the 16th and 17th of December for examination by the council and the pastors of the city. Storch himself refused to come, and left the city in company with Thomas Drechsel and Marcus Thomas Stübner. Their destination was the center of the Reformation movement, Wittenberg itself. The council received a rather full catalogue of Storch's teachings from other leaders who did appear. Two refused to change their views on the grounds that Storch was more godly than any of the examining pastors, who were incapable therefore of proving Storch to be heretical. These two were imprisoned until early in January, after which they were exiled. Two other leaders, Caspar Teucher and his wife who was a prophetess for the group, were not punished because Teucher was the master builder for the renovation of St. Mary's Church. The remaining leaders were threatened with a citation to appear before Duke John. But the threat was never carried out; the council was still too divided to act. Despite the lack of disciplinary action, the council and pastors felt it necessary to apply to Duke John for a guard to protect them against vengeance from the radicals. No violence developed. Indeed, with its principal leader and inspiration in flight, the movement tended to subside. It did not completely disappear in Zwickau; it went underground. As for Storch himself, after his Wittenberg fiasco he wandered about in Central Germany and even tried to return to Zwickau. In 1525 the council refused him permission to return. In 1536 he was certainly in the town again, but his further whereabouts are uncertain. It is even possible that he was executed in Zwickau in mid-1536 with another radical.[1]

What did the Storch party teach and believe that aroused so much enthusiasm among some and antagonism among others? It will not be necessary here to examine the teaching of Müntzer and his effect upon the group since his ideas will be treated elsewhere. Rather, Storch's ideas will be examined here, since the fundamental doctrines of the "Zwickau Prophets" came primarily from him.

The idea in Storch's thought that overshadowed all others was his conviction that God spoke directly to men, certainly not through the medium of the church but also not through Scriptures. He probably first entertained the idea as a Nicholite in his youthful Bohemian

[1] *Ibid.*, pp. 23–24, 40–43.

sojourn. He believed that God revealed his will to him through dreams and visions. He claimed to have held familiar conversations not only with angels but also with God himself. Such conversations and dreams enabled him to predict future events: large, world-shaking occurrences such as the imminent destruction of Christian Europe by the Turks as well as smaller, less significant matters such as the content of a man's thought at a given moment. Storch's subjectivity led to a vision of a new church of which he was to be the leader, designated for the task by Gabriel himself. Luther had not gone far enough in his reformation of the church. He, Storch, would complete the task, and lead men to a newer, higher righteousness. He gathered around him his new elect, whom he claimed to be able to detect by spiritual intuition. He laid down to his followers a three-fold rule of behavior, obedience to which could assure them of election in his new church. They were to speak little, clothe themselves meanly, and demand the Holy Spirit from God with invective. His followers claimed visions, voices, and the like, but they did not normally attain the distinction as conversationalist with divinity that Storch did.[1]

Storch's reliance on revelations led him to reject Scripture as a divine power in itself. He called it a dead letter. One learned of God through the Spirit directly, which could teach through illuminating Scripture, but which could teach directly.[2] It is probably fair to say that Storch relied, in his mature years, more on the direct communication from the Spirit than on its illumination of Scripture. But it remains a curious fact that his mastery of the Scripture was phenomenal, which would suggest considerable reliance on it. Storch opposed his source of authority especially to what he considered Luther's reliance on a literalistic interpretation of Scripture. If God had wanted to use the Bible as the major medium for teaching us of himself, he would have sent us one directly from heaven.[3]

A third consequence of Storch's spiritualism was his rejection of outward ceremonies as media of grace. First and foremost he rejected the rite of infant baptism. The reasons for the selection of baptism rather than, say, the Lord's Supper, are not altogether clear. Wappler hints that he got the idea from Müntzer.[4] It might be argued that, since

[1] *Ibid., passim.*
[2] Letter of Nikolaus Hausmann, pastor at Zwickau, to the Duke, December 18, 1521, in Theodore Kolde, "Ältester Bericht über die Zwickauer Propheten," *Zeitschrift für Kirchengeschichte*, V (1881–82), 323–25.
[3] Wappler, *op. cit.*, pp. 12, 20, 39.
[4] *Ibid.*, p. 20.

he suggested the formation of a new church, he singled out infant baptism for attack because it was the means by which the individual entered the church, Roman or Lutheran. Logically he therefore should have instituted adult or believers' baptism as a sign of admission into his new church. One document from 1597 suggests that he did advocate adult baptism.[1] It is obvious that he did not advocate it with much force during his encounters with the Zwickauers and with the Wittenbergers, else their rather full reports would have mentioned it. It is likely that he did not advocate it at all.

In point of fact Storch rejected infant baptism in the first instance because he did not believe that the *fides aliena* could in any way substitute for an absence of faith in the infant. He interpreted Mark 16:16 to mean that baptism may be performed only after faith is engendered. Infants are incapable of faith. Therefore do not baptize infants. A logical consequence of Storch's spiritualism would have been the complete rejection of baptism. Nikolaus Hausmann, a Luther follower and pastor at Zwickau, reported that the Storch party denied the efficacy of the act, not only for infants.[2] Wagner's description of Storch's view on baptism includes his rejection of it because the act itself carried no grace. Water remained water, no matter how much blessed. If poured over a child it had no different effect than if it was poured over a dog.[3] Such a view again appears to be a logical outgrowth of Storch's spiritualist approach.

It appears that Storch also denied the doctrine of original sin. Infants were incapable of believing. Baptizing them in no way saved them; indeed, it did nothing at all, spiritually, for them. Therefore it followed that in God's economy infants had no sin. Storch added that the infant's destination, if it should die, would be determined by the spiritual life of its father. If the father was pious, the infant would be saved. A pious father always procreated a pious child.[4]

---

[1] *Ibid.*, p. 30, who uses Marcus Wagner's *Einfeltiger Bericht wie durch Nicolaum Storcken die Auffruhr in Thüringen vnd vmbligenden Revir angefangen sey worden, etc.* (Erfurt, 1597). Wagner obtained his information, according to his own testimony, from Johann Chiomusus (Schneesing), pastor at Friemar. Wagner claimed that Chiomusus disputed with Storch and knew him quite well. Wappler believes that Wagner took some liberty in interpreting the oral and written reports of Chiomusus. Wappler, *op. cit.*, p. 36. Wagner's formal presentation of Storch's doctrine included matters not mentioned in other documents – for example polygamy and free will. It is obvious that Wagner was a hostile critic whose account must be used with caution. He considered Storch to be the founder of Anabaptism, the accepted Lutheran view by his time.

[2] Letter to the Duke, December 18, 1521, *Zeitschrift für Kirchengeschichte*, V, 323–25.

[3] Wappler, *op. cit.*, p. 38, quoting Wagner.

[4] *Ibid.*

Storch the spiritualist and the rejector of infant baptism was also radical when he dealt with the social-political order. He customarily approached strangers to his message with strong attacks on the existing rulers, civil and spiritual. It was his habit to move quietly and humbly among the simple people in a town or village, dressed in a long gray robe and a broadbrim hat, denouncing the authorities for their unethical behavior, their voluptuous living, and their pride. He pronounced woe upon them and predicted their imminent destruction at the hand of the Turks who were God's emissaries for the task. He denounced the seigneurs for cruelty toward their serfs. Such lords treated their hounds better than their serfs. Aldermen in the towns were no better. He preached that all worldly possessions should be held in common. These were very effective words to people long oppressed by servile conditions and penury.[1]

There is some reason to believe that Storch eventually urged the use of violence to overthrow the constituted civil and spiritual authorities. Marcus Wagner reported that he instructed his followers to prepare to kill magistrates, priests, and lords, and to plunder their mansions.[2] It is not likely that Storch was urging revolution of this sort in Zwickau and Wittenberg in 1521 and 1522, else the reports would have indicated such information and the degree of alarm would have been much greater. It is entirely possible that he urged revolution before and during the Peasants' Revolt. This is difficult to confirm or deny because Storch drops from the records for the most part after 1522.

Storch preached strange doctrine concerning the marriage bond. Early in his career he advocated caution in the selection of a spouse. One should carefully ascertain the piety of the prospective mate, since the children procreated would invariably reflect that piety or lack of it. God alone would reveal to one whom he ought to marry.[3] Later he tended to take a liberal view in regard to the dissolubility of the marriage bond. Husband and wife were not, in his opinion, bound together for life. Moreover one could add spouses as often as he wanted to, as often as passion drove him to it. Storch was accused of being an adulterer.[4]

Fearing the consequences of the council-sponsored hearing, Storch fled Zwickau and headed toward Wittenberg with his two companions.

[1] *Ibid.*, pp. 28, 30, 38.
[2] Wagner in Wappler, *op. cit.*, pp. 37–38.
[3] *Ibid.*, p. 19.
[4] *Ibid.*, p. 36.

Little is known of Drechsel, other than that he was an unlettered weaver. Stübner,[1] on the other hand, was a student who had been quite impressed with Luther's teachings. He had studied for a time at Wittenberg, which he left after a dispute with Melanchthon.[2] Stübner met Müntzer in Thuringia, and later Storch in Zwickau. He was much impressed with them, particularly with the latter. He accompanied Müntzer on preaching trips to Bohemia where they met with no success. He returned to Zwickau and absorbed more of Storch's influence. He was reported to have had an excellent command of Scripture, one which surpassed even that of Melanchthon. These three "Prophets," then, arrived in Wittenberg on December 27, 1521, under the conviction that they were chosen of God to bear the true gospel to the center of the Reformation.[3]

Some in Wittenberg heard them gladly. Storch moved quietly among the laborers of the town, and in the surrounding countryside. Stübner talked to the university students and professors. Melanchthon offered him living quarters with himself, and Stübner used the status such a dwelling gave him to advantage among the students. After a short stay in Wittenberg, Storch and Drechsel quitted the town, leaving Stübner behind to carry on his work with the learned. His most important convert was Martin Cellarius, a scholar whom Melanchthon had brought to Wittenberg to help prepare students for the university.[4] He made a great impact on Melanchthon and Amsdorf also. Melanchthon was at first overwhelmed by the spiritual pretensions of the Prophets, their claim to spiritual authority. Gradually he came to see their visions as ridiculous and sometimes self-contradictory. The deepest impression he received was from their challenge to infant baptism. On this point he was sorely troubled and felt himself unable to withstand the Prophets without the intervention of Luther.

Amsdorf also was awe-struck by the spiritual claims of the Prophets. He did not care to dispute with them because he felt himself less proficient than they in the use of the Scriptures. He shared with Melanchthon the apprehension that the Elector might use force in dealing with the Prophets.[5] The Elector was less inclined to view the

---

[1] Stübner was a nickname. The man's real name was simply Marcus Thomae. He was called Stübner because his father managed a *Bathstube* in Elsterberg.

[2] Alluded to in Melanchthon's letter to the Elector, January 1, 1522, *CR*, I, 533-34.

[3] Wappler, *op. cit.*, p. 25.

[4] *Ibid.*, pp. 28-29.

[5] Amsdorf's report to Einsiedeln, *CR*, I, 534-35. Luther also cautioned the Elector, through Spalatin, against the use of force. Letter to Spalatin, January 17, 1522, *WB*, II, 444.

Prophets' dreams favorably, though he was struck with horror at the thought of acting against God.[1] He was reasonably certain that the Prophets were not of God, for he knew well the disturbances they had caused in Zwickau. Melanchthon and Amsdorf had advised that a hearing be conducted, in which the Prophets' teaching might be thoroughly examined. Frederick opposed this suggestion on the grounds that it would settle nothing and rather provoke more disputations. One senses a note of sarcasm when he reminded Melanchthon and Amsdorf that St. Augustine had long ago settled the baptism issue, and since the Augustinian Order controlled education at the University of Wittenberg, Augustine's word should be the final one. Surely the Prophets did not know more about baptism than Augustine did! As for the use of force, he denied any intention of trying to punish the Prophets; indeed, he seemed to resent Melanchthon's and Amsdorf's insinuation that he might consider it.[2]

Melanchthon reported his impressions of the Prophets to Luther in the Wartburg.[3] Luther was not nearly as excited about them as Melanchthon was. He chided Melanchthon for his irresolution, which he felt was inexcusable in view of Melanchthon's erudition. Apparently in response to a request, he gave Melanchthon advice on how to ascertain the calling of the Prophets. Luther strongly suspected that their master was Satan rather than God. He also provided Melanchthon with arguments on the question of infant baptism.[4]

Luther was obviously disturbed by the course of events in Wittenberg. He felt a strong sense of responsibility for he had begun the reform there. The activities of the Prophets together with those of Carlstadt and Zwilling caused him much alarm, especially when he learned that Carlstadt was paying heed to Stübner. He did not expect a combining of forces here, because he believed that Carlstadt could not accept the full teaching of the Prophets. But the situation was getting out of hand. He therefore made his decision early in March to leave the Wartburg and return to the leadership of the reform movement in Wittenberg. He did

---

[1] Wappler, *op. cit.*, p. 27, quoting Frederick from *Georg Spalatin's Historische Nachlass und Briefe*, eds. Neudecker and Preller (Jena, 1851), I, 30.

[2] *CR*, I, 535–38.

[3] I can find no copy of such a report. It is obvious from Luther's letter of January 13, 1522 to Melanchthon that he was writing in response to some communication about the Prophets from Melanchthon. In 1911 Müller declared that the letter was not extant. Nikolaus Müller, *Die Wittenberger Bewegung, 1521 und 1522* (Leipzig: Heinsius Nachfolger, 1911), p. 135, n. 7.

[4] Letter to Melanchthon, January 13, 1522, *WB*, II, 424–28. Translated and printed in part in Preserved Smith and Charles Jacobs, *Luther's Correspondence and Other Contemporary Letters* (Philadelphia: Lutheran Publication Society, 1918), II, 84–86.

so against the wishes and counsel of the Elector who was somewhat embarrassed that the outlaw of Worms should return to the Electoral seat. Frederick requested that Luther provide him with a statement of his reasons for returning which he could show to the princes, probably to prove that he, Frederick, had not wanted him to come. Frederick also requested that Luther exercise self-restraint.[1]

During the course of the next seven months Luther had occasion to meet all three of the Prophets. First and foremost, Stübner. By the end of March at the especial urging of Melanchthon, Luther had designated a day and hour for meeting Stübner. Luther anticipated no good results from such a meeting and therefore did not want one. Stübner opened with an explanation of the soul's progress from sin through dissatisfaction with sin and anger with self to a desire for God's righteousness and finally to the direct righteousness of God – a mysticism which Stübner imbibed from Müntzer who got it from the late Medieval mystics. Luther wanted to know how one could ascertain which stage he was in. Stübner replied that he revealed such information only to students with aptitude or talent. Luther's talent lay in the first stage of mobility, but he was about to enter the first stage of immobility, where Stübner himself was, so Stübner informed him. Luther considered Stübner's ideas impertinent and foolish and called upon him to abandon them. His refusal to accept Stübner's claim of miracle-working powers provoked Stübner to the further claim of ability to read a man's mind. Luther asked him to reveal what he was thinking. "You are considering that my teaching is true," Stübner replied. Luther was so startled he dismissed Stübner abruptly. For he had momentarily entertained precisely that thought. After a later exchange of letters, Stübner, who sensed defeat, took his leave not only of Luther but also of the town.[2]

Later Luther met Drechsel. Drechsel treated Luther to a sample of fanciful visions with equally fantastic interpretation. Luther handled him curtly and told him to cease his frivolity with the name of God. Drechsel angrily predicted the destruction of Wittenberg within six weeks.[3]

Finally in September of 1522 Luther met Storch himself. The conversation, quiet and orderly, concerned only the baptism of infants. Storch

[1] See Elector Frederick to Jerome Schurff, March 7, 1522, Smith and Jacobs, *op. cit.*, II, 96–97, and Luther to Elector Frederick, March 12, 1522, *ibid.*, 98–101.
[2] Wappler, *op. cit.*, p. 33, and Preserved Smith, *The Life and Letters of Martin Luther* (Boston: Houghton Mifflin Co., 1911), p. 150, who quotes from Bindseil, *D. Martini Lutheri Colloquia* (Lemgo and Detmold, 1863–66), II, 21.
[3] Wappler, *op. cit.*, p. 35.

laughingly scorned the spiritual efficacy of a handful of water, nor would he pay heed to Luther's insistence that the water was indeed powerless unless accompanied by the Word. Again the results of this encounter were meager. Luther did not meet the Prophets again, nor did he wish to. He considered their Spirit to be satanic, and he wished to be rid of it.[1]

The activities and teachings of Thomas Müntzer formed the second decisive element in Luther's *Schwärmer* concept. Müntzer, schooled at the Universities of Leipzig and Frankfurt, appeared on the Reformation scene at Leipzig in 1519 at the time of the Luther-Eck debate. Luther apparently was sufficiently impressed with him to recommend him to Egranus, pastor at Zwickau. Kolde suggests that it was Luther who pointed him to the *Theologia Deutsch*, and possibly to other mystics such as Tauler. He appears to have embraced the Reformation with enthusiasm, but also in his own individualistic fashion. Müntzer was a restless individual, firm to the point of complete stubbornness in his opinions, gifted as a speaker, well-versed in Scripture. He tended to be violent in his speeches. He was therefore frequently asked to move on to other places.[2]

During his ministry in Zwickau he tried to build a community of his elect, who distinguished themselves by their spiritualism. Conflict with Catholics and then with Egranus forced him to leave in April, 1521. He turned to Bohemia, particularly Prague, in an attempt to build his spiritual communities and there met with indifferent success. Many were inclined to accept his ideas but were alienated by his wild invective against the clergy. He enjoyed no settled existence until Easter of 1523 when the council of Allstedt accepted him as preacher at St. John's Church. It seems likely that he met Luther in December, 1522. The two could not come to terms, principally because of Müntzer's stubborn attitude.[3]

His first act of importance in the imperial city of Allstedt was the reformation of the church service, particularly of the mass. He rendered it into German, and introduced a much larger amount of singing. The work revealed his artistic taste and originality. It was a highly constructive piece of work for a man usually regarded by historians as

---

[1] *Ibid.*

[2] Most of the factual detail in the following account of Müntzer comes from Theodore Kolde, "Thomas Müntzer," *The New Schaff-Herzog Encyclopedia of Religious Knowledge* (Grand Rapids, Mich.: Baker Book House, 1956), VIII, 47–50.

[3] Wappler, *op. cit.*, p. 35.

essentially destructive.[1] But his activity was still held in disfavor by many because of the Wittenberg opposition to Müntzer. Luther disapproved of his spiritualism and of his strongly polemical attitude. Count Ernst of Mansfeld prohibited attendance at Müntzer's services. Müntzer responded with an appeal addressed to the Elector for a trial. The Elector, though he had not approved of Müntzer's activities at Zwickau, hesitated actually to challenge Müntzer with an ecclesiastical trial, so Müntzer won his point. Müntzer promised the Elector he would desist from violent attacks from the pulpit.

Allstedt was the place of origin for several of Müntzer's theological works. It was here also that he developed his ideas of social reform to the point of advocating revolution. He did incite a burst of iconoclasm in the spring of 1524, though he denied any part in it for a time. Mobs descended upon a chapel containing a miracle-working picture of the Virgin Mary, located at near-by Mallerbach, and burned and looted the shrine. Subsequent action against a member of the council who approved of Müntzer brought forth violent tirades against the princes from Müntzer.

Still the princes of Saxony did not move to stop him. Frederick only urged him to cease his iconoclastic activity else he would incur Frederick's displeasure. Müntzer openly prepared his followers for the use of force against the godless by organizing them into a *Bund*. Finally, on July 13, 1524, Duke John and his son, John Frederick, journeyed to Allstedt to hear Müntzer preach. Müntzer had constantly urged the princes to give heed to his message. For this occasion he chose to preach from Daniel 2. He laid before the princes his interpretation of historical epochs derived from the figure of Daniel's vision. Müntzer believed himself to be the chosen leader for a fifth epoch, after Christ the stone smashed the image. Christ had been unable to establish the Kingdom of the fifth epoch because the princes retarded him. Now was the time for the clear emergence of the epoch, with Müntzer as leader. Müntzer appealed to the princes to join with him in the realization of the Kingdom of Christ. But he also threatened them: if the princes would not join they must accept the consequences. The entire appeal was addressed with that boundless assurance that he, Müntzer, was the

---

[1] See Carl Hinrichs, *Luther und Müntzer* (Berlin: de Gruyter, 1952), pp. 5–10. An otherwise excellent piece of research and interpretation is marred slightly by an overemphasis upon Müntzer's rivalry with Luther. The fact of the rivalry is undeniable. But Hinrichs goes too far when he tends to suggest that the principal, and indeed sole, motivation for Müntzer's constructive work was the intense desire to wrest leadership of the Reformation from Luther and carry it himself.

chosen messenger of God. As such it must have been in part convincing. We cannot ascertain the attitude of the princes upon hearing it. They undoubtedly did not approve of it, for they did not place their power at Müntzer's disposal for the purpose of ushering in the Kingdom as Müntzer had suggested. On the other hand they raised no objection to the printing of the sermon.[1]

The sermon brought from Luther his "Letter to the Princes of Saxony against the Revolutionary Spirit" near the end of the month. He warned Elector Frederick and Duke John that the spirit of Allstedt intended to enforce his will, not only with the Word, but also with the sword. When religious fanaticism turned to the use of physical force to support it, the matter was no longer religious only but more essentially political. The princes must act to curb rebellion; to do otherwise would be unchristian. God demanded a reckoning from that prince who used his sword carelessly. For his part Luther was convinced the spirit which drove Müntzer was satanic.[2]

The upshot of the Allstedt disturbances was that Müntzer finally fled early in August to settle in Mühlhausen. Here he met Heinrich Pfeiffer, a native Evangelical preacher with gifts of eloquence and violence. The two supplemented each other in stirring the mobs to action against the church order and the aristocratic town council. They agitated for the deposition of the council, but failed to win enough support. Both left the town and Müntzer wandered for a time in southern Germany. Both returned to Mühlhausen by early 1525, where they once more embarked upon a revolutionary course. They drilled men as soldiers and preached a social revolution. Gradually, in the spring of 1525, the peasants around Mühlhausen, in Thuringia and the Harz region, were drawn into open revolt. On May 15 occurred the bloody battle of Frankenhausen in which the peasants were dispersed and slaughtered by the princes. Müntzer had incited them to attack by assuring them that the appearance of a rainbow was a sign from God that the victory would be theirs. Müntzer was captured the following day, tried, and executed.[3]

The central pivot of Müntzer's religious thought was his mysticism-

---

[1] *Ibid.*, pp. 57–65. The sermon has been translated into English and newly published in George H. Williams and Anton Mergal, *Spiritual and Anabaptist Writers*, Vol. XXV of *The Library of Christian Classics*, eds. J. Baillie, J. T. McNeill, and H. van Dusen (Philadelphia: Westminster Press, 1957), pp. 49–70.

[2] Letter translated and printed in Smith and Jacobs, *Correspondence*, II, 241–47.

[3] See letters Nrs. 88 and 89, May 12, 1525, H. Bœhmer and P. Kirn, *Thomas Müntzers Briefwechsel* (Berlin: Teubner, 1931), pp. 122–24 for examples of Müntzer's boldness with the princes before the battle. He commanded them to cease their tyranny else they would experience the wrath of God. He signed his letters "T. M. with the sword of Gideon."

spiritualism. He believed that all men, as beings created by God, had within them the kernel of faith which the Spirit from without sought to enliven and to make grow. This immanent religion was in no way dependent upon Scripture for its life and growth. It existed in men long before Scripture was written – prior to the patriarchs – and it existed in Müntzer's day in even the infidel Turks. The Spirit came from without to awaken the kernel of faith, which otherwise would sleep on undisturbed. But the manner of the Spirit's visitation was radically different from Luther's concept of a once-and-for-all justification. Müntzer called Luther's Christ the sweet Christ, because he believed faith in Luther's Christ required no personal suffering. His own bitter Christ, on the other hand, took him through degrees of spiritual experience that were extremely painful. One was made aware of his sins, was amazed at his thoughts of sin and grace, studied to become better, and finally reached *Gelassenheit:* that degree of self-denial and resignation whereby man was made ready for godly things. But Christ further required a *Nachfolge.* Müntzer's *Nachfolge Christi* was a turning from all created things to contemplate and experience the suffering of Christ on the cross.

Müntzer was cynical and scornful of Luther's justification by faith, for it was absolutely contingent on an understanding of the Bible. And the Bible could be properly interpreted only by the theologians, who were in turn hand in glove with the civil authorities. A racket if there ever was one! The civil authorities were determined to so influence the interpretation of the Scripture that the masses of the people would not be enabled themselves to understand its social implications. Müntzer believed in a radical amelioration of the misery of the lower classes, and he believed Christianity, rightly interpreted, meant a complete equality of all men. The ways of God and his Spirit were freer and more direct. They could come to anyone; though he spoke of his followers as the elect, he did not use the term in a deterministic, predestinarian sense, for he believed firmly in freedom of the will in contrast to Luther. Scripture to the mystic-spiritualist Müntzer was a dead letter unless the Spirit breathed life into it. The Spirit could breathe into man without his reading the Scripture at all.[1]

Müntzer was enough of a spiritualist to prize visions and dreams. Perhaps he followed Storch at this point. It appears that he relied little on such manifestations of God's will before he met Storch in Zwickau. He believed that God revealed himself through dreams and faces of the

---

[1] Hinrichs, *op. cit., passim*, especially pp. 94–95; Neff and Hege, "Thomas Müntzer," *ML*, III, 188.

elect especially in the end-times (Joel 2:27–32). Müntzer went out among the simple people to read their faces and listen to their dreams. The results were spectacular enough to convince him he lived in the end-times.[1]

It is difficult to tell whether it was religious or social ideas that were uppermost in driving Müntzer to embrace a theory of revolution. He possessed a strong dislike of the misery and poverty of the lower classes. He held the princes and lords to be ultimately responsible for thievery, since their excess was an inducement and temptation to the poor peasants. If the lower classes wrested control from the lords and distributed their wealth, the lords had only themselves to blame. There was a strong social note in Müntzer's appeals. But the goal of revolution was not only to free the lower classes and to relieve their economic distress; it was also, and perhaps even primarily, to give the lower classes a chance to realize that they were the dwelling place of God and should give evidence of this by their manner of living. For Müntzer the church of the elect and the state eventually would become coterminous.

Müntzer's church was a group of persons chosen by the Spirit. It was classless and propertyless. Its prototype was the early church. One suspects that the *Bund* which was organized at Allstedt in June, 1524, was the realization of his concept of the church. It is difficult to learn many details of the *Bund* with accuracy, since there is little source material on it. It appears very likely that within the *Bund* there was to be community of goods, an idea based on the practice of the early church. There was equality within it; if the princes would join – and Müntzer hoped and expected the Saxon princes to join as a result of his July 13 sermon – they would enter as equals and be allowed only slightly greater privileges. Anyone could enter the *Bund*, since God sent his Spirit freely to awaken faith in those who wanted it. But the *Bund* was also exclusive in the sense that anyone not in it was not of the elect. Moreover God willed that such persons were to be extirpated. The time was at hand when the elect should take the sword and kill the rulers who opposed them and thereby usher in the fifth epoch, the Kingdom of Christ.

Müntzer used Romans 13 to justify revolution. He obviously could not rely on verses 1 and 2, in which Paul enjoined all believers to obey their rulers. He used verses 3 and 4:

---

[1] Hinrichs, *op. cit.*, pp. 54–56.

For rulers are not a terror to good conduct, but to bad. Would you have no fear of him who is in authority? Then do what is good, and you will receive his approval, for he is God's servant for your good. But if you do wrong, be afraid, for he does not bear the sword in vain; he is the servant of God to execute his wrath on the wrongdoer.

Müntzer interpreted Paul's words to mean that civil authority to legitimately wield the sword must be godly. A godly government would protect the righteous. If the government was not godly, then the elect must overthrow it and wield political authority righteously themselves. By such interpretation Müntzer posited the elect, his elect of course, as the bearers of God's sovereignty. Hence he made a bold plea to the Saxon princes to join his group and help direct the revolution from Saxony throughout all of Germany.[1]

A mystic-spiritualist like Müntzer could not be expected to honor outward ceremonies as media of grace. He not only rejected them, but he did so with a vigor that turned him into an iconoclast. Veneration of Mary, or of relics, was grossest superstition. He believed the Lord's Supper should be celebrated and received only in a spiritual sense. But he continued to consecrate and administer the sacrament.[2] He early opposed infant baptism as unscriptural. Neither the Virgin Mary nor Christ was baptized as an infant. He considered much of the error in the Catholic Church to have developed from a misunderstanding of baptism. Infant baptism served as a means of admission to the church. Müntzer of course believed that it was the presence of the Spirit in the individual which made him a member of the true body of the elect. Müntzer used the Fourth Gospel's words on baptism to show that, in his opinion, the motive power in the act of baptism was the Spirit. He seemed to believe the Spirit could move a person without baptism.[3] He placed little reliance on the ceremony itself; yet he continued to administer it to infants throughout his preaching ministry.[4]

The activities and teachings of Andreas Bodenstein von Carlstadt formed the third basic element in Luther's *Schwärmerei*. Carlstadt was schooled at Erfurt, Cologne, and Wittenberg in scholasticism.[5] He was

---

[1] *Ibid., passim*, in chapter i.

[2] Boehmer and Kirn, *Briefwechsel*, p. 161, for Müntzer's confession at his trial, May 16, 1525.

[3] See his *Protestation* printed in Otto Brandt, *Thomas Müntzer, sein Leben und seine Schriften* (Jena: Diederichs, 1933), pp. 134–35.

[4] See below, p. 107, n. 7.

[5] Much of the factual information on Carlstadt is taken from H. Barge, "Carlstadt," *The New Schaff-Herzog Encyclopedia of Religious Knowledge*, II (New York: Funk and Wagnalls, 1908), 413–16. Barge is not an unbiased observer. In attempting to counteract the hostile view of Carlstadt perpetrated by generations of Luther admirers, he tends to attribute too

an enthusiastic supporter of absolute Thomist authority in theological matters until some years after his visit to Rome in 1515. There he was shocked by the worldliness of the papacy. In Wittenberg he encountered and eventually accepted Luther's rejection of the Schoolmen.[1] As archdeacon at the Collegiate Church, which required that he preach once a week and lecture at the university, he began to uphold the Bible as the prime and absolute source of authority. He also began to deny the ability of the human will unaided to attain favor with God. Augustine taught him to attribute redemption of the soul to divine grace exclusively. Unquestionably Luther's influence here was decisive.

Carlstadt participated in the 1519 Leipzig Debate with Eck. Indeed, the debate was set up originally with Carlstadt, rather than Luther, as principal protagonist among the Wittenbergers. He was no match for the dialectical skills of his opponent, though his arguments were not without substance and effect.[2] In 1521 he journeyed to Denmark at the request of King Christian II. He worked for a time on ecclesiastical laws, but was forced to leave by the opposition of nobles and clergy. Back in Wittenberg he gradually moved to a position of advocating radical changes in religious practice. He attacked clerical celibacy; indeed, all seculars must be married. He attacked monasticism, and urged votives to leave the cloistered life. He finally denounced certain aspects of the mass: private masses in general, withholding of the cup from the laity, the adoration of the Host, and the exclusive use of the Latin language in the recitation of the mass. On Christmas Day, 1521, he administered the mass in both kinds, eliminated the elevation of the Host and that portion of the ceremony which suggested the mass was a sacrifice, and recited part of it in German. The congregation was electrified. Carlstadt was driven to this action both by his convictions and also by the demands of some of the people. There can be no doubt that he was motivated in part by a desire to exercise leadership in the Wittenberg reform movement during Luther's absence at the Wartburg. A spirit of rivalry permeated his relations with Luther; they were never warm friends. But it is incorrect to visualize Carlstadt as the originator of changes in the mass and other practices for the sole purpose of grasping leadership and discomfitting Luther. In the pre-

much to Carlstadt's originality and too little to the influence of Luther. See the dispute with Karl Müller, in Müller, *Luther und Karlstadt* (Tübingen: J. C. B. Mohr, 1907), and Barge, *Frühprotestantisches Gemeindechristentum* (Leipzig: M. Heinsius Nachfolger, 1909).

[1] H. Barge, *Andreas Bodenstein von Karlstadt* (2 vols.; Leipzig: Brandstetter, 1905), I, 70–72.

[2] Ernest Schwiebert, *Luther and His Times* (St. Louis: Concordia, 1950), pp. 396–97.

ceding October Carlstadt had declared himself more conservatively than Melanchthon in respect to the Augustinians' refusal to celebrate the mass. At that time he decided that the celebration of the mass could be changed only by the civil authorities.

Carlstadt continued with innovations in the next several months. He wished auricular confession abolished. In January he married. He joined with Gabriel Zwilling, a former Augustinian monk, to attack the use of images in the churches. But the disturbances which followed in his wake, coupled with those from the Zwickau Prophets, turned Wittenberg into a stormy center indeed. Luther therefore left his Wartburg refuge and returned to Wittenberg early in March, 1522.[1] In a series of remarkable sermons Luther won the populace to his more conservative position. The cup was withheld from the laity, and the Host was elevated again. Carlstadt remained as a professor in the university but his influence had melted. He had not had the wisdom to anticipate the extent of the tumult his innovations would arouse.[2] The explosive situation called for a conservative approach to change, in order, as Luther put it, to show forbearance to the weak.

By 1524 Carlstadt was preaching at Orlamünde, having left Wittenberg to assume the pastoral responsibility in that parish from which he had formerly received a stipend.[3] He had earlier developed views about the lay character of the ministry. He dressed in a simple long gray cloak, and worked as a peasant. Now he returned to the problem of the

[1] Luther intended to return to Wittenberg anyway by Easter of 1522. For his projected translation of the Old Testament he wanted help from the Hebrew scholars among his Wittenberg colleagues. The disturbances provided the occasion; the town council issued the invitation; Luther accepted. Roland Bainton, *Here I Stand* (Nashville: Abingdon Press, 1950), pp. 210–11.

[2] It is only fair to note that Luther also did not anticipate the amount of disorder the changes would provoke. On his secretive return to Wittenberg early in December, 1521, he reported himself pleased with the changes that had been made up to that point (some marriage of priests, cup to the laity, non-celebration of private masses in some places). He warmly supported the marriage of priests, and his theses concerning monastic vows were the most important influence in emptying the cloisters in Wittenberg. He objected to private masses, and considered it Scriptural to give the cup to the laity. When rioting accompanied these changes, Luther wanted an abrupt return to the traditional church practices to ensure public order. Clearly in his mind change would have to be introduced slowly, with the utmost caution. See *ibid.*, pp. 198–204.

[3] Carlstadt's position as archdeacon at the parish church at Wittenberg brought with it the income of the parish at Orlamünde. Part of that total income of course went to the vicar at Orlamünde. Barge declares that Carlstadt went to Orlamünde because of the pressure of friends and for conscience sake: the religious leader should aspire to the highest religious office, namely, the preaching of the Word. (Barge, *Frühprotestantisches Gemeindechristentum*, pp. 228–31.) Karl Müller suggests that Carlstadt went to Orlamünde for financial reasons: in order to be assured of a regular income of sufficient size. (Karl Müller, *Luther und Karlstadt*, p. 143.) It seems reasonable to expect Carlstadt to leave Wittenberg at least partly because he had lost his influence there.

mass, and determined that Christ was not corporeally present in the elements. He also denied that baptism was a conveyor of grace. His preaching and his suspected connections with the unrest in Allstedt induced the Wittenbergers to move against him. Luther met him in August of 1524 in Jena. The next month Carlstadt was expelled from the Saxon lands.

There followed for Carlstadt a period of wandering in southern Germany and Switzerland. In 1525 he appealed to Luther to intervene on his behalf with the civil authorities so that he might be allowed to return to Saxony. Carlstadt was allowed to return if he would recant his position on the Lord's Supper, which he did. But he retracted the recantation and was forced to flee again in 1529. His wandering took him finally to Switzerland, first Zurich and then Basel, where he spent the remaining years of his life teaching and writing. He died in 1541.

Carlstadt differed substantially with Luther in interpreting the meaning and purpose of the Lord's Supper.[1] Late in 1521 he inaugurated radical changes in the performance of the mass, changes which he intended should conform to the new Evangelical teaching. Luther did not object so much in this instance to Carlstadt's re-interpretation of the mass; he opposed rather the rapidity of change on the grounds that a quick tempo tended to incite disorder. Far more crucial for the progress of the entire Reformation was their bitter conflict over the meaning of the Lord's Supper. By 1524, when Carlstadt published some half-a-dozen pamphlets on the subject,[2] he was denying the corporeal presence of Christ in the sacrament. This denial developed from his earlier conviction that the mass could in no way be a sacrifice. Christ had suffered and died on the cross and thereby earned salvation for all who believed in the atonement. This experience had a once-and-for-all character which certainly did not require repetition for the salvation of a soul. Indeed, to try to repeat it through the Lord's Supper was to suggest, thought Carlstadt, that the cup contained a new executioner bent on shedding Christ's blood afresh. Faith compels us to reject such an idea; it tells us Christ's blood was shed on the cross and cannot therefore be poured from the cup. Though Carlstadt was certainly not inclined to reject mystical thought, he completely refused to accept the

---

[1] The selection of issues which divided Luther and Carlstadt plunges one into an immediate controversy. Luther and Carlstadt and their respective twentieth-century supporters did not agree in their analyses of the differences between them. See Barge, *Karlstadt*, II, 267. For this study the twin issues of the Lord's Supper and the appropriate tempo for changes in religious practice are the most significant.

[2] Barge, *Karlstadt*, II, 151-52. The first one appeared late in 1523.

mystery of transubstantiation. Faith in such mystery was not faith at all; it was superstitious belief in magic.[1]

Carlstadt grounded his denial of the real presence primarily on the impossibility of fitting it into his framework of experiential apprehension of Christ's atonement. In mystical stages Carlstadt perceived the efficacy of Christ's atonement: upward glance at the crucified one, acknowledgment of the immensity of his burden, remembrance of his Lordship, burying of one's own will within the will of Christ, and finally the inner new birth.[2] Such an apprehension of Christ's suffering and death made it a living experience, far removed from the barren materialistic apprehension of the flesh of Christ in the sacrament of the altar. Without such a personal inward experiencing of Christ's atonement there could be no such thing as justification. Certainly the mere eating of consecrated bread and drinking of the wine could not contribute in any way to the soul's justification in the sight of God.[3]

Carlstadt supported his denial of the real presence by declaring that the New Testament repudiated such an idea. Essentially his argument was based on the absence of evidence that the apostles and Paul actively supported a doctrine of the real presence. None of those who wrote in the New Testament canon of Christ's life, teaching, suffering, death, burial, and resurrection suggested that Christ's body and blood were in the sacrament, or that the sacrament was in any way necessary for salvation.[4]

Carlstadt had earlier agreed with Luther that the Eucharist accompanied by the Word contained the promise that Christ would give his body for the remission of sins to the faithful.[5] In his later explanations Carlstadt declared that this promise was nothing more than one of Christ's many allusions to his suffering and death. He intended to give his body in death – once, but not necessarily in bread and wine corporeally throughout succeeding centuries. His death on the cross forgave the sins of men. But Christ did not give himself in such a manner that he who partook of the sacrament of the altar had his sins therefore forgiven. The sacrament in itself remitted no sins. To believe and teach such a doctrine was not only contrary to the prophets, the apostles, and Christ, but constituted also a denial of the efficacy of the

---

[1] *Ibid.*, II, 153–56.
[2] *Ibid.*, chapter viii.
[3] *Ibid.*, II, 154–56.
[4] *Ibid.*, II, 153.
[5] Matt. 26:26–28; Luke 22:19–20.

historic Calvary.[1] What then did Christ mean when he said: "This is my body?" He referred to that body which was given to the Jews for crucifixion. He did not refer to an eternal, glorified body. Barge reminds us, and rightly so, that Carlstadt's ultimate authority was not a literal interpretation of Scripture. It was rather his own religious conviction. He believed that he, as the apostles, was given final assurance as to the truth or falsity of a given doctrine by the Spirit.[2]

What then was the meaning and purpose of the Lord's Supper to Carlstadt? He certainly did not intend to do away with its celebration. To him it was two things: a reminder and a proclamation of the saving death of Christ. The celebration of the first communion of course could not have had this meaning, for Christ was then still alive. Hence the disciples did not understand what Christ did on that occasion. Celebrants of the Lord's Supper after Christ's death were to regard the occasion with greatest reverence as a reminder of the entire saving work of Christ. As such the celebration should be a joyful occasion. Moreover it was one with a certain power of its own: the power, through an earnest, conscious effort at recollection, which accompanied the realization of Christ's lordship, love, wisdom, and obedience even to the cross. This power, aroused by the reminder of Christ's saving work, should impel the participant to proclaim Christ's saving work. Carlstadt conceived of a line of spontaneous force generated by recollection, moving from a worshipful remembrance of Christ's work to an oral testimony to it.[3]

A second major disagreement between Carlstadt and Luther arose over the problem of the rate at which change in religious practices should be inaugurated. The new Evangelical teaching made untenable some of the traditional church practices. Carlstadt and Luther could agree on that point. But there was a certain firmness, amounting to a legalistic rigidity in Luther's eyes, in Carlstadt's approach to the problem of how rapidly church practices should be altered. Let us examine a few of the changes made in Wittenberg in 1521 and 1522 with Carlstadt's thoughts on them.

How should the Lord's Supper be celebrated and named, late in 1521?

[1] Barge, *Karlstadt*, II, 156–57.

[2] *Ibid.*, II, 161–62, 169.

[3] *Ibid.*, II, 171–73. Carlstadt tended to regard any external religious act, any sacrament in the Roman tradition, as a sign, having no power in itself. The act of baptism to him conveyed therefore no grace. I have chosen not to discuss his views on baptism primarily because Luther did not try to refute them so much as he opposed Carlstadt's views on the Lord's Supper. Luther met views on baptism which were determinative for his Anabaptism in the Zwickau Prophets.

Carlstadt thought in the first place, that the name *Messe*, which to him meant sacrifice, absolutely must be changed. The Lord's Supper was above all not a sacrifice. The name must be changed immediately. Or the Host, should it be elevated or not? The Roman practice demanded its elevation. Carlstadt demanded on the other hand that it not be elevated for to do so retained the sacrificial character of the Roman mass. He who elevated the Host committed sin.[1] Roman practice in communion was to distribute only the Host to communicants. Carlstadt demanded the distribution of both elements in the communion service. Indeed, "He who partakes only of the bread sins in my opinion." [2] He considered partaking of neither bread nor wine preferable to receiving only the bread. Here Carlstadt foreshadowed his later teaching that the wine represented Christ's death and power to forgive sins, and the bread his resurrection and power over death; therefore both were necessary.[3] But above all, Carlstadt was convinced late in 1521 and early in 1522 that the order of the mass must be changed with celerity in order to conform to the new Evangelical doctrines. In this persistence he met the firm resistance of the Elector who was disturbed both by the absence of unanimity among the religious leaders in regard to the order of the mass and also by threats of further violence among the people. Frederick declared the liturgy must remain unchanged for a time. But Carlstadt announced he would change the mass. He recited the mass on Christmas Day, 1525, clothed in a plain black robe. He did not elevate the Host, and he omitted those sections of the mass which referred to the act as a sacrifice. He recited part of it in German. And he distributed both elements to the people, some two thousand who gathered in the Castle Church. His prior announcement of intended changes in the conduct of the mass unloosed a crowd of rioters in the church on Christmas Eve. Drastic change in religious practice met a riotous reception on the part of the common people.[4]

So it was with images and pictures too. Carlstadt was convinced already in October, 1521, that images in the churches had to go. They stood as a threat to Christianity as a spiritual force. For they threatened to turn the Evangelical religion into superstition and idolatry. The first commandment forbade the erection of pictures and images. What then should be done with them? They should be taken out of the churches

---

[1] *Ibid.*, II, 270.
[2] *Ibid.*, I, 290.
[3] *Ibid.*, II, 145.
[4] *Ibid.*, I, 357–61; Bainton, *Here I Stand*, pp. 205–207.

and destroyed. The Augustinian monks did precisely that in January, 1522. Partly through the influence of Carlstadt the Wittenberg city ordinance of January 24, 1522, directed that all pictures and all altars in excess of three per church should be removed.[1] But removing pictures and images was not done quietly; Carlstadt's iconoclasm incited riots among the people.[2]

There was in Carlstadt a radical tendency, a desire to quicken the tempo of change in religious practices irrespective of the consequences. It is probably not fair to accuse Carlstadt of deliberately provoking riots, but on the other hand he did not oppose them with much force.

What was Luther's mature reaction to the *Schwärmer*? On what grounds did he oppose them? Luther met in the Zwickau Prophets a serious denial of the validity of infant baptism. They used Mark 16:16 to discredit infant baptism. They argued from this passage that baptism was contingent upon the faith of the baptized for its validity. Infants were not capable of having faith; therefore it was useless to baptize infants. Luther, in the first instance, rejected their exegesis. Mark 16:16 could in no way be used to prove that infants were incapable of faith. Then on what grounds could the Prophets prove that infants did not believe? Because they could not speak and declare their faith? How many hours in twenty-four did Christians declare their faith, or were they even conscious of it? Surely not very many. Did this mean that men could not be Christians when they were asleep, or eating, or thinking of something other than their relation to God? Such an argument was ridiculous. God was able to maintain faith in children during their infancy "as though it were a continuous sleep." [3]

The Prophets also challenged the Lutheran view of the *fides aliena* being a substitute for an infant's inability to believe. Luther was provoked to develop further his doctrine of the *fides aliena* in this instance.[4] The earnest desire and prayer for faith to be infused in the infant, prayer by the entire congregation, was assuredly rewarded by God, according to Matt. 18:19. Indeed, to him that believed, everything was possible. When a child was presented for baptism, it was in fact offered to a Christ who was in reality present among men showing them his grace.[5]

---

[1] The ordinance applied only to the *Pfarrkirche*.
[2] Barge, *Karlstadt*, I, 386–90; K. Müller, *op. cit.*, pp. 49, 64–65.
[3] Letter to Melanchthon, January 13, 1522, *WB*, II, 424–28. Also letter to Spalatin, May 29, 1522, *WB*, II, 545–47.
[4] Wappler, *op. cit.*, p. 31.
[5] Letter to Melanchthon, January 13, 1522, *WB*, II, 424–28.

Luther rejected the Prophets' arguments in the third instance because they did not understand the nature of a sacrament. The Prophets wished to make baptism contingent on the faith of the recipient. The faith of any human was at best a weak, vacillating thing. No act of divine grace could be grounded on such a flimsy foundation. Luther believed that the sacraments were based on the command of God.[1] As such they were true; accompanied by the Word they became the certain conveyors of God's grace.

Finally Luther based his defense of infant baptism on the long-standing practice of the Christian church. Indeed, I Cor. 7:14, "else were your children unclean; but now they are holy," was a clear indication to Luther that infant baptism was the practice of the apostolic church. Throughout the intervening centuries the practice continued. Even the heretics did not oppose it. That the entire church of Christ could err at the point of baptism throughout the centuries of its existence under the leadership of Christ was to Luther an absolute impossibility.[2]

Luther turned both to the Old and New Testaments for substantiation of his belief in infant baptism. Baptism served the Christian church as circumcision did the children of Israel. Surely the "Prophets" must condemn circumcision in the Old Testament if they denied the validity of infant baptism.[3] By May of 1522 Luther's strongest New Testament support was the passage in Matt. 19 where Christ said: "Suffer the little children, and forbid them not, to come unto me: for of such is the kingdom of heaven." If the Kingdom was given through circumcision in the Old Testament, why would it not be given through baptism in the New Testament – in both instances with children included? Luther repeated his conviction that infants received faith through the prayer and faith of the congregation, and therefore were numbered among the faithful in the Kingdom of Heaven. He even suggested, as he had earlier in his commentary on Galatians, that it was easier for the infant to possess faith than for the adult; for the adult discovered seeds of rebellion against the Word in his own ability to reason.[4]

Despite a certain bravado which characterized Luther's dispatches to his friends on the Prophets' denial of infant baptism, Luther was

---

[1] *Ibid.*
[2] *Ibid.*
[3] *Ibid.*; letter to Spalatin, May 29, 1522, *WB*, II, 545–47.
[4] *Ibid.*

troubled. "I have always expected Satan to touch this sore, but he did not will to do it by the papists." [1] He was disturbed because an attack on inconsistency between justification by faith and infant baptism arose within the Evangelical camp.

Luther discerned and condemned the subjective character of the *Schwärmer's* religion. He was immediately scornful of the Prophets' spiritual pretensions. That they testified concerning their own spiritual powers made him suspect that their spirit was not of God. Everything they had done could have been inspired by Satan. Therefore their spirit must be tested as John required. [2] Luther laid it down that no one was sent by God, to the accompaniment of extra-Scriptural revelations, unless God granted him also the ability to perform miracles. Here was the problem of office. "The ancient prophets had their authority from the law and from the prophetic rank, as we now have ours from the appointment of men." But by what authority did these Zwickau Prophets preach and teach? They were not appointed by men to the holy office. They usurped it on the basis of their pretensions to revelations. But these pretensions were not supported by miracle-working powers.

If the Prophets received special revelations and held familiar conversation with God as they claimed, what was the nature of their spiritual experience? Did they suffer pain and torture in their encounters with the Divine? Luther cited Old Testament passages to show the terror and pain experienced by those to whom God revealed himself. It was not possible for God to speak familiarly with man without first slaying him and drying him up, so that the evil odor of the old Adam might not be a stench in his nostrils. But the Prophets experienced a bland, smooth God. They were caught up in ecstasy into the Third Heaven, painlessly and without fear. Therefore to Luther their spirit was not the bonafide Spirit of God. All this Luther discerned from reports written by friends to him in his Wartburg retreat. [3] His personal encounters with the three Prophets, later in 1522, served only to confirm his earlier rejection of their spiritualism. [4]

Müntzer also displayed a subjectivism which was extremely distasteful to Luther. Müntzer, in Luther's estimation, relied overmuch on the Spirit. This Spirit could indeed be found in the Scriptures, but it

---

[1] Letter to Melanchthon, January 13, 1522, *WB*, II, 424–28.
[2] I John 4:1.
[3] Letter to Melanchthon, January 13, 1522, *WB*, II, 424–28.
[4] See above, pp. 15–16.

ranked above the Scriptures as a source of authority. It carried with it immense conviction of its absolute worth and authority. Luther's "Word" was not inflexible, but it was much more fixed and certain than Müntzer's Spirit. Behind Luther's Word stood always the concept of an historical revelation which had been recorded in the Scriptures.[1] Certainly the Word bore the Spirit of God; indeed, it was that Spirit that gave the unlimited power and might of God to the Word whenever and wherever the Word was spoken. But Luther grounded his notion of the Spirit much more firmly in the Bible than did Müntzer. Luther did not so much deny the reality of a spirit which motivated Müntzer as he suspected that spirit was satanic. When Müntzer turned to revolution, in theory and fact, Luther was certain of his analysis.[2]

Luther did not chide Carlstadt for his subjectivism as much as he did the Prophets and Müntzer. Carlstadt was a mystic. In fact his developed theology appears to have been more influenced by late Medieval mysticism than by Luther's principle of justification by faith. He shared with the Prophets and Müntzer some of their distaste for what they considered Luther's too objective and impersonal approach to the manner of God's communication of grace to man. But he did not share their enthusiastic reliance on dreams, visions, and reading of faces as true media for the revelation of God's will to man. He had, moreover, a much higher regard for the Scriptures as the source of revelation of God's will.[3] The point in Carlstadt's theology at which his mysticism provoked Luther was the issue of outward forms as media of grace. Carlstadt clung to his inward personal experiencing of the Divine will, beginning with the medieval emphasis on quietism and vacancy of thought (*Langweiligkeit* and *Gelassenheit*) as the ultimate means whereby God's grace was communicated to mankind. Such a view tended to exclude the traditional sacraments as media of grace. Luther considered such a view excessively subjective; he ridiculed it.[4]

Luther was irate at the amount of disorder this unholy trio of forces instigated. The Prophets, although not the originators of riotous iconoclasm in Wittenberg, were somewhat gleeful promoters of it. They helped to foster a revolutionary temper among the people which Luther

---

[1] Hinrichs, *op. cit.*, pp. 44–45.

[2] Julius Köstlin, *Luthers Theologie in ihrer geschichtlichen Entwicklung* (2 vols.; 2d revised ed.; Stuttgart: J. F. Steinkopf, 1901), II, 220; Letter to the Princes of Saxony concerning the revolutionary Spirit, Smith and Jacobs, *Correspondence*, II, 241–47.

[3] Barge, *Karlstadt*, II, 24–25.

[4] Luther's "Wider die himmlischen Propheten" as paraphrased and quoted in Barge, *Karlstadt*, II, 272.

sensed and pronounced dangerous. The Prophets were able to stir the populace to such a fever pitch that mob violence resulted. This had been true especially in Zwickau. Luther's opposition to them was based more on their rejection of infant baptism and their spiritual subjectivism than on revolutionary tendencies. He tended later to associate their type of iconoclasm with revolution.[1]

Carlstadt drew more fire from Luther. His insistence on rapid change in matters of celebration of mass, removal of pictures and images, release of votaries from monastic vows, and marriage of priests and monks brought riots in its wake late in 1521 and early in 1522. Luther approved of many of the changes in Wittenberg inaugurated by December, 1521.[2] He was far more disturbed, at that time, by the revolutionary temper among the people as he journeyed to Wittenberg. It was this concern and apprehension of insurrection that prompted him to write his "Earnest Exhortation for All Christians, Warning Them against Insurrection and Rebellion." [3] There is no evidence to support a theory that Luther blamed Carlstadt in this instance for the disturbances. But a brief examination of his brochure will be instructive, for in it he laid down his basically conservative convictions about the nature and justification of civil rebellion.

Luther analysed the rebellious temper of the people as being directed primarily against those among the clergy who refused to reform themselves. He railed against the tyranny of the unreformed, particularly the papacy itself, but he did not justify the use of force against them. In fact, the existence of spiritual despotism was God's visitation of wrath upon the people for their sins. Thus the people should confess their sins, pray, and proclaim the gospel. In any event insurrection even against a despotism was both unprofitable and wrong, in the sense that God forbade it. It was of the devil.[4]

If the "Earnest Exhortation" was not directed against the work of Carlstadt, the eight sermons of March, 1522 certainly were. On eight successive days, starting on March 9, Luther preached to the Wittenberg populace about changes in religious practice. He dealt with marriage of clergy, monastic vows, destruction of images, the order of the mass, and the nature of confession. The principle on which his attitude

---

[1] In "Wider die himmlischen Propheten."

[2] "Everything that I see and hear pleases me very much." Letter to Spalatin, early December, 1521, Smith and Jacobs, *Correspondence*, II, 79.

[3] *Ibid.*

[4] "An Earnest Exhortation for All Christians," translated and printed in *Works of Martin Luther* (6 vols.; Philadelphia: A. J. Holman, 1930), III, 206–22.

toward change was based was that of forbearance to the weak. "All things are lawful for me; but not all things are expedient." [1] Some folk took offense when changes were made too rapidly; these could lose their Christian faith thereby. One should first preach the Word until it had time to do its work in the hearts of men. When those hearts were united against the mass, it could of course be abolished. Until that time those who did not believe in its efficacy were not harmed if they continued to allow its celebration. There remained the possibility of reclaiming those who still clung to it. [2]

Luther possessed an unbounded faith in the ability of the Word to perform unaided the task of reform. No one should be constrained by force; faith must come freely, without compulsion.

Take myself as an example. I have opposed the indulgences and all the papists, but never by force. I simply taught, preached, wrote God's Word; otherwise I did nothing. And then while I slept, or drank Wittenberg beer with my Philip and with Amsdorf, the Word so greatly weakened the papacy, that never a prince or emperor inflicted such damage upon it. I did nothing. The Word did it all. Had I desired to foment trouble, I could have brought great bloodshed upon Germany. Yea, I could have started such a little game at Worms that even the emperor would not have been safe. But what would it have been? A fool's play. I did nothing; I left it to the Word. [3]

Late in 1524 Luther waxed vehement against the tendencies of Carlstadt to provoke civil disturbance. Carlstadt believed it better to remove images immediately than to run the risk of people lapsing into idolatrous worship of them. That such removal touched off rioting seemed not too serious a matter to him. Luther, on the other hand, laid the greater emphasis on the manner of removal, riotous or peaceful, than on whether or not they were removed at all. He even pleaded for the retention of a few pictures as memorials. [4] But the extreme iconoclasm of Carlstadt in Orlamünde convinced Luther that the man was a revolutionary. He would move from iconoclasm to civil insurrection. Even if Carlstadt did not have rebellious ideas in mind, still: "I must declare that he had a revolutionary and murderous spirit, as the Allstedter had, so long as he remains with the iconoclastic mischief." [5] Luther indulged in sharp invective against this demon.

---

[1] I Cor. 6:12.

[2] "The Second Sermon," translated and printed in *Works*, II, 398–99.

[3] *Ibid.*, pp. 399–400.

[4] Barge, *Karlstadt*, II, 268. Probably Luther's reception by the parishioners of Carlstadt at Orlamünde in 1524 influenced his estimation of Carlstadt's riot-stirring potential. Luther was met with stones and mud and verbal threats to his safety. Letter to the Christians at Strassburg, December 17, 1524, trans. and printed in Smith and Jacobs, *Correspondence*, II, 278.

[5] Barge, *Karlstadt*, II, 269, quoting from "Wider die himmlischen Propheten."

In Müntzer Luther faced a committed agitator against the civil order. Müntzer developed a justification for revolution based partly on Scripture and partly on his recognition of social injustice. Even before his public announcement of the right and necessity for revolt against the princes, Luther anticipated it. With Müntzer, as with Carlstadt, Luther judged that violent iconoclasm would inevitably lead to open insurrection.[1] Consequently his letter to Elector Frederick and Duke John of Saxony in July, 1524, warned them of this possibility. Luther re-emphasized his belief that the warfare in which he was engaged was a spiritual one. Let the spirits fight it out. God would certainly emerge the victor over Satan. But if the satanic force took up the sword, then the matter was no longer a purely spiritual affair. It belonged in this instance to the civil authorities to exercise the power of their office, for which they were held responsible by God. Any appeal to force in order to advance the Kingdom of God must immediately be met and repulsed by force. It was precisely for such situations that God provided the civil office.[2]

After the death of Müntzer Luther wrote a brief history of his latter days. He included a few of Müntzer's final letters, in which Müntzer scolded several of the princes for martyring the Christians (i.e., Müntzer's followers) and threatened them with extinction. Müntzer believed these princes would be delivered shortly into his hands by the living God, and thereby they would become the devil's martyrs. Luther turned at the end to contrast Müntzer's brazen and boastful talk with his ignominious defeat in the Frankenhausen battle. This was surely the judgment of God. Indeed, the major purpose for publishing the account was to warn people with a concrete example of how God damned and punished revolutionaries. He rejoiced that in this instance the judgment of God was so unmistakable.[3]

A fourth issue which separated Luther from the *Schwärmer* was that of the Lord's Supper. In this instance Luther's arguments were directed solely against Carlstadt.

Luther's earliest objections to Carlstadt's interpretation of the Lord's Supper centered around the matter of how rapidly changes in its celebration should be introduced. By 1524 the problem was much more fundamental: was Christ corporeally present in the elements? Carlstadt

---

[1] Hinrichs, *op. cit.*, pp. 146-48; 156-58; 163.

[2] Letter to the Princes of Saxony concerning the Revolutionary Spirit, July, 1524, trans. and printed in Smith and Jacobs, *Correspondence*, II, 241-47.

[3] "Ein schrecklich Geschicht vnd Gericht Gotes über Thomas Müntzer, darinnen Gott offenlich desselbigen Gayst Lügenn strafft vnnd verdammet," *EA*, LXV, 12-22.

denied the real presence; Luther affirmed it. The conflict set the stage
for growing disagreement among the Reformation forces, culminating
in failure at union in the Marburg Colloquy of 1529. It took Luther the
better part of four years to settle his own doctrine of the Lord's Supper.
It was the challenge to the real presence by Carlstadt, and earlier
Honius, that provoked him to a clarification.

Luther had objected to the Catholic view of the sacrament on the
grounds that the outward act, completed by the priest, had added to it
the salvation-working power without proper attention given to the faith
of the recipient. Faith in the believer was the product of God's grace and
power only, Luther believed; no external act of itself could dispense such
faith to one who did not have it. The Roman church based salvation too
much on outward ceremonies which were established and regulated by
rule of the church. In fact, the entire character of the church was
externalized.[1] But he could not accept Carlstadt's view that the
sacrament of the altar had only a spiritual character and meaning. The
words of Scripture were too unyielding. He even declared in 1524 that
he had tried to adopt the view that the elements remained unchanged
because he thought thereby to damage the papist's position more
severely. But he had found the words of Scripture unmovable.[2]

"This is my body" meant precisely what it said. It did not mean
"This represents my body." The recipient of the bread and wine
partook of the real body and blood of Christ: both the divinity and
humanity of Christ were present, for in the God-man divinity and humanity were inseparable. To declare that Christ was only spiritually
present was to deny that inseparable character of the two natures of
the incarnate Christ. Christ was perfectly capable of being present at
one time in ten thousand places. Luther called this real presence of the
God-man the bodily sign. It was made into a bonafide objective medium
for God's transmission of grace to man through the addition of the
Word. Combined they wakened and strengthened one's faith. The
external part, the sign, was the visible bread and wine become body and
blood of Christ. To receive it was to receive the historic Christ, and
thereby forgiveness of sins and eternal life.[3]

Luther did not profess to be able to understand clearly how God
worked in the sacrament. He was convinced that the New Testament

---

[1] Köstlin, *op. cit.*, I, 402.
[2] Letter to the Christians of Strassburg, December 17, 1524, trans. and printed in Smith
and Jacobs, *Correspondence*, II, 277.
[3] Köstlin, *op. cit.*, I, 405; Schwiebert, *op. cit.*, pp. 701–703.

firmly laid out the fact of the real presence.[1] "How all this is possible, or how he can appear in the bread, we do not know, nor are we able to comprehend it; we are to believe God's Word rather than order standards or ways for God." [2] He regarded any denial of the real presence as an attempt to rationalize divine matters. Such attempts, he believed, not only denied one of the blessing and comfort of a sacred communication of God's grace; they also tended generally in the direction of a Pelagian works-righteousness: without the faith in the grace of the external act, the individual looked to the earning of his salvation through his own power.[3] So it was with Carlstadt, thought Luther.

The fifth charge that Luther made against the *Schwärmer* was that of works-righteousness. Again the principal target was Carlstadt. It is difficult to ascertain how seriously Luther believed the charge himself – not that there existed no grounds for it. But he condemned Carlstadt on the one hand for relying too heavily on a mystical inner experience for his salvation, described in jargon incomprehensible to Luther. His concurrent accusation that Carlstadt relied ultimately on a performance of certain acts, or a denial of others, for his salvation does not logically fit with the charge of excessive mysticism. It is well to remember that when Luther wrote against Carlstadt in the mid-1520's, he wrote intemperately. In fact his invective against Carlstadt, early in 1525, turned some of the Swiss Reformers to a defense of this man whom they otherwise might not have helped.[4]

Luther's charge of works-righteousness was based on his assertion that Carlstadt's preaching and teaching were directed entirely at externals. Carlstadt preached and wrote about images, excessive ornamentation of churches, the necessity for humble garb, and the absolute impossibility of grace being mediated through the sacrament of the altar. Where then were the expositions on faith or the exhortations to love? Where were the words on the cardinal points of Christian doctrine? Luther had been impressed in 1522 with what he considered Carlstadt's devotion to external matters to the neglect of the basic Christian teachings. How do people become Christians then? By wearing gray robes, smashing pictures and burning churches, and refusing the Eucharist? This was nothing but a new monasticism.

---

[1] Luther used I Cor. 10:16 as the best explanation.
[2] Schwiebert, *op. cit.*, p. 866, n. 121, quoting Luther from *WA*, XVIII, 87.
[3] Köstlin, *op. cit.*, I, 405.
[4] Barge, *Karlstadt*, II, 277, 272.

Where was the freedom of the Christian man? Luther's entire religious experience cried out against such a development.[1]

Finally, the *Schwärmer* provoked Luther to a further clarification of his view of the devil's activity in this world. Luther viewed all history as a struggle between the power of the devil and that of Christ. This cosmic struggle would end only on Judgment Day. In the meantime the world was the center of Satan's power, the devil's hostel. History was in its third and worst period of the struggle. This period was characterized by the antichrist, the papacy, reigning as a godly, majestic devil, revered and worshipped as if it were God himself. Luther believed that those who wished to enlist on the side of God should above all act so as to release the mighty power of God. This was nothing else but to release the Word, and allow it to take its course unhindered.[2]

But when the Word was truly released so that it changed the hearts of men, it also brought forth the bitter wrath of the devil. This was to be expected. First he attacked through his agent the pope. But he was not successful; for the Word continued to flourish and to win men's hearts. He knew that the more the Word was attacked, the more it would spread and grow. Later, after a barren sojourn in dry places, he attacked through the *Schwärmer*. The *Schwärmer* did not originate from the camp of the papists; nor did they quite originate from the Lutheran party, for which Luther was thankful.[3] They apparently drew their origin directly from the devil. This was the true meaning of their revelations: their visions, dreams, and the like were sent by the devil. As such the *Schwärmer* became the true minions of Satan, the angels of Satan incarnate.

By 1524 Luther held no hope for the winning of Müntzer from the grasp of Satan. He did entertain the hope that Carlstadt could be reclaimed.[4] For Luther the decisive point, at which the individual human's diabolical origin could be unalterably ascertained, was that point where disorder was deliberately fostered.[5] Here then were

---

[1] "Wider die himmlischen Propheten." I have used Barge's paraphrases of, and quotations from, it. *Ibid.*, II, 264–77, especially p. 267. See also Letter to the Christians of Strassburg, December 17, 1524, in Smith and Jacobs, *Correspondence*, II, 276–78.

[2] Hinrichs, *op. cit.*, pp. 152–53.

[3] Letter to the Princes of Saxony, Smith and Jacobs, *Correspondence*, II, 242.

[4] Barge, *Karlstadt*, II, 265, interpreting Luther's "Wider die himmlischen Propheten."

[5] For the satanic origin of:

a. the Prophets, Letter to Melanchthon, January 13, 1522, *WB*, II, 424–28.

b. Carlstadt, Letter to Nicholas Gerbel, December 17, 1524, trans. and printed in Smith and Jacobs, *Correspondence*, II, 273–74; Letter to the Christians of Strassburg, December 17, 1524, *ibid.*, 278.

c. Müntzer, Letter to the Saxon Princes, *ibid.*, 241–47; "Ein schrecklich Geschicht vnd Gericht Gotes," *EA*, LXV, 12–22.

Luther's *Schwärmer*, those religious enthusiasts who swarmed over the land usurping to themselves the right to preach and teach and whose trail was marked by successive waves of disorder and unrest. Luther condemned them in bitter words, for they relied ultimately on their own religious experience as authoritative, to which they subjected even the Bible.

Melanchthon was not as prompt as Luther in rejecting the *Schwärmer* on his first encounter with them. He displayed an initial hesitancy in condemning them which was a compound of his own uncertainty in the face of their spiritual pretensions, and of his natural irenic temperament. Intimations have already been given of his reactions. It will be necessary here to give only a summary view of the position he developed.

Melanchthon faced in the Prophets a series of spiritual claims based ultimately on revelations to them in person. Storch and Stübner held conversations with the Lord.[1] They called into question the uniqueness of Scripture as a means of imparting knowledge of God to men. Scripture was valid insofar as the Spirit spoke through it. But God's essential means of revelation was more directly personal; the kind of revelation the Scriptural writers themselves had had was available to any one.[2] Melanchthon was at once speechless before and chary of these pretensions. It took him several days to recover, and particularly to find arguments to use against this part of the Prophets' doctrine. Later he considered their claims silly.[3]

The challenge to infant baptism was even more difficult to withstand. The Prophets questioned the existence of faith in the infant. They decried the validity of the *fides aliena* for the infant. And they contended that the candidate for baptism must have faith. Melanchthon was troubled. He was reasonably certain that the arguments were diabolical, but he had to admit that Satan had chosen a soft spot in the Lutheran defenses for the attack.[4] Above all he was disturbed because he discovered what he thought was indecision on the question of infant baptism in Augustine. He observed that Augustine eventually came around to defend the act on the basis of original sin and ancient

---

[1] Report to Spalatin and Einsiedeln, January 1, 1522, *CR*, I, 533–34.

[2] Record of conference between Einsiedeln, Spalatin, Melanchthon, and Amsdorf, January 2, 1522, *CR*, I, 536–37.

[3] Letter to Spalatin, December 27, 1521, *CR*, I, 514–15. Cellarius' dreams were inconsistent with his doctrine. He denied the existence of Purgatory, yet dreamed of Chrysostom suffering in Purgatory and apparently considered the dream a valid indication of Chrysostom's disposition after death. Melanchthon found this ridiculous. Joachim Camerarius, *De Philippi Melanchthonis ortv, totius vitae cvrricvlo et morte...* (Leipzig, n.d.), p. 50.

[4] Report to Spalatin and Einsiedeln, January 1, 1522, *CR*, I, 533–34.

practice.[1] In Melanchthon's own writings of this period the question was not answered. Luther supplied him with some arguments, but it is not likely that he did not know all of these anyway. He considered it both futile and dangerous to debate the problem publicly in January of 1522; the Prophets would not be dissuaded, and the common folk might easily be misled. He discovered in Storch a degree of spiritualism that made the performance of the rite of baptism relatively unimportant.[2] The experience reminded him of the highly personal character of faith; it was a personal experience. Melanchthon did not agree with this subjective emphasis of the Prophets; far from it. But in counteracting it he was forced to rely on church tradition more than he was accustomed to at this stage of the Reformation.[3]

Subjectivism on the questions of Biblical authority and baptism led to subjectivism and individualism with respect to the civil authority. Not that he predicted or even anticipated revolution in 1521 or early 1522. But the Peasants' Revolt, and Müntzer's role in it, were crowning events in a radicalism that depended all too frequently on highly individualistic interpretations of faces or visions or even of the Scriptures. Above all, the radicals paid no heed to the restraining influence of tradition with the result that change in church practice led to violence. Melanchthon approved of many of the changes advocated by persons like Carlstadt and Gabriel Zwilling. He publicly defended the marriage of priests at a time when it was radical and perhaps even dangerous to do so. Earlier he had declared against the continuing validity of monastic vows for one who had come to know and experience Evangelical truth.[4] Late in 1521 he tended toward approval of Zwilling's attacks on the mass. Zwilling wanted it abolished among the Augustinians.[5] But the cumulative effect of the acts of Carlstadt and the Prophets produced a feeling of uneasiness in Melanchthon. By February of 1522, he was ready to move with greater caution. He agreed to keep the old forms of church worship until a more propitious time appeared.[6] He considered himself unable to stem the flood of radicalism which Carlstadt, Zwilling, and the Prophets had unleashed in Wittenberg.[7]

[1] *Ibid.*

[2] Record of conference between Einsiedeln, Spalatin, Melanchthon, and Amsdorf, January 2, 1522, *CR*, I, 537–38.

[3] Georg Ellinger, *Philipp Melanchthon, Ein Lebensbild* (Berlin: Gaertner, 1902), pp. 164–66 for a good discussion of Melanchthon's reactions to the Prophets.

[4] *Ibid.*, pp. 148–49.

[5] Chancellor Brück to Elector Frederick, October, 1521, *CR*, I, 459–61; Manschreck, *op. cit.*, pp. 73–75.

[6] Müller, *op. cit.*, pp. 188–89.

[7] Letter to Einsiedeln, February 5, 1522, *CR*, I, 546.

He even feared that the good progress of the Reformation would be utterly destroyed by the violence which followed in the wake of reforms; the light would be extinguished.[1] Melanchthon had learned through a disillusioning and somewhat bitter experience that change in church practice must be introduced with caution and much careful preparation. The radicals moved too fast. Their kind of program culminated in the twelve articles of the peasants, and in the full plans of Müntzer to seize civil control and destroy the princes. By 1524 and 1525 he was so wary of change, and particularly of social change under the banner of Christianity, that he could scarcely recognize the justice of some of the peasant demands.[2] Müntzer's fury stemmed from an earlier *Schwärmerei*.[3] The pattern of radical change to the point of revolution developing from a religious subjectivism was fixed in Melanchthon's mind.

Melanchthon moved from uncertainty with respect to radicals to a position of immense distrust and ultimately passionate hatred. He was willing and even eager to lend an ear to their words at first.[4] But his suspicion of their irrationality deepened and was strengthened by the disorder they unloosed. He could see only civil revolt as the ultimate result of *Schwärmerei*.

---

[1] Letter to Spalatin, printed by Manschreck, *op. cit.*, p. 79. Melanchthon later tried to give the impression that he had disapproved earlier of the activities of Zwilling in particular. Ellinger, *op. cit.*, p. 151.

[2] "Eyn Schrifft Philippi Melanchthon widder die Artickel der Bawrschafft," 1525, *CR*, XX, 641–62. Elector Ludwig of the Palatinate had requested Melanchthon's advice in treating the demands of the peasants expressed in the twelve articles because Melanchthon was a native of the Palatinate, because he was well-versed in Scripture, and because he had been named as arbitrator by the peasants themselves. Ludwig wanted Melanchthon to attend the session of the Palatine Diet when the question would be discussed. Melanchthon declined the invitation but sent his written opinion. Letter from the Elector to Melanchthon, May 18, 1525, *CR*, I, 742–43.

[3] "Philipp Melanchthons Historie Thomae Müntzers," printed in Johann Walch, *D. Martin Luthers... sämtliche Schriften* (24 vols.; Halle: Gebauer, 1739–1753), XVI, 199–217. Melanchthon's authorship of the brochure has been questioned in recent years. See Brandt, *op. cit.*, p. 223. Boehmer's view seems to me the most plausible. Melanchthon wrote it, not so much as history, but to give his students an example of humanist public speaking. Heinrich Boehmer, *Zur Feier des Reformationsfestes und des Übergangs des Rektorats ... Studien zu Thomas Müntzer* (Leipzig: Edelmann, 1922), pp. 3–4. Melanchthon was at some pains to show that Müntzer's revolutionary goals were the natural result of *Schwärmerei*. The connecting link between a milder radicalism and the wild civil revolt was of course the devil.

[4] A gossip sheet of the times, the "Zeitung aus Wittenberg," declared that Melanchthon spent much time with Stübner. The latter lived in Melanchthon's house for a time. Melanchthon came to his defense when the students teased him. N. Müller, *op. cit.*, p. 160.

CHAPTER II

ANABAPTISM IN CENTRAL GERMANY I
THE RISE AND SPREAD OF THE MOVEMENT

The *Schwärmer* of Central Germany were only one manifestation of a larger radicalism which accompanied the Reformation wherever it found root. Everywhere there were men who were dissatisfied with what they considered the half-way measures of the Reformers, or non-Catholics who differed fundamentally with the theological formulations of the Reformers. One scholar has recently analyzed the extremists under the name Radical Reformation. As a fourth form of religious expression in the sixteenth century the radicals have had a pervasive influence on contemporary Protestantism.[1]

Within the broader stream of radicalism Anabaptism finds its rightful place. It made its formal appearance in Zurich in January, 1525. For more than a year previously a small number of Zwingli's followers had shown traces of disaffection because of his slow rate of progress in abolishing Catholic practices. Their irritation had been particularly evident at the second public disputation held in October, 1523. Here several of the radicals objected to state interference in what they considered purely religious matters. These radicals assembled for the first time as a unified body of believers only after the city council formally declared in January, 1525, against their opposition to infant baptism. Thereafter the movement took shape and spread through Switzerland and southern Germany, attended by much persecution.

In recent decades a large amount of research has been done on

---

[1] George H. Williams, "Introduction" to *Spiritual and Anabaptist Writers*, p. 19. Williams has the best current typology of the Radical Reformation. He distinguishes among the Anabaptists (evangelical, revolutionary, and contemplative), the Spiritualists (evangelical, revolutionary, and rational), and the Evangelical Rationalists. He considers Nürnberg (Denk) and Amsterdam (Hoen on the Eucharist) as hearths of Anabaptism entirely unrelated to Zurich and equal to it as points of geographical origin and spiritual influence in the early stages of the total movement. There is much to be said in favor of both his typology and his theory of origins. His ideas are best expressed in "Studies in the Radical Reformation: A Bibliographical Survey," *Church History*, XXVII (1958), 46–69; 124–60.

Anabaptism. The discovery of substantial deposits of source materials in archives scattered throughout Europe has led to the publication of a large number of monographs.[1] More recently some of the source materials have been printed in the *Täuferakten* series.[2] In this study our concern lies primarily with the sources and monographs on Anabaptism in Central Germany.

Within the larger revival of the study of Anabaptism in recent decades, relatively less attention has been given to an interpretation of the movement in Central Germany, the region where the Reformation was born. An impressive number of source materials on Anabaptism in the old Stem Duchy of Thuringia and adjacent regions have been uncovered and printed during the past sixty years. Some of these source publications were accompanied by narrative and interpretive accounts of the movement. The most extensive editor of such materials was Paul Wappler,[3] who covered over four hundred pages with printed source materials from the archives of Weimar (Ernestine Saxon Archives), Dresden (Royal Saxon State Archives), Mühlhausen (City Archives), and to a lesser extent Marburg (Royal Prussian State Archives) and Nürnberg (Royal Bavarian Kreis Archives). The wealth of this material is all the more apparent today in view of the relative unavailability of most of these sources behind the Iron Curtain. Sources aside, Wappler's delight in displaying Luther and Melanchthon in an unfavorable light provoked outcries from some scholars at his interpretation.[4] It is clear to any reader of his narrative

---

[1] See (1) Wilhelm Pauck, "The Historiography of the German Reformation during the Past Twenty Years," Part IV, *Church History*, X (1940), 305–40. (2) Walther Koehler, "Das Täufertum in der neueren kirchenhistorischen Forschung," *ARG*, XXXVII (1940), 93–107; *ibid.*, XXXVIII (1941), 349–64; *ibid.*, XL (1943), 246–70; *ibid.*, XLI (1948), 164–86. (3) Eberhard Teufel, "Täufertum und Quäkertum im Lichte der neueren Forschung," *Theologische Rundschau*, XIII (1941), 21–57, 103–27, 183–97; *ibid.*, XIV (1942), 27–52, 124–54; *ibid.*, XV (1943), 56–80. (4) H. S. Bender and C. Krahn, "Historiography," *ME*, II, 751–67. (5) Williams, "Studies in the Radical Reformation," *op. cit.*

[2] H. S. Bender, "The Täufer-Akten Publication Series of the Society for Reformation History," *MQR*, XXIII (1949), 48–52.

[3] *Die Stellung Kursachsens und des Landgrafen Philipp von Hessen zur Täuferbewegung* (Münster: Aschendorff, 1910) and *Die Täuferbewegung in Thüringen* (Jena: Fischer, 1913) are the principal works of value for this study. In both he relied somewhat on an earlier work, *Inquisition und Ketzerprozesse in Zwickau zur Reformationszeit* (Leipzig: Heinsius Nachfolger, 1908) for the basic attitudes of Luther and Melanchthon toward treatment of heresy.

[4] So Walter Sohm, *Historische Zeitschrift*, CXVII (1917), 126–28, who devoted half a dozen lines to the praise of his printed sources and the remainder of a three-page review to the incompetence of his interpretation. Sohm challenged the accuracy of Wappler's transcriptions in a few instances. Robert Stupperich, "Melanchthon und die Täufer," *Kerygma und Dogma*, III (1957), p. 150, n. 1, dismisses him as virtually useless because he is too partial. The fact of his bias is incontestable, although his antipathy to Luther and Melanchthon appears to be based more on humanistic than on confessional grounds. Wappler did not like religious persecution.

on Thuringian Anabaptism that he was overwhelmed by the amount and diversity of his material. He did not work through his materials enough to disclose the thought of the movement, but presented a series of relatively unconnected pictures of local groups and persons. It must be admitted, however, that the contradictory positions of Anabaptists in his sources present unusually difficult problems in interpretation.[1]

Georg Berbig printed the pertinent source materials on Anabaptism in the Electoral Saxon enclave in Franconia.[2] He provided his sources with a commentary, not a narrative in the fullest sense of the word; his passion for disclosing the radicals as incipient revolutionaries eclipsed his interest in providing an account of their activities and particularly of their religious life. Wappler considered his work of little value because it contained too many errors and the geographic area of his Anabaptist treatment was too limited.[3] More recently Clauss has attempted to trace the movement in its larger Franconian setting, in areas controlled by the Bishops of Bamberg and Würzburg.[4] His treatment is marred by a strong antipathy to the radicals; it discloses little of their doctrine and is directed largely to describing the severity of the punishment meted out to them.

For the region of northern Thuringia and beyond, the monograph of Eduard Jacobs gives excellent coverage.[5] Although confessionally opposed to what he felt was excessive subjectivism in the Anabaptists, Jacobs succeeded in drawing a comprehensive picture of the movement uncolored by bias. His delineation of their doctrine and life is especially commendable. Jacobs appended some forty pages of sources.

For Hesse, which in the sixteenth century included a section of western Thuringia, the old monograph by Hochhuth still has value as a narrative, although it is full of error.[6] It is largely superseded because

---

[1] See the review by Hecker, *Neues Archiv für sächsische Geschichte und Altertumskunde*, XL (1919), 200–202.

[2] His most important collection is found in "Die Wiedertäufer im Amt Königsberg in Franken in den Jahren 1527/28," *Deutsche Zeitschrift für Kirchenrecht*, hereafter *DZK*, XIII (1903), 291–353. Collections of lesser value: "Die erste kursächsische Visitation im Ortsland Franken," *ARG*, III (1905–06), 336–402; "Die Wiedertäuferei im Ortslande zu Franken, im Zusammenhang mit dem Bauernkrieg," *DZK*, XXII (1912), 378–403.

[3] Wappler, *Thüringen*, p. 3.

[4] "Kleine Beiträge zur Geschichte der Wiedertäufer in Franken," *Zeitschrift für bayrische Kirchengeschichte*, XV (1940), 105ff., and XVI (1941), 165ff.

[5] "Die Wiedertäufer am Harz," *Zeitschrift des Harz-Vereins für Geschichte und Altertumskunde*, XXXII (1899), 423–536.

[6] "Mittheilungen aus der protestantischen Secten-Geschichte in der hessischen Kirche: Landgraf Philipp und die Wiedertäufer," *Zeitschrift für die historische Theologie*, XXVIII (1858), 538–644, and XXIX (1859), 167–234. Hochhuth wrote a monograph on the movement

its sources have been included in the *Täuferakten* volume on Hesse, which becomes of course a major source for any treatment of the Anabaptists of Central Germany.[1] A shorter, less comprehensive treatment of the movement in Hesse can be found in the article by Christian Hege; [2] however, he tends to overlook the spiritualism and the radicalism of some of the Anabaptists.

Wilhelm Wiswedel included persons and pictures from Central German Anabaptism in the first volume of his work.[3] Wiswedel is highly sympathetic, to the point of sometimes being uncritical, since he wrote for the spiritual edification of the Baptists in Germany rather than for the scholarly world. This does not, of course, imply that he neglected the best sources.

With the publication of the *Täuferakten* for Hesse in 1951 the interest of scholars has been focused afresh on Anabaptism in Central Germany. A few monographs based on these materials have appeared in the last few years. Gerhard Zschäbitz applied the "method of historical materialism" to these materials.[4] Among Marxist interpretations his is probably better than average. Some of his observations are stimulating and useful.

Ruth Weiss is the latest to publish. Her excellent monograph, "Die Herkunft der osthessischen Täufer," appeared in two installments in the *Archiv für Reformationsgeschichte*.[5] Mrs. Weiss emphasizes the religious character of this essentially religious group, in contrast to the interpretation of her Marxist compatriot, Zschäbitz. She gives us a sympathetic and penetrating analysis of the group.

Although the richness of source materials is undeniable, the historian still faces large problems in interpreting them. Since almost all of these materials came from the ecclesiastical and judicial examinations of the Anabaptists, or from letters of officials reporting either these trials or private conversations with Anabaptists, the sources are universally

---

in the County of Solm: "Die Wiedertäufer in der Grafschaft Solms, im Reformations-Zeitalter," *Archiv für hessische Geschichte und Alterthumskunde*, X (1863–64), 360–92.

[1] Günther Franz, *Urkundliche Quellen zur hessischen Reformationsgeschichte*, IV (Marburg, G. Braun, 1951) hereafter *TA, Hesse*. Walther Koehler, Walter Sohm, and Theodor Sippell uncovered and edited many of the documents.

[2] "The Early Anabaptists in Hesse," *MQR*, V (1931), 157–78.

[3] *Bilder und Führergestalten aus dem Täufertum* (3 vols.; Kassel: Onken Verlag, 1928–1952).

[4] Gerhard Zschäbitz, *Zur Mitteldeutschen Wiedertäuferbewegung nach dem grossen Bauernkrieg*, Band I, Reihe B of *Leipziger Uebersetzungen und Abhandlungen zum Mittelalter*, eds. E. Engelberg and H. Kusch (Berlin: Rütten und Loenig, 1958).

[5] Jahrgang L, 1–16, 182–99. She has since published "Die Herkunft und Sozialanschauungen der Täufergemeinden im westlichen Hessen," *ARG*, LII, 162–88.

hostile to the Anabaptists. Rarely does one find a tract or letter in which an Anabaptist can declare himself freely on a topic of his own choosing. Rather the Anabaptists of the available sources always speak in reply to specific questions put to them by interrogators who are thoroughly convinced that Anabaptism is both heresy and sedition, and whose only purpose is to discover the degree to which a given prisoner has been infected by this poison. This type of information seriously limits the historian. For example, a full view of the doctrines of the twenty-five Anabaptists tried at Petersberg near Sorga in August, 1533, is blocked by the limited scope of the questions. Of the nine questions put to each in turn, the first, designed to identify the individual with the radicals, was: Do you attend the services of the Evangelicals and their distribution of sacraments? In explaining why they refused spiritual fellowship with the Lutherans, some of the Anabaptists touched the area of theology. But in the subsequent eight questions there was no opportunity to do so because the questions concerned only civil matters, at least as the interrogators viewed them. The authorities were obviously fishing for replies which they could label seditious.[1] Again, Anabaptism's mind on the Lord's Supper cannot be ascertained from the trial records because this view of the Lord's Supper was always presented negatively: Why did the Anabaptists not recognize the bodily presence of Christ in the elements? Both on such questions as the meaning of, or the reason for, its observance the Anabaptists were given no opportunity to express themselves. Their interrogators were interested only in determining whether or not their prisoners deviated from established truth, the truth of the real presence.

The validity of the court testimony of the Anabaptists is further compromised by the use of torture. Did the Anabaptist, after being racked, say what the interrogators wanted him to say in order to avoid further torture and in the conviction that he would be executed anyway, or was his fresh information the truth reluctantly revealed? How much of the testimony given under torture is trustworthy?[2] In

---

[1] *TA, Hesse*, p. 64. See the questions put to the Anabaptist leader Alexander, Wappler, *Thüringen*, pp. 348–51. Here the interrogators were interested in detecting new adherents of the sect, and in determining the sedition of Alexander. Alexander was a leader who could have given a more carefully developed theology than could most of the Anabaptists, if he had been given the opportunity.

[2] Thomas Spiegel von Ostheim, questioned and tortured on March 3, 1527, declared only after torture that the Anabaptists were to help the Turks extirpate ungodly nobles and civil officers. Beutelhans, a member of the same Franconian group, and like Thomas a disciple of Hut, revealed teachings of Hut that were apocalyptic but not revolutionary – i.e., the Anabaptists were not to use the sword in the great final struggle between Turk and European. Wappler, *Thüringen*, p. 235; Berbig, *DZK*, XIII, 313.

some instances the recorder of the testimony made no attempt to distinguish between what was confessed before and after torture.[1]

Finally, most of the Anabaptists questioned were simple people, without formal education, and not at all adept at formulating replies to the sometimes tricky questions. Moreover some of them had obviously received little religious instruction, for they freely admitted that they did not know the answers to even simple questions.[2] Some of this, of course, may have been evasion. But since the Anabaptists met clandestinely and infrequently, some who were baptized immediately after their introduction to Anabaptist teaching could not possibly have known much of the group's doctrines.

For this study the Anabaptism of West Thuringia is most important and will be given special attention. Described in terms of political boundaries, the Anabaptist area embraced southwestern Electoral Saxony, southeastern Hesse, and the northeastern part of the Fulda holdings. Geographically it is a strip approximately thirteen miles from north to south, and extending from Eisenach in the east to Hersfeld in the west. There are a number of reasons for concentrating the analysis of Anabaptism here. In the first place the degree of Anabaptist infiltration in this region was greater than in any other section of Central Germany. Georg Witzel testified to the prevalence of Anabaptists in this region; he declared that every village and town between Fulda and Erfurt had been infected by Anabaptism.[3] Part of the region, Amt Hausbreitenbach, was under the joint administration of the Hessian Landgrave and the Saxon Elector; hence those Anabaptists who wished to flee the sterner treatment meted out by the Saxons could find some refuge here, as well as fellowship with their established brethren. Because of sharp differences of opinion on how to treat captured Anabaptists, there is a sizable correspondence between the Hessian and Ernestine Saxon courts, with as a consequence a more detailed description of Anabaptists both in person and in doctrine than one finds for other areas in Central Germany. Eberhard von der Thann, the civil officer at the Wartburg, in particular wrote often to Philip in an effort to persuade him to be more severe in punishment.

This region was the center of Anabaptism in Central Germany. Many of the Anabaptist leaders in neighboring regions began here or es-

---

[1] Thus Caspar Spiegel von Ostheim hearing, 1527, Berbig, *DZK*, XIII, 309–10.
[2] See Sorga hearing, *TA, Hesse*, pp. 64 ff.
[3] From Keller, "Der sog. Anabaptismus am Harz im 16. Jahrhundert," *Monatshefte der Comenius-Gesellschaft*, IX (1900), 182.

tablished contacts with the Anabaptists here; e.g., Heinz Kraut, Alexander, Georg Köhler, Ludwig Spon. It displayed a vitality not always found elsewhere, primarily because of the ability of its first great leader, Melchior Rink, but also because of the influence of Fritz Erbe's steadfastness in his sixteen-year imprisonment at Eisenach and the Wartburg.

Finally the region is important for this study because the Lutheran Reformers learned to know Anabaptism here. For Menius this is especially true. He lived during his mature years as a Reformer in Eisenach. As superintendent of the region he had many first hand contacts with the Anabaptists here. It was a little east of this region that Melanchthon visited the churches in the summer of 1527, after which he began to write against the Anabaptists. West Thuringian Anabaptism is pre-eminently the Anabaptism of the Lutheran Reformers.

Anabaptism first appeared in Central Germany in 1526, in northern Franconia, where the intrepid missioner, Hans Hut, began his distinctly Anabaptist preaching.[1] Most of the Anabaptism in this region reflected his influence, even though the scene of his most intense activity was Austria. Hut was a native Thuringian, born in the village of Haina, near Römhild. He served as sexton in the village of Bibra, and there plied his trade as bookbinder and book salesman. The latter business took him on long, extended travels in Germany, where after 1517 he eagerly sold pamphlets and books propagating the new Evangelical faith. He even visited Wittenberg, the geographical center of the new movement, where according to his later testimony, he was disturbed by the absence of improvement in life among the Lutherans and by their failure to satisfy his objections to infant baptism. Already in 1524 Hut encountered serious objections to infant baptism, as a result of which he eventually refused to have his own child baptized. This led to his expulsion from Bibra and initiated the wanderings which lasted throughout the remainder of his short life. He observed the battle of Frankenhausen in May, 1525, where he was captured and released by the conquering lords. He had gone there to find a market for his books,

---

[1] For Hut I have relied primarily on Herbert Klassen, "Some Aspects of the Teaching of Hans Hut (*ca.* 1490–1527)" (unpublished M.A. thesis at the University of British Columbia, April 1958); Johann Loserth and Robert Friedmann, "Hans Hut," *ME*, II, 846–50; Wappler, *Thüringen*, pp. 26–30. There is a biography of Hut, written as a doctoral dissertation (Bonn) in 1913: Wilhelm Neuser, *Hans Hut. Leben und Wirken bis zum Nikolsburger Religionsgespräch*. Two chapters of six (Nos. iii and vi) were published in 1913 by Hermann Blanke, Berlin.

and had become enthusiastically converted to Müntzer's eschatological views. Immediately after the disaster he preached revolution at least at Bibra and possibly elsewhere. He then dropped from sight until May, 1526, when he was baptized at Augsburg by Hans Denk. This reception of adult or believers' baptism was a turning point in his life. Müntzer's socially revolutionary eschatology was now more and more replaced by one which eliminated the call to arms in favor of an intense conviction that the Turks would inadvertently help to usher in the Kingdom by destroying the German nobility in a decisive battle near Nürnberg. With this conviction he retraced his steps to southern Thuringia and began, in the summer of 1526, a preaching and baptizing mission which was to carry him far beyond his native regions into Bavaria, Moravia, and Austria on what was probably the most extensive and most vigorous of all early Anabaptist missionary campaigns. Hut won and baptized, in something over one year's time, more persons to the Anabaptist cause than any other leader–indeed, more than all the rest put together.[1] He was arrested at Augsburg and tried in September, 1527, after the "Martyrs' Synod." After severe torture he died in his cell in early December, either as the result of an attempt to escape or else as the victim of a fire ignited while he lay unconscious from severe torture. He was condemned posthumously as a heretic, and his dead body was committed to the flames.

The manner of Hut's preaching was impassioned, the content inflammatory. Court testimonies of his converts give evidence of the profound impression made by his preaching. A group of simple peasants and artisans would meet secretly in solitary houses on a village edge, in isolated farmsteads or mills, some already adherents of the new teaching, but most of them not. When Hut appeared he greeted those assembled with the words: "Go ye into all the world and preach the gospel to every creature. He who believes the gospel and is baptized will be saved; and this is baptism – to endure anxiety, want, sorrow, and all tribulations in patience." Then he preached on the imminence of Christ's return: the Turks were about to wreak a most awful punishment upon Christendom, and this was to signal the return of Christ. Other tribulations, revolts, earthquakes, plagues, would harass the land, which scarcely one man in three would survive. All who repented would ultimately survive, though not without severe persecution, and would assemble with the faithful to possess the land with the triumphant Lord. Hut's theme, being thus a mixture of Biblical apoca-

[1] *ME*, II, 849.

lypticism with the contemporary political setting, successfully played upon the fears of Europe in the face of the Turkish threat. This is not to suggest that Hut's theme was a deliberate attempt at deception. He was earnest, and undoubtedly believed with utmost sincerity that what he preached was God's holy truth. Hut concluded his sermon with a call to repentance and baptism. Those who wished were baptized, unto suffering as Hut interpreted it, and then Hut moved on to other places. His genius was that of the fiery revivalist; he did not remain to carry on the more painstaking work of instruction.

Hut's effectiveness in his native regions was instantaneous. A few of his earliest converts – men like Georg Kolerlin, Kilian Volkaimer, Eucharius Binder, and Joachim Mertz – either attended Hut in his further ministry or were sent out by him to do the work of "apostles." He left behind, however, a series of devoted though poorly instructed bands of adherents in Franconia. Probably the center of the movement was Königsberg, within the Saxon enclave. Here the magistrate first detected Anabaptism in January, 1527, and by February had made several key arrests. Under torture the Anabaptists confessed that they were planning revolution.[1] The Bishop of Würzburg, in whose territory some of those Anabaptists were seized, executed two of them, and Elector John of Saxony followed suit with two more. Other Anabaptists, as well as certain suspects, were required to undergo the "Schamstrafe": each Sunday, until service began the culprits were to stand barefoot before the church door; then during the service they were to stand with bowed head and eyes in a row before the chancel; after the service they were to confess their sins publicly. Their property was confiscated and sold, though they were allowed to live from the proceeds. Each had to spend a day or two monthly in prison, where they were to renew their abjuration of the Anabaptist error. The promptness and dispatch with which the movement was detected and its adherents punished, together with the severity of that punishment, frightened the

---

[1] Berbig, *DZK*, XIII, 295, declares that the sect was essentially political under the guise of religious motivation. Wappler (*Thüringen*, p. 33), following Berbig's sources at this point, insists that at least the group thrived on planned insurrection. Hege ("Königsberg," *ME*, III, 220) finds the movement essentially a peaceful, religious one, with ideas of civil revolt appearing only when the prisoners were tortured. What Hege says about confessions of revolutionary ideas only under torture I find demonstrable only for Thomas Spiegel von Ostheim (Wappler, *Thüringen*, Urkunden i, pp. 228–235). The other Anabaptists were indeed tortured, but the court recorder did not distinguish between what they confessed before and after torture (Berbig, *DZK*, XIII, 309–316). Wappler and Berbig do not give consideration to the strong element of nonresistance in Thomas Spiegel's testimony, nor to the later unequivocal nonresistant stand of Hut against Hubmaier. See below, p. 96.

fledgling movement and scattered its members. There is evidence of further arrests and executions in the region in 1527, but most of those who remained faithful to the cause fled to more hospitable territories.[1]

From Königsberg Anabaptism fanned out to the north and northwest late in 1526 and 1527. In the regions of western Electoral Saxony, Ducal Saxony, and eastern Hesse the movement worked against the background of Müntzer's religious enthusiasm and the Peasants' War. Some of its first leaders and adherents had participated in the Peasants' War. In its earliest forms, under the impress of Hut's eschatological expectancy, it won adherents rapidly because it seemed to echo Müntzer; but it quickly alarmed the rulers. Hans Römer, a battlefield comrade of Müntzer's, led a band of radicals in the region slightly to the south of Mühlhausen. He began peacefully enough to build a congregation of Christians, preaching repentance in the homes of the simple folk. But his eschatology took a dangerous turn when he announced the impending return of Christ as only eleven months away. He and his followers, feeling themselves called of God to realize the coming Kingdom of Jerusalem and to aid in its restoration, planned and began to execute an attack on the city of Erfurt for January 1, 1528. The plot was discovered and judicious arrests made. Römer himself escaped, but was reapprehended in Göttingen in 1534.[2]

Anabaptism of West Thuringia, in contrast to that of Römer and his followers, generally followed more moderate channels. It had a robust eschatology but tended to pour its energies into evangelistic activity and in some instances into the creation of an active congregational life. The Anabaptists attacked infant baptism, the real presence, and the doctrine of original sin in their teaching. They endeavored to follow simple worship patterns, led by men chosen by the congregations or sometimes self-appointed. The movement was discovered and arrests

---

[1] Wappler, *Thüringen*, pp. 25–37, is the principal source here. He should be supplemented by the sources, though not the narrative, in Berbig, *DZK*, XIII, 309ff.

[2] There are as usual enough contradictions in this case to cause difficulties in interpretation. In the first place it is very clear that Römer's converts were required formally to renounce revolution. How could he then make a complete turnabout and not only justify but also advocate revolution? Secondly, one of Wappler's sources, a chronicler of the times, declares that the conspirators were Anabaptists and Lutherans, which gives the movement the appearance of a general revolt ("qui partim Lutherani partim Anabaptistae erant," Paul Lang in J. B. Mencke, *Scriptores rerum Germanicarum praecipue Saxonicarum*, II, 71, Ab. Wappler, *Thüringen*, p. 43, n. 4). One could try to make a case for Römer's being more a captive than a leader of the movement, but this is useless in view of his prominent role in the plot. Moreover there can be no doubt but that Anabaptists – i.e., persons who had received adult or believers' baptism – were deeply and actively involved. No matter how pious the beginnings, the eschatology grew to fantastic proportions and carried the erstwhile nonresistant Christians into revolution. Wappler, *Thüringen*, pp. 38–44, and the pertinent printed sources.

were made in 1528. Some of the captives recanted and nine of these were arrested a second time near the cloister of Reinhardsbrunn south of Gotha. Friedrich Myconius, the Lutheran superintendent at Gotha, conducted an ecclesiastical hearing. Six of the captives refused to recant, and were consequently executed in January, 1530, by order of the Saxon Duke Elector.[1] But the executions served as much to strengthen the movement as to curtail it. Objections were raised in various quarters to the execution of persons who were apparently not guilty of sedition in doctrine or deed. Even Myconius was more than a little disconcerted at the severity of punishment.[2] Justus Menius, Lutheran superintendent at Eisenach, thereupon wrote a book [3] to justify rigorous punishment of the sect by refuting Anabaptist doctrine and revealing the enormity of Anabaptist error. As for the Anabaptists, their growth was checked by neither execution nor polemic; they did, however, make a judicious move to Landgrave Philip's territory, or at least to Amt Hausbreitenbach.[4]

Throughout the 1530's the spiritual center of Anabaptism in Central Thuringia was the congregation at Sorga in Hesse a village three miles east of Hersfeld, where an aggressive missionary activity was carried out by a group of forty to fifty persons. The principle of love meant for them a sharing of goods with those who were in need. They broke their bread together with thanksgiving in commemoration of the death of Christ. For them the reception of the true body and blood of Christ was a consequence of doing the will of God and it had no connection with their communion service. Here too there was a strong eschatology. These simple folk lived in the expectancy of the impending judgment of the world by God. They spread their doctrines vigorously, working especially in the regions to the east in Amt Hausbreitenbach, and on into Electoral Saxony proper. A succession of leaders is to be found

---

[1] The rationale for punishment was based on previous Electoral mandates which forbade Anabaptist activities of every variety, and on the imperial mandate of January, 1529, which decreed death to Anabaptists.

[2] Wappler, *Die Stellung Kursachsens*, pp. 12–13. Also Justus Menius, *Der Widdertauffer lere und geheimnis* (Wittemberg: Nickel Schirlentz, 1530), pp. G4r.-Hr. Menius gives a vituperative account of the event, charging the Anabaptists with being followers of Müntzer and of publicly threatening to stone one of their number who did not agree to recant the second time. Menius could not understand their fearlessness in the face of death. Apparently, as was frequently the case with Anabaptists being executed, they rejoiced at death. He calls them "insanely frivolous" at death.

[3] *Der Widdertauffer*. See below, pp. 181–197.

[4] On the Reinhardsbrunn affair see Wappler, *Thüringen*, p. 221; Wappler, *Die Stellung Kursachsens*, pp. 12–13, and Anhang I, Nr. 6, pp. 134–37; Menius, *Der Widdertauffer*, p. G4r. I have not been able to find a detailed account of the trial, or of these Anabaptists' articles of faith.

here, but the most influential one, despite his early arrest and the cessation of his activity, was Melchior Rink. Rink was the most important leader of Thuringian Anabaptism.[1]

Melchior Rink [2] was born in Hesse in 1494. Despite a peasant background he attended the University of Leipzig where he received the degree of *baccalaureus artium*. He achieved a reasonable proficiency in the use of the classical languages. His Latin poetry, in a book published in 1516, displayed a competence with the language, although the poetry itself was little above doggerel.[3] From his nickname "the Greek," and from rumor about him, it is certain that he knew Greek well enough to lecture on Greek poetry. He had a reputation as a competent humanist.[4]

Rink appears in the records in 1523 as schoolmaster and chaplain at

---

[1] Ludwig Spon in his trial at Mühlhausen in 1533 gives the best information on the congregation at Sorga (Wappler, *Thüringen*, p. 50, who relies on Hochhuth here). Rink had the dubious distinction of appearing in the Catholic Index, through an error however. The 1550 Index of the University of Louvain, approved by Charles V, included the works of a certain Melchior Clinck or Kling. A later transcriber changed the name to Rinck. Fr. Heinrich Reusch, *Der Index der verbotenen Bücher* (Bonn: Max Cohen, 1883), I, 120.

[2] His name is spelled in many ways in the sources: Rink, Rinck, Ring, Ringk, Reick. There is no good biography of Rink. Wappler's account in *Thüringen* (pp. 50–58) is the best, and Friedrich zur Linden, in *Melchior Hofmann* (Haarlem: De Erven F. Bohn, 1885) pp. 171–78, makes a good attempt to save the man from obscurity. Zur Linden made several errors. He had Rink in the Elector's hands after 1531, which is manifestly impossible because the Elector certainly would have killed him immediately; although he rejected Hochhuth's assertion that Rink was killed at Münster, he believes that Rink participated in the Münster kingdom, whereas Rink was in Philip's hands at the time. Wappler relied too much on zur Linden's account of Rink's theology and thus made him out to be a complete spiritualist. Zur Linden's concept of Rink as a spiritualist comes perhaps from his discovery that Rink and Hofmann are sometimes confused in the records because, as zur Linden surmised, their theology was similar. I suspect that zur Linden transferred some of Hofmann's spiritualism to Rink (*ibid.*, pp. 95–96, 176–79). It is admittedly difficult to deal with Rink because of obscurities in the sources. Rink was the victim of a major attempt at defamation in his trial by Balthasar Raidt in 1528, unless he was completely dishonest in his rejection of Raidt's charges against him. In view of the various character depositions on Rink, and because the Marburg theologians did not protest or contest Rink's rejection of the charges, such purported dishonesty is difficult to accept. Ottius, *Annales Anabaptistici* (Basel: J. Werenfelsius, 1672), p. 7, declares that Rink came with the Zwickau Prophets to Wittenberg in December, 1521. It seems incredible, in view of the tremendous excitement these men caused in Wittenberg, that Melanchthon and Amsdorf did not mention him by name if he was in Wittenberg at that time. But it is precisely such misinformation, which tends in general to connect Rink to the more violent manifestations of Anabaptism, that makes the historian suspicious of adverse criticism of Rink in the primary sources, especially since both Bucer and Philip of Hesse were impressed with the man's integrity.

[3] Otto Clemen, "Zur Geschichte des 'Wiedertäufers' Melchior Rink," *Monatshefte der Comenius-Gesellschaft*, IX (1900), 113–16.

[4] A memo of the Tübingen theological faculty to Duke Ulrich of Württemburg on punishment of Anabaptists in 1535 referred to Rink as learned in both Latin and Greek, enough in the latter to lecture on Greek poetry. Printed by Wappler, *Die Stellung Kursachsens*, p. 240. Georg Witzel called him a man of excellent learning. Letter to MBF, December 24, 1531, printed by Wappler, *ibid.*, p. 35, n. 2.

Hersfeld, where he and a colleague, Heinrich Fuchs, early began to preach the Evangelical doctrine. It was received with mixed reactions. On the one hand the common people received the teaching gladly. On the other hand the canons were enraged because Fuchs and Rink fulminated against tithes and the fornications of the canons. On one occasion Fuchs was physically beaten by the canons. The abbot was not opposed to the new teaching; he had even invited Luther to stop and preach at Hersfeld on his return from Worms in 1521. But the wrath of the canons was more than he could withstand. Fuchs and Rink were forced to leave. Their departure, following a farewell address, was attended with violence. The people broke in upon the canons and drove out the concubines. Fuchs and Rink earned the sentence of exile from the Hessian Landgrave because they had aroused the people to violence. But the Hersfeld region rapidly became Evangelical as a consequence, to the obvious joy of Wittenberg.[1]

Rink appeared next at Oberhausen, and then very soon at Eck- hardtshausen, about ten miles southwest of Eisenach, where he was installed as pastor. Fuchs obtained the pastorate at Marksuhl, a few miles west of Eckhardtshausen. Both were awarded their pastorates through the influence of Jakob Strauss at Eisenach. The records do not mention any significant contact between Strauss and Rink, but the similarity of their interest, besides the fact that Strauss was instru- mental in procuring a pastorate for Rink, indicates a considerable exchange of ideas. At Eckhardtshausen Rink married Anna, the daughter of Hans Eckhardt. He began to be critical of the Lutheran faith and to favor the more virulent, active doctrines of Müntzer, whom he considered a true hero in preaching, through whose word the power of God was mighty. Small wonder that Rink participated in the Peasants' War, along with Fuchs, who was killed at Frankenhausen.[2] It is not easy to determine to what extent Rink understood what he was doing at Frankenhausen. Eberhard von der Thann declared in a letter to Landgrave Philip in 1532 that Rink had not properly under- stood the consequences of what he had done in 1525. Eberhard had hoped for some improvement in Rink's attitude, and became indignant when Rink did not implore the mercy of the government for his participation in the war. Indeed, Rink not only failed to repent, but even proclaimed that Müntzer's great cause had not collapsed with the

[1] Zur Linden, op. cit., pp. 172–73.
[2] Wappler, Thüringen, p. 51.

leader's death [1] and that God had spared him at Frankenhausen in order that he might carry on the work.[2] Rink himself had written earlier to Eberhard in protest against the charge that he was inciting revolution, for no one could prove that he had incited the Peasants' Revolt. Whatever he thought in 1525, by the 1530's he clearly regarded civil insurrection as contrary to the will of God.[3] Rink probably joined the Revolt in 1525, however, with a religious fervor derived from Müntzer.

Rink dropped from sight for several years after the Frankenhausen debacle. Wappler says that he returned to the area around Hersfeld in Hesse.[4] He comes to light again in Worms.

There in 1527 Jakob Kautz, an erstwhile Lutheran preacher who had begun to embrace Anabaptist views, challenged his Reformed opponents to a disputation by the publication of seven theses. He attacked outward forms, such as baptism and communion, as having no power to comfort or assure one of salvation. His own preference was for the inner life, which was the basis of religious striving, and which should be directed toward absolute obedience to God. In a foreword to the theses Kautz gave brief credit to three brethren who had helped him: Ludwig Hätzer, Hans Denk, and Rink.[5] Hätzer and Denk, of course, were known to have been in Worms, working with Kautz on the German translation of the Prophets in the first several months of 1527. There is no evidence whatsoever that Rink helped with the translation. The records give us no indication of his reasons for living in the Palatinate, beyond the obvious fact, derived from a comparison of his theology with that of Denk, that the association with Denk must have been decisive in enabling him to restructure his theological outlook after the catastrophe in Central Germany. While in the Palatinate he developed a relationship with Johannes Bader, the Reformed pastor at Landau. Denk together with several of his friends, including Rink in all probability, met with Bader on several occasions and had almost persuaded him to renounce infant baptism. The bitterness with which Rink later denounced Bader indicates that Rink thought that Bader had been completely convinced of the rightness of the Anabaptist cause.

---

[1] Letter of Eberhard to Landgrave Philip, March 1, 1532, printed *ibid.*, pp. 333–34.
[2] Letter of Eberhard to Elector John, November 25, 1531, printed in Wappler, *Die Stellung Kursachsens*, p. 145.
[3] Letter of Rink to Eberhard, undated, *ca.* 1530, *TA, Hesse*, p. 31.
[4] Wappler, *Thüringen*, p. 52.
[5] Zur Linden, *op. cit.* p. 174 and note 1. On Kautz see Hege, "Jakob Kautz," *ME*, III, 159–60.

Rink went through a conversion experience, sealed by the ceremony of baptism, in close fellowship with Bader. Indeed, it appears that Bader was among the sponsors at Rink's baptism, and Rink singled him out as the one to whom he made confession of his sins. Since Bader gave Rink spiritual counsel,[1] Rink was the more keenly disappointed at his "defection."

But Bader had not gone over to the Anabaptists. In 1527 he wrote a book attacking Denk's views on baptism.[2] Rink took it upon himself to reply in a short pamphlet entitled *Widderlegung eyner Schrifft So Johannes Bader, vermeynter pfarrher zu Landau, newlich than hat, den Kindertauff als Christlich zuerhalten.*[3] Both men were rash and intemperate despite the protestation of each that what he was doing was for the spiritual edification of the other. Neither wrote a very systematic account of his position. For Rink this was an occasion to refute the Reformed instead of the Lutheran view on baptism. He encountered the Zwinglian argument on covenants, in which baptism was compared to circumcision. Rink spiced his account with sharp warnings to those who did not heed the truth. The pamphlet is extremely useful to the researcher because it collects the most pertinent arguments of Rink on his favorite theological topic.

The records do not tell us when Rink left the Palatinate, but by 1528 he was proclaiming the Anabaptist cause in the regions of West Thuringia. He not only worked with individuals in isolated places in customary Anabaptist secrecy – harvesters in fields, charcoal burners in the forests, peasants in their cottages – but also demanded the right to proclaim the Anabaptist faith openly before the Evangelical congregation in Hersfeld. For the latter he was summoned by Philip to a personal interview at his hunting lodge, Friedewald, east of Hersfeld. The upshot of the discussion was that Rink would either have to renounce his views publicly at Hersfeld or submit to a cross-examination by the theological faculty of the University of Marburg. Exile

---

[1] *Widderlegung*, pp. 6–7.

[2] *Brüderliche warnung für dem newen Abgöttischen orden der Widertäuffer*, n.p., 1527.

[3] The tract was discovered in handwritten manuscript form by Adalbert Goertz in the library of the University of Frankfurt in 1958, bound with ten other works in a *Sammelband* collected by an opponent of the Anabaptists sometime after 1563. The collection included another handwritten work by Rink: *Vermanung vnd warnung an alle so in der Obrigkeit sind.* Gerhard Neumann transcribed the manuscript, and it is printed in *MQR*, XXXV (July,1961), 197–217, together with introductory comments by Gerhard Neumann and Harold S. Bender. The tract is undated. It was probably written late in 1527 or early in 1528, before Rink left southern Germany. There is no evidence that it was ever printed. (Hereafter this work will be referred to as *Widderlegung*. Citations from the work will refer to the page number of the manuscript, which is indicated in the reproduction printed in *MQR*.)

was to be the penalty for not responding to either of the alternatives. Rink chose the second, and the hearing took place on August 17 and 18, 1528, presided over by the rector.[1]

Two sets of theses served as the basis for the hearing. Upon request, Rink had drawn up his doctrines in a brief, five-point statement. But the hearing began with the consideration of a twelve-point statement of Rink's doctrines composed by Balthasar Raidt, the Lutheran pastor at Hersfeld, on the basis of the earlier conversations between Rink and the Landgrave at Friedewald. Raidt's bitterness toward Rink is apparent; it was undoubtedly due to Rink's former work in and around the Evangelical congregation at Hersfeld, where Raidt now had the cure of souls. But Rink also displayed some bitterness, namely toward Luther and the Evangelical faith. He denied that he had said that the recipient of the Lutheran sacrament received not God but the devil, but he let stand Raidt's charge that the infant recipient of baptism received the devil. He did not unequivocally deny that he had said Luther at first had had the Spirit but later became the devil and the true antichrist. The area of disagreement between Raidt and Rink on the latter's doctrines, indicated by the frequent refutation and qualification of the twelve points by Rink, was very wide. Either Raidt grossly misunderstood Rink, which seems very unlikely, or he was deliberately trying to defame him. Rink's refutation of Raidt's charges was allowed to stand in the court records, which show no trace of a real discussion on the question of whether or not Rink believed what Raidt asserted he did. Rink apparently tried to be scrupulously accurate. For instance, in reply to Raidt's assertion that he had taught the people at Hersfeld that Christ's body and blood were not present in the sacrament, Rink challenged Raidt to produce witnesses whom Rink could question. The problem to Rink in this instance was not belief in the real presence; he rejected that completely; it was rather that he was not absolutely certain he had taught this at Hersfeld, but if witnesses would testify that he had, he would accept the charge. Rink's distrust of Raidt is obvious.[2]

Before the end of the first day the theologians had moved to an examination of Rink's statement. On the first three points he attempted a Pauline statement of man's creation, sin, and justification through Christ. On these points there was no disagreement between the Anabaptist and the Lutherans. Rink's fourth point criticized and re-

---

[1] Wappler, *Thüringen*, pp. 47, 53; Raidt report of the proceedings, *TA, Hesse*, p. 4.
[2] *Ibid.*, pp. 4–7.

jected infant baptism, and here the hearing bogged down. Rink's critique of infant baptism was answered by Raidt. But the rector did not permit Raidt to proceed to a full justification of infant baptism itself, probably because Raidt was not very persuasive; he let the Marburg theologians justify the practice. Rink never accepted the Lutheran arguments and refused to acknowledge the verdict of Lutheran victory. Hence the hearing did not move on to a consideration of Rink's fifth point, i.e., the Lord's Supper.[1] Rink was adjudged in error and was banished.[2]

Rink, however, did not heed the sentence of exile, but continued to work in the border area of Hesse and Electoral Saxony. In April, 1529, Eberhard von der Thann was requested by the Electoral Prince John Frederick to keep a sharp eye out for him in the region between Eisenach and Marksuhl. Shortly thereafter Rink was apprehended in Hessian territory. Imprisoned at Haina for almost two years, he was released and banished a second time, despite Eberhard's appeal to Philip to punish more severely the dangerous revolutionary.[3] John also wrote to Philip, requesting that he, at the very least, order Rink in John's name to leave forever the Electoral lands.[4] During his imprisonment Rink's marital problems came to light. His wife, who claimed he had not visited her at Eckhardtshausen since the Peasants' War,[5] wanted a legal separation. Philip would not hear to this without Rink's assent. Rink's father-in-law visited him in prison to obtain this consent, but Rink would not give it. Rink wrote a sharp rejoinder to Eberhard, who apparently had urged Hans Eckhardt to press for a separation, protesting that Eberhard could not in good conscience advise separation of marriage partners whom God had joined together.[6] Later Rink gave his version of the controversy. Hans Eckhardt, wishing for his daughter a respectable and quiet life as the wife of a pastor, had arranged the marriage with Rink, and all hands were satisfied. When Rink abandoned the life of a settled pastor in the Evangelical faith, the true motives of the parent and daughter were revealed. At first, so it was rumored in Rink's hearing, Anna attempted a flat denial of her marriage to him. He heard that she even claimed he had refused to

[1] *Ibid.*, pp. 8–15.
[2] *Ibid.*, p. 4.
[3] Letter of Eberhard to Elector John, November 25, 1531, printed in Wappler, *Die Stellung Kursachsens*, pp. 145–47.
[4] Letter of Elector John to Philip, December 4, 1529, printed *ibid.*, p. 134.
[5] Rink denied this. *TA, Hesse*, p. 36.
[6] Letter of Rink to Eberhard, *ca.* 1530, *ibid.*, pp. 31–32.

acknowledge the marriage. Then she modified her stand to claim that she had never really wanted to marry Rink, but that her parents had forced her into it; for the sake of peace she had not protested at the time.[1] Finally she wanted Rink to agree to the dissolution of the marriage. Rink declared that to give herself in holy marriage unwillingly was no less than fornication, and that Hans Eckhardt was guilty of pandering, for he had sold his daughter against her will. Rink confessed his relief and joy at being spared such a dishonorable marriage by the vagaries of life as an Anabaptist apostle. He placed the burden of guilt for their separation squarely on his wife; she did not choose to remain with him, although she knew he was harried and driven about for no misdeeds of his own. Rink cried out strongly against the wolves who forced him constantly into hiding for the sake of the gospel. This abomination of persecution could not stand up before the judgment of Christ. His entire defense is redolent of the emotion of one who felt himself deceived and maligned. There was even a hint that Rink had been accused of sexual immorality by his wife and father-in-law. But the letter tells us too that Rink was not fair to his wife in this instance, a type of situation repeated many times in early Anabaptist history, when she who did not share her husband's faith and conviction could not take on the persecution of her harassed spouse. The only possible solution to the problem would have been Rink's renunciation of his faith. This he would not do. "He that loveth father or mother more than me is not worthy of me: and he that loveth son or daughter more than me is not worthy of me" (Matt. 10:37). Despite the unnatural separation Rink would not agree to a legal action making the separation a binding one. He considered remarriage to be adultery; hence divorce was to him but the prelude to adultery. He believed the injunction of Christ, "What therefore God hath joined together, let not man put asunder" (Matt. 19:6), to be absolutely binding.[2]

Rink composed a tract on baptism during his imprisonment at Haina.[3] Designed as an exhortation to the brethren on the subject of

---

[1] It is difficult to reconstruct the picture with accuracy both because many of the facts of the case must be derived by implication only and also because Rink's sentence structure leaves something to be desired.

[2] Rink's untitled defense of his refusal to sanction divorce, sent to Eberhard von der Thann, 1531, *TA*, *Hesse*, pp. 33-37.

[3] Baptism tract in *Sammelband*, pp. Kr.-K3r. Translated by J. C. Wenger, *MQR*, XXI (1947), 282-84. The tract was published anonymously in an undated *Sammelband* edition. See R. Friedmann's description of the *Sammelband* in *MQR*, XVI (1942), 82-98. It is preceded by a one-page letter of which Rink declares himself the author. Friedmann assumed Rink to

baptism, it was in effect a polemic against the Lutherans and Catholics. He denounced both the Lutheran and the Roman faiths as false; they allowed Satan, that great corrupter of souls, to enter their flock through the medium of infant baptism. But even in his polemic Rink's passion for evangelism displayed itself. He invited his readers to leave the errors of Wittenberg and Rome and to join the flock of true believers. The tract implies a rigorous discipline for the Anabaptists, in contrast to a complete absence of discipline, in Rink's view, within the Roman and Lutheran churches. The issue of baptism was the subject matter for both his evangelistic appeal and his polemic. He wrote the tract by way of exposition of Mark 10:14: "Let the children come to me, do not hinder them; for to such belongs the kingdom of God."

Rink remained in prison until approximately May, 1531. His release and banishment were followed by an Anabaptist mandate of Philip dealing explicitly with Rink's type of case: i.e., an Anabaptist leader who returned to Hesse despite a previous order of exile. The mandate threatened loss of life to such a person.[1] Undaunted, Rink returned to his former work around Hersfeld, and in Amt Hausbreitenbach. Eberhard's brother Martin arrested him with eleven others at worship in Vacha on November 11, 1531. Vacha at that time was under Philip's jurisdiction; Rink was either fortunate or foresighted in always being caught by Philip's men, not those of the Elector. The arrest provided the occasion again for a spirited exchange of letters among Eberhard, Elector John, and Landgrave Philip. Eberhard wrote Philip a lengthy description of Rink's crimes and errors, designating him as an impenitent instigator of the Peasants' Revolt who advocated the abolition of all civil authority and rejected the explicit commands of civil authority, since he had deliberately re-entered Hessian territory despite his banishment. All of this Eberhard considered revolutionary. If that

be the author of the following tract as well (ibid., p. 91). It seems likely that the tract was written by Rink, probably during his imprisonment at Haina. The tract exhibits Rink's special interests which can be ascertained from other sources. Its author uses certain phrases and terms as Rink used them (e.g., "... dieweil er die creatur vnd sich selbs also liebet..." Sammelband, p. Kv.). Its position in the Sammelband suggests that the editor of the collection considered Rink to be the author and therefore included the brief letter in which Rink identifies himself as author in order to identify the tract which follows. The cover letter has Rink imprisoned at Haina, and we know from other sources that Rink was imprisoned at Haina from April, 1529, to May, 1531 (letter of Rink to Eberhard, ca. 1530, TA, Hesse, p. 31; letter of Eberhard to the Elector, Nov. 25, 1531, ibid., p. 48). It is possible that this tract was one of the two writings that Eberhard forwarded to the Elector in November of 1531 (ibid.). There is also the possibility that the tract was written several years earlier. A letter from the governor and council of Kassel, written on March 10, 1529, to Philip of Hesse, speaks of Rink circulating his "booklet" in an effort to win converts (ibid., p. 19).

[1] Issued June or July, 1531, ibid., pp. 37-38.

was not sufficient to condemn him to death, he charged Rink with blasphemy. Eberhard argued, as Melanchthon did, that although erroneous belief in itself was inculpable, the public proclamation of religious error was blasphemy and deserved most severe punishment; [1] a lighter sentence than death would be an admission to the common people that Rink's cause was a just one and would enable Rink to win even more for his nefarious sect. Eberhard counseled death; [2] he advised John of the culprit's apprehension and urged him to press Philip for Rink's execution. [3] The Elector urged Philip to adhere to the imperial mandate of April, 1529, condemning Anabaptists to death. [4] But Philip persisted in regarding the matter not as sedition, attempted or real, but as erroneous religious opinion. Although Philip did not condone those opinions, he could not execute Rink for matters of religious faith, nor even for blasphemy. If he did so he would be bound to execute all Jews and Catholics, because he considered them the worst possible blasphemers of Christ. Philip therefore sentenced Rink to life imprisonment. [5]

Sometime in 1530 or 1531, probably during one of his enforced periods of leisure in jail, Rink wrote his *Vermanung vnd warnung an alle so in der Obrigkeit sind.* [6] The burden of the tract was Rink's protest against the persecution of the Anabaptists by the magistrates. He attempted to lay bare the limitations imposed on government as it was ordained by God. It had no right to regulate or govern in religious

[1] Letter to Philip, *ca.* March 1, 1532, printed in Wappler, *Thüringen,* pp. 333–36.
[2] Letter to Philip, March 1, 1532, *ibid.,* p. 333.
[3] Letter of Eberhard to John, November 25, 1531, printed in Wappler, *Die Stellung Kursachsens,* pp. 145–47.
[4] Letter of Elector John to Philip, December 21, 1531, *ibid.,* pp. 152–53.
[5] Letter of Philip to Elector John, January 3, 1532, *ibid.,* p. 155.
[6] Unpublished handwritten manuscript in the *Sammelband* referred to above, p. 55, n.3 . (Hereafter referred to as *Vermanung.* Citations will refer to the page number of the manuscript, which is indicated in the reproduction printed in *MQR.*) I date the *Vermanung* in 1530 or 1531 because of Rink's repeated brushes with the magistrates in those years, and because of its similarity in tone and content with his letter to Eberhard, *TA, Hesse,* p. 31, which was probably written in 1530. But the only certainty in the dating of the pamphlet is that it was composed after his conversion to Anabaptism, i.e., after late 1527. There is no evidence that it was ever printed. Eberhard von der Thann reported to Philip of Hesse around March, 1532, that Rink had written a number of books, some printed and some still in handwritten form. Eberhard sent some of these writings to Philip (letter to Philip, printed in Wappler, *Thüringen,* p. 335), as he had done earlier to Elector John of Saxony (letter to Elector, Nov. 25, 1531, *TA, Hesse,* p. 48). The writings of Rink which Eberhard sent to Elector John are known to be his brief tract on marriage and his cover letter to Eberhard on the same subject (*TA, Hesse,* p. 33). It seems probable that Eberhard forwarded the *Vermanung* to Philip, because he wanted to prove to Philip that Rink was a rebel at heart, and the *Vermanung* had enough bitter criticism of magistrates in it to add weight to Eberhard's charge. Beyond this conjecture, there is no evidence of a reference in other available source materials to either the *Vermanung* or the *Widderlegung.*

affairs. Characteristically, Rink could not omit a discussion of baptism even when writing on a subject that had no obvious relation to the issue of baptism. He sprinkled the writing with sharply-worded denunciations of the Christian princes and their confessional advisers, because they were presumptuous enough to think that God sanctioned their persecutions of his own people.

Various attempts were made to regain Rink for the Evangelical faith. The first of these was undertaken by Georg Witzel, probably in 1531 while Rink was still in the Vacha region.[1] Witzel was attracted to Anabaptism because of its ethical message. He wanted to restore the early church of the Acts account and bitterly charged Lutheranism with moral laxity. But he could not accept the Anabaptist practice of rebaptism or their break with the church. With his passion for the constitutional unity of the church, he tried to win Anabaptists from their error. But he had no ultimate success with Rink, though there is no information about his arguments or possible relative success.[2]

A second attempt to convert Rink was made in 1538 or 1539 by Peter Tasch, an erstwhile Anabaptist who had recently rejoined the state church under the persuasive arguments of Martin Bucer. Bucer had discovered that former Anabaptists were more effective than state church theologians in persuading the Anabaptists to recant, and therefore recommended to Philip of Hesse that he use such persons.[3]

---

[1] It is possible that the discussion with Witzel occurred before Rink's arrest. See testimony of Hans Werner at the Vacha trial, in Wappler, *Thüringen*, pp. 331–32. Wappler (*ibid.*, p. 79) declares he was visited by Witzel in prison.

[2] Witzel was much abused both in his own time and by historians since. Part of his bitterness toward Lutheranism can be laid to the manner in which he was treated while occupying a pastoral charge at Niemegk, near Wittenberg, a post which Luther obtained for him. He was suspect in Wittenberg because he did not try to get close to the theologians there, because he openly criticized the absence of an ethical concern both in Lutheran theology and also in church practice, and finally because he entertained Campanus in 1529. After the latter event the Elector ordered him seized and imprisoned, as a suspected anti-trinitarian. Subsequently released as not guilty, he returned as a layman to his native town, Vacha, bitterly determined to wage verbal war on Lutheranism. He thereby supplied Catholics with much ammunition. His attachment to Reformation ideas and to clerical marriage was too firm to permit a return to Catholicism, but he could not tolerate Lutheranism nor was he tolerated by it, and Anabaptism was too sectarian for him. Witzel was a pastor-theologian without a church, a distressing predicament in the sixteenth century. G. L. Schmidt calls him aptly an Old Catholic of the sixteenth century. He wandered about seeking positions with Catholic princes who had Reformation inclinations. As to Anabaptism, he blamed the Lutherans for having occasioned its rise, i.e., he probably accepted at full value the Anabaptist charge of moral laxity among Lutherans as the reason for their separation from the Reformers' Church ("Erroris huius omnis occasio a Luthero est"). A. Ritschl, "Witzel's Abkehr vom Luthertum," *Zeitschrift für Kirchengeschichte*, II (1878), 399. See also P. Tschackert, "Witzel," *Allgemeine Deutsche Biographie*, XLIII (1898) 657–62.

[3] Letter to Philip, printed in Karl Rembert, *Die Wiedertäufer im Herzogtum Jülich* (Berlin: Gaertner, 1899), p. 456, n. 2.

Philip ordered the governor of Marburg to release Tasch from prison, after Tasch's so-called recantation, and to send him to convince Rink of his error.[1] Tasch had been a disciple of Hofmann, working mostly in West and Central Hesse.[2] Again details of the attempt are missing; the mission failed, for in 1540 there is good evidence of Rink's continued imprisonment.[3]

Little is heard of Rink after his arrest in 1531. He was confined eventually to a cell in Bärbach in the County of Katzenelnbogen,[4] some distance from the regions where he had worked. In 1540 Bucer interceded with the Landgrave for milder treatment of the prisoner;[5] Philip had Rink put into a private and more comfortable room.[6] This intercession by Bucer suggests that Bucer himself may have had conversations with Rink and tried to get him to recant. His final end is uncertain. Wappler says that he was still a prisoner in 1545, but his evidence is very slight.[7] It is probable that Rink died for his faith, a "prisoner of Christ" as he styled himself.[8]

What was the character of this man? That he was steadfast and faithful to his cause and calling as he understood them goes without saying. That he was learned and reasonably able in argument is seen in his trial in 1528 and is corroborated by his friend Witzel, who greatly admired Rink's courage and erudition, but called his insistence on rebaptism madness.[9] But what of the fact of his refusal to obey the order of exile? Twice he was banished, and twice he returned to his Anabaptist work within Hesse despite the fact that he probably was required both times to offer an oath that he would not return.[10] Eberhard in particular added this disobedience to his accusation of sedition.[11]

---

[1] Letter of Philip to the Statthalder in Marburg, December 26, 1538, *TA, Hesse*, p. 261.

[2] Zur Linden, *op. cit.*, pp. 463–66.

[3] Max Lenz, *Briefwechsel Landgraf Philipps des Grossmüthigen von Hessen mit Bucer* (3 vols.; Leipzig: Hirzel, 1880–1891), March 17, 1540, I, 156.

[4] Wappler, *Die Stellung Kursachsens*, p. 35. Today Bärbach is a small, agricultural village, the seat of a former nunnery which lies in ruins. It is likely that Rink was incarcerated in the convent.

[5] Bucer to Philip, March 17, 1540, Lenz, *op. cit.*, I, 156.

[6] Philip to Bucer, March 22, 1540, *ibid.*, p. 161.

[7] Wappler, *Die Stellung Kursachsens*, p. 82.

[8] Letter of Rink to Eberhard, *ca.* 1530, *TA, Hesse*, p. 31.

[9] Witzel to MBF, December 24, 1531, printed in Wappler, *Die Stellung Kursachsens*, p. 35, n. 2.

[10] I could find no record of his having taken such oaths, except a reference in a letter from Elector John to Philip of Hesse, Dec. 21, 1531, advising the death penalty for Rink because he had broken his oath about returning (letter printed in Wappler, *Stellung*, p. 153). Philip usually demanded an oath from the Anabaptists captured in his lands, that they would honor the sentence of exile.

[11] Eberhard to Philip, *ca.* March 1, 1532, printed in Wappler, *Thüringen*, p. 335.

If it was a moral issue to Eberhard, was it not likewise one to Rink? Rink did not counsel disobedience to civil authority. On the contrary, he taught his followers to obey the government as long as its demand was not against the command of God.[1] He believed that the order to leave forever a given territory was contrary to the Lordship of God over the entire world.[2] What belonged to the Lord was meant to belong also to his children. He could not accept the verdict of expulsion from any land, for this would have meant that Rink did not consider himself one of the Lord's children, an impossible conclusion. Any government, he said, that judges a child of God either with the sword or with expulsion is itself judged by that very act; for such government is acting contrary to its ordination, to its Christian mandate. God never intended that the authority of civil office be used to kill his children. Rink was not surprised that governments so acted; indeed, he believed that the true Christian must expect unjust suffering constantly at the hand of government.[3] But no one had a right to argue for such persecution in the name of the Lord, a point intended as a thrust against Eberhard's arguments. In all this Rink had the firm conviction that he was called to warn the civil authorities of his time of their impending judgment and doom if they persisted in the persecution of God's children.[4] His reference was to eternal punishment rather than to a specific act of judgment on the princes on earth. On one occasion he denounced the magistrates for their use of torture to compel the Anabaptists to perjure themselves by promising, against their own convictions, to remain in exile. Of course they denied the validity of oaths taken under duress. He likened the Anabaptists to the subjects of a prince who was driven from his lands by a murderer, who in turn compelled the subjects to swear allegiance to him. When the hereditary prince recovered his domain, both prince and subjects considered the oaths of allegiance to the usurper of no validity.[5]

Conviction that exile for an Anabaptist was a contradiction of God's purpose and therefore not to be obeyed leads to another trait in Rink's character – anger. His fulminations against Eberhard in particular, and magistrates in general, are full of wrath. He called the Lutheran princes, whom Eberhard served as magistrate, bloodthirsty false prophets who worshipped not the Lord of Heaven but their own bellies;

[1] Testimony of Heinz Ot, Vacha hearing, *ibid.*, p. 330.
[2] Eberhard to Philip, *ca.* March 1, 1532, *ibid.*, p. 335.
[3] Ot testimony, *ibid.*, pp. 330–31.
[4] Letter of Rink to Eberhard, *ca.* 1530, *TA, Hesse*, p. 31.
[5] *Vermanung*, p. 18.

any inconvenience which they suffered brought down their wrath upon innocent offenders. Rink struck a blow against the widespread use of the term *Schwärmer* as a damning cover for all persons not in a-greement with the Lutheran princes and theologians.[1] Moreover, Rink was especially provoked by a series of false charges, unspecified for us, by his father-in-law and wife, and also by the persistent attempts to arrest and persecute him and his people. The vigor of his language, somewhat unusual for an Anabaptist, in his warning to Eberhard can be explained at least in part on the ground that he was speaking the warning of pending judgment from heaven. It is also probable that latent hatred of the lower classes toward the nobles in Central Germany found an echo in Rink's words. Rink was, however, rarely angry. At his trial in 1528 there is a notable absence of provocative language on his part. But on occasion one feels the sting of a sharp tongue.

Even when he was not provoked to anger by special circumstances, Rink's passionate nature found expression in flaming epistle and fervid speech. He could convert a group of peasants into ardent Anabaptists with his harangues against the Lutherans. His prison letter to his flock was not a quiet pastoral exhortation to stand firm against the per-suasive arguments of the state church theologians and pastors, with some timely instruction on crucial points of doctrine, although the circumstances of his followers called for such a letter. It was rather a bitter attack against the state church in the course of developing his favorite theme of baptism.[2] His followers often displayed a marked hostility to state church doctrine, but were ill-equipped to discuss its major shortcomings, from the Anabaptist viewpoint, let alone its errors on finer points. Rink was fitted by nature for the task of the fiery evangelist, the itinerant missioner who called people from the darkness of an inadequate faith to the light of the full gospel. But he was not disposed by nature to abandon his restless wanderings for the quieter task of building his converts into a band of dedicated believers. His doctrine called for the creation of a highly disciplined brotherhood; but he was not the man to develop such a body.

Rink was an intensely dedicated proclaimer of the Word, a man ready and willing to suffer without developing a martyr complex. His impression on Philip and Bucer, both of whom kept a sharp eye for revolutionaries among the Anabaptists, was highly favorable. He emerges as a conscientious worker in the Anabaptist cause.

[1] *Ibid., passim*, esp. pp. 10 and 12.
[2] Baptism Tract in *Sammelband*, pp. Kr.–K3r.

The activity of the Anabaptists in western Thuringia by no means disappeared with Rink's departure. Other leaders, though generally less capable, came to the fore. The Hutterian Brethren sent missioners to evangelize Hesse. Georg Zaunring and Christoph Gschäll (Christoph von Mähren) were two of these in the early 1530's. They began a relation between Anabaptists in Hesse and Moravia that was to produce both harmonious fruit and discord. In the latter half of the decade the Brethren even sent Peter Riedemann, who wrote his *Rechenschaft* while in a Hessian prison.[1] Other men, such as Georg Stein, Jakob Schmidt, Ilgen, and Hans Bott, all natives of Central Germany, were also leaders in this region. Alexander, whose major area of activity was farther north, around Mühlhausen, also did some work in this region.[2]

The arm of the law was not idle while Anabaptism was spreading. In July, 1533, a group of nineteen Anabaptists was arrested at Berka, west of Eisenach and north of Vacha, in the district of Hausbreitenbach. Some of these were disciples of Rink. At the hearing on July 19 to 21 they could not be dissuaded from their opinions. They refused to attend the Evangelical church at Herda on July 20, where their errors were to be exposed and refuted in the sermon. They displayed an extreme suspicion of their captors; their leaders, they said, had warned them against fellowship with the Evangelicals. Again Hesse and Electoral Saxony were at odds on the type of punishment to be accorded. John Frederick counseled execution; but Philip had the jurisdiction in this instance, and he released all but one, Margarete Koch, who had been apprehended and released before. She was confined to prison for a longer period.[3]

One month later twenty-five Anabaptists of the Sorga center, east of Hersfeld, were caught. This was Rink's major congregation, and many of the people arrested were his followers. A hearing was conducted by the Hessian authorities at Petersberg near Sorga on August 9, 1533. At Philip's direction the questions put to the twenty-five were directed to two major problems: their attitude toward the Evangelicals, and their attitude toward the state. Philip was not at all convinced that they were seditious, but thought them obviously sectarian, for they would have nothing to do with the Evangelicals. Whereupon Philip banished them from Hesse, because he was convinced that Sorga was

---

[1] Robert Friedmann, "Hutterian Brethren," *ME*, II, 855. Letter of Hutterite elders to Mathes, 1538, *TA, Hesse*, pp. 180–84.

[2] Wappler, *Thüringen*, p. 85.

[3] Trial printed in Wappler, *Die Stellung Kursachsens*, pp. 168–76. Wappler, *Thüringen*, pp. 88–89.

an Anabaptist center which lent personnel and enthusiasm to the cause elsewhere in his territory.[1]

Both before and after this trial at Sorga, many of the western Thuringian Anabaptists emigrated to Moravia, the "promised land" of Anabaptists and other Reformation radicals in the sixteenth century.[2] A group of Sorga Anabaptists traveled to Moravia in September, 1533, under their leader Hans Bott.[3] But they found no happy fellowship with the Hutterian Brethren. Bott and his followers were reluctant to surrender all of their possessions, as the Hutterites demanded, but eventually consented. Then the Hutterites, displeased with Bott's preaching, told him to desist, whereupon he declared that they were stopping streams of living water [4] and withdrew in favor of fellowship with Gabriel Ascherham and Philip Plener. He and his group, disatisfied with Moravia, returned to their old homes later in 1533, but without having their material possessions restored to them.[5]

---

[1] Trial in *TA, Hesse*, pp. 64–69. Wappler, *Thüringen*, p. 102.

[2] See Robert Friedmann, "Moravia," *ME*, III, 747–50.

[3] Bott was not among the twenty-five tried in August, 1533. He is an elusive figure, about whom one can get very little positive information. His dispute with the Hutterian Brethren offers the only source of substantial information on his doctrine, and this does not provide a full view at all. He claimed to represent the views of Rink, whose mantle of spiritual authority over the Sorga congregation he apparently inherited. But in these fluid, formative years of Anabaptism there were too many differences of opinion between master and disciple to assume that Rink's doctrines were also Bott's. He got his start in Anabaptism with a strong eschatology in the days immediately following Müntzer's heyday of power among the peasant masses. See Neff, "Hans Both," *ME*, I, 395–96.

[4] Bott accused the Hutterites of maligning Rink in their repudiation of his own doctrines. The charge was undoubtedly the result of Bott's attempt to maintain a party of followers among those who had come, and were coming, from Hesse and Thuringia. The Hutterites accused Bott of spiritualism and rejection of Scripture, plus error on matters of the flesh. *TA, Hesse*, pp. 180–84.

[5] It is obvious that the conflict between Bott and the Hutterites can be laid in large part to the internal struggle among the brethren in Moravia at the time. Bott went over to Ascherham and Plener, who did not agree with each other, not because he accepted their views but because he rejected, and was rejected by, the followers of Hutter. (See Friedmann, "Hutterian Brethren," *ME*, II, 854–55.) The Hutterites appealed to Mathes Hasenhan, an Anabaptist leader in Hesse, against Bott and his false witness concerning them among the brethren in Hesse. They referred to Rink's moderate Anabaptism, even though they did not know Rink well, but had only heard that he remained steadfast in the faith. They did not trust Bott's representation of Rink's thought. (See letter from the elders in Moravia and Austria to Mathes in 1538 [*TA, Hesse*, pp. 180–84]. Testimony of Georg Knoblauch, April 15, 1534, printed in Wappler, *Thüringen*, p. 358. Also *ibid.*, pp. 103–05.) Mathes is even more elusive than Bott; they both had to be elusive, or else sacrifice their necks. One meets Mathes almost only as a baptizer or teacher of others who were caught. (Thus from the archives, *TA, Hesse*, pp. 156, 205, 262, 291; Wappler, *Thüringen*, p. 426.) He was obviously a trusted and faithful leader of the Anabaptists. (Letter of Moravian elders referred to above in this note; also letter of Tasch to Schnabel, 1538, in *TA, Hesse*, p. 161.) Mathes was caught in 1540; Bucer and Tasch argued with him to the point that he admitted he had no certain word from Scripture against infant baptism. He agreed to cease directing people away from the state church on grounds of faulty or improper baptism – i.e., as infants. But he requested time to

Thuringia could offer examples of Anabaptism less moderate than Bott. In 1532 the notorious "Prophet" and his followers were brought to heel by the authorities in the Abbacy of Fulda. A group of forty followers fortified a house and provisioned it with food enough to withstand a siege of six months, but with only stones to throw against the forces of the state who attacked them. When their supply of stones was exhausted, they threw substantial pieces of their provisions of meat and cheese. Soon the defenders were led off to prison at Fulda, after suffering the loss of three dead, three mortally wounded including the "Prophet" himself, and many more with minor wounds. No amount of persuasion could induce them to recant, except for the few fellow travelers who had come only to see the "Prophet" perform miracles. Six were beheaded in the hope that others would recant when they realized the punishment that awaited them. They remained steadfast. Probably others were subsequently executed.[1]

The "Prophet" and his followers met the minimum requirements of Anabaptism by submitting to adult baptism. It is impossible to discover what the act meant for them; probably they regarded it as a formal initiation into the group. Beyond some details of their exaggerated spiritualism and use of mass hypnosis, nothing is known of their doctrine. In prison they experienced visions of the Comforter's arrival. In ecstasy some shouted, "I see him"; one bayed like a hound; another bellowed like an ox; one neighed like a horse. One of the fellow-travelers testified after the ordeal that he had cried out with the others, though he did not want to; he was conscious of his involuntary involvement with the frenzied radicals. In their frenzy they even requested death; death held no threat for them. The "Prophet" himself was reputedly the worker of miracles, having healed a girl of leprosy, turned water into wine, and even raised people from the dead. All the while he was surrounded by his ecstatic followers who shrieked out his virtues and pronounced his miracles a glorious success.[2] Here was spiritualism gone to seed.

A later manifestation of excessively radical Anabaptism was the movement, again in the southwestern fringes of Thuringia, in the

---

consider his own rejoining the state church because he was not fully convinced it was a true church (letter of Bucer and Tasch to Philip, Feb. 7, 1540, *TA, Hesse*, pp. 269–70). No more is heard of him after this date.

[1] Wappler, *Thüringen*, pp. 81–85. He relies for his information on the correspondence between Abbot Johann of Fulda and Count Wilhelm of Henneberg, March 25, 1532 to May 5, 1532, printed on pp. 336–44. Schannat, *Historia Fuldensis* (Frankfurt, 1729), III, 255, reports briefly on the incident.

[2] Wappler, *Thüringen*, pp. 81–85.

Abbacy of Fulda, under the leadership of Hans Krug, Hans von Fulda, and Peter the Baptist. This group was a mob of robbers and cutthroats who for unknown reasons adopted adult baptism and were called Anabaptists by the civil authorities. Krug confessed that their spirit was not of God, but of the devil. They spent their time burning, killing, raping, and pillaging. Krug himself murdered, or helped to murder, at least five persons. He raped a woman who would not submit to baptism and burned an entire village himself. Again the researcher is thwarted by absence of sources which explain motives and origins. Could this be a group born within evangelical Anabaptism? What was its relation to other Anabaptist groups? The sources are silent on these questions.[1]

One of the foci for moderate Anabaptism in the 1530's was Fritz Erbe. He himself was not a leader of the movement. But his steadfast-ness through sixteen years of imprisonment was an inspiration to Anabaptists in all of western Thuringia. Erbe became to the Anabap-tists a symbol of the invincibility of truth. First arrested at Haus-breitenbach in October 1531, he was interrogated by Justus Menius. His testimony gives some insight into the manner in which Anabaptists spread their faith. Erbe first encountered Anabaptism in the person of a woman whom he met walking on the road to Berka. She spoke of many things and finally of baptism. She referred him to a Nicholas [2] at Wünschensuhl for further information. He met the man, received instruction, and was baptized. Erbe was not as adamant on the ne-cessity for believers' baptism as were some Anabaptists, but thought it should be left to the individual conscience. He personally considered the baptizing of infants useless, and he felt himself conscience-bound to receive baptism as a believer. Erbe appears, in his brief recorded testimony, to have held the customary Anabaptist position on most subjects. He disclosed a mild eschatology, which was characteristic of Thuringian Anabaptism.[3] The six Anabaptists apprehended on this occasion were divided between Philip and Elector John for punishment, since the two rulers could not agree on a common disposition of the problem. Saxony's three were executed. Erbe recanted and was released by Philip in January, 1532.[4]

But Erbe was reapprehended one year later for refusing to have his newborn child baptized. His arrest was followed by the arrest of the

---

[1] Testimony of Hans Krug, obtained without torture, September 11, 1533, *TA, Hesse*, pp. 71–73.

[2] Nicholas Schreiber.

[3] Trial, October 9–11, 1531, printed in Wappler, *Die Stellung Kursachsens*, pp. 138–39.

[4] *Ibid.*; letter of Eberhard to John Frederick, December 14, 1540, *ibid.*, p. 210.

nineteen Anabaptists at Berka, including Margarete Koch, the *alte Garköchin*, to whom he had given refuge on occasion in his home at Herda, some two miles east of Berka. While the other eighteen were ultimately released, Erbe and Margarete were retained in prison for a long time, he until his death in 1548, and she for an unknown period.[1] John Frederick advised death for Erbe, but Philip wanted exile; meanwhile Erbe lay in prison in a tower of the Eisenach city wall. People for miles around regarded him as a martyr. Wappler declares that half of Erbe's village of Herda was converted to Anabaptism by his steadfast courage.[2] Even Eberhard von der Thann, the hardheaded civil officer for the district of Eisenach, who encountered Anabaptism often and found it extremely odious, was moved by Erbe's plight. He probably admired the courage of a man who had much to lose for the sake of his faith, for Erbe was a farmer with considerable property and of course had a family.[3] Eberhard provided religious instruction for Erbe in the vain hope that he would recant. For a time during the instruction Erbe was transferred to more comfortable quarters in Eisenach. After his refusal to recant he was recommitted to the tower in the Wartburg which had been his prison since 1540. Here Erbe died in 1548.[4]

While he was in the Eisenach tower, Erbe was visited by Anabaptists for the purpose of mutual encouragement. This was of necessity done clandestinely; on two occasions persons were caught at the wall conversing with the prisoner. In November, 1537, two men were surprised at night by the guard outside Erbe's tower cell in conversation with Erbe. Menius conducted the examination of the men. The record of their trial shows them to have been moderate Anabaptists who emphasized a righteous walk for the Christian and eschewed fellowship with preachers whose lives were sinful. They rejected infant baptism and the real presence for the usual reasons, and looked forward to persecution for the true Christian; for to suffer persecution was the true Lord's Supper, the true communion with Christ. The two were not found guilty of any subversive plots against civil authority, but were found

---

[1] Koch was reinterrogated in 1537. She drops from the records after this time. *TA, Hesse*, pp. 152–53.

[2] Wappler, *Thüringen*, p. 87.

[3] Letter of Eberhard to John Frederick, January 8, 1541, printed in Wappler, *Die Stellung Kursachsens*, p. 211. *Ibid.*, p. 94 "... Dyweil er dan Leibs vnd halber ... vast vnuormugelich vnd ... das er biss auff diese seine misshandlunge Einen guten wandel gefurth vnd sich je vnd allewege billichs gehorsames gehalten, Er auch mit weib vnd kinder vnd zimlicher Bauerssnarunge ... besessen ..."

[4] *Ibid.*, pp. 91–94.

guilty of seditious views, as defined by the Lutherans. They rejected private property on the grounds that everything belonged to the Lord. Oaths and suits at law they considered forbidden the Christian. They were skeptical about a Christian serving as magistrate, although they would not declare themselves unequivocally on the point. Despite torture they refused to recant. At the order of Elector John Frederick they were executed in January, 1538, as blasphemers and revolutionaries.[1]

A second group, this time of three men, was apprehended in May, 1539. These men displayed an aggressive spiritualism that scorned Scripture as authority; the Spirit of God, they maintained, instructed man apart from Scripture, which was a dead letter. They heaped abuse on the Evangelical Lord's Supper, styling the bread the bite of Judas and the cup the curse of the Babylonian Whore (Rev. 17:5). True communion was persecution for Christ's sake and discipleship. They denied the bodily resurrection from the dead. Government they considered unnecessary for Christians. Oaths were forbidden except in a few instances. Concerning private property they said it was permissible if it was shared with people in need. The Wittenberg court decreed torture to induce recantation. The treatment was successful, and thereby saved the trio from execution for blasphemy.[2] But the common people tended all the more to regard Erbe and those who visited him as bearers of the truth. Precisely in this geographical region where the princes disagreed on how to handle errors in religious doctrine they were suspicious of the use of force to induce a restoration of true faith. They were convinced that Scripture was on the side of Erbe, both because Erbe would not recant despite persecution, and also because the Evangelicals were reduced to the argument of force. "If he could be overcome by [arguments from] God's Word, he would not be a captive for so long a time." [3] Erbe was a prophet and martyr to the common

[1] Trial record from Menius' pen printed in Wappler, *ibid.*, pp. 196–98. Narrative in Wappler, *Thüringen*, pp. 172–74. The order of the court is missing and the precise grounds for execution are therefore unknown. Elector John Frederick, in his letter of November 22, 1537, to the Mayor and Council of Eisenach on the case describes the captives' beliefs as "unchristian and revolutionary." Wappler, *Die Stellung Kursachsens*, p. 199.
[2] Account of the trial, June, 1539, in Wappler, *ibid.*, pp. 203–04. The three were required to do public penance on two or three successive Sundays in Eisenach. They were commanded to remain with the Evangelicals throughout their lives; they were never to go over to the Catholics. *Ibid.*, p. 91.
[3] Mayor Johann Ley and the Eisenach Council paraphrasing the attitude of the common people in a letter to Elector John Frederick and Duke John Ernest, end of July, 1539, printed *ibid.*, p. 208.

folk of western Thuringia. Because of his fame, he was moved to the less accessible Wartburg fortress.[1]

Interminable imprisonment or banishment in Hesse, execution in Electoral Saxony, but still the movement did not die, although it was retarded. Early in 1544 there were fresh arrests in Berka, Erbe's home community. His wife was one of sixteen caught here. Some recanted; others refused. There ensued the usual dispute between Hesse and Electoral Saxony on treatment. Philip used an ex-Anabaptist in an effort to induce more recantations. The Saxons, led in this instance by Menius, argued for execution. Menius charged Philip with contributing to the spread of Anabaptism in the region because of his refusal to adopt sterner measures against the radicals.[2] But during the remaining 40's the movement died down throughout Thuringia. Persecution had taken its toll. The steadfast among the brethren had emigrated to more hospitable regions,[3] and those who remained made their peace with the state church.

Central German Anabaptism was not, of course, confined to western Thuringia. It spread to the northern part of the old Medieval Stem Duchy and on beyond into the region of the Harz Mountains, and appeared in West and Central Hesse. Although the movement in these regions need not detain us long, a brief overview might be useful at this point.

Anabaptism spread early to northern Thuringia, probably from Franconia. One finds traces of it in the records in 1527. It reached its high point in the 1530's. All of its most influential leaders had connections with Anabaptism farther south. Georg Köhler originated near Zwickau, and spent some time among the Anabaptists around Vacha and Herda.[4] Alexander, the most influential of the northern Thuringian leaders, ranged from Göttingen to Weimar and Sorga in his itinerant mission.[5] Hans Bott was a leader of the Sorga Anabaptists after the incarceration of Rink. Ludwig Spon gives us a description of congregational life at the Sorga Anabaptist center; obviously he had been there.[6] Heinz Kraut was arrested, tried and executed in the region

---

[1] *Ibid.* I can find no evidence of a sentence of life imprisonment on Erbe. In effect this is what he received.

[2] *Ibid.*, pp. 97–100.

[3] Wappler, *Thüringen*, p. 105, says that many emigrated to Moravia, particularly the disciples of the Hutterian apostles like Riedemann.

[4] Jacobs, *op. cit.*, pp. 78, 81, 86; Wappler, *Thüringen*, p. 118.

[5] Wiswedel, *op. cit.*, I, 89.

[6] Wappler, *Die Stellung Kursachsens*, p. 47.

around Jena.[1] Here, and farther north in the Harz, the brethren called themselves the "Beloved of God," or the "Friends of God."[2] There were the usual arrests, trials, and executions. There were centers of Anabaptists at various times at Mühlhausen, Sangershausen, Frankenhausen, Esperstedt, and Emseloh. The movement at Mühlhausen received special attention because three princes had political control in successive years, each for one year at a time after the Peasants' War; and they did not agree on how to handle the sectarians. Saxon Duke George and the Saxon Electors generally followed the imperial mandate of 1529. Philip of Hesse always sought to obtain recantations, which were followed by release from prison. The Anabaptists in these regions were very similar to those in western Thuringia with respect to doctrine and practice. One finds traces of what may well have been a large amount of intercourse between the regions, e.g., the peregrinations of the leaders mentioned above. After the death of Duke George in 1539, his lands became Protestant. With this process and its concomitant persecution the movement died out.[3]

In Central and West Hesse a movement is discerned which mixed and meshed with that of West Thuringia to its east. But this movement probably originated, and was certainly nourished, from different sources. Here is found the influence of Melchior Hofmann and the whole line of prophets and teachers from the Lowlands and the Rhineland. Hofmann's spiritualism, including his peculiar view of the incarnation, is found among the Anabaptists in this region. In this region there were five principal leaders, four of whom were captured and examined at the same time. Georg Schnabel, Peter Lose, Hermann Bastian, and Leonhard Fälber were surprised with twenty-six other Anabaptists at worship in an abandoned church near Gemünden on the Wohra. These five were imprisoned with six others at Wolkersdorf, where they were dealt with so leniently that they were able to enlarge the opening through which their food was given them, so that they could pass in and out. They returned to the prison from time to time, but spent long periods of time outside at their missionary activity. It

---

[1] *CR*, II, 997–1003. Jordan, "Wiedertäufer in Mühlhausen," *Mühlhäuser Geschichtsblätter*, XV (1915), 42, 44, considers these five men the most important leaders of Anabaptism north of the Eisenach-Berka line. One could add Bernhardus, who influenced Alexander, and Volkmar von Hildburghausen who baptized Alexander; but very little is known of the activity and doctrines of these men. "Alexanders Confession," printed in Wappler, *Thüringen*, pp. 348–49.

[2] Jacobs, *op. cit.*, p. 472.

[3] For detailed coverage of the movement in these regions see Jacobs, *op. cit.*, and Wappler, *Thüringen*, chapter i of Book i and chapters iv, v, and vii of Book ii.

is reported that Schnabel baptized thirty persons during the period of one year before the opening was discovered. A dispute between the four and Bucer, who represented the state church, was held at Marburg from October 30 to November 1, 1538. Bucer was admirably suited for the task, since he did not feel compelled to defend the Lutheran church at every point against which the Anabaptists raised their complaints. He admitted the necessity for church discipline; he did not try to justify ecclesiastically the practice of persecution of Anabaptists; he even admitted that the church must be more conscientious in its efforts to give religious instruction to children as a follow-up to infant baptism. He repeatedly put before these Anabaptists the evil of separation from the church, a church which, though not pure in every respect, nevertheless proclaimed God's truth. These Anabaptists succumbed, agreed to receive instruction, and were received back into the church, but not without maintaining a certain bargaining position, i.e., they would return to the church only if the church made changes. After a series of written exchanges, the Anabaptists were convinced that the state church theologians were in earnest. Besides the return of these Anabaptists to the church, together with Peter Tasch, the fifth leader of importance, this affair resulted in the adoption of a discipline for the Hessian church in 1538 which instituted confirmation and introduced the idea of the ban. Not all of the Hessian Anabaptists accepted the compromise; inured by years of persecution they were suspicious of any dealings with state church officials. Consequently Bucer proposed that the leaders who recanted should be sent out to induce their erstwhile flocks to re-enter the state church. Tasch and others were subsequently dispatched on such missions with some measure of success. As a settled church life spread throughout these regions of Hesse, the Anabaptist movement gradually subsided.[1]

It must be noted in passing that the Anabaptist leaders in this region had the ability and opportunity to articulate their views more satisfactorily than did most of their brethren in Central Germany. They could speak a theological language. One need mention only the "Confession" of Peter Tasch [2] and the "Vindication" of Georg Schnabel. [3]

[1] The most substantial narrative of the movement here described is that of Hochhuth, *op. cit.* Much of this has been summarized by Hege, "The Early Anabaptists in Hesse," *MQR*, V (1931), 157–78, and in "Hesse," *ME*, II, 719–27. Rembert, *op. cit.*, pp. 450–53, has worthwhile discussions of Tasch and Fälber.

[2] "Glaubensbekenntnis der in Marburg gefangenen Wiedertäufer," *TA, Hesse*, pp. 247–57. Earlier printed in part as "Bekenntniss eines Wiedertäuffers," by zur Linden, *op. cit.*, pp. 463–66.

[3] "Verantwortung und widerlegung der artikel, so jetzund im land zu Hessen uber die armen Davider (die man widertaufer nennt) usgegangen sind," *TA, Hesse*, pp. 165–80.

One final development must be at least mentioned here. This is the group called the "Blood Brothers," [1] led by Klaus Ludwig of Tüngeda, a native of the Gotha region; it spread in the 1540's and 1550's in the region between Gotha and Mühlhausen. It combined a critique of infant baptism with libertinism and murder, and terrorized the land. It had no connections with any ecclesiastical group nor with the Anabaptists, although it was confused with Anabaptism by the common people. Menius published a refutation of the sect in 1551.

Anabaptism as a movement faded in Central Germany from 1540 on. The spread of authority and chains of responsibility within the state churches was too much for the beleaguered brethren. Deprived of vigorous leadership by persecution and emigration the movement disappeared. It had never commanded a large following,[2] although its ability to capitalize on peasant grievances and dissatisfaction with the embryonic state churches made it a formidable threat to the magisterial Reformation in its early years. It left its imprint on the state churches in the institution of confirmation and in the idea of the ban.[3]

---

[1] *Blutsfreunde*. Hochhuth, *op. cit.*, p. 182, declares that these are the "Freie Brüder" of Bullinger. See below, pp. 205–09.

[2] Jordan, *op. cit.*, p. 49, rightly challenges Wappler's assertions that Anabaptism found many supporters. Jordan cites six executions in Mühlhausen, a city of 8500 inhabitants and a reputed Anabaptist center. Wappler builds numerical strength on the theory that the court records of Anabaptist examinations cover only a small percentage of the total Anabaptist population. This theory is plausible but dangerous. Nor should one build numerical strength on the degree of concern of the princes. The civil authorities were worried, almost panicked, because they saw in the movement the constant threat of another peasant war. O. A. Hecker in a review of Wappler's Thuringia book in *Neues Archiv für sächsische Geschichte und Altertumskunde*, XL (1919), 201, counted ninety martyrs in the entire region. Ninety martyrs to a cause is no small number; but one cannot speak of this movement as a mass one.

[3] See Hege, "Hesse," *ME*, II, 726–27 for the opinion of Walter Sohm. See also Franklin Littell, *The Anabaptist View of the Church* (2d revised ed.; Boston: Star King Press, 1958), p. 36 for the influence of Anabaptism on the state church.

CHAPTER III

ANABAPTISM IN CENTRAL GERMANY II
FAITH AND LIFE

We turn next to a discussion of the religious ideas of the Anabaptists. What did the brethren believe? Any discussion of Anabaptist doctrines is made difficult by the fact that most Anabaptists were not theologically oriented or minded. There were exceptions to this, of course; individual figures can be found with an aptitude for, and interest in, theology. Some of the more promising of the younger intellectuals met early deaths. But the entire emphasis of the brethren was far more on the manner of Christian life than on a systematization of their religious ideas. Yet a presentation of Anabaptist thought is essential if one is to understand them against the background of the larger Reformation movement. In the account which follows the ideas of Melchior Rink will receive the principal attention, for several reasons. Rink was the only leader of strictly Thuringian Anabaptism capable of careful and systematic formulation and articulation of religious ideas.[1] Moreover, there is more material from the sources on his ideas than on those of any other leader. He speaks to us in a few writings of his own, in the account of his hearing in 1528, and in the testimonies of his followers.

For Rink's soteriological views one must begin as he did with a rejection of Luther's view of faith. Rink is reported to have spoken, in 1525, with some vehemence against the dead faith of the Lutherans and in favor of the living heroic faith of Müntzer.[2] By 1528 he was still rejecting the Lutheran doctrine of justification because it was lifeless, but the vehemence is less evident.[3] His disciples carried enough distaste

---

[1] Alexander is a possible exception to this generalization. But the sources on Alexander are too scanty to build upon.

[2] Menius, *Der Widderlauffer*, p. H4r. Rink was a disciple of Müntzer at the time.

[3] Raidt charged him with blaspheming the gospel of Christ on the basis of his declaration that Luther's teaching led one to the devil (*TA, Hesse*, p. 4). Rink denied the charge, but the records do not make clear which part he denied (*ibid.*, p. 6). Rink was certainly capable of intemperate outbursts against Luther.

for Lutheran dogma on justification to warrant the assertion that such rejection constituted a rallying cry of their faith.[1] Rink meant that Lutheran justification did not produce good works in the lives of those who claimed its healing powers.

On the occasion of the 1528 hearing Rink addressed himself briefly to the soteriological question he was most impressed with the quality of love in God's nature. Man created in the image of God meant therefore a creature of love whose essential nature was love itself. God intended that man should love him wholly, without restraint. But man built up a false love to disfigure and replace the true love of God in himself; he set up himself and his own acts as the means and power to his own salvation. Having made himself more important than he really was, he was not prepared to accept the mercy of God because he felt he did not need it. He needed no outside aid to stand righteous before the throne of God. "This attitude, this sin, was prefigured in Eden ... in the revelation of the law." The law was given to teach men that "judgment came upon all men to condemnation" (Rom. 5:18). It was to be a schoolmaster to bring men to understand the fact of their sin (Gal. 3; Rom. 5). This sin was overcome so that man could stand righteous before God only when he could return to the original image of love. Rink did not explain how man could return to the true image. The two most necessary elements in that return were a true faith in Christ and a return to God's Word. Whereas in his delineation of sin Rink had used predominantly Pauline Scriptures, in this instance he turned to Johannine and Old Testament passages. Unfortunately the records do not give his explanation of them.[2] Rink's declaration was an adroit mixture of Paul and John, of Luther and Denk.

Rink's insistence that the essential nature of God was love did not exclude other attributes; they were merely not as important to him. In Raidt's summary of Rink's discussion he inserted some rather more Lutheran terms. Man was created in the image of God, which meant not only love but also wisdom, holiness, and righteousness. Rink offered no objection to this formulation. It is most significant that to Rink's doctrinal position up to this point his examiners, Raidt and the Marburg theologians, could find no grounds for objection.[3] Anabaptist and

---

[1] For example, see the testimony of Adam Angersbach, November, 1531, printed in Wappler, *Thüringen*, p. 328.

[2] *TA, Hesse*, p. 8.

[3] *Ibid.*, p. 9. Zur Linden (*op. cit.*, p. 177) errs in ascribing to Rink the completely mystical view that Christ was not satisfaction for sin but example; he who will be saved must follow Christ's example in act and suffering. Although Rink's approach to soteriology is more

Lutherans agreed in this instance on a minimal soteriological formulation.

Rink's critique of Lutheran faith as dead is amplified by an examination of his use of the term resignation (*Gelassenheit*). It was impossible for Rink to dissociate ethics from salvation. The individual Christian in his approach to God must be divested of every remnant of self, desire, or attachment to temporal things – created things – and become completely resigned before God. He must renounce all sin, in the form of love of material goods, love of self, love of feasting, love of the world, else he was not ready for the grace of God. Rink did not believe that man was capable in himself of achieving complete resignation; indeed, if man were capable he would thereby be induced to return to his basic sin of pride and self-importance. God alone granted him the ability to become resigned. Man must first be instructed from the Word, through which God gave faith.[1] Rink nowhere defined faith, nor did he possess a bonafide doctrine of the atonement. It is surprising that the theologians did not uncover this deficiency.

He did declare himself on the controversial issue of faith versus works as a means of salvation. He was accused of teaching salvation by works, a charge which he vigorously denied.[2] Yet despite his denial, his insistence on defining the gospel as God's promise of salvation to those who improved themselves morally leaves him at least suspect on the point.[3] For the most part, however, his emphasis on the necessity for good works in the life of the Christian cannot be taken to mean that he believed the Christian relied on good works at least partially for his salvation; he bitterly castigated the Catholics as teachers of this kind of salvation.[4] It is understandable that Rink's opponents accused him of teaching works-righteousness; they did not often hear him emphasize the distinctive work of God in man's salvation. To the Lutherans Rink spoke critically of their failure to sufficiently teach good works. The absence of spiritual fruit in their lives could be laid to an absence of teaching on works within their doctrine of justification. But to the Anabaptists, on the other hand, Rink emphasized man's absolute

mystical than Luther's, it is inconceivable that the theologians at the Marburg hearing would have pronounced themselves in agreement with a doctrine as thoroughly mystical as the one described by zur Linden. Rink tried to steer his course between Pelagianism, and, in his view, Luther's dissociation of justification and sanctification.

[1] See Rink's baptismal formula as reported by Menius, *Der Widdertauffer*, pp. E2v.–E3r. Also testimony of Angersbach, in Wappler, *Thüringen*, p. 329.

[2] Nos. 1 and 12 of the points formulated by Raidt, *TA, Hesse*, pp. 4, 6, 7.

[3] *Widderlegung*, p. 3.

[4] Tract on Baptism, *Sammelband*, p. Kv.

reliance on God's mercy, as over against any reliance whatsoever on self or works.[1]

Rink's soteriology was inseparable from his view of baptism. The man who became saved began his spiritual renewal with a desire to live a better life and a desire to abstain from sin. He developed a willingness to repent, and was brought to a belief that God forgave his sins and considered him righteous.[2] Baptism was an appropriate capstone to this process in that in the act the man sealed his confession of faith in the mercy of God toward himself. The act of baptism carried no grace of God by itself; divorced from the larger process of which it was a part, probably it had no meaning at all.[3] But as part of the larger process it was both valid and necessary.

It was necessary primarily because Christ had commanded that men who believed should be baptized. This was the minimum obedience that Christ demanded.[4] It had both a two-fold ceremonial character and a two-fold meaning. Ceremonially it represented man's death with Christ [5] and also his marriage with Christ, the Bridegroom.[6] Rink believed that baptism both sealed one's confession of faith and also was a solemn promise on the part of the candidate to follow Christ in holiness of life and also in death if necessary.[7] Rink's insistence that there was a sharp distinction to be made between the baptism of Christ and the baptism of John underscores this two-fold meaning of the act. The distinctive characteristic of Christ's baptism was an ethical commitment in obedience and discipleship to the Master. The baptism of John required only the realization of one's sin, of one's inadequacy as over against God's person and his demands in the law. The baptism of Christ demanded a complete surrender of oneself and one's material goods to him in loving obedience.[8]

---

[1] Rink's baptismal formula as found in Menius, *Der Widdertauffer*, pp. E2v.–E3r.

[2] Rink's meaning is not entirely clear for this last point, the sixth step. He speaks of the candidate being "uffgericht." But the context would make it appear that his meaning was very close to Luther's when the latter used the term "rechtfertigt" (*TA, Hesse*, p. 8. Also *Widderlegung*, p. 2).

[3] Testimony of Bilg Scherer on what Rink taught, November, 1531, in Wappler, *Thüringen*, p. 330.

[4] *Vermanung*, p. 17.

[5] I assume he was alluding to Romans 6. He cited it in his general introduction to the passage, but he cited 19 other Scriptural passages as well. I take it from his rejection of Lutheran baptism in which he accused them of not dying with Christ. It is also implied in his reference to the purification of the congregation in its marriage with Christ (*Vermanung*, p. 19).

[6] *Ibid.*

[7] Testimony of Hans Werner on what Rink taught, November, 1531, in Wappler, *Thüringen*, p. 331. Also Angersbach, *ibid.*, p. 329.

[8] The passage is difficult. "Auffs erste/ das sie einen fragen/ Bistu ein Christ? Antwort er/

Because the Christian was truly wedded to Christ, he partook of the inheritance of Christ as a bonafide Son of God. In this connection Rink made a sharp distinction between the practice of baptism and that of circumcision, in an attempt to refute Johannes Bader's arguments against Hans Denk. Rink argued that God instituted circumcision through his servants Abraham and Moses. But baptism was given to men through his Son. Circumcision therefore was the symbol of the yoke, by which even the unwilling were compelled to adhere to the people of God, if not to the law itself. But baptism was pre-eminently the symbol of the free relationship that existed between a father and his son. There was no duress in it; men might join with God's people because they wanted to. If one justified infant baptism on the grounds that it was the New Testament parallel to circumcision in the Old Testament, as Bader and Zwingli did, and if one then continued to practice the baptism of infants, he clearly rejected the superior status of Son for the inferior one of menial servant in his relationship to God.[1]

But baptism signified not only the bond of the Christian with Christ; it also brought the Christian into a covenant relation with his brethren. Indeed, Rink's point about the ceremony of baptism being in fact a wedding ceremony posited Christ as the Bridegroom and the entire congregation as the bride. He meant also to emphasize the fact that, as the ceremony obligated the bride to obey her husband, so the brethren as the Bride of Christ had a corporate obligation to obey and to remain pure.[2]

Not that the Anabaptists, via baptism or any other means, could be perfect. They came to Christ as a bride unspotted, following Paul's line of thought as Rink interpreted it in Ephesians 5:27 and II Corinthians 11:2.[3] But Rink did not argue for a perfected people in perpetuity. He

---

Ja/ So fragen sie weiter/ was gleubestu denn? Antwort/ Ich gleub an Gott/ meinen Herrn Jhesum Christ etc. Fragen sie aber/ Wie wiltu mir deine werck geben? Antwort/ Ich gebe sie einem alzumal vmb einen groschen/ Denn fragen sie weiter/ Wie wiltu mir deine guter geben/ auch vmb einen groschen? Antwort/ Nein/ So fragen sie abermals/ Wie wiltu mir denn dein leben geben/ auch vmb ein groschen? Antwort/ Nein/ So sagen sie denn/ Ey sihestu/ so bistu auch noch kein Christen nicht/ denn du hast noch keinen rechten glauben/ vnd stehest nicht gelassen/ sondern nimmest dich noch der Creaturen vnd dein selbst an/ Darumb bistu auch nicht recht jnn Christus tauffe mit dem heiligen geist/ sondern nur allein jnn Johannes tauff mit dem wasser/ getauffet/ Wiltu aber selig werden/ so mustu warlich entsagen/ vnn dich zu uor verzeihen/ aller deiner werck/ aller creaturen/ vnd zuletzt auch dein selbst/ vnd muss allein jnn Gott gleuben." Menius, *Der Widdertauffer*, pp. E2v.–E3r.

[1] *Widderlegung*, p. 4.

[2] *Vermanung*, p. 19. Other Central German Anabaptists on the *Bund*, testimony of Angersbach, in Wappler, *Thüringen*, p. 329.

[3] *Ibid.*

insisted on the absolute necessity for obedience to Christ in ethical life as a consequence of one's calling as God's child.[1]

Baptism carried with it also the outpouring of the Spirit. The records do not show how significant this outpouring of the Spirit was in Rink's theology; it is mentioned on only one occasion.[2] This outpouring may have been a singularly strong Pentecostal visitation, or perhaps only one of many already experienced visitations of the Spirit.

The larger part of Rink's recorded opinion on baptism is devoted to the subject of infant baptism. Thus in the 1528 hearing Rink formulated the baptism issue negatively: infant baptism was wrong. Indeed, it was blasphemy against God.[3] For to baptize infants was to pervert an act instituted by God to solemnize a relationship and a promise between God and man by changing it into one of lesser importance. Such perversion constituted a denial in the face of God of the purpose and worth of baptism. Infant baptism was contrary to reason and to the Biblical order and relationship between faith and baptism.

Baptism of infants was against reason precisely in that the candidates were utterly incapable of reason and understanding. Without reason and understanding the infant could not possibly comprehend the distinction between good and evil, the nature of sin, and the necessity for repentance and faith. To baptize apart from the preaching and experiencing of repentance and faith was unthinkable to Rink. Nor could an infant make any kind of commitment to Christ. Rink insisted that the act pointed back to an experience of repentance and forward to a promise to live in obedience to Christ. [4]

It would not do, said Rink, to argue that baptism of infants had its validity in the washing away of the guilt of original sin. That guilt had been completely removed for all mankind by the sacrificial death of Christ. Original sin itself was a different matter. Rink believed in its damning power as an inherent, congenital desire to do evil. It came to light slowly in a child, as the child gradually learned to distinguish between good and evil. But it damned no one until he sinned of his own will. Rink used Ezech. 18:20: "The son shall not bear the iniquity of the father, neither shall the father bear the inquity of the son," to

---

[1] *Widderlegung*, pp. 7–8.

[2] Menius, *Der Widdertauffer*, pp. E2v.–E3r.

[3] *TA*, *Hesse*, p. 5. Angersbach declared that Rink taught that infant baptism was introduced by the papacy at the same time that it forbade clerical marriage. Testimony of Angersbach, in Wappler, *Thüringen*, p. 329.

[4] This is what he meant when he described infant baptism as being opposed to the baptism of John and the baptism of Christ. *TA*, *Hesse*, p. 8.

demonstrate the impossibility of the newborn baby's being damned for what Adam had done. An individual was neither damned nor saved until he reached the age of accountability.[1] If the infant really required a sacramental act, as the Lutherans taught, why not insist on infant communion also? [2]

A highly important reason for the rejection of infant baptism developed from the Scriptural sequence on faith and baptism. The brethren quoted Mark 16:16 interminably: "He that believeth and is baptized shall be saved." They would not move from their literalistic interpretation of the verse: faith must absolutely precede baptism. Salvation was contingent upon following the correct sequence.[3] This same literalism meant that the rite itself was a necessity, almost a requirement for salvation.

In their inauguration of believers' baptism the Anabaptists of course rejected the concept of its being a rebaptism, as the originators of the nickname "Anabaptist" intended. They were instituting the true baptism.[4] On one occasion Rink went so far as to suggest that, since proper baptism was a wedding in which the church was married to Christ, improper baptism, namely that of infants, was comparable to an illicit sexual union. Should not the wench who repented of her fornication be expected to rejoice at the prospect of a proper marriage ceremony with her erstwhile paramour? Of course a new ceremony was incumbent upon the pair as soon as they understood the sinful nature of their previous relationship.[5] Rebaptism was not rebaptism at all; it was the institution of the only correct baptism, believers' baptism, which the Reformers chose erroneously to call "rebaptism."

Rink was dedicated to the issue of baptism as central in Anabaptist life and doctrine to a degree that is lacking in Swiss and South German Anabaptism. Rink had what can only be described as a passion for the topic. It is possible that the issue was more crucial for the Anabaptist-Lutheran conflict in Central Germany than for the Anabaptist-Swiss Reformed struggle. Rink believed that the devil entered the Lutheran body at the point of baptism. Even though the Lutherans

[1] Hearing of 1528, ibid., pp. 4, 5, 8, 11, 13. Testimony of Heinz Ot, November, 1531, Wappler, Thüringen, p. 330.

[2] Testimony of Angersbach, ibid., p. 329.

[3] Hearing of Rink in 1528, TA, Hesse, p. 11; Angersbach testimony, in Wappler, Thüringen, p. 329; Werner testimony, ibid., p. 331; Thomas Spiegel von Ostheim testimony, ibid., p. 230; Schnabel in the "Verantwortung," TA, Hesse, p. 168.

[4] Rink's letter to Eberhard von der Thann, ca. 1530, in TA, Hesse, p. 31; so also the Anabaptists in the Harz, Jacobs, op. cit., p. 469.

[5] Vermanung, pp. 19–20.

tried to eliminate persons of erroneous doctrine from their midst through cleansing and reforming the church, they did not strike at the devil's foothold in their midst, the practice of infant baptism. So important it was to Rink.[1] Luther in turn considered the Anabaptist attack on infant baptism to be nothing less than an attack on the power and majesty of the Divine Word, and even on the omnipotence of God.[2] The issue was also hotly debated in the formative years of the Anabaptist movement in the Swiss environment, but usually as a part of the larger issue, the church.[3]

Rink was unrestrained in his fanatical zeal to condemn infant baptism and to laud believers' baptism. Those who practiced infant baptism thereby proffered their allegiance to the devil, to the Great Whore of the Revelation account, and to the pope.[4] He compared the baptism of infants, not to the Old Testament practice of circumcision, but to the idolatrous practice of the Jews who offered their children to Baal.[5] He insisted that the Protestants only aided the cause of Rome by continuing a sacrament which he apparently thought began with Rome. In strong terms he denounced the practice as putting the mark of the Beast on the foreheads of the infants who were baptized (Rev. 13: 16–17).[6] Baptism was for him the absolute means of determining who belonged to the Kingdom of God. This was always a sensitive question for the Anabaptists: were they divinely commissioned to read the hearts of men, to determine who belonged? Bader put the issue to them emphatically on one occasion.[7] Rink faced the issue well enough in his reply to Bader. He insisted that Christ's declaration that all power belonged to him (Matt. 28:18) meant that the Spirit revealed to the true followers of Christ who belonged and who did not.[8] But Rink usually solved the problem in a much more facile, almost flippant, manner: all those who practiced infant baptism did not belong to the Kingdom, while those who baptized believers only were the chosen of the Lord. The former did not obey the Lord's commands, and the latter

---

[1] Tract on Baptism, *Sammelband*, pp. Kv., K3r.

[2] *Tischreden*, undated, *Dr. Martin Luther's sämmtliche Werke*, ed. by J. G. Plockmann *et al.* (67 vols.; Frankfurt and Erlangen: Heyder und Zimmer, 1829–1857), LVII, 66; Sermon on I Cor. 15: 35–38, *ibid.*, XIX, 114; Luther, *Von der Widertauffe an zwen Pfarherrn, Ein brieff*, p. E3r.

[3] Heinrich Bullinger, *Der Widdertöufferen vrsprung/ fürgang/ Secten/ wäsen* (Zürich: Froschower, 1561), p. 15b.

[4] *Vermanung*, pp. 18–21.

[5] *Ibid.*, p. 20.

[6] *Widderlegung*, p. 6.

[7] *Brüderliche warnung*, pp. M4r.–N3r.

[8] *Widderlegung*, p. 3.

did; it was that simple.[1] But this also tells us why Rink was so fanatical on the issue of baptism. Even in a tract written for the ostensible purpose of clarifying the church-state issue, Rink launched out on the baptism issue, precisely because with it he could determine that the governments with which he was acquainted were damned since they universally supported the practice of infant baptism. Rink warned them accordingly.[2]

Concerning the mode of baptism the records on Rink are silent. The Anabaptists in Central Germany generally followed a pattern of questioning the candidate as to his desire for baptism, his experience of repentance and faith in Christ, and his desire to follow Christ. Then the candidate was requested to kneel. The officiating minister dipped his finger in water and made the sign of the cross on his forehead and possibly on his breast. He was baptized in the name of the Father, the Son, and the Holy Ghost. Afterwards he was admonished to remain dissociated from the world but still to consider himself a sinner, to obey God, and to follow the brotherhood. One formula from around 1528 required the candidate to confess his acceptance of most of the articles of the Apostles Creed.[3]

Rink's soteriological ideas were valid for most of Thuringian Anabaptism. To be sure, many of the captured brethren could not explain them as fully as he did. For most of them the matter was simple: the Lutherans separated salvation from good works and thereby destroyed a God-ordained unity. Simple men like the two captured outside Erbe's cell in Eisenach in 1537 assumed without any question that ethics and soteriology were inseparable. Thus they held that the preacher whose life was sinful could not possibly proclaim the truth; Christians should not listen to sermons from such a man. They even went so far as to say that the death of Christ had no validity for the individual who did not imitate Christ in purity of life.[4]

The group in Central Hesse, i.e., Tasch, Schnabel, and others, added a new dimension to the controversy on faith and works. Before their hearing in 1538 they were given Lutheran literature to read in jail,

[1] *Ibid.*, pp. 8 and 9.
[2] *Vermanung*, pp. 17–21, especially p. 20.
[3] See the discussion in Jacobs, *op. cit.*, pp. 469–70; the formula printed in Wappler, *Thüringen*, p. 305; Rink's formula (exclusive of the baptismal act itself) in Menius, *Der Widdertauffer*, pp. E2v.-E3r.; a truncated version of Römer's practice in testimony of Hans Lodewig, December 19, 1527, in Wappler, *Thüringen*, p. 262. The brethren around Römer began the service with wine and ended with a tankard of beer.
[4] Testimony of Köhler and Scheffer, November 12, 1537, in Wappler, *Die Stellung Kursachsens*, p. 197.

including Melanchthon's *Loci*. They rejected his doctrine, and one of the reasons they gave was that it damned anyone who believed salvation was possible on the basis of his own works. Did they believe that man was saved because of his good works? There is more than a hint of such belief in this and similar statements.[1]

Anabaptist refusal to separate faith and works meant for a few the achievement of perfection through the purification experience of baptism; whatever they did after baptism could in no wise be reckoned as sin. The followers of the "Prophet" believed this,[2] and certainly the libertines in the camp of Hans Krug must have held the same view. Rink's successor at Sorga, Hans Bott, was reported to have believed that the flesh was not evil; this sounds like a variation on the same theme.[3] For the majority of Thuringian Anabaptists, however, the opinion prevailed that one remained a sinner as long as he lived in mortal flesh.

On baptism there was little of consequence beyond what Rink, or his followers testifying specifically to his doctrine, had said. The most important difference between Rink and some of the other Anabaptists was on the relative importance of the various reasons for initiating believers' baptism. Rink emphasized in baptism the bond of the believer with Christ, to follow Christ in life and suffering. Hut's followers in Franconia and other Anabaptists in Thuringia emphasized the union (*Bund*) of the baptized. The *Bund* meant different things to different persons. Caspar Spiegel von Ostheim and the Aurachsmüller, both disciples of Hut, spoke of baptism as the sign of the *Bund* of those who would reign after the Turkish demolition of the European political structure.[4] Did this *Bund* constitute a union of potential revolutionaries? This was always the crucial question for the interrogating officials,

---

[1] See Peter Lose testimony, 1538, in *TA, Hesse*, p. 191. Also Bucer-Schnabel dispute, 1538, in Hochhuth, *op. cit.* (1858), 631. Schnabel declared that Melanchthon said in a visitation report that teaching on repentance had been neglected. Lose quoted from the *Loci*, "vermaledeiet seie der, so us eigen werken vermeint selig zu werden." I could not find this in the *Loci* although there are statements similar in character and meaning.

[2] Wappler, *Thüringen*, p. 85.

[3] I find it difficult to believe that a man so close to Rink could have taught this kind of libertinism. The Hutterite charges are not always consistent or clear. In their letter to Mathes in 1538 they accused Bott and his people of believing that human flesh was not sinful but the flesh of Christ was sinful. Bott was accused in addition of spiritualism, which sounds much more likely. None of these charges was carried in the Hutterite Chronicle. Rather they accused Bott there of denying the existence of devils and angels. Bott was obviously the object of an attempt at defamation. It is also clear, however, that there was genuine difference of doctrine between Bott's Thuringian Anabaptism and that of the Hutterites. (See *TA, Hesse*, p. 181; Chronicle in Wappler, *Thüringen*, p. 103, n. 5.)

[4] Testimony in Berbig, *DZK*, XIII (1903), 309–10.

whenever they uncovered talk of a *Bund*. This question can be answered however only in the context of individual Anabaptists' views on revolution. In one instance, the trial of the revered Anabaptist apostle Alexander, the authorities were obviously fishing for evidence of a revolutionary conspiracy in the *Bund* for the baptized. Alexander firmly denied such intent.[1] But for some of the early Franconian disciples of Hut, such denial would have been difficult to make.

For some Anabaptists baptism was a part of their eschatological thought. In a fanatic like Römer baptism into the *Bund* was a prelude to greater things; the act opened the eyes of the person baptized. Through dreams and visions the believer would be enabled to see and predict in detail the cataclysmic events of the near future. God would most assuredly reveal to his own the coming judgment.[2] But even the more moderate Anabaptists interpreted the act as an entrance into the *Bund* of those whom God would especially protect during the imminent punishment of the world. Fritz Erbe believed that God's judgment would break furiously over the world in the form of an army striking unheralded and unexpected by all except the baptized, whom the Lord would preserve.[3] One senses here the pious expectancy of a persecuted flock, reading the Old Testament accounts of Israel's deliverances by Jehovah, eagerly awaiting the promised return of their vindicating Lord. Believers' baptism was the act of initiation into fellowship with the Lord's people.

Soteriology and baptism lead to a third problem: the place and work of the Spirit in the life of the Christian. It touches our treatment of Anabaptist theology at numerous places, the most important of which are the process of salvation already discussed and the problem of ultimate authority in Christianity. Rink's interpretation of man's reconciliation with God laid more weight on the free course of the Spirit than did Luther's interpretation of justification.[4] The Spirit had to move the individual, else one could not properly speak of reconciliation with God.

---

[1] Testimony printed in Wappler, *Thüringen*, p. 349.

[2] *Ibid.*, pp. 39–40.

[3] Testimony of Erbe, October 9–11, 1531, printed in Wappler, *Die Stellung Kursachsens*, p. 139. Erbe did not scornfully reject infant baptism in the customary Anabaptist manner. He was inclined to be tolerant on the point. He thought the individual should decide for himself, when he came to an understanding of God, whether he wanted baptism as a believer or wanted to remain with only baptism as an infant (*ibid.*, p. 138). Rink was too furiously opposed to infant baptism to have made such a concession.

[4] Rink never wrote or spoke on the subject of the Spirit; it is therefore difficult to reconstruct a doctrine of the Spirit for him. Luther was influenced profoundly by mysticism and spiritualism, particularly in the *Theologia Deutsch*. Some of his statements sound very spiritualistic.

Rink characterized Lutheran faith as dead because he thought justification was a formalistic act which hampered the Spirit. When the Spirit worked in an individual it produced fruit in the form of holiness of life and conduct. Precisely because the Lutherans did not exhibit holiness of life and conduct, as Rink required, he was certain that the Spirit had not moved. But if Rink believed in a free Spirit, he also limited that freedom by an insistent reliance on the Spirit's adherence to Scripture; i.e., the Spirit did not act contrary to Scripture. How then did Rink interpret Scripture? A detailed analysis of his exegetical principles is impossible owing to the absence of substantial writings and exegetical works from his pen.[1] Several observations, however, can be made.

Rink's rejection of the real presence in the Lord's Supper was based on a more spiritualistic exegesis of Scripture than was Luther's affirmation of the real presence. Rink taught that the body of the Lord was no more bound or contained in the sanctified bread than it was in any other created thing. God was everywhere present. Rink did not preach pantheism, however. He intended the argument on divinity in created things purely as a negative one: to deny a unique presence of Christ in the Host. The true presence, and thus the true Lord's Supper, was the itinerant mission of the proclamation of the good news, from house to house. This the apostles had done. Only in preaching the gospel could the life-giving power of the Spirit be loosed; this was the true bread. Rink relied on the sixth chapter of the Fourth Gospel for his view.[2]

In his exposition of one passage in the Sermon on the Mount, which most Anabaptists interpreted quite literally, Rink added an allegorical interpretation. One of his followers, testifying on the question of Rink's attitude toward the exercise of justice, gave the usual literalistic view of Matt. 5:40: "And if a man will sue thee at the law and take away thy coat, let him have thy cloak also"; i.e., the Christian must expect injustice. But Rink found more than an example to be followed literally. The coat stood for all temporal goods, the cloak for life itself. The Christian must be willing to surrender both his goods and his life.[3]

---

[1] Generally one is compelled to determine Rink's exegetical ideas by examining his use of Scripture; for he commented on an aspect of Scriptural interpretation on only one occasion, and that in a limited way. Bader, following Zwingli, declared that since Scripture did not forbid infant baptism, the practice was permissible. Rink repeated the argument used by the South German and Swiss Anabaptists: that which is not explicitly commanded by Scripture is, by its omission, forbidden to the Christian. He displayed his customary literalism in this instance. *Widderlegung*, p. 5.

[2] Testimony of Heinz Ot, 1531, in Wappler, *Thüringen*, p. 331.

[3] *Ibid.*

But Rink was adamantly literalistic on at least those Scriptures which touched baptism. Infant baptism was wrong because it denied the sequence given in Scripture. Baptism must necessarily follow faith, and faith is impossible in infants.[1] Throughout the argument on baptism, Rink thought in terms of a literal interpretation of Scripture. He buttressed his charge against infant baptism in the 1528 hearing with a large array of Scriptural quotations, and demanded that any attempt to refute his argument must be based on sufficient Scripture. Scripture stood as final authority.[2]

Rink was literalistic in his interpretation of Scripture on marriage. No matter how unpleasant and unnatural his situation was, he could not consent to a legal alteration because divorce was forbidden by Scripture. One senses here not only literalism but also legalism: certain New Testament Scriptures comprised a new set of rules on conduct replacing those of the Old Testament; the wrath of God would surely descend on him who transgressed.[3]

What then was final authority for Rink: Spirit or Scripture? Rink's interpretations ran the range from spiritualism to legalism. Authority was not an either-or proposition to him. Authority was Scripture always; but it was also a lively Scripture, one in which the Spirit moved. Indeed, otherwise it would have been no authority at all. This is, to be sure, an evasion; but the question of authority was never put to him directly. Behind it one must recognize the earnestness of a man who believed Spirit and Scripture could be, indeed must be, combined in a manner different from that of Luther, who quenched the Spirit. There was un-questionably a strong personal element in what Rink appeared to regard as objective Scripture. Because God, through the Spirit, spoke with a certain directness to him in the Scripture, Scripture became authoritative to him. Like the Reformers, he had the bland conviction that his interpretation of the Scripture was the correct one.[4] He de-manded from his opponents not only "sufficient Scripture" to disprove his views on infant baptism, but also "unfalsified Scripture." [5] There is nothing in the records to indicate that he relied on extra-Scriptural revelations in visions, or dreams, or writings on the heart.[6]

---

[1] See above, p. 81.

[2] Hearing of 1528, in *TA, Hesse*, pp. 11–12, 9; letter of Rink to Eberhard, *ca.* 1530, *ibid.*, p. 31.

[3] Rink's defense of his marriage views, 1531, *ibid.*, pp. 34, 35.

[4] See H. Fast and J. H. Yoder, "How to Deal with Anabaptists: An Unpublished Letter of Heinrich Bullinger," *MQR*, XXXIII (1959), 83–95, for an example of one Reformer's ideas on how to interpret Scripture.

[5] Hearing of 1528, in *TA, Hesse*, p. 9.

[6] Zur Linden (*op. cit.*, pp. 176–78) sees Rink as a mystic in soteriology and a complete

Other Thuringian Anabaptists did rely on dreams. The "Prophet" and Römer believed in and utilized extra-Scriptural revelations.[1] Jacob Storger, a Mühlhausen Anabaptist who was tried and executed in 1537, admitted the validity of dreams which touched the gospel, as he put it. Storger also used the Inner Word as a touchstone for doctrine.[2] One sees here only the reliance on the subjective elements, without explanation as to the extent of their use, the kind and number of persons to whom they were vouchsafed, or the possible limitations of such media through Scripture. A similar inadequacy of information attends the record of one Kunne Zinderlin, whose choice of the Anabaptist way was verified for her by a voice.[3]

Another expression of spiritualism can be found in the ideas of the three Anabaptists caught conversing with Erbe in 1539. On the one hand they admitted – probably as the result of some argument with Menius – that the Christian's knowledge of God must derive from the Scriptures. Nevertheless the Spirit for them was capable of instructing quite without Scripture. Obviously they insisted that Scripture, which taught about God, must be interpreted by the Spirit; Scripture by itself was a dead letter.[4] For these men marriage, too, was primarily a spiritual affair. A truly spiritual union lasted through eternity, and

---

spiritualist in authority. But zur Linden relies on Raidt's formulation of Rink's soteriology, without reference to Rink's qualification and refutation of parts of it. Thus Rink is purported to believe in a salvation process which originated in man's own power: man could bring himself to the Spirit of God. Rink denied flatly that he ever taught salvation in any way through one's own power, a denial in direct response to the statement which zur Linden uses (*TA, Hesse*, pp. 5–6, 7). Zur Linden also relies on Menius to say that Rink declared that all books of the New Testament in all languages – Greek, Latin, German, etc. – were false; no true Scripture existed on earth any more (Menius, *Von dem Geist der Widerteuffer* [Wittemberg: Nickel Schirlentz, 1544], p. Jv.). If Rink actually said this, and Menius declared he had heard him personally, it is in complete contradiction to his practice of regarding Scripture as authoritative. It is inconceivable that a man who rejected Scripture completely would quote it as frequently as Rink did, or would bother with it at all. Menius did not make the charge in his 1530 book. Only in 1544, after the Lutheran picture of Anabaptism as excessively subjective had become well fixed, did he make the charge. Perhaps Menius, reflecting on the configuration of his charge of Anabaptist rejection of Scripture, recalled a 1525 attitude of Rink, a practice which he followed on other occasions. It is significant that he referred to Müntzer's reliance on the Spirit and rejection of Scripture immediately prior to the charge against Rink. It is convenient to handle Rink as a mystic and spiritualist; but a closer examination of his ideas discloses too many uncomfortable contradictions to a mystic or spiritualist position. These require explanation which zur Linden does not give.

[1] For the "Prophet," see Wappler, *Thüringen*, pp. 81 ff. For Römer, *ibid.*, p. 40.

[2] Storger hearing, October 12, 1537, printed *ibid.*, p. 429.

[3] Trial at Frankenhausen, January 30, 1530, printed *ibid.*, p. 314. She was baptized by Hans Hut. The Hutterites charged Hans Bott with a spiritualism which included a reliance on dreams as revelations. I am inclined to concede the charge of spiritualism in the area of Scriptural interpretation in the case of Bott. But the rest of the evidence is too questionable.

[4] Hearing printed in Wappler, *Die Stellung Kursachsens*, pp. 203, 204.

contrasted sharply with the inadequacies of a purely fleshly union.[1] The records give no clue as to what direction their marriage views took.

The spiritualism of Erbe's friends of 1539 is all the more impressive because of its contrast to the literalism of Köhler and Scheffer, who visited him in 1537. They adhered to a literal rendition of Matthew's account of the sending out of the twelve on a healing ministry. "Freely ye have received; freely give" (Matt. 10:8) meant that a minister should not receive wages for his labor; he was to live from charity. The Sermon on the Mount was also to be literally understood and obeyed. With these men there was no trace of excessive spiritualizing, at least according to Menius.[2]

Hessian Anabaptism inherited some of Melchior Hofmann's spiritualization of the incarnation. Christ's humanity did not derive from his mother, Mary. Schnabel argued that Christ's spirit became flesh, but he did not provide a satisfactory explanation of the origin of Christ's humanity. Together with this spiritualizing Schnabel placed a heavy reliance on Scripture, citing it often in the manner of one who assumed it to be of decisive authority.[3] The Anabaptists in general accepted the Reformation principle of *sola Scriptura*, but differed from the Reformers on its interpretation. In Central Germany they insisted on putting both a more spiritualistic and at the same time a more literalistic construction on it than the Reformers did.

An indissoluble part of repentance and salvation for the Anabaptists was their insistence on newness of life in the regenerated Christian. For them, faith manifested itself in holiness of life, else it was not faith but hypocrisy. Again and again the Anabaptists told their interrogators that they rejected the new Evangelical teaching precisely because it did not induce its adherents to abstain from sin in all forms; it could not be true.[4] Adam Angersbach in Rink's Sorga congregation considered the wickedness of the people greater after the new teaching than it had been under the papacy. He was attracted to Rink and his followers because they made an earnest effort to abstain from sin; one found

---

[1] Heinz Kraut and others captured at Kleineutersdorf and interrogated by Melanchthon in 1535 held a similar position. *CR*, II, 1001–02.

[2] Hearing 1537, in Wappler, *Die Stellung Kursachsens*, pp. 197–98.

[3] "Verantwortung," *TA, Hesse*, pp. 165–80, *passim*, especially pp. 171–73.

[4] This was one of Rink's favorite appeals to draw people into the Anabaptist brotherhood. He sharply condemned the Evangelicals, who, boasting of a new life in Christ, had not even been buried with Christ. This was probably a reference to the ceremony of believers' baptism following Paul in Romans 6, but perhaps also a reference to the necessity for suffering with Christ. The Evangelicals gave no evidence of newness of life in their daily living, he thought. *Widderlegung*, pp. 8–9.

purity of life among them. He was certain therefore that they had the Spirit.[1] Brother Adrian in the Harz region cried to God in anguish at the enormity of the sin around him and God in his infinite mercy led him to the Anabaptist brotherhood.[2] This insistence on purity of life and conduct has appropriately been called discipleship.[3] What did discipleship mean to the Anabaptists?

Discipleship meant in the first place separation from the world. He who would not separate from the wickedness around him was not worthy to bear the name of Christ. The Anabaptists decried the gluttony, drunkenness, cursing, and vice in all forms around them; and they were especially indignant when such conduct touched the lives of the Lutheran pastors. True Christianity was always identical with spiritual fruit in the form of an earnest repudiation of the sins of the world. "Ye shall know them by their fruits. Do men gather grapes of thorns, or figs of thistles?" (Matt. 7:16) [4]

Discipleship meant a community life in which the sharing of material goods was the accepted practice. Yet these Anabaptists did not practice community of goods.[5] They meant that sharing with the brother in need was done so frequently as to make it virtually impossible for one to call his own goods strictly private. The only absolute for them in this respect was the lordship of God over everything; because of that lordship strictly private property was non-existent.[6] In their practice of sharing there was something of a leveler attitude; they regarded riches with scorn. He who was rich must distribute to those who were less fortunate. In one instance an unfavorable contrast was made with

---

[1] Testimony, 1531, in Wappler, *Thüringen*, pp. 328–29.

[2] Jacobs, *op. cit.*, p. 485. Hans Hut declared at his trial that dissatisfaction with the ethics at Wittenberg led him to seek a faith different from that of the Lutherans (Wappler, *Thüringen*, p. 26).

[3] Harold S. Bender, "The Anabaptist Vision," *MQR*, XVIII (1944), 67–88.

[4] This point needs no further elaboration. It is implicit and explicit in the numerous Anabaptist complaints against Lutheranism. See the testimonies of Angersbach and Adrian, cited above. See the hearing of Otilia Goldschmidt (or Rüdigern) for an example of an Anabaptist call to repentance from the sin of the world (December 7, 1537, printed in Wappler *Thüringen*, p. 456).

[5] Berka hearing, July, 1533 (Wappler, *Die Stellung Kursachsens*, pp. 168–76, *passim*). Brethren have a right, they said, to the goods of other brethren. But they did not pool all their material resources and live a communal life. At the Sorga hearing, August, 1533 (*TA, Hesse*, pp. 64–69, *passim*), the Anabaptists could not clearly answer the question on private property. Their confusion came obviously from a practice of sharing so frequently that one could not in truth say his goods were his own. Yet private property was not forbidden, technically. One must remember that the Sorga group under Bott had the greatest difficulty accepting the absolute community of goods of the Hutterites during their Moravian sojourn.

[6] They used the same grounds to refuse to obey any sentence of banishment. This is the direction of the Koch testimony (Wappler, *Die Stellung Kursachsens*, p. 174).

Lutheranism which, in one brother's eyes, was all too tolerant of its rich extorting even more from its poor.[1]

Discipleship also meant suffering. Just as Christ had suffered, so must the true Christian inevitably endure suffering and the cross. When it came one was assured that he was following the truth.[2] Rink expected to seal his faith with his life.[3] One of his followers declared that he recognized Rink's teaching as true because it was attended by suffering.[4] At the moment of execution Anabaptists spoke of their joy at being able thus to testify for their Lord.[5] For the most part Thuringian Anabaptism did not develop a martyr complex. Death at the hands of the world did not become a part of the salvation process. On the contrary, many recanted, including some of those closest to Rink, whose ideas were most typically Anabaptist.[6] One suspects that their recantation was the result both of fear and the realization that Philip released those who recanted in his lands. This practice came to be condemned by the Anabaptists.[7] Of course there were many Anabaptists in Thuringia who suffered martyrdom.

Discipleship further meant nonresistance, the repudiation of the Christian's participation in war, even in the classic Augustinian just war, on the grounds that killing even in self-defense was sinful. On this point the Thuringian Anabaptists were not of one mind. The brethren were interrogated extensively on the question, always in reference to their attitude toward civil authority. Indeed, the civil servants who handled the questioning regarded the topic as political, not religious. It was overemphasized in the hearings because the authorities were naturally anxious to ferret out and destroy anything that might lead to a renewed peasant uprising. The Anabaptists were repeatedly accused of having been participants in the Peasants' Revolt. They were accused of teaching sedition and fostering revolution. They were tortured in an effort to induce them to confess their true motives, and to reveal

---

[1] So Schnabel in "Verantwortung," *TA*, *Hesse*, pp. 174-75. For other testimony on this issue see Alexander, in Wappler, *Thüringen*, p. 349; Heinz Ot on Rink, *ibid.*, p. 330; Köhler and Scheffer, in Wappler, *Die Stellung Kursachsens*, p. 198; the trio caught in 1539, *ibid.*, p. 204.

[2] This is what Ot meant when he spoke of suffering unjustly (Wappler, *Thüringen*, p. 330). The Anabaptists undoubtedly had Matt. 5:10-12 in mind when they spoke on the point.

[3] Hearing of 1528, *TA*, *Hesse*, p. 6.

[4] Angersbach, in Wappler, *Thüringen*, p. 329.

[5] For example, see Hans Heutrock testimony, January 17, 1538, *ibid.*, p. 456.

[6] So Angersbach and Ot, *ibid.*, pp. 330, 331.

[7] Hans Bott remonstrated with Hans Quinger the Elder for the latter's recantation. This was an act against the Heavenly Father. Quinger did not recant the second time. Wappler, *Die Stellung Kursachsens*, p. 140.

the names of other persons who might harbor seditious intentions. Against this onslaught of accusation the Anabaptists were hard pressed to clear themselves; they never succeeded in convincing the authorities that matters of civil obedience were essentially matters of conscience, of Christian conviction, to them. An examination of their view on civil obedience is in order at this point.

One of the major sources of information on Rink's attitude toward civil authority is Eberhard von der Thann's report to Philip of Hesse in March, 1532. Eberhard's avowed purpose for writing was to induce Philip to execute the recently captured leader of the Anabaptists.[1] He therefore set about to picture Rink in the blackest possible colors as a long-standing revolutionary from whom no reform could be expected; the report is full of exaggeration. Eberhard's stated reasons for declaring the prisoner to be a revolutionary were as follows: (1) Rink was an open instigator of the Peasants' War, a leader second only to Müntzer and Pfeiffer, who never repented of his activity. (2) He left his wife in order to propagate rebaptism. (3) He propagated rebaptism secretly despite the absence of a Scriptural basis for the act. (4) He taught that there should be no civil authority. (5) He taught that no Christian should or could be a magistrate. (6) He taught that the community should install, or dismiss, the magistrate. (7) He persistently refused to desist from teaching these doctrines despite the earnest commands of the civil authorities.[2]

The fourth charge was by far the most serious one. Eberhard qualified it, however, by observing that Rink had ceased proclaiming it since the Peasants' War. Eberhard listed it because he considered Rink's new line, that no Christian could be a magistrate, the same idea as Rink's earlier injunction against all civil authority.[3] Eberhard's confusion and alarm on these points can be laid to his inability to understand Ana-

---

[1] Eberhard to Elector John, November 25, 1531, *ibid.*, pp. 145–46. Philip of Hesse did not find Eberhard's proof of Rink's revolutionary intentions very convincing. He insisted on regarding Rink as a man badly mistaken in matters that were purely religious; he was guilty of blasphemy, but he was not seditious (Philip to Elector John, January 3, 1532, *ibid.*, p. 155). No mention was made of seditious ideas at Rink's hearing of 1528.

[2] Printed in Wappler, *Thüringen*, pp. 333–36. "Gemeine" in Point 6 can of course be congregation.

[3] "... so hat itztgedachter Rinck, man soll keine obrigkeit haben, volgends aber, als er den armen einfeltigen dieses aus dem, das sie furnemlich umb diesen und dergleichen artickeln in vergangenem paurischen aufrur seint gestraft worden, nicht hat unvermarkt der aufrur einbilden mogen, an des stat, ein christ soll oder moge kein oberherr sein, item die gemeine sol dieselbige zusetzen und entsetzen haben, wilchs zweierlei rede und ein meinung, zwu hosen und eines tuchs ist, offentlich geleret" (*ibid.*, p. 334). I have interpreted this much as zur Linden did, except for the different consequences. Zur Linden considered Rink to be a revolutionary (zur Linden, *op. cit.*, p. 178).

baptist ethics. Rink was not saying that the contemporary princes should not serve as magistrates; i.e., that they should either resign or be forcibly expelled from office. He was rather saying that since they were magistrates they were not Christians. It was common Anabaptist belief that the office of the sword was denied to the Christian.

Rink denied outright that he was an instigator of the Peasants' War.[1] The charge of disobedience he could not deny. He did say that one should disobey government when it commanded that which was contrary to the commands of God. Since Rink, like Luther, considered himself divinely commissioned to preach the Word, the command to cease teaching and baptizing was for him directly contrary to God's commands. The remaining charges were insignificant. Rink's ideas, as derived from Eberhard's report, were revolutionary in the sense that they were radical, but not in the sense of constituting a plot to overthrow the existing government. Eberhard, however, put the latter construction on them.

Rink declared himself more fully on the nature and legitimacy of government, its prerogatives and the limitations to its authority, in his pamphlet *Vermanung vnd warnung an alle so in der Obrigkeit sind.* He accepted the Pauline explanation of the divine origin of the institution of government (Romans 13:3-6). And he repeated the usual Christian explanation for the suffering of the righteous: if God's people suffered under a tyrant, it was because God wanted to punish them for their sins. But Rink was not inclined to accept that punishment without demur. If he did not question the right of magistrates to rule, at the very least he felt himself compelled to speak the prophetic word of warning to them. To punish unjustly, or to step beyond the circumscribed boundaries of one's authority as a magistrate, was to abuse one's ordination from God, the consequences of which were eternal.[2] What were those boundaries?

Rink was not writing a treatise on government. He did not attempt to formulate a definitive statement on the authority of government. He was distressed by the spectacle of civil magistrates punishing men for their religious persuasions. The only limitation of authority that concerned him at the moment was the restricting of political rulers to political affairs at the exclusion of any activity on their part in religious matters. He appears to have relished using Luther's argument: since faith was a gift of God, it could not be forced on anyone. Therefore the

---

[1] Letter to Eberhard, *ca.* 1530, *TA, Hesse,* p. 31. He did not deny his participation in it.
[2] *Vermanung,* pp. 2-3. See also his letter to Eberhard, *ca.* 1530, *TA, Hesse,* p. 31.

magistrates exceeded their God-ordained authority if they compelled
men to accept a particular religious confession.[1] Rink insisted also that
their authority did not cover church property.[2] He probably had in
mind the financial aspects of the church visitations in Central Germany,
which were under the direction of the princes. Against the usurpation
of authority by the secular rulers in church doctrine and finance he
proposed a spiritual authority. Just as Christ acted on his own spiritual
authority, without mandate or license from Caesar or the Sanhedrin, so
also the Christian should imitate his Master and obey a spiritual
authority which was not bound to the political arm. And the only
spiritual authority of Rink's time that he considered competent to
decide questions of faith and practice was the congregation. He did not
specify the means by which the congregation made and registered its
decisions; his own flocks were much too scattered to carry on an active
congregational program. But he did insist that their leaders were not
to make decisions for them; the spiritual leaders were pre-eminently
servants of the congregations, bound to do their bidding.[3]

Rink was irate at the political rulers of his time because they persecuted God's people. He held those rulers in very low esteem. They were
greedy for power to the point of arrogating to themselves an authority
which God never intended them to have.[4] He referred with sarcasm to
unnamed persons who declared that they were not aware of any limitations to the authority of government, especially the imperial government.[5] Their villainy was such that Rink was reduced to intemperate
language. And along with his central complaint, he took the occasion to
excoriate the magistrates of his time for their taxation schemes. He did
not object to legitimate taxation. What he disliked was the fact that
influential persons in both Protestant and Catholic lands paid little or
no taxes, and some actually received money from the government,
while the poor Anabaptists were taxed beyond their means.[6] Here was
perhaps a strain of Rink's Peasants' War days coming to the surface
again. He contemptuously scored the rulers for not granting what the
pagan Romans had granted, namely, the right of an accused person to
face his accusers and to give a public answer to them. Even the Turks
were better than the "Christian" princes of Germany, and compared

---

[1] *Vermanung*, p. 16.
[2] *Ibid.*, p. 13.
[3] *Ibid.*, pp. 12–13.
[4] Letter to Eberhard, *ca.* 1530, *TA, Hesse*, p. 31; *Vermanung, passim*, especially p. 17.
[5] *Ibid.*, p. 15.
[6] *Ibid.*, p. 11.

to the latter Pilate was a saint.[1] He objected also to being called a *Schwärmer* and a revolutionary and a heretic by people, both magistrates and religious leaders, who did not know what they were talking about.[2] But his central concern, to which he returned repeatedly in his pamphlet, was the impropriety of secular rulers deciding matters of faith, and proceding by force to impose religious conformity. Precisely because they employed force, they were not the ministers of the Lord. Did anyone need further proof of their alienation from God? They behaved as if Christ had said: "The bishops and rulers are to defend their teaching with compulsion, so that if anyone does not want to accept the doctrine from love, he is compelled to accept it anyway" instead of "You know that the rulers of the Gentiles lord it over them, and their great men exercise authority over them. It shall not be so among you; but whoever would be great among you must be your servant, and whoever would be first among you must be your slave." (Matt. 20:25–27) The power and authority of the true Christian leader was his servanthood, or, although Rink did not use the phrase one may legitimately say for him, his suffering servanthood.[3] As for the Romans and the Wittenbergers, precisely because they required the use of force for maintaining their religions, those religions could not be identified with the gospel of Jesus Christ. For the true gospel of Jesus Christ was sustained entirely by the power of God and his Word, not at all by the arm of man.[4]

If Rink was rash and intemperate when writing to the magistrates directly, to his own followers he counseled patience and nonresistance to the persecutions of the secular authorities. He insisted that one must obey the magistrate as long as he did not demand that which was contrary to God's commands. The Christian must suffer persecution. If one's coat was unjustly confiscated, the Christian should freely surrender his cloak too. No Christian could sue at law.[5] But he did not lack boldness to the point of recklessness in his admonitions to the magistrates for not filling their God-ordained offices properly.

Anabaptism in its early days in Franconia presented a mixed position on the question of the attitude toward government. The movement in Franconia was the result of Hut's missionary work. Hut's mature views

---

[1] He referred to Festus (Acts 25:1-12) and Gallio (Acts 18:12–17). *Vermanung*, pp. 14, 11, 13.

[2] Letter to Eberhard, *ca.* 1530, *TA, Hesse*, p. 31; *Vermanung*, pp. 10, 12.

[3] *Ibid., passim*, especially p. 12.

[4] *Ibid.*, pp. 13, 14–15.

[5] Heinz Ot on Rink, in Wappler, *Thüringen*, pp. 330–31.

on revolution and rebellion are clear enough: the Christian must be
completely nonresistant.[1] But what he taught in the summer of 1526
immediately after his conversion, and how his ideas were received and
understood by the many who had participated a year earlier in the
Peasants' War – these questions are more difficult to answer. One finds
among his followers advocates for Christian nonresistance and advocates
for civil insurrection. Caspar Spiegel von Ostheim and his brother
Thomas both confessed that the Anabaptists were to help in extirpating the princes after the Turks should have destroyed the flower of
the German chivalry in a cataclysmic battle. Thomas did so only after
torture. Beutelhans and Wolf Schreiner, members of the same group
with the Spiegel brothers, denied the right of Anabaptists to participate
in the slaughter. They agreed that the slaughter was to come soon.
Beutelhans went so far as to say that those among them who had
participated in the Peasants' War had erred.[2] One cannot explain this
inconsistency on grounds of pre-torture and post-torture differences in
testimony, as Hege does.[3] These differences are clear only in the case
of Thomas Spiegel. It seems more reasonable to explain them on other
grounds. Hut and his fellow preachers visited their converts rarely. The
converts lacked adequate instruction. Some of them, placing Hut's
pronounced eschatology against the background of the recent revolt,
advocated a fresh rebellion in connection with the awaited Turkish
visitation. Others got some teaching from Hut forbidding the use of the
sword and retained that idea despite torture.

One of the strangest mixtures of revolution and nonresistance was
found in Hans Römer and his followers. Their baptism customarily
concluded with admonitions to the new brother to live a good Christian
life and to abstain from revolution.[4] Yet the group, with Römer fully in
league if not in command, once conceived an elaborate plot for the
forcible overthrow of the city government of Erfurt and were proceeding with its execution when they were discovered. Here were
Anabaptists completely carried away by their own eschatology.[5]

[1] Klassen, *op. cit.*, pp. 71–81.
[2] Testimony in Berbig, *DZK*, XIII, 309–16, *passim*; and in Wappler, *Thüringen*, pp.
228–35.
[3] Hege, "Königsberg," *ME*, III, 220. Hege refers to a later hearing conducted by a different
civil officer, without torture, where the Anabaptists recanted their earlier statements which
they had made for fear of the rack. While it is true that Caspar Spiegel appeared at this
hearing, it is not at all clear that he was one who recanted. Beutelhans, Wolf Schreiner, and
the Aurachsmüller did retract certain of their previous statements (Berbig, *DZK*, XIII, 335).
[4] Testimony of Hans Lodewig, Dec. 19, 1527, Wappler, *Thüringen*, p. 262.
[5] *Ibid.*, pp. 38–44.

The rest of Thuringian Anabaptism presents a confused picture on the issue. Alexander, Erbe and Schnabel exemplify the usual Anabaptist position: nonresistance, obedience to civil authority, and no Christian could serve as a magistrate.[1] Others, like Margareta Koch or Erbe's visitors of 1539, present other views. Koch believed that princes universally had usurped more power than God intended them to have. The three friends of Erbe held much the same view; namely that the civil authorities behaved as Pilate toward Christ. They believed Christians had no need for government at all. Such views had religious roots like those of Rink: no government had the right as an agent of God to persecute his children. But there were also social-economic roots. Koch felt that the abused peasants had a right to raise the banner of revolt in the Peasants' War. All material goods belonged to the Lord and should not be withheld from the many by the few.[2] On his way to the executioner's block at Jena, Heinz Kraut quoted the social revolutionary jingle of John Ball and the German Peasants' War: "When Adam delved and Eve span, who then was the gentleman?"[3] Clearly Anabaptism presented no unified set of ideas on the Christian's attitude toward the civil order. The disunity can probably be attributed to insufficient instruction and the all-pervasive influence of the Peasants' War among the lower classes from which Anabaptism drew much of its membership.

The best illustration of this confusion and disunity can be found in the testimony of around twenty-five members of the Sorga congregation in 1533. To a relatively simple question as to whether or not a Christian ought to go to war, they achieved a unified no. They could not answer so unequivocally the question whether the Peasants' War was right or wrong. Some of them declared it ungodly; others thought it justified; still others did not know. The most difficult question for them was whether or not a Christian could admit the right of civil authority to rule him. One thought that government was necessary and that a Christian serving in government could in good conscience execute thieves. Another ruled out capital punishment, but not the right of a government to exercise judgment. A third believed the existence of government was permissible but that it should never wage war or call

---

[1] Of the three, Schnabel gives the fullest report: "Verantwortung," *TA, Hesse,* pp. 169–70; Erbe, in Wappler, *Die Stellung Kursachsens,* p. 139; Alexander, in Wappler, *Thüringen,* p. 348; and Jacobs, *op. cit.,* pp. 479–81.

[2] Koch testimony, July 21, 1533, in Wappler, *Die Stellung Kursachsens,* p. 174.

[3] Wappler, *Thüringen,* p. 417. "Da Adam reute und Eva spann, wer war die Zeit ein Edelmann?"

up its people to kill for any purpose. Others were not sure enough to answer. Most of them believed government should be obeyed except when conscience forbade obedience. This question on civil authority was too tricky; they did not understand its implications.[1] Nonresistance – revolution; obedience to government – no government at all; Thuringian Anabaptism had not fully made up its mind.

The interrogators of Anabaptists sometimes put the questions of oath-swearing and suits at law into the category of articles which could be labeled seditious. Thuringian Anabaptists generally condemned the oath as unnecessary and sinful. Christ had commanded a simple yes or no in the speech of his followers.[2] Occasionally an Anabaptist admitted that perhaps the civil oath was not forbidden by Christ.[3] In the one instance when the question of lawsuits was raised, the Anabaptists condemned the practice for the Christian.[4]

On Christological and Trinitarian issues Anabaptist hands were generally clean, apart from the docetic view of the incarnation obtained from Melchior Hofmann.[5] This doctrine was widely spread geographically, but it was not supported by all Anabaptists in any given area. Peter Pestel, who worked from Austria to Zwickau, in 1539; Erbe's Anabaptist friends of 1539; possibly Hans Bott; these in addition to the Schnabel-Tasch group in Central Hesse accepted the doctrine.[6] All attempts to prove Trinitarian heresy against captured Anabaptists failed. On one occasion Alexander accepted the idea of the Trinity without question.[7] In general, the non-theologically minded Anabaptists were not aware of the existence of either a Trinitarian[8] or a Christological problem.

Rink was well aware of a distinction between the two natures of Christ. He posited Christ's agony in Gethsemane as a struggle between flesh and spirit in which the ultimate victory went to the spirit. Raidt

---

[1] Sorga hearing, in *TA*, *Hesse*, pp. 64–69, *passim*.

[2] For example, Köhler and Scheffer, 1537, in Wappler, *Die Stellung Kursachsens*, p. 198.

[3] Schnabel's "Verantwortung," *TA*, *Hesse*, p. 171.

[4] Köhler and Scheffer, in Wappler, *Die Stellung Kursachsens*, p. 198.

[5] For an explanation of this view, see zur Linden, *op. cit.*, pp. 286–91. Menno Simons defended the same view. (See I. E. Burkhart, "Menno Simons on the Incarnation," *MQR*, IV [1930], 178–202.) Hofmann and Menno held that Christ became flesh *in* Mary but not *of* Mary. His flesh was somewhat spiritualized.

[6] Pestel, in Wappler, *Inquisition und Ketzerprozesse*, pp. 78–79; Erbe friends, Schultheiss Ley to Elector John Frederick, July 9, 1539, in Wappler, *Die Stellung Kursachsens*, p. 206; Bott in Letter of Elders of Moravia to Mathes, 1538, *TA*, *Hesse*, p. 181. The 1539 friends of Erbe also denied the resurrection of the flesh, both in Christ and subsequently in everyone. The resurrection was only spiritual (Wappler, *Die Stellung Kursachsens*, pp. 203–04).

[7] Hearing, 1533, in Wappler, *Thüringen*, p. 349.

[8] So the Kleineutersdorf Anabaptists interrogated by Melanchthon (*CR*, II, 998).

tried to interpret this as a declaration of Christ's disobedience in the flesh, and therefore in essence to God. Rink denied the charge. Later Raidt attempted to interpret Rink's ideas as a denial of Christ's divinity; Christ was a created being, and therefore less than God. Again Rink insisted he did not depart from orthodox Christian thought on Christological matters.[1]

On the Lord's Supper Rink opposed both Lutherans and Catholics by denying the presence of Christ's body and blood in the elements. The doctrine of the real presence was idolatry; it was an attempt to fashion an image of God out of created materials. This much is clear from the hearing of 1528, the testimony of his disciples, and his pamphlet against Bader.[2] What is not clear is Rink's idea of the purpose of the ceremony, having repudiated the real presence. He was reported to have likened the communion to the preaching of the gospel; this was the true communion because it handled the true word of life as in John 6.[3] Rink's reference to apostolic practice in this connection led zur Linden to say that Rink taught the communion in the daily breaking of bread, any bread, among the believers.[4] This may well have been the case. But the records give small basis for any positive concept of the Lord's Supper in Rink's thought. He regarded it as a great mystery and of secondary value in Christian doctrine. Only those individuals well along in their faith should receive instruction on it.[5] Perhaps Rink said little about it because most of his work was to dispense milk rather than meat.

An examination of the statements of other Anabaptists in Central Germany is of little help in reconstructing their observance of the Lord's Supper. One finds a variety of reasons for opposing the real presence: Christ was in heaven and therefore could not be in the elements; the elements tasted and smelled like wine and bread; the real presence was idolatry. But the nearest approach to a positive doctrine paralleled Rink's in kind: he who followed Christ in holiness of life truly ate and drank Christ.[6] It was spiritualized in this instance.

Of all the available sources Menius gives the fullest account of general Anabaptist practice in the celebration of the Lord's Supper in Central

---

[1] Hearing of 1528, *TA, Hesse*, pp. 5, 7, 10.

[2] *Ibid.*, pp. 5, 6–7, 9; Ot testimony, 1531, in Wappler, *Thüringen*, p. 331; *Widderlegung*, p. 6.

[3] *TA, Hesse*, pp. 5, 6–7, 9; Wappler, *Thüringen*, p. 331.

[4] Zur Linden, *op. cit.*, p. 177.

[5] Testimony of Hans Werner, 1531, in Wappler, *Thüringen*, p. 331.

[6] Berka hearing, printed in Wappler, *Die Stellung Kursachsens*, pp. 168–76, *passim*.

Germany. They used the service as a sign of love and brotherly unity. They began their celebration of communion with a sermon on brotherly love. They admonished one another on Christian behavior and charity to the brother. After reading Romans 12 they ate and drank the bread and wine. All those who participated were part of the true body of Christ. But the service symbolized more: it symbolized the suffering inevitable for the Christian. Hence the Anabaptists celebrated it when they thought they were about to be caught or punished in the expectation that it would strengthen them for the ordeal.[1]

Another element of Thuringian Anabaptist thought that requires our attention is its eschatology. This appeared in vigorous form as an integral part of the appeal of the new movement in its earliest days. The Anabaptists in Franconia were harangued with Hut's opinions of the time and manner of approach of the end time. Hut taught his followers that the Turks would engage the political leaders of Christendom in a decisive battle near Nürnberg, in which most of Germany's princes and lords would be destroyed; the remaining few would be destroyed later, either by the Turks or, as some Anabaptists said, by the Anabaptists themselves. The Lord would then come to rule the world with his Anabaptist helpers.[2]

Echoes of this theme can be found in Anabaptism throughout Central Germany in succeeding years among both moderate and radical elements. In the extant writings of Rink there are no details on the manner and time of the Lord's coming, or on the role of the Anabaptists in preparing for him. But Rink did use the Revelation account to embellish his charges that both Catholics and Protestants were disciples of antichrist.[3] Other Central German Anabaptists supplied more detail. Erbe spoke of a huge army bringing the judgment at midnight.[4] Hans Bott proclaimed much the same in his early ministry.[5] Margarete Koch held fervently to the conviction that the princes who slaughtered

---

[1] Menius, *Der Widdertauffer*, pp. T3v.–T4v.

[2] Hearing at Königsberg, 1527, which is given fully in Berbig, *DZK*, XIII, 309–16, *passim*, and Thomas Spiegel von Ostheim hearing, 1527, in Wappler, *Thüringen*, p. 231. Hut's eschatology was much more elaborate in the minds of the authorities. They were certain he designated the time: within three and a half years; and they believed he taught the participation of all Anabaptists in the final extirpation of the lords. These views do not agree with Hut's testimony in court, with his writings, or with the testimonies of the majority of his responsible followers who had more than a fleeting acquaintance with him. Hut agreed at the Martyrs' Synod in Augsburg, August 1527, to stop preaching eschatology of any sort. See Klassen, *op. cit.*, pp. 71–74.

[3] *Widderlegung*, p. 6.

[4] Testimony, 1531, in Wappler, *Die Stellung Kursachsens*, p. 139.

[5] Neff, "Hans Both," *ME*, I, 395.

the peasants in 1525 would receive their reward in the pending visitation of the Lord.[1] Hans Römer developed his eschatology in fantastic detail with the help of John's Revelation: heaven would rain grasshoppers to devour the unbaptized (i.e., non-Anabaptists). A strong wind would destroy most of the remaining offenders. Finally the faithful were expected to restore Jerusalem, and for this Römer and his people devised a plot to capture Erfurt. He anticipated help from Zwingli and Oecolampadius against the Lutherans.[2] Römer's exaggerated eschatology is the best available explanation for the contradiction between his avowed nonresistance and his assistance in the attempt to seize Erfurt by force. There was the equally fantastic expectancy of the "Prophet's" group for the immediate return of the Bridegroom.[3] All of this contrasted sharply with the moderate eschatology of the Moravian Hutterites. They likewise awaited the return of the Lord, but for them his return was less predictable in time or relation to an historic occasion than it was in the thought of the Thuringians. It was less attached to the extirpation of political leaders. There was less desire to see the Lord's own vindicated here and now. The Hutterites looked with anticipation toward the judgment, but emphasized the bliss of heaven.[4] Thuringian Anabaptism was born and nourished among a peasantry smarting from the defeat and butchery of the Peasants' War. It clamored for retribution, and sometimes was not willing to permit the Lord to vindicate his children in his own time and manner.

Finally there remains the question of congregational life and practice, particularly with respect to discipline. Anabaptism of the sixteenth century regarded the church as a brotherhood of the believers. The church was necessary and useful not only for worship and fellowship, but also for discipline. This implied the existence of a set of standards of faith which could be applied to individual members of the brotherhood. Did Thuringian Anabaptism possess such standards, and did it discipline its members? There are many evidences of attitudes which could be maintained only by the exercise of discipline. The Anabaptists experienced an enormous tension between themselves and the state church because of their emphatic rejection of the doctrines and practices of the state church. The conflict forced both sides to clarify and sharpen their doctrines. The Lutherans were better qualified than

---

[1] Testimony, 1533, in Wappler, *Die Stellung Kursachsens*, p. 174.
[2] Wappler, *Thüringen*, p. 42.
[3] *Ibid.*, p. 83.
[4] Letter of the Elders of Moravia to Mathes, 1538, *TA, Hesse*, p. 180.

the Anabaptists for such a task. But how could the Anabaptists maintain their position against the use of persecution to force a return to the state church? The effort to maintain a unity of doctrine, despite intense conviction, would of necessity be an immense one if it were to succeed against the forces of opposition. The situation called for stern discipline.[1]

There are evidences of such a discipline, but the instances are surprisingly few and are found mostly outside the geographical center of Thuringian Anabaptism. Menius reported briefly on the use of the ban, presumably in the Thuringian Anabaptist heartland. They counseled with each other and practiced the ban against the sinning member before the observance of communion. They were especially careful to require repentance and confession of a member who had recanted.[2] Other records on western Thuringian Anabaptism's use of discipline are virtually nonexistent. In border regions there is more to be found. An Anabaptist of the Harz testified that they did not permit any lewd or unchaste person among them. A brother with a bad reputation was always investigated. Since gossip was forbidden among them, one can suppose that they were fair enough to judge an accused brother on the basis of good evidence. Another Anabaptist denied that a specified individual, a local miller, belonged to their brotherhood, on the grounds that the miller beat his wife.[3] These instances point unquestionably to the exercise of discipline. By far the best evidence is found in Central Hesse. In an argument with Bucer on why the Anabaptists separated from the state church, Georg Schnabel gave as one reason the state church's failure to practice the ban against a sinning member. He declared that Luther at one time wanted to establish a true church, presumably with discipline, but that he was unable to do so because he could not find enough of the right kind of people for it. Schnabel accused Luther of a lack of courage.[4] The group led by Schnabel and

---

[1] The necessity for discipline is as apparent in Rink's tract on baptism as it is anywhere in the records of Thuringian Anabaptism. Rink believed, as Luther did, that wherever true Christian doctrine and worship were established, the devil tried to invade in order to tear down and destroy the work of the Lord. He likened the body of believers to a flock of sheep who undertook the work of reform, driving out the wolves, lions, and bears, because the Protestant pastors, the sheep-dogs, refused to perform the task. Tract on Baptism, *Sammelband*, pp. K2r.–K3r.

[2] Menius, *Der Widdertauffer*, p. T4r.

[3] Jacobs, *op. cit.*, p. 485; Hochhuth, *op. cit.*, (1858), pp. 627–31.

[4] The reference is undoubtedly to Luther's *Vorrede* to the *Deutsche Messe*, 1526, in *WA*, XIX, 75. Luther feared that separate secret conventicles of earnest Christians would develop factionalism in the church, to the detriment of the many who needed instruction. Schnabel overstated Luther's desire to found such a separated church.

Tasch must have practiced the ban. But it is significant that it was precisely the leaders of this group who were induced to return to the state church, not without concessions of course on the practice of the ban in the state church.[1]

Within a given congregation in Anabaptism's geographical heartland one notices considerable variation in belief and understanding of faith and doctrine. Twelve persons including Rink were apprehended on November 11, 1531, at the house of Hans Werner at Vacha, having gathered to hear Rink preach. At the subsequent hearing three of them displayed an excellent grasp of Rink's thought and showed obvious signs of having had some instruction from him. Two others were somewhat less well instructed. Of the remaining six, two disclaimed any relation to the movement except that of passing curiosity. The other four were bonafide Anabaptists, but either knew little about the faith or were not given an opportunity to display their knowledge. Two of the most ably instructed, Adam Angersbach and Heinz Ot, recanted on the ground that they were not absolutely sure Rink's teaching was correct. They were willing to receive instruction. Rink, needless to say, must have been discomfitted. But what can one say about congregational life and discipline here? It is questionable that there existed at this place a congregation in the usual Anabaptist sense of the word. Their meeting on this occasion was for the purpose of evangelism. Rink spoke on baptism, undoubtedly within the context of individual salvation, in an effort to win new members. It was reported that their meetings during the previous summer were for the same purpose, and that they did not meet alone as a congregation.[2]

---

[1] One of the crucial areas in which discipline could have been exercised was that of mixed marriage. Could an Anabaptist consider his marriage to a non-Anabaptist a valid one? Generally the attitude prevailed that a mixed marriage was not valid. This meant in some instances that an Anabaptist deserted his non-Anabaptist spouse. See, for example, the tangled affair of Hans Zwinger the Younger, whose wife deserted him when he recanted (Berka hearing, 1533, Wappler, *Die Stellung Kursachsens*, p. 172). It sometimes meant further that the Anabaptist partner could remarry, this time of course an Anabaptist. See the case of Georg Volck, in Marx Mayı's testimony, in Wappler, *Thüringen*, p. 323; or the case of Adam Schwabe, Frankenhausen hearing, 1530, *ibid.*, p. 313. Volck was accused of teaching that wives should be had in common. He took a second one because his first one disagreed with him. Schwabe confessed to having two wives, the second of whom was an Anabaptist. Although there is evidence of marital problems, there is still no direct evidence of discipline administered by a congregation in a case of mixed marriage. There is even no evidence of congregational counsel on the matter.

[2] The magistrate, Martin von der Thann, and Council of Vacha reported this in a letter to Philip, November 12, 1531. It is doubtful that the authorities could have known the exact character of all the Anabaptist meetings in Vacha during the preceding summer, but the generalization is not without validity and significance. Wappler, *Thüringen*, pp. 326–27. The report of the hearing follows, pp. 327–33.

For the other congregations, such as Sorga or Berka, the evidence is not so clear one way or the other. Here again one finds substantial differences in degree of spiritual growth and understanding. The contrast is not so great as at Vacha, partly at least because the interrogations at Berka and Sorga in 1533 did not cover as broad a scope of doctrine.[1] It is interesting to observe differences in doctrine between the two groups of men apprehended while conversing with Fritz Erbe, in 1537 and 1539. These men probably had connections with the Berka group at least. The pair caught in 1537 were Scriptural literalists with what appears to be a traditional Anabaptist position against the use of force in war or at law. The trio of 1539 were spiritualists with an attitude toward government suspiciously like revolution.[2] Could these five men and Erbe have been in the same congregation if a consistent discipline had been exercised? For that matter, the rise in esteem of a man like Erbe, replacing somewhat, or at least standing beside, the veneration given to Rink by the rank and file Anabaptists, is significant. Erbe did not possess the fire of Rink in denouncing infant baptism and insisting on believers' baptism. Anabaptism had to maintain a vigorous sanction with respect to believers' baptism or fall prey to the blandishments of state church theologians. This is exactly what happened to Mathes Hasenhan, one of the leaders of Thuringian-Hessian Anabaptism in the 1530's. In Thuringian Anabaptism's dying days in 1540, he capitulated to Bucer's arguments on baptism. He agreed not to proselyte within the state church membership on the traditional arguments of error in baptism. For himself he could not accept the full validity of infant baptism.[3] Needless to say, no Anabaptism could continue to exist on such a position.

To question the existence of a vigorous discipline among the Thuringian Anabaptists is not to deny a sense of brotherhood or to rule out some sort of congregational life. Their sense of brotherhood is testified to by the warmth of their greeting. Always they called one another "Brother" or "Sister." [4] Among some of them the greeting was

---

[1] Sorga hearing, August 9, 1533, in *TA, Hesse*, pp. 64–69; Berka hearing, July 19–21, 1533, in Wappler, *Die Stellung Kursachsens*, pp. 168–76.

[2] Köhler and Scheffer hearing, 1537, *ibid.*, pp. 197–98; 1539 trio's hearing, *ibid.*, pp. 203–04.

[3] Letter of Bucer and Tasch to Philip, February 7, 1540, *TA, Hesse*, p. 269. Mathes is a silent but influential figure in Thuringian Anabaptist history in the second half of the 1530's. It was to Mathes that the Moravian Hutterites appealed, against Hans Bott, as one whose doctrine, as they heard from others, was sound. The Tasch-Schnabel correspondence on the question of the trip to England mentions Mathes as a leader.

[4] Hans Römer's group made it "Dear Christian Brother" (Wappler, *Thüringen*, p. 41. Franconian Anabaptists, hearing of Beutelhans, in Berbig, *DZK*, XIII, 313).

more elaborate. One said: "The peace of the Lord be with you, brother"; to which the other replied: "And with your spirit." [1] The fuller greeting was utilized as a means for otherwise unacquainted brethren to recognize each other as members of the same brotherhood. It was a kind of password. In a brotherhood scattered by persecution, constantly drawing in fresh members, one could not be expected to recognize every brother on sight. There were without question some meetings of the brethren for mutual edification. Alexander reported that they spoke to each other of godly righteousness on such occasions.[2] They were certainly aware of each other's needs; their testimony on sharing material goods is as unanimous in all of Thuringian Anabaptism as on any other point. They felt themselves bound to proffer financial aid to their traveling ministers.[3] But their entire congregational life as such was constantly threatened by the spectre of capture; they were constantly on the move.[4]

The written evidence for discipline among the Thuringian Anabaptists is scarce. One can safely say that they practiced no consistently vigorous discipline; it was at most sporadic. Internal weakness, the absence of a consistent discipline, must be added to the previously given reasons for the relatively early demise of Anabaptism in this region. It was certainly a factor in the relatively large number of recantations and in the absence of a common mind on certain pivotal doctrines such as nonresistance.

The relative absence of discipline among Thuringia's Anabaptists requires some explanation. This lack cannot be laid to intention on the part of the brethren. Several plausible reasons suggest themselves. Harried from place to place, the brethren could not develop a normal congregational life. Secondly, their sense of mission led them to build most of their activity around evangelistic endeavor. The wandering preacher visited a village one evening, preached on repentance and the need for commitment to Christ, baptized those who requested it, and then moved on to another village. His converts lacked

[1] Fritz Erbe hearing, in Wappler, *Die Stellung Kursachsens*, p. 139.
[2] Testimony of 1533, in Wappler, *Thüringen*, p. 349.
[3] *Ibid.* Also hearing of Thomas Spiegel von Ostheim, 1527, *ibid.*, p. 234.
[4] Testimony of Veit Weischenfelder, March 18, 1527 (*ibid.*, p. 242). Some of them defended themselves against the charges of being clandestine, and their ministers having no proper call to preach, with Scripture. It was not only the pressure of persecution but also the necessity for obeying the gospel that led them to such a life. They likened themselves to Christ's disciples who were sent out to move from place to place (Matt. 10:8-13). Their ministers were called of God, like the Apostle Paul (Gal. 1:1), not by men as in the state church. (Köhler and Scheffer, in Wappler, *Die Stellung Kursachsens*, p. 197; Schnabel, "Verantwortung," in *TA, Hesse*, pp. 176-78.)

consistent instruction. Finally, it is likely that those Anabaptists who were most amenable to the idea of, and necessity for, discipline were attracted by the Hutterite example and emigrated to join the brethren in Moravia. The move to Moravia had a dual motive: persecution at home as against relative freedom in Moravia, and the existence of a strong brotherhood there with an active discipline.

However, absence of discipline in Thuringian Anabaptism was a relative matter. The brethren charged the state church with its complete absence. But compared to Anabaptism elsewhere in Europe, the Thuringian variety was a somewhat undisciplined stepchild.

An examination of the problem of Anabaptist origins in Central Germany is in order. This problem is traditionally answered in Protestant historiography by pointing to Thomas Müntzer as the originator of the movement, or at least the person of most decisive influence in its origin. The Zwickau Prophets, Müntzer's spiritual predecessors, are also frequently added as forerunners of the Anabaptists. A substantial number of writers support the theory that Müntzer initiated the Anabaptist movement.[1] The existence of this literature compels one to begin the inquiry into Thuringian Anabaptist origins with a fresh examination of the evidence for the Müntzer theory. It is unquestionably true that Müntzer had some influence on certain persons who later joined the Thuringian Anabaptists. The degree of that influence is more difficult to ascertain. We can begin with an examination of his earlier influence on the most important leaders of the movement.

A number of the later Anabaptist leaders, including some of the most important ones, had fallen under the influence of Müntzer in his heyday. Rink and Hut were his disciples in 1525. Both were at Frankenhausen, the one as participant and the other as itinerant book-peddler and interested spectator. Both escaped unscathed in body, but changed in spirit. The extent of change in Hut has already been thoroughly investigated in another monograph.[2] Here we must discuss the relation between the matured theology of Rink and the ideas of Müntzer in order to learn how much Rink changed since his days as a disciple of Müntzer.

In the ideas of repentance and forgiveness of sins their ways parted. By 1528 Rink had abandoned Müntzer's mysticism for an approach dominated by the twin ideas of repentance and commitment to Christ

[1] Much of this literature derives from the efforts of Karl Holl and Heinrich Boehmer to re-examine Müntzer. See above, p. 2.
[2] Klassen, *op. cit.*, pp. 87–104.

in holiness of life.[1] His ideas on repentance were Pauline in origin. This does not mean that his soteriology contained no elements of mysticism; the absence of a clear doctrine of atonement, a reliance on primarily Johannine ideas on conversion, and the continued use of the terminology of the mystics (*Gelassenheit*, for example) suggests a not insignificant degree of mysticism. But his preoccupation with the theme of love as the framework both for man's separation from and reconciliation to God suggests Denk [2] rather than Müntzer [3] as its author. Müntzer built his concept of salvation around the suffering of the cross. Through suffering and pain the soul was made ready to receive the Spirit of God.[4] Rink did not reject the cross as suffering. But to him the cross was the consequence of becoming a Christian, the persecution which the true Christian must expect, rather than an integral part of the redemption process.[5] Rink did not reject Müntzer's idea of resignation (*Gelassenheit*) in redemption. Indeed, it is at this point that he sounds the most like Müntzer. But his insistence on the necessity for divine aid in achieving *Gelassenheit* suggests at least an alteration of Müntzer's idea in the direction of a Pauline theology. He did not work through the relationship carefully. There is no explanation in Rink's writings of the respective shares of man and God in the work of man's redemption; there is no discussion of free will and determinism. His soteriology is a mixture of Luther and Denk, with very little of Müntzer remaining.

In baptism also the differences appear greater than the similarities. Müntzer condemned the practice of infant baptism with his customary vehemence. Rink agreed with his arguments that it reduced to nonsense the ceremony of inception into the Christian church, a ceremony that ought to be invested with the greatest solemnity, and that salvation could in no sense be dependent upon infant baptism.[6] But Müntzer did not take the subsequent step of inaugurating adult or believers' baptism, nor did he even cease baptizing infants.[7] It has been suggested

---

[1] The emphasis on repentance is found especially in his use of Scriptures to buttress his case, Scriptures in which the call to repentance predominates (*TA, Hesse*, p. 8, point 4).

[2] Jan J. Kiwiet, "The Theology of Hans Denck," *MQR*, XXXII (1958), 3–27. See particularly the section "The Law of God," pp. 15–17.

[3] Annemarie Lohmann, *Zur geistlichen Entwicklung Thomas Müntzers* (Leipzig: B. G. Teubner, 1931), p. 33.

[4] *Ibid.*, pp. 33, 44–45.

[5] Hearing of 1528, *TA, Hesse*, p. 6; Angersbach testimony in Wappler, *Thüringen*, p. 329. See also R. Friedmann, "Thomas Müntzer's Relation to Anabaptism." *MQR*, XXXI (1957), 83.

[6] "Protestation oder Entbietung Thomae Müntzers," in O. Brandt, *op. cit.* pp. 134–35.

[7] Müntzer's post-*Protestation* practice is not altogether clear. In 1524 he told Oecolampadius that he baptized infants but not shortly after their birth; he held a baptismal

that the basis for his protest against infant baptism did not lead logically to adult or believers' baptism,[1] since Müntzer's excessive reliance
on the Spirit obviated the necessity for any outward ceremony. On the
one hand there is little or nothing in his theology that would lead to
believers' baptism either as a seal of one's faith in Christ as Redeemer,
or as a sign of commitment to Christ in holiness of life. Rink got these
ideas elsewhere. On the other hand, however, adult baptism was not
illogical from Müntzer's theological viewpoint.[2] If adult baptism was
not inevitable in his position, it was at least not impossible. Adult
baptism could have become the basic sign of reception into Müntzer's
Bund, a sign of election. It may be suggested that for those later
Anabaptists who sang the praises of Müntzer as prophet and leader,
the rite of baptism was essentially the sign of reception into a *Bund*.[3]
Hut's followers in Franconia, for whom the rite was first and foremost
a sign of entrance into a *Bund*, could have derived the idea from
Müntzer's theology if not from his explicit teaching.[4]

Baptism led Rink secondarily to the *Bund*. Müntzer practiced a
conventicle Christianity during his residence in Zwickau and instituted
a *Bund* at Allstedt. He intended to pattern his church after that of the
New Testament. It was at once the body of the elect and co-terminous
with society in a geographical locale. For Müntzer believed that the
elect should expel and even extirpate the ungodly. Hence the Allstedters
who did not join were expelled from the town. In imitation of the early

---

service every two or three months for all those born within that time (C. Hege, "Thomas
Müntzer," *ML*, III, 189). He appears to have wanted to hold baptismal services twice annu-
ally for children around six or seven years of age (Jordan, "Die Wiedertäufer in Mühlhausen,
Mühlhäuser Geschichtsblätter, XV [1915], 38). It is clear that he did not practice adult baptism;
technically he was not an Anabaptist. On these grounds Sebastian Franck excluded him from
Anabaptism proper (*Chronica, Zeytbuch vnd geschychtbibel* [Strassburg: Balthassar Beck, 1531],
p. 394 *verso*).

[1] Müntzer laid more weight on the inner baptism of the Spirit than the outward ceremony
(Lohmann, *op. cit.*, p. 48. See R. Friedmann, "Thomas Müntzer's Relation to Anabaptism,"
MQR, XXXI [1957], 80; also Harold S. Bender, "The Zwickau Prophets, Thomas Müntzer,
and the Anabaptists," *MQR*, XXVII [1953], 4). It is significant that Conrad Grebel interpreted Müntzer's rejection of infant baptism as a rejection of the entire act, under any
circumstances whatsoever, and protested against this rejection. (See H. Fast, "The Dependence of the First Anabaptists on Luther, Erasmus, and Zwingli," *MQR*, XXX [1956],
p. 114 and n. 58.)

[2] *Ibid.*, pp. 113–14 and note 58.

[3] So Margarete Koch's testimony in Wappler, *Die Stellung Kursachsens*, p. 174, and Jacob
Storger's testimony in Wappler, *Thüringen*, p. 429.

[4] At this point the treatment of Müntzer-Anabaptist relations by H. S. Bender (*MQR*,
XXVII, 3–16) is not entirely valid because it deals more specifically with Müntzer and the
Swiss Brethren, and the purported genetic relationship between Müntzer and Anabaptist
origins in Zurich. It is clear enough that Müntzer was of some influence on Thuringian
Anabaptism.

church Müntzer inaugurated community of goods. He insisted on a
leveling of social classes within the *Bund*. Müntzer's *Bund* bore a para-
military character in line with its purpose to usher in the Kingdom of
God. This meant to Müntzer a defense against the ungodly who attacked,
and an eventual offense against them in order to wreak the righteous
extirpating justice of the Lord upon them.[1] Both activities required
military force. Müntzer's *Bund* in its final, fullest development bore a
resemblance to the later group around Hans Römer. But Rink and his
followers held a different view. Rink could have gotten from Müntzer
the bare idea of a church of believers built on New Testament lines,
together with eschatological expectancy. But the ends to which he
turned the body, to an earnest quest for a more holy life, and his
drastically different means to enlarge the Kingdom make a deeper
reliance on Müntzer most unlikely at this point.

With respect to eschatology Müntzer and the Anabaptists show
similarity.[2] Some Anabaptists were filled with a great expectancy of
the Lord's return. There was difference in the delineation of the manner,
time, and particular method of the return. The majority of the peaceful
Thuringian Anabaptists would have rejected Müntzer's use of force to
usher in the Kingdom. But there were a few who sanctioned it.

There was similarity too in the matter of spiritualism. Müntzer
believed in a lively Spirit which manifested itself in dreams and visions.
On the one hand he was willing to go beyond the limits of the Scriptural
lines in his pursuit of the freely coursing Spirit. On the other hand he
believed that dreams could originate from ungodly sources, and therefore must be judged on the basis of Scripture.[3] In general the Anabaptists laid a sharper insistence on Scriptural limitations to the Spirit as
authority. Nor did they rely as much as Müntzer on visions and dreams;
Rink not at all. They did not condemn the Scripture as a dead letter as
much as Müntzer did. They found a doctrine of repentance in the
Scripture, and ethical injunctions in the Sermon on the Mount. Müntzer
used Scripture mainly for his ethical and social ideas. And he relied in
the first instance on Old Testament personages as examples worthy
of imitation, or on Old Testament law. Christ was to be followed in

---

[1] Hinrichs, *op. cit.*, chapter I.

[2] Friedmann ("Thomas Müntzer's Relation to Anabaptism," *MQR*, XXXI [1957], 85) also
does not touch the Central German picture of Anabaptism and its relations to Müntzer
because he is dealing with the Zurich circle. Hut agreed to cease preaching his apocalypticism
only at what turned out to be the end of his mission; he was imprisoned and died shortly after
the agreement. Prior to that he had unquestionably inspired many with his eschatology, including his disciples in Franconia. (See Klassen, *op. cit.*, pp. 70–74).

[3] Hinrichs, *op. cit.*, pp. 54–56; Lohmann, *op. cit.*, 33–34, 47.

suffering.[1] The Anabaptists could accept the example of Christ in suffering; but they insisted on using Christ as example for holiness of life as well. But if the Anabaptists went beyond Müntzer in reliance on Scripture, and curtailed the effervescence of Müntzer's Spirit, their kinship with him is still apparent. Similarity in kind remains, if degree is different.

Two final issues require only passing mention. On the Lord's Supper Müntzer retained a conservative practice; he retained the Catholic service with few changes, and even called it the mass.[2] The Anabaptists were firm rejectors of the real presence. On the use of military force their ways parted. The majority of Thuringia's Anabaptists acquired their doctrine of nonresistance from other sources.

In summary, one can observe a considerable dependence on Müntzer in Rink's spiritualism and general Anabaptist eschatology. A lesser measure of dependence can be found in Rink's mysticism, and in his idea of a believers' church. But in Rink's ideas on salvation, baptism, Lord's Supper, and nonresistance the dependence is so slight as to be unnoticeable, or the attitude is in direct contrast to Müntzer's. In the four areas where dependence can be shown, Rink changed his ideas to a considerable extent. There were decisive changes in Rink's post-1525 theological development. The total change is of such magnitude that one can safely postulate a kind of conversion for Rink after 1525. Logically it would have centered around his acceptance of believers' baptism. This is not to deny that Müntzer led Rink to the living water, a water somewhat apart from the stream which nourished the Lutheran reform. For this guiding hand Rink must have been grateful. But his subsequent development, under the guidance of Denk's religion, took him far from Müntzer's paths. It is not correct to call the Rink of 1528 a disciple of Müntzer.

The second Thuringian Anabaptist leader of influence who was an earlier disciple of Müntzer was Hans Hut. In his case one observes also a decisive change in his religious ideas. On the most crucial issues, the nature of the church and the attitude toward the state, Hut's divergence from the teachings of Müntzer is the most complete. Hut retained a larger measure of Müntzer's expectancy of a violent return of the Lord than did Rink. But in Hut's church the disciplining brotherhood function can be discerned more clearly than in Rink's religious circle.[3]

---

[1] Brandt, *op. cit.*, p. 28.

[2] Friedmann, "Thomas Müntzer's Relation to Anabaptism," *MQR*, XXXI (1957), 84.

[3] For Hut's ideas and for a comparison of these with the theology of Müntzer, I have relied on H. Klassen, *op. cit.*, particularly pp. 87–104.

Both Hut and Rink discovered other, more decisive, sources for their religious views after the disaster at Frankenhausen.

What about those Anabaptists who openly declared themselves followers of Müntzer? Some were obviously unreconstructed rebels. They referred with approval to Müntzer's battlefield activities.[1] Those who insisted that only Christ or God was fit object for the title Lord were perhaps following Müntzer's final pamphlet, in which he paralleled Luther's appeal of July, 1524, to the Saxon princes with an appeal to Christ; only God and Christ were worthy of the title Lord.[2] This type of social egalitarianism, however, appeared seldom among the Thuringian Anabaptists. Influence is more difficult to trace in the case of the Anabaptist who praised Müntzer and yet insisted on obedience to government.[3] His inconsistency may be explained on grounds of torture or simple mental confusion. The appeal to Müntzer may also have been an admission of respect for his spiritualism or his mysticism. The Anabaptists never looked at society in terms of the problem of maintaining order. In this sense they were not socially responsible. They did not always insist on regarding Müntzer as the political authorities did, that is as a rebel. The fact that to any prince he symbolized rebellion did not mean that his social and political aims were uppermost in the minds of all the Anabaptists who respected him.[4]

Of major importance in the ideas of the Anabaptists was the theology of Hans Denk.[5] Some of Rink's points of divergence from Müntzer's ideas show similarity to Denk's teachings. Denk's emphasis on the law of God as given in love and for the purpose of bringing men to God's love is echoed in Rink's soteriology.[6] Far more striking is the emphasis on a Christian life of obedience to and imitation of Christ.[7] Rink's mysticism and his ethical concern seem likely derivatives from Denk. Denk is much more explicit and detailed than Rink in his infrequent statements; a detailed comparison is therefore impossible. But the gaps in our knowledge of Rink's theology could logically be filled with

---

[1] So Margarete Koch, testimony printed in Wappler, *Die Stellung Kursachsens*, p. 174.

[2] "Hoch verursachte schutzrede und antwort wider das geistlose, sanftlebende fleisch zuo Wittenberg...," Lohmann, *op. cit.*, p. 64. See the interrogation of Kraut and others, presided over by Melanchthon, below, pp. 165-67.

[3] Jacob Storger case, October 12, 1537, printed in Wappler, *Thüringen*, p. 429.

[4] Boehmer, *op. cit.*, p. 221, considers Müntzer's connection with the Peasants' War, i.e., revolution, to be a circumstantial accident. His mystic-spiritualist ideas were the dominant ones for himself and his subsequent followers.

[5] See Jan Kiwiet, "The Life and Theology of Hans Denck," *MQR*, XXXI (1957), 227-59; *ibid.*, XXXII (1958), 3-27.

[6] *Ibid.*, XXXII, 17.

[7] *Ibid.*, p. 18.

Denk's ideas, for example in soteriology. Hut likewise received decisive ideas from Denk.[1]

As a second line of influence, one might suggest Jakob Strauss.[2] Geographical proximity makes it appear most probable that Rink had far more personal contact with Strauss than with Müntzer. Strauss got Rink his appointment as pastor at Eckhardtshausen. Rink worked for more than a year at a distance of twelve miles from Strauss' center of activity at Eisenach. Strauss is remembered primarily for his rigoristic opposition to the charging of interest, and the social unrest which his condemnation of the practice unleashed. But Strauss' objection to interest must be seen within the larger context of his advocacy of an enthusiastic sharing of material goods among the brotherhood of Christians, almost to the point of community of goods. In addition there is more than merely the germ of the believers' church in Strauss' thought.[3] His views on baptism, too, were very close to those of later Anabaptists.[4] If Rink got the fire of his opposition to Luther from Müntzer, he could have gotten a fuller body of reasons for opposition from Strauss.[5] Though Müntzer was admittedly the leading figure for turbulence in Central Germany in the mid-1520's, it does not follow that all radicals in the same geographical area and time descended from him.

Finally there remains the theory of the existence of Anabaptism in Central Germany before 1525, which postulates a completely different explanation of origins. The slight possibility that Müntzer's colleague

---

[1] Klassen, op. cit., pp. 108–12.

[2] Strauss is a much neglected figure of importance in the early Central German Reformation. Joachim Rogge, Der Beitrag des Predigers Jakob Strauss zur frühen Reformationsgeschichte (Berlin: Evangelische Verlagsanstalt, 1957), is the latest work on Strauss. Rogge suggests his conflict with Luther is the reason for the absence of interest in him by historians.

[3] Ibid., pp. 21–24, 71 ff., 168. His idea of the church, according to Rogge, is an expanded version of Luther's "Ein Sermon vom Sakrament und von den Brüderschaften," 1519 (WA, II, 738 ff).

[4] Rogge, op. cit., pp. 54–60. Rogge thinks a number of Strauss' distinctive points came from Luther's "Sermon von der Taufe," 1519 (WA, II, 728). Strauss laid great weight on inner baptism to bring fruit and salvation. Inner baptism, the baptism of Christ, was a daily requirement. His ideas led logically to the performance of the rite itself on the basis of individual experience of the inward baptism. It was precisely this kind of subjectivism in the later Anabaptists to which Luther objected.

[5] Other ideas which were similar to those of the Anabaptists: a strong emphasis on works (in deliberate contrast to Luther), and a conviction based on the Sermon on the Mount that the Christian must necessarily endure unjust suffering. Strauss' reverence for the Sermon on the Mount paralleled the respect of the Anabaptists. Lutheran Rogge criticizing Strauss for a failure to come to the heart of Lutheran sola fide sounds much like the orthodox Lutherans criticizing Anabaptism on the same grounds (Rogge, op. cit., p. 149). To Rogge Strauss' friendship with Rink implicates Strauss with Müntzer (ibid., p. 113). There is no evidence that Rink was in any way a disciple of Müntzer in 1523 when he took the Eckhardtshausen pastorate.

Heinrich Pfeiffer began the practice of adult baptism very early in 1525 [1] has been rejected by the editor of one of the major sources [2] used to support the suggestion.[3] One early case of adult baptism is more difficult to explain. The Anabaptist Anna Reichard declared in September, 1535, that she had been baptized more than ten years earlier by a certain Bernhardus.[4] This was enough for Ludwig Keller to repeat his theory of Anabaptism being a continuation of the Old Evangelical Brotherhoods, coming in particular from the Bohemian Brethren.[5] The total evidence is too slight to postulate a pre-1525 existence for Anabaptism in Central Germany, although the possibility of a connection with pre-Reformation groups must not be excluded. In the absence of further evidence one must accept Wappler's conclusion that Anabaptism in Central Germany derived from the activities of Hans Hut in northern Franconia in the summer of 1526. Here began the systematic baptism of adult believers.

---

[1] So Wappler, *Thüringen*, p. 17.

[2] *Chronik der Stadt Mühlhausen*, edited by Jordan.

[3] Jordan, "Wiedertäufer in Mühlhausen," *Mühlhäuser Geschichtsblätter*, XV (1915), 39. Jordan used negative evidence to reject the assertion: if Pfeiffer had baptized adults, his later accusers in court would have been delighted to mention this as evidence against him. They did not.

[4] Hearing on September 21, 1535, printed by Jacobs, *op. cit.*, p. 529. Wappler, *Thüringen*, p. 90, n. 1, declares the date to be false, but produces no proof.

[5] L. Keller, "Der sog. Anabaptismus am Harz im 16. Jahrhundert," *Monatshefte der Comenius Gesellschaft*, IX (1900), 183–84.

CHAPTER IV

LUTHER AND THE ANABAPTISTS

Luther embarked upon his radical criticism of the Roman church with the conviction that the Word of God had been hampered and needed a path cleared for its free and unhindered course. Men had always tried to make themselves and their own inventions more important than the Word itself. So the Roman church had done. Over the centuries it had raised formidable blocks to the progress of the Word. In the first rank stood the blockade of Pelagianism: the Romans had developed the notion that a man could obtain salvation through the performance of good works. Another blockade of equal stature was that of institutionalism. The church had built itself into an authority so absolute that no secular or spiritual power could shake it. Thus the papacy, at the top of an imposing hierarchy of ecclesiastical power, reserved for itself the sole right to interpret Scripture and to summon councils in order to preserve its power. Through these human additions the Word of God was made to suffer. It needed to be released from human encumbrances. That is precisely what Luther set about to do.

Although he sought to recondition the church, he did so with the rather naive confidence that it would allow itself to be reconditioned by a German monk. Above all he did not seek to break with the church. That the events from the posting of the ninety-five theses to the papal bull of excommunication made such a break inevitable and even necessary became a matter of surprise to him, and also a matter of painful concern. Not the concern of prospective burning. Luther always feared the wrath of God more than that of man. But it was for him a terrifying, awful thing to break with the church. Perhaps the severity of his *Anfechtungen* in later years can be laid partly to this cause.

Luther was convinced that the Word had captured him and virtually forced him against his own will to purify the church. The power of the Word was to him unlimited. Therefore he developed a supreme confidence in the ability and power of the Word to run its course unaided, once it was set free. He translated the Bible into the German language to enable the Word to speak with even greater force to more people. He published books of sermons to enable pastors to release the Word ever more effectively. He expected the political rulers to allow the Word its free course by permitting the preaching of it and allowing those modifications of Roman church practice which were necessary. But in the end it was the Word alone that worked; it alone could speak the good news of forgiveness by God to the hearts of men. Nothing in his encounter with the papists caused him to change this fundamental view.

There is a vast difference between criticizing the defects of an existing institution and building a structure to replace it. So Luther discovered when he was forced, in the 1520's, to build a church. This is not to suggest that he offered nothing of a constructive nature with his criticism of the Roman church. But he faced problems in the reconstruction task which he had not anticipated, and which caused him to appear as a new pope to some. He actually faced the necessity for rebuilding with the appearance of criticism from the left, from the *Schwärmer*. Hitherto he had relied so heavily on the creativity of the unaided Word to first convict and then build that he had almost regarded the task of building a church an automatic one. Almost, but not quite. He did write about certain changes in church practice, such as release from monastic vows, marriage of clergy, and celebration of the Lord's Supper. But the radicals, who declared that Luther had not gone far enough, forced his hand. From the Wittenberg debacle of early 1522 through the Peasants' Revolt, and indeed for the rest of his life, Luther sought in building to steer between the Charybdis and Scylla of excessive institutionalism and excessive subjectivism. One suspects that he actually feared the left more than he did the papists, for Luther, conservative by nature, utterly abhorred the threat, always implicit among the radicals, of insurrection. The *Schwärmer* had impressed and shocked Luther deeply. For the remainder of his life he was deeply suspicious of any idea or person that appeared similar to that diabolical trio of forces. So it was when he turned his attention to the Anabaptists.[1]

By mid-1525 the threat from the left appeared to have subsided, though not without its trail of blood. Müntzer was dead, the Prophets were badly dispersed and discomfited, and a discouraged Carlstadt

---

[1] For this characterization of Luther's outlook I have relied on Bainton, *Here I Stand*, chapters xii and xiii, *passim*, and certain lectures of Prof. Wilhelm Pauck on Luther.

appeared willing to recant his Lord's Supper views in order to return to Saxony. Central Germany began to settle down; but not for long. For in 1526 the vigorous missioners of that new sect, Anabaptism, penetrated northward as far as Franconia, to the edges of the Thuringian Forest. By 1527 they were in Saxony itself. Everywhere with amazing rapidity they won converts, principally among the common people. Luther was impelled afresh to counteract a radicalism which threatened the progress of reform in Central Germany. He did so fully within the context of Anabaptism conceived as a continuation of the work of the *Schwärmer*.

Luther wrote or spoke on many occasions against the Anabaptists. Most of his references to the group were short, with little description of their ideas. He wrote only one tract which was devoted exclusively to a discussion and refutation of Anabaptism. Otherwise his remarks appeared in sermons, letters, or prefaces to books written by others. As one would expect under such circumstances he repeated himself endlessly. Most of his utterances could be described as miscellaneous diatribes against their teachings on baptism or the Christian's relationship to the state or as brief, troubled discourses on how to treat these poor deluded souls. His one basic pamphlet against the radicals should be treated as a unit. The remainder of his utterances can be handled better within the framework of the ideas he touched when he approached the subject of Anabaptism.

Luther took up his pen early in 1528 to write against the Anabaptists. He was invited to the task by two of his followers who labored for the cause in Catholic lands. They apparently asked him for aid in refuting the arguments of the Anabaptists.[1] This invitation fitted the general apprehension of Luther that disgruntled peasants might flock to the standard of new radicals after their defeat in 1525. Hence he complied in the expectation that simple and pious people might be helped thereby to detect error.[2] He announced his intention to write the tract in a letter to Wenzel Link, the Austin General in Nürnberg, late in December, 1527. He intended the brochure on Anabaptism as a kind of prelude to

---

[1] *Von der Widertauffe an zwen Pfarherrn, ein Brief* (Wittemberg: Georg Wachter, 1528). Luther addressed the two pastors as "the worthy esteemed gentlemen N. and N., my dear brothers in Christ." The editors of the Weimar edition of Luther's works were unable to suggest who the men might be. (*WA*, XXVI, 139.) There are no other clues in the pamphlet itself. The tract was issued in at least five editions in 1528. (*WA*, XXVI, 141.) The first edition was off the press sometime between January 27 and February 5, 1528. See letter to J. Hess, *WB*, IV, 371–72; and letter to Spalatin, *WB*, IV, 376.

[2] Letter to Spalatin, February 5, 1528, *WB*, IV, 376. Also letter to Conrad Cordatus, March 6, 1528, *WB*, IV, 402–03.

his next attack against the sacramentarians.[1] It is clear that he considered the relationship between the Anabaptists and those who rejected the real presence in the Lord's Supper to be an exceptionally close one.

Throughout the entire tract Luther's attitude was stiffly authoritarian and archly conservative. He appeared to be almost a Romanist. He blandly accepted many of the Roman doctrines without any kind of qualification. Thus he declared as true the Romanist teachings on Scripture, baptism, sacrament of the altar, forgiveness of sins, office of minister, and catechetical formulae such as the Lord's Prayer, Ten Commandments, and the Confession of Faith. He did not specify which confession; probably he meant one of the early creedal statements, such as the Apostles Creed or the Nicean. Why then leave Rome? Luther gave only one answer in this tract: the pope was antichrist because he worked against the true Christian faith, albeit from within the body of Christ, namely Christendom. Indeed, the pope had tried to kill Luther after excommunicating him. But the church over which the pope presided had collected and preserved many truths which were still universally valid.[2]

Luther certainly did not intend to indicate that he found no fault in Catholic views on, say forgiveness of sin, or the Eucharist. What he did intend to do was to spell out a conservative approach to the matter of change as over against what he considered the extremely radical attitude of the Anabaptists. Thus he declared that they intended to discard all vestiges of popery, in doctrine and practice, for no better reason than because they smacked of popery.[3] They threw out the baby with the bath. They discarded the body of Christ. Luther rallied his readers to the truth of a church damaged by popery but not irreparably so.

Luther also displayed a tendency to relegate *sola fide* to a relatively inferior position. But again he did so because the Anabaptists were radical in its interpretation. They turned faith into a highly subjective experience, without which there could be no salvation, and certainly no baptismal ceremony. Against such immoderation Luther posed the command of God in his Word. Faith was at best fickle and transient compared to the Word of God. It could not become the basis for baptism.[4]

---

[1] Letter to Link, December 29, 1527, *WB*, IV, 310. Also letter to Hausmann, December 31, 1527, *WB*, IV, 312-13.
[2] *Von der Widertauffe*, p. A2v.
[3] *Ibid.*, p. A3r.
[4] *Ibid.*, p. E2v.

If Luther was conservative, it was primarily because the radicals, the Anabaptists, wanted to go too far. There is a note of exasperation in his vituperation.[1] He thought the Anabaptists tried to claim a spiritual kinship with himself. He was particularly angry because Balthasar Hubmaier had referred to Luther's views in a book on "rebaptism," as if Luther agreed with Hubmaier on the issue. He took pains therefore to clear himself of any identity of opinion with the Anabaptists on the issue of baptism.[2]

Luther was dictatorial partly in jest. His anonymous soliciters apparently had performed the baptism ceremony the second time, in Latin, for the children of some of their followers who were not quite prepared to accept the earlier ceremony which used a baptismal formula in German. What was that if not "Anabaptism"? If they insisted on reversion to popery, via the Latin formula, Luther could act the pope for them: he had never enjoined such conduct on them. He turned serious when he reminded them that their own behavior, in reverting to popery, was an inducement for others to become Anabaptists, since the people wanted to leave the Roman church.[3]

But what did he say about baptism, the main business of the tract? Luther wrote hastily, and his organization of material suffered as a result.[4] Essentially his method was to discuss the Anabaptists' reasons for rejecting infant baptism and then to refute those reasons. He devoted very little space to a systematic clarification of his own views on the subject. Probably he expected his readers to know his position, and therefore he considered it best to provide them with arguments for refuting the radicals. The reasons he cited for the Anabaptists' rejection of infant baptism were somewhat fanciful. Luther deplored his uncertainty about Anabaptist doctrines. His pastor friends had not given him any information,[5] and the Anabaptists themselves operated so clandestinely that he could not learn of their teachings.[6] He hoped the

---

[1] *Ibid.*, p. E3r.

[2] *Ibid.*, p. Av. Luther referred to Hubmaier's *Der Vralten vn gar neüen Leeren Vrtail, Das man die jungen kindlen nit tauffen solle biss sy jm glauben vnderricht sind.* 1526. The editors of the Weimar edition point out that Hubmaier, in quoting a sermon of Luther's, badly misinterpreted him. This leads the editors to the conclusion that Luther had not read Hubmaier's pamphlet to which he referred. It is not likely that Luther would have failed to point out the misinterpretation, had he read the tract. (*WA*, XXVI, 144–45.)

[3] *Von der Widertauffe*, p. A2r.

[4] Letter to Spalatin, February 5, 1528: "I send herewith my letter against the Anabaptists, or Catabaptists, which was composed hastily because I had other things to do. Perhaps if one of their leaders is angered [by it], he will be aroused to write most diligently of their doctrines. Meanwhile this will be of use to the simple and the pious." *WB*, IV, 376.

[5] *Von der Widertauffe*, p. A2r.

[6] *Ibid.*, p. E3r.

tract would antagonize them sufficiently to reply, so that he could learn what they believed.[1]

The Anabaptists rejected infant baptism in the first place, so Luther heard, because they wished to vex the pope. Individuals who wanted to separate themselves completely from the antichrist often joined the Anabaptists for this reason. Luther placed the sacramentarians in the same category: people who desired primarily to vent their spleen on the papacy by rejecting a major tenet of Romanist doctrine. He asserted that such grounds were completely false. It was at this point that he listed Romanist doctrines, the product of centuries of careful theological development, which were in fact true. Christ did not change everything in the religious practice of his times, though he discovered much abuse among the Pharisees. One should not change merely for the sake of change. The Anabaptists, thought Luther, ought to lend aid to the general movement of reform which Luther initiated. Instead of helping with the Reformation, they hindered it. Luther recounted a folk tale of two brothers who met a bear in the Thuringian Forest. The bear pinned one of them to the ground. The other drew his sword to help his brother. But his thrust missed the bear and ran his brother through. The Anabaptists resembled the second brother: good intentions, commendable zeal, but faulty aim.[2]

A second reason for rejecting infant baptism was the Anabaptists' uncertainty as to the actual performance of a first baptism. Luther paraphrased their attitude as follows: How do you know you were baptized? Someone told you that you had been. One cannot believe men, but only God. Your baptism, to be a sure and true one, must be certified to you by God. Luther sensed here the demand for a radical experiential relationship with God, excessive subjectivism. He denounced it as anarchic. If men could never believe the testimony of humans, the entire structure and fabric of society would vanish. For the social order was built upon at least a minimal amount of mutual trust. He taunted the Anabaptists with the suggestion that they should deny the authority of their feudal lord or civil magistrate on the same basis: some human testified that a certain man was lord or magistrate. Luther laid down a test for the validity of human testimony. When an individual bore witness of God's work, work not created or done by man, such testimony was to be believed, especially if it was that type of

---

[1] Letter to Spalatin, February 5, 1528, *WB*, IV, 376.
[2] *Von der Widertauffe*, pp. A2r.–A3v.

activity which invited the opposition of Satan. A case in point was baptism.[1]

Thirdly: "He that believeth and is baptized shall be saved" formed a basis for the Anabaptist rejection of infant baptism. Their argument, one should observe, carried beyond that of the Prophets, in that they not only rejected infant baptism but they also insisted upon baptism of adults or believers. They used the verse as the basis for the correct sequence: baptism came after faith. But they used it also to insist that the physical act of baptism was required for salvation, something the spiritualist Prophets did not do. Luther caught the point. He turned first to question their believers' baptism, and then to a defense of the historic practice of infant baptism.[2]

Believers' baptism was too subjective. How could one be certain of the faith of the candidate for baptism, were he a minister – or of his own, if he were a candidate? It required the omniscience of God to ascertain the presence of faith, or lack of it, in a man's heart. But the man confessed and professed his faith, the Anabaptist might argue. Men are inveterate liars. One could baptize a man one hundred times on the basis of his confession of faith, and yet he could never be absolutely certain of that faith. Luther chided the Anabaptists for inaugurating believers' baptism without being able to ascertain their candidates' faith or lack of it. He also suspected that rebaptism on the basis of personal faith could disintegrate into the desire for daily baptism, on the grounds that faith had increased since the last previous baptism. Foolish, fickle subjectivism![3]

Luther grounded his defense of infant baptism on long-standing practice. He dated the practice from the time of the apostles. He believed that no heresy remained permanently active in the Christian church. For one thousand years infant baptism had been practiced. Surely God would not have allowed a heretical practice to exist for that long a period of time. The burden of proof for the necessity for changing this practice rested entirely with the Anabaptists. He was certain they could not prove it erroneous.[4]

Scripture also testified to the reliability of infant baptism. He cited the occasion when the pregnant Elizabeth hailed the Virgin Mary as the mother of her Lord because Mary's salutation had caused the unborn

---

[1] *Ibid.*, pp. A3v.–B2r.
[2] *Ibid.*, pp. B2r.–v.
[3] *Ibid.*, p. B2v.
[4] *Ibid.*, pp. B3r., Dr.–Er.

John to leap in his mother's womb (Luke 1:41–44). Even the foetus had faith. For Christ himself had spoken the greeting through the mouth of his mother. In the same manner Christ could speak through the mouth of a priest, and the infant candidate for baptism could respond as the unborn John had done. In second rank, to Luther, stood the words of Christ to his disciples: "Suffer the little children, and forbid them not, to come unto me: for of such is the kingdom of heaven" (Matt. 19:14). Christ intended to indicate that salvation belonged to children and not only to adults. Luther also referred to the passage in Psalms (106:37–39) where the Jews sacrificed innocent children to idols to prove that infants possessed faith. The Scriptures declared the children to be innocent; innocence bespoke purity and holiness; purity and holiness did not exist without faith.[1]

Baptism under the New Covenant occupied a place parallel to circumcision under the Old. In both instances the act was prescribed as a sign of God's covenant with man. This promise and command of God was the ultimate basis for baptism. To compare God's command with the faith of a human as the basis for baptism was foolish and perhaps sacrilegious. Faith should be present at baptism, indeed. But the ceremony was performed because of God's command, and not because of the faith of humans. "We are baptized, not in order to become certain of faith, but rather because it is God's command and will that we be baptized." [2] Luther constantly challenged the Anabaptists to prove, from Scripture or church practice, that infants should not be baptized.

What other issues were touched by Luther in this tract? He was primarily concerned with his task of providing arguments to use against the Anabaptists' rejection of infant baptism. Consequently he did not deal exhaustively with any other issues. He merely touched a few. In one instance he directed his argument on baptism to include a charge of works-righteousness. He reported that the Anabaptists relied so confidently on the efficacy of the act of rebaptism that the ceremony itself did not in any way engender or increase faith. But his meaning is not clear. Perhaps he meant that their emphasis upon rebaptism, i.e., believers' baptism, was so great that they left no room for Christian growth after the act. This is a curious charge in view of the fact that the Anabaptists were usually accused of perpetuating a kind of monastic works-righteousness because of their

---

[1] *Ibid.*, pp. B3v.–Cv.
[2] *Ibid.*, pp. B4v.–Cr., C4r.–v.

unusual emphasis upon post-conversion ethical behavior. So some of the Swiss Reformers analyzed it.[1] Luther was normally hypersensitive to such conditions because of his own experience with monasticism as a means of finding a gracious God. But the charge is even more puzzling when it is compared with his other pronouncements on their doctrine of baptism. He tended on the whole to spiritualize or subjectivize their interpretation of the act. How then could it bear, in itself, an efficacy so satisfying as to lull the baptized person into a false trust in its power? This was popery; Luther even called it that.[2]

Luther had sensed subjectivity in the Anabaptists' approach to baptism, a subjectivity which he believed carried logically to the collapse of civil order. He observed that the Anabaptists left family and home in order to wander in company with their fellow religionists. Here was real anarchy.[3] It is surprising that he did not develop this charge, which was a common one leveled by the Reformers against the Anabaptists. He did elaborate the charge a bit in a letter to Johann Hess, written during or immediately after the composition of the *Von der Widertauffe*. He reported to Hess that in Bavaria these Anabaptists, the devil's captives, ran wild, leaving wives and children and goods with no concern. Luther declared further that these people agreed with Müntzer that Christians should kill the godless. They bore the spirit of Cellarius. They were completely seditious.[4] But why not develop the charge in *Von der Widertauffe*? Again one must remember his major purpose. He wrote to provide arguments for refuting the Anabaptists in their major error, baptism. Luther was not attempting to draw up a composite list of Anabaptist errors. He did not know enough about them to do that, as he freely admitted.[5]

It is clearly evident that Luther was thinking of his experiences with the *Schwärmer* when he wrote this tract. His attempt to subjectivize the Anabaptists' teachings on baptism, to the point of blindness to their excessive Biblical literalism, stands as one piece of evidence. He made the identification even more complete by calling them *Schwärmer* in the tract.[6] In his letter to Hess he declared that they had in them the

---

[1] John S. Oyer, "The Reformers Oppose the Anabaptists," *The Recovery of the Anabaptist Vision*, ed. Guy Hershberger (Scottdale, Pa.: Herald Press, 1957), pp. 207–09 for opinions of Zwingli and Bullinger.

[2] *Von der Widertauffe*, pp. C2v.–C3r.

[3] *Ibid.*, p. A4r.

[4] Letter to Hess, January 27, 1528, *WB*, IV, 371–72.

[5] *Von der Widertauffe*, p. E3r.

[6] *Ibid.*, p. A3r.

spirit of Müntzer.[1] He further identified them with the sacramentarians, meaning those who opposed the idea of the real presence in the sacrament.[2] As between the two groups, the sacramentarians and the Anabaptists, the latter were slightly worse. The two agreed in rejecting the real presence, but they disagreed on the baptism issue. Whereas the sacramentarians turned it into a mere symbol, which Luther called a nothingness, the Anabaptists made something entirely new out of it.[3] He did not explain the point, but he must have meant their insistence on believers' baptism, a baptism based not on the command of God but on the frivolous faith of man. Luther was inclined to regard the entire collection of groups to his left as one group, though he recognized some differences among them. They were the sectaries, whose unity consisted of common opposition to Luther.[4] "All the sectaries think they are a hundred times wiser than I, and do not listen to me; I am more at war with them than with the pope, and they do more harm."[5]

No systematic picture of Anabaptism emerges from Luther's treatment of the movement in his 1528 tract. He presented an indiscriminate mixture of ideas on baptism which he ascribed to Anabaptism, ideas which not only were inharmonious with each other, but were even contradictory. One contradiction is of special significance. Luther portrayed the Anabaptists on the one hand as insisting upon the performance of baptism (adult of course),[6] and on the other hand as regarding the act as a human trifle in the same category of popish devices as the application of salt, the blessing of crosses, and the use of holy water.[7] For the soul's salvation baptism was both necessary and useless.[8] How can one account for this contradiction? A number of reasons suggest themselves.

(1) Luther was pressed for time. He was in the process of composing a more important work against the sacramentarians. He was trying, above all, to provide frontier pastors with ammunition for refuting

[1] Letter to Hess, January 27, 1528, *WB*, IV, 371–72.
[2] *Von der Widertauffe*, p. A2r.
[3] *Ibid.*, p. E3r.
[4] *Ibid.*
[5] Letter to William Pravest, March 14, 1528. Trans. and printed in Smith and Jacobs, *Correspondence*, II, 433. Pravest, a pastor at Kiel, apparently accused Luther of having fathered the sectaries. Luther wanted to declare his independence of them, and theirs of him. Pravest was uncertain about following the Evangelicals and Luther wanted to win him to the cause. Pravest eventually elected to remain with the Catholics.
[6] See above, p. 120 and n. 2.
[7] *Von der Widertauffe*, p. Er.
[8] See another statement of the same type of contradiction – baptism regarded as efficacious for salvation and yet spiritualized to virtual meaninglessness – above, pp. 121-22.

Anabaptists on their major error, the issue of baptism. The Anabaptists were a motley crew whose ideas on baptism were very dissimilar. As the pastors met different arguments of Anabaptists they could select the appropriate refutation.

(2) The contradiction was not Luther's but that of the Anabaptists themselves. He was merely a faithful recorder of their arguments, on the basis of which he provided refutations. They did not agree among themselves, and there was little useful purpose served in trying to draw the fine lines of distinction among the various groups.

(3) Luther identified the Anabaptists with the earlier spiritual enthusiasts, the *Schwärmer*. The Anabaptists were radical in the sense that they wanted to go further than he did. That much he knew. He did not know all of their directions, or precisely how far they wanted to go. But he was disturbed because he feared an outbreak of violence similar to those which attended the trails of the *Schwärmer*. He abhorred violence. The Word of God could only be hindered through violent means. Because he saw in the Anabaptists in 1528 a reappearance of the *Schwärmer*, he ascribed to these later radicals some of the same ideas of the former ones. But he attempted to spiritualize and subjectivize even their literalistic use of Scriptural passages on baptism because the Prophets had used at least one of the same passages (Mark 16:16) and the Prophets were too spiritualistic.

Luther's 1528 pamphlet contained his basic declaration against the Anabaptists on the issue of baptism. In most of his later writings about baptism or rebaptism he relied on the major arguments he had used in 1528, though they were much more briefly stated.[1] There were a few embellishments and additions, however. These probably came as the result of Luther's hearing or reading more about the Anabaptists.

One can distinguish an increased emphasis on the Anabaptists' denial of the sacramental character of baptism in Luther's later works. They insisted on regarding the water of baptism as simply water, no more or less. It did not carry with it any form or degree of saving power, no matter what was spoken during the ceremony or how earnestly God's grace was invoked.[2] This conviction derived from their insistence on regarding the performance of the act as contingent upon the faith of the candidate, faith which saved without any external aid. Luther believed

---

[1] Four Sermons on Baptism, February, 1528, *WA*, XXVII, 32–60; Greater Catechism, 1529, *EA*, XXI, 137–38; *Tischreden* item, undated, *EA*, LVII, 66.

[2] For examples see Sermon on John 3 and 4, sometime between 1537 and 1540, *EA*, XLVI, 114; Sermon on I Cor. 15:35–38, 1544, *EA*, XIX, 114; *Vorre de* to Menius' *Von dem Geist*, 1544, pp. A2v.–A3r.

that the Anabaptists did not hold God's Word and work in sufficient honor. They relied on a weak, human experience rather than on the power and majesty of the Divine Word and activity.[1] This was probably Luther's most important objection to the Anabaptists on the issue of baptism. He had used it, stated in slightly different form, in his 1528 pamphlet.[2] He pushed the point to its most extreme form in 1544, when preaching on I Cor. 15:35–38. All of the radicals – the sacramentarians, *Schwärmer*, and Anabaptists – essentially denied the omnipotence and even the existence of God by refusing to recognize the sacramental character of baptism and the Lord's Supper. For they refused to take God at his Word. With respect to baptism Luther used Mark 16:16. Whereas the Anabaptists had emphasized the relationship between belief and baptism to produce salvation, Luther emphasized baptism and salvation. It was to him a promise that salvation attended absolutely upon the ceremony of baptism. It was useless to try to understand how God fulfilled this promise, but to deny its fulfillment was to call into question both the omnipotence and existence of God.[3]

In an earlier sermon Luther developed a new charge to level against the Anabaptists. They relied overmuch on human reason. The cornerstone of their rejection of infant baptism he decided was their denial of understanding or reason in the infant. He protested that they used reason as a lamp to guide one to faith. Luther referred to the account of Christ blessing the children to demonstrate that reason was not a prerequisite for the reception of salvation. But Luther went further. Reason was not only not a necessary guide to faith; it was an actual hindrance to faith. For it was precisely the absence of reason in the child that Christ referred to when he said: "Whosoever shall not receive the Kingdom of God as a little child, he shall not enter in" (Mark 10:15). Man must bury his reason in order to enter the Kingdom of Heaven. For reason and faith were antithetical. Luther cited a number of examples to illustrate the unreasonableness of Christian faith. The idea of trinity was contrary to reason, and yet it was true. This was a stumbling block to the Turks. Or the incarnation itself – who among the heathen could ever understand and therefore accept the fact of God becoming man? In order for faith to hold absolute sway in these instances, reason must be killed.[4]

---

[1] *Tischreden*, undated, *EA*, LVII, 66.
[2] *Von der Widertauffe*, p. E3r.
[3] Sermon on I Cor. 15:35–38, *EA*, XIX, 114.
[4] Sermon on Matt. 19:14–15, sometime between 1537 and 1540, *EA*, XLIV, 154–57.

Error in baptism was not the only reason for condemning the Anabaptists, although it was the principal one. Luther added the charge of sedition early in his conflict with the Anabaptists. He first called their activity seditious in a letter to Myconius and Menius in February, 1530. In 1529, ten Anabaptists had been captured at Gotha. Upon their recantation they were released, only to return to the Anabaptist faith. Six were later recaptured and executed at Reinhardsbrunn on January 18, 1530. Myconius, superintendent at Gotha, was disturbed at the severity of punishment. He wrote to Melanchthon for a theological explanation.[1] Melanchthon replied in the sternest possible terms: not only should rebels he executed, but also those who were guilty of blasphemy. What then was blasphemy? Any public teaching of heretical doctrines, such as the rejection of infant baptism.[2] It was in this context that Luther also pronounced on the subject of sedition. He wrote to Myconius and Menius together to commend their intention of writing a book against the Anabaptists.[3] Then he added that the Anabaptists were not only blasphemous, but also seditious. They should be executed.[4]

What did sedition mean to Luther? He expressed himself the most clearly on the nature of sedition in his "Exposition of the Eighty-Second Psalm," published in 1530. He began the exposition with a discussion of secular authority, particularly as opposed to the tyranny of Romanist spiritual authority. Secular authority had a divine origin which was entirely self-sustaining; it needed no corroboration from the spirituals. If Luther intended the princes to be free from religious authority vested in an overbearing institution, he did not mean they should be free to do whatever they wished. They were bound in conscience and fact to preserve peace and order. If they did not, if they were remiss in their obligations, subjects were permitted nothing but obedience or flight. But those who occupied the office of the Word should publicly rebuke the princes. For rulers ought to obey God and the Word. Luther laid down three virtues of princes. The ruler ought to support the Word of God, to administer justice, to protect subjects and maintain peace. Luther had no illusions about the possession and practice of these virtues by the rulers of his time. Indeed, they practiced the very opposites. But if the rulers were to support the Word of God,

---

[1] See above, pp. 50–51.
[2] Letter to Myconius, February, 1530, *CR*, II, 17–18.
[3] *Der Widdertauffer Lere vnd Geheimnis*, composed by Menius alone, and published later that year.
[4] Letter to Menius and Myconius, February, 1530, *WB*, V, 244.

what precisely did this involve when heretics appeared? How should they be handled? Luther faced this problem in his own conscience, for he had often repeated his belief that faith cannot be forced upon people. He faced it apart from theoretical considerations in the Anabaptists who obstinately would neither recant nor cease proselytizing.

Seditious heretics were those who taught that: (1) no ruler should be tolerated; (2) no Christian could occupy a position of political authority; (3) private property was sin; (4) the Christian ought to leave his family and private goods; (5) all property should be held in common. Persons who advocated one or several of these ideas should be treated as rebels; they should not be tolerated. Luther condemned blasphemers to capital punishment also.

Blasphemy was the public proclamation of heretical doctrines. Luther would not punish heretics who kept their ideas to themselves. But in this category of blasphemers came the secret preachers, those who covertly moved about in the cottages of the poor, or among the workers in the fields, to dispense their poisonous words. He was irate at these sneaks principally because they were not called to the task. Nothing should be done as a result of one's own decision, but only as a result of a command or call. Luther was moved to strong words in discussing the problem of office. All Christians might be priests, but not all were pastors. Each pastor had his own parish, and to allow anyone to enter that parish to teach without permission was to allow disorder. Luther always expected civil disorder to follow in the wake of the sneaks because he had experienced the unrest and turmoil which attended the activities of Müntzer and Carlstadt. Though both men had been ordained to office, they nevertheless preferred to sneak clandestinely among the people to spread their most radical views.[1]

Luther meant his catalogue of seditious doctrines to cover the activities and doctrines of the Anabaptists as well as others. He did not accuse the Anabaptists of teaching that no ruler should be tolerated. But on all remaining counts they were guilty. Early in 1528 already he noted their tendency to forsake wife and children and worldly goods in order to wander about in their teaching ministry.[2] These wolves in sheep's clothing put on an appearance of great piety by dressing in gray robes, a reference no doubt to Carlstadt's action, and complained to the peasants and simple folk that the Lutheran teachings did not produce

---

[1] An Exposition of the Eighty-Second Psalm, 1530, trans. by C. M. Jacobs and printed in *Works of Martin Luther, op. cit.*, IV, 285–315.

[2] Letter to J. Hess, January 27, 1528, *WB*, IV, 371–72.

fruit in terms of improved ethical conditions. People were impressed.
But what came next? The denial of the right of a Christian to wield the
sword, and thus to perform in political office. Nor was the Christian
allowed private property. Rather, he must share all goods in common
ownership with others of his persuasion. Such were Luther's charges,
repeated often but elaborated little.[1] He left the elaboration to others.

The Anabaptists went further. They actually preached revolution. In
1528 he believed them possessed of Müntzer's spirit, who determined to
kill the godless.[2] In his 1530 foreword to Menius' book against the
Anabaptists he declared that they preached the destruction of the
godless by the cohorts of Christ. They taught that Christ entrusted the
sword specifically to themselves, bound together in a Confederation.[3]
Luther repeated the identical charges later.[4] The presence of bonafide
rebels among the Anabaptists, as reported to him apparently by others,
convinced Luther yet more firmly that the sneak who began with
purely theological matters would become an inciter to revolution.

Luther's most substantial diatribe against the clandestine character
of the Anabaptist missioners was his "Open Letter to Eberhard von der
Thann concerning Sneaks and Corner-Preachers." Eberhard was the civil
officer at the Wartburg. He encountered Anabaptists from 1528 on, and
constantly reminded the Elector of their presence. Eberhard was of the
opinion that the Anabaptists should be punished severely on the theory
that severity would create fear of the government in the hearts of the
remaining brethren.[5] His theory was not attended with notable success.
It is not clear why Luther wrote to Eberhard; the latter required no
particular encouragement in abiding by his belief in severity of punishment. But the "Open Letter" did achieve a wide circulation. Four
editions were published in 1532, two in Wittenberg and one each in
Erfurt and Nürnberg.[6]

Luther inveighed against only one aspect of Anabaptist activity:
their furtive and clandestine movement among the people to spread
their doctrine. Luther was convinced that they were messengers of
Satan because they did not come out into the open. They sneaked in

[1] These charges are best expressed in Luther's exegesis of Matt. 7:15, 1532, *EA*, XLIII,
317–21. See also exposition of John 6, 7, and 8, 1530–1532, *EA*, XLVII, 313.
[2] Letter to J. Hess, January 27, 1528, *WB*, IV, 371–72.
[3] *Vorrede* to Menius' *Der Widdertauffer*, p. A4r.
[4] See *Tischreden*, undated, *EA*, LXI, 82–83; and Sermon on Matt. 13:24–30 (Parable of
the Tares), February 7, 1546, *EA*, 2d ed., XX, 541.
[5] Gustav L. Schmidt, *Justus Menius, der Reformator Thüringens* (Gotha: Perthes, 1867),
I, 145 ff.
[6] Introduction to the Letter in *WA*, XXX, Part 3, 510–15. See above, chapter ii on
Anabaptism, for information on the Anabaptists and Eberhard.

among the harvesters in the field, or to charcoal burners and isolated people in the forests, to sow their poisonous seed. In point of fact the Anabaptists were driven underground by persecution; Luther was not altogether fair. It was obvious to him that they were afraid of the light. Luther spoke of office: these who operated secretly had no command or call of God to teach. The true teaching of the church could be maintained only with the utmost diligence. Hence the importance of the call to office, which came from God generally through men. The Anabaptists claimed a call in the manner of Paul's exhortation: "If a revelation be made to another sitting by, let the first keep silence" (I Cor. 14:30). Luther countered by insisting that Paul referred only to those visited with the gift of prophecy. The Anabaptists should plainly announce that they were prophets, if that is what they believed. But if they claimed prophetic powers, these must be attested to by the ability to produce miracles or by other God-given signs. In the absence of miracles, the power of God worked through those who were divinely ordained to the office of preacher or teacher. Luther was sensitive to the Catholic inquiry as to his own authority -- especially in those areas outside his Wittenberg parish. "God and the world must bear witness that I began openly in my office of Doctor and preacher, and that I have continued by the grace and help of God." [1] He had never wanted to spread his ideas but felt compelled to do so by his appointment as doctor in the university. It was Staupitz as Vicar of the Augustinians who first commanded Luther to take the doctor's degree. Luther complied reluctantly. A university professor was sworn to expound the Scriptures for the entire world. The university charter was granted by pope and emperor. Hence Luther was commanded by pope and emperor to expound Scripture. A more certain call could not exist, since the entire series of events which took him from simple monk to university doctor was against Luther's own will. He felt compelled absolutely by the will of God to continue his preaching and teaching ministry in view of that initial reluctance. [2]

The Anabaptists erred on the question of baptism; they were also seditious. In third place among Luther's charges against them was that of works-righteousness. As an issue dividing Luther and the Anabaptists it was greatly inferior in importance to baptism and sedition -- at

[1] "Ein Brieff D. Mart. Luthers, Von den Schleichern vnd Winckelpredigern," *WA*, XXX, Part 3, 515–27. Another expression of the same, more condensed, in Letter to Johannes, Prince of Anhalt, December 15, 1534, *WB*, VII, 111–12.

[2] Exposition of the 82nd Psalm, *Works*, IV, 315.

least within the framework of the historical debate. The Anabaptists laid great emphasis on *Nachfolge*, the attempt of the committed Christian to follow his Master, not only in suffering but also in ethical behavior. This led them to reject not only prevarication, theft, adultery, and the entire spectrum of sins, major and petty, against which the entire Judeo-Christian tradition bore testimony. But because they interpreted the Sermon on the Mount as literally designed for Christians in this world, they rejected also the swearing of oaths and bearing of arms even in a "just" war, which to them was a contradiction to fact. Moreover their nonresistance led them to reject the use of power, the sword, by any committed disciple of Christ. Therefore no Christian could wield political authority. Most of the Reformers were aghast and then irate at the radical turn the Anabaptists put to Christian ethics. The entire political-social order was jeopardized by their insistence on no Christian participation in the political affairs of men. This was to abdicate the control of society in favor of the non-Christians, a proposal utterly abhorrent to religious figures of the sixteenth century. Luther shared the apprehension of the other Reformers concerning the sedition of the Anabaptists, as we have seen. But he did not make much of the Anabaptists' own basis for sedition, namely their attempt to develop rules of personal and social conduct from the Sermon on the Mount. Zwingli regarded this attempt as a new legalism.[1] We would expect Luther to see not only this legalism, but also to suspect it was nothing but a renewed attempt to define and practice the medieval counsels of perfection. Within the context of his own spiritual pilgrimage, a new monasticism among erstwhile Protestant forces would seem to be the most abhorrent of all of the Anabaptist doctrines. He did not regard it so in fact. He always related it primarily to sedition, and only second-arily to a doctrine of works-righteousness. The issue of baptism revealed the Anabaptists' subjectivity; insistence on Sermon on the Mount ethics pointed to sedition.

Luther's first remarks that approach a charge of works-righteousness among the Anabaptists came in his preface to the 1530 book of Menius. Here Luther merely repeated what Menius developed more fully. Menius declared that the principal error of the Anabaptists was their teaching on salvation through works. Luther charged the Anabaptists with neglecting to teach the cardinal points of Christian faith because of their overemphasis on the temporal, mundane things of life which the masses loved to hear. In this category of crowd-pleasing doctrines was

---

[1] Oyer, "The Reformers Oppose the Anabaptists," p. 208.

their eschatological view of the approaching end-times, in which they would erect a kingdom on earth and slaughter the godless. Luther was nettled that the Anabaptists, so he heard, accused him of teaching that good works were not worth a farthing. They took his insistence on *sola fide* to mean that he despised good works heartily. Luther angrily replied that he did not despise good works, but that moral betterment was the product of one's faith and not a means in itself to God.[1]

Two years later Luther repeated his accusation with more clarity, in his exegesis of Matt. 7:15 ("Beware of false prophets ...."). The Anabaptists were such false prophets. For they began enticing the common people by crying out against the lack of spiritual fruit among the Lutherans. Since the rank and file among the followers of Luther were arrogant, avaricious, and as bad as, or worse than, before, it followed that the gospel was not preached rightly by the Lutherans. For when the gospel was rightly preached, those who heard with gladness showed evidence of their acceptance of the truth by a radical change in their pattern of living. Spiritual fruit ensued from such changed lives. And of what, inquired Luther, did this fruit consist? Dressing poorly, wandering about in a gray coat, suffering hunger and persecution, renouncing private property, leaving wife and children, denouncing sword-bearing: these were their spiritual fruits. The tragedy lay in the acceptance of such rubbish by so many of the simple folk. It irked Luther that people tended, as he reported it, to ascribe holiness to poverty and rags, and to despise neatness of appearance in the respectable pastors and term it hypocritical. Why were people unable to detect the wolf in sheep's clothing, the hypocrisy of these new mendicants? So it was with the monks. They, too, tried to appear more holy by dressing in rags.

The Anabaptist technique, according to Luther, was to insinuate themselves into the good graces of the people by a show of piety. Then they spread their poisonous teaching and subverted the hearts and minds of the people. As such they were worse than rulers who openly persecuted the Christians, depriving them of life and goods. The Anabaptists dispensed a concentrated dose of trivia once they had gained their audience. They were more malicious than Luther's theological opponents who debated openly with him. "The Anabaptists outwardly bear our name and admit well enough that we have the gospel." [2]

One of Luther's more curious charges was that the Anabaptists who decried the use of the sword nevertheless thirsted for battle and blood.

---

[1] *Vorrede* to Menius' *Der Widdertauffer*, pp. A4r.–v.
[2] Exegesis of Matt. 5, 6, 7, 1532, *EA*, XLIII, 317–21.

Here was an absolute contradiction which Luther did not try to explain. It could have been explained on the basis of the existence of different groups of people, all labeled Anabaptists. There were, for example, non-resistant Anabaptists and there were also the Münsterites. Luther did not draw a clear distinction among kinds of sectarians, so he did not explain the contradiction. He usually related their desire for bloodshed with Müntzer. One suspects that nonresistance appeared as hypocrisy to Luther: merely another attempt to put on a semblance of holiness in order to gain adherents.[1]

On the issue of the Lord's Supper Luther had little to say against the Anabaptists. Not that they accepted his own teaching on the sacrament. His tracts against the sacramentarians were directed primarily against Carlstadt, Zwingli, Oecolampadius, and Schwenkfeld.[2] It was enough to disclose the inadequacy of the sacramental view of the Anabaptists in the baptism issue. He was aware of the symbolic view the Anabaptists took of the sacrament of the altar. He considered the Anabaptists and the Zwinglians to be one and the same because both were guilty of a refusal to recognize grace in the sacrament.[3]

In general it can be said that Luther discussed only one theological issue when he discoursed on Anabaptism: the issue of baptism. He analyzed briefly their ideas on social conduct from a political rather than a theological vantage point: they were seditious. Other potential theological issues between himself and the Anabaptists, such as works-righteousness or the sacrament, Luther only touched and dismissed with a casual comment. This dearth of theological discussion from a man who was essentially a theologian surprises us. It can be laid partly to the quality and quantity of his information concerning the Anabaptists, and partly to his conviction that the degree of their error in baptism and affairs in social conduct was already so patent that they could be condemned without further inquiry into theological matters. Luther had heard enough to convince himself that the Anabaptists were pointing toward the same goals that the *Schwärmer* had had. His comments to that effect were numerous.

What was the character of the Anabaptists as Luther regarded them?

---

[1] *Tischreden*, undated, *EA*, LXI, 82; also Exegesis of Matt. 5, 6, 7, 1532, *EA*, XLIII, 317–21.

[2] Sermon von dem Sakrament des Leibes und Blutes Christi, wider die Schwärmgeister, 1526, *WA*, XIX, 474–523; Das diese Wort Christi, "Das ist mein Leib," noch fest stehen, wider die Schwärmgeister, 1527, *WA*, XXIII, 38–320; Vom Abendmahl Christi, Bekenntnis, 1528, *WA*, XXVI, 241–509.

[3] *Vorrede* to Menius' *Von dem Geist*, 1544, p. A2v. Also Sermon on I Cor. 15:35–38, 1544 , *EA*, XIX, 114.

What kind of people were they? First of all they were sneaks and corner preachers (*Schleichern und Winkelpredigern*).[1] Their intense determination to subvert men's souls led them to operate secretly in places where they were forbidden by law to teach. Secondly, they were audacious and outspoken. On one occasion a pious woman of Freiburg told Luther of an Anabaptist prisoner in Freiburg who raved against his accusers, and even railed against Luther. He refused to allow himself to be examined, declaring that he was holy and his accusers were not.[2] Again, they were rabidly anti-intellectual. Luther told of a revered Anabaptist brother who preached in a village after a three-day fast in the wilderness. He gathered all the learned people in one place, and bitterly denounced worldly wisdom before them. The lesser folk, the rabble, he assembled at another place. These he praised excessively for their simplicity and piety. Luther opined that the Anabaptists had no leaders who by virtue of their learning were capable of disputing with him. They were a simple, but radically anti-intellectual people.[3] On another occasion Luther described them as the thieves and murderers spoken of in John 10. This time Luther clearly identified them with Müntzer.[4] Finally, they were like the Donatists and Cathari in their attempt to pursue what they considered to be a purer spiritual existence, either by withdrawal from society, or else by extirpation of the godless.[5]

But the Anabaptists were more than radicals, rogues, and Donatists. They were devils. Satan manifested himself in various forms in this world. One of those forms was the human being. The Anabaptists were the minions of Satan himself, the devil's angels incarnate. Whenever Christ raised up a true church, the devil came along and built a chapel immediately beside it. Luther believed that the entire spectrum of left-wingers built to some extent on his own work. They took what he had discovered and twisted its meaning or practice, sometimes subtly and sometimes openly, and thus simulated a true spiritual beginning.[6] Scripture made plain to the true Christian that the devil would come eventually in some guise or mode. He always brought the gates of hell to bear directly upon the presence of the true gospel. Previously he had

---

[1] Terminology used in the "Open Letter to Eberhard v. d. Thann."

[2] *Tischreden*, August 14, 1538, *EA*, LXI, 89–90.

[3] *Tischreden*, undated, *ibid*, 90–91.

[4] Letter to Johannes, Prince of Anhalt, October 20, 1534, *WB*, VII, 111–12.

[5] *Tischreden*, September 2–17, 1540, *WT*, V, 19. Trans. by Preserved Smith and Herbert Gallinger, *Conversations with Luther* (Boston: Pilgrim Press, 1915), p. 206. See also his Sermon on the Parable of the Tares, Matt. 13:24–30, February 7, 1546, *EA*, 2d ed., XX, 541.

[6] *Ibid*.

worked through the papists, through whom he had established a market for souls. He was able to turn the mass into a hellish sacrifice. He built upon an imposing edifice of good works. But since the gospel had been released to run its course freely, the devil tried to build upon the new teachings. He appeared in the Anabaptists and the radicals. Luther believed the constant strife between the gospel and the devil redounded eventually to the glory of God. For through strife with the devil the Christian learned to handle the Word more carefully. The Word, burnished by strife, shone ever brighter to the world.[1]

But some were misled and destroyed through the activities of the devil. How could it be said that the gospel triumphed? Luther did not deny there would be casualties. There were in every kind of battle. The fallen demonstrated the wrath and punishment of God exercised against the godless and hard of heart. Luther's determinism was not quite absolute at this point, however. He clung tenaciously to the belief that there was real hope for those who were simply misled. He was inclined to regard obstinacy in error as a sign that the individual was more than merely misled.[2] He believed firmly that the judgment of God was not reserved entirely for the hereafter. Some of the devil's human agents felt the wrath and judgment of God in the form and manner of their deaths on earth. He had earlier used the death of Müntzer as a sign of God's judgment.[3] So also was the execution of the Anabaptists, and the death of Zwingli.[4] The Anabaptists went to their deaths with steadfastness and joy, Luther was informed.[5] Some of them even seemed to develop a martyr complex: they begged for death.[6] It was always the way of Satan to delude his followers with the belief that their deaths were those of martyrs. Luther was convinced for his part that their constancy was nothing but the stubbornness of Satan. For some of them died blaspheming the holy sacrament.[7]

Luther did not try to establish formally the link between Satan and the Anabaptists. He did not consider it necessary.[8] It is difficult to

---

[1] *Vorrede* to Menius' *Der Widdertauffer*, pp. A2r.–A3v.

[2] *Ibid.*

[3] See above, p. 34.

[4] Letter to Prince Albert of Prussia, 1532, *WA*, XXX, Part 3, 550.

[5] Letter to Link, May 12, 1528, *WB*, IV, 457. Trans. in Smith and Jacobs, *Correspondence*, II, 443–44. Luther's letter to Link is obviously a reply to Link's inquiry about the deaths of Anabaptists.

[6] *Tischreden*, September 2–17, 1540, *WT*, V, 19. Or in Smith and Gallinger, *Conversations*, p. 206.

[7] Letter to Link, May 12, 1528, *WB*, IV, 457.

[8] In his *Vorrede* to Menius' *Der Widdertauffer*, pp. A3v.–A4v., he did list several reasons for thinking they were devils. And his letter to Eberhard von der Thann is devoted to disclosing the diabolical origin of sneak-preachers.

ascertain the decisive factor which led him to conclude their ultimate origin was diabolical. He perceived Satan in both rebaptism and sedition.[1] He probably made the discovery when he identified the Anabaptists with the earlier *Schwärmer*. Luther called the Anabaptists devils in some of his earliest references to them.[2]

Luther did not believe that all of the Anabaptists were damned, or to put it more accurately, that all of them were in advanced stages of deviltry. Some could be reclaimed: i.e., those who were simply misled. But obstinacy in error to the moment of execution he regarded as a clear sign that the individual was more than merely misled.[3] For the really convinced Anabaptist-devil any question of ultimate salvation was foolish. Peter Waller once put the question to him: are the Anabaptists saved? Some of Waller's friends were disturbed and impressed by the joy with which the Anabaptists died at the stake. Was there not *some* truth in their doctrines? Luther replied that men were able to judge others only on the basis of the gospel. Since the Anabaptists erred, since they did not believe truly, they were damned by God.[4]

Despite their heresy, and even their diabolical origin, Luther moved very slowly and reluctantly to the conviction that Anabaptists should be executed.[5] In the early years of the Reformation Luther spoke out sharply against the execution of heretics. Already in the 1518 version of the ninety-five theses he declared: "The burning of heretics is against the will of the Holy Spirit." [6] He was undoubtedly influenced by the fact that by the Catholic laws on heresy he was condemned to the stake. He regarded his attempt to reform the church as God-directed and inspired. Clearly the administration of the Catholic heresy laws therefore militated against the very working of God. He was confirmed in this conviction by his study of church history, particularly the case of John Huss. Luther believed that the state did not have the power to handle spiritual matters. A spiritual means must be found to deal with heretics. Luther believed in the early days that the proper spiritual

---

[1] *Von der Widertauffe*, pp. A4r., Ev.
[2] *Ibid.*, p. Av. Letter to Jacob Probst, December 31, 1527, *WB*, IV, 313.
[3] See above, p. 134, n. 2.
[4] *Tischreden*, undated, *EA*, LXI, 89.
[5] There are a number of excellent essays on Luther's attitude toward heretics. It does not seem necessary therefore to treat the topic here in an exhaustive manner. The best essay, in my opinion, is that of Walther Koehler in his article "Luther" written for the *Mennonitisches Lexicon*, II, 703–708. (This article was translated for the *ME*, III, 416–22.) Koehler devotes half of his essay to Luther's attitude toward the Anabaptists as heretics. Another excellent treatment of the problem is the article by Roland H. Bainton, "Development and Consistency of Luther's Attitude to Religious Liberty," *Harvard Theological Review*, XXII (1929), 107–49.
[6] *WA*, I, 624.

means was the use of the Word; let the Word be proclaimed, in disputation or in sermon, and it would work its own way into the hearts of even the heretics. So in 1520 in his "Address to the Nobility of the German Nation" he wrote: "One should overcome the heretics with Scripture and not with fire. If it were scholarly to overcome heretics with fire, then the executioners would be the most learned doctors on earth." [1] And three years later, on the use of force in matters of faith: "The soul's thoughts and reflections are revealed to no one but God; therefore it is impossible to compel one with physical force to believe this or that. Another kind of compulsion does it; physical force does not." [2]

A turning point for Luther's thought on punishment of heretics came in July, 1524, when he wrote to the Princes of Saxony about Müntzer. He still held to the conviction that in the spiritual realm the Word would suffice to foist off the machinations of the devil. But if the heretic began to use the fist, if he turned to iconoclastic violence or raised the standard of insurrection, then the matter was no longer one for the Word alone. Then indeed the political authorities must act with dispatch. Sedition in heretics deserved physical repression and punishment. Still, it was the sedition, not the heresy with respect to articles of faith, that warranted punishment – a rather fine distinction but an important one.[3]

This distinction Luther tried to apply throughout the remainder of his life in dealing with the Anabaptists. Insofar as they were guilty of sedition, they were subject to punishment by the civil authorities. Error in faith alone was a matter for the ecclesiastical order to handle. His increasing harshness against them, after 1528, was due to his growing conviction that the latter type of case, the "heretic only," did not exist among the Anabaptists. There were no Anabaptists who did not preach some form of sedition, according to Luther's definition of the term. Luther developed the idea that blasphemy, the open proclamation of a heretical view, constituted a form of sedition. If he could not accuse the Anabaptists in certain circumstances of disrupting the civil order in any other manner, he could always condemn their vigorous missionary outreach as blasphemous, and therefore seditious. Still one must notice that Luther did not appear at all pleased with his or Melanchthon's harsh pronouncements against the Anabaptists. Let us briefly trace the development of his thought.

---

[1] *WA*, VI, 455.
[2] Von welltlicher Uberkeytt, wie weyt man yhr gehorsam schuldig sey, *WA*, XI, 264.
[3] See above, chapter 1, p. 18.

In 1528, in his *Von der Widertauffe* he declared that the punishment of hell was enough for heretics; it was not necessary to execute them. He advocated tolerance in matters of faith. He was particularly distressed at the pitiless slaughtering of poor, deluded folk. He held back from the death sentence because he feared that they might be martyrs in a just cause; he could not be absolutely certain.[1] Later that year, or in 1529, he wrote a letter to Johannes Brenz in response to Brenz's question concerning the treatment of heretics. Brenz, the reformer of Swabian Halle, then stood alone among the Lutheran Reformers against the death penalty for the Anabaptists, a position he did not retain throughout his life. This did not mean that he encouraged the Anabaptists, or that he liked them. But he could not quite accept the view that their punishment was merited because of sedition among them. He thought they were being killed for their faith – certainly they regarded it so. It is interesting therefore to notice Luther's careful answer to his inquiry.

You ask whether the magistrate may kill false prophets. I am slow in a judgment of blood even when it is deserved. In this matter I am terrified by the example of the papists and the Jews before Christ, for when there was a statute for the killing of false prophets and heretics, in time it came about that only the most saintly and innocent were killed. ... I cannot admit that false teachers are to be put to death. It is enough to banish.[2]

By 1530 with his Exposition of the Eighty-Second Psalm Luther's position had hardened. Here he declared that the Anabaptists were to be condemned by the state for sedition and blasphemy. Luther's opinion on sedition we have examined.[3] Blasphemy for him meant public teaching or preaching against an article of the creed plainly founded on Scripture. It might well be argued that the Anabaptists accepted the historic creeds of the church. Luther did not so analyze the sect. On this occasion he specified the Anabaptists and the Turks as people who taught that Christ was not God, but only a man like other prophets.[4] Hence the Anabaptists warranted the sternest penalty

[1] *Von der Widertauffe*, pp. Av.–A2r.
[2] Quoted from Bainton, *Here I Stand*, p. 314. In *WB*, IV, 498–99. This letter has been erroneously dated July 14, 1528, and appended to Luther's letter of that date to Wenzel Link. The editors of the Weimar edition pay their thanks to N. Paulus for first demonstrating that the section here quoted does not belong to the Link letter. They decide it must belong to the period from 1528 to March, 1530, when Luther finished his Exposition of the Eighty-Second Psalm which delivered a judgment of blood against the Anabaptists. The inquiry from Brenz is not extant.
[3] Above, pp. 126–129.
[4] It is the only occasion on which Luther charged the Anabaptists with Christological error. See *Works of Martin Luther*, IV, 310.

from the state. Why did he decide they should be killed? Partly because
they appeared to him as increasingly seditious, and partly because he
was losing faith in the belief that the mere releasing of the Word would
bring about the defeat of heresy. The Word could not do it alone.
Luther apparently decided the Anabaptists must be stopped before
they became openly revolutionary. He probably accepted Melanchthon's
view that Anabaptist types were but stages in their development: all
would eventually preach revolution. Luther called for the punishment
for blasphemy found in the Mosaic Law.[1]

In 1531 Elector John asked the Wittenberg theologians for advice
on the treatment of several captured Anabaptists, notably Melchior
Rink and others. The Saxon Elector had issued several mandates forbidding the Anabaptists to preach and teach. John was angered at their
stubbornness and disobedience to his earlier mandates. Melanchthon
replied for the theologians advocating the sternest possible punishment
for the Anabaptists, reserving mercy only for those who had been led
astray and could be recalled from their error.[2] Luther signed Melanchthon's statement. He appended a short one of his own in which he
specified the counts on which the death penalty was necessary. The
Anabaptists damned the ministry of the Word, had no true teaching of
their own, suppressed the true teaching, and wanted to destroy the
civil order.[3] He probably added this statement because John had
specifically requested advice from Luther himself.

In 1535 Luther concurred with an appended statement in another of
Melanchthon's judgments, this time directed to Eberhard von der
Thann, about several Anabaptists in Eisenach. The judgment was
delivered in general terms. Eberhard was advised to regulate the severity
of punishment in accordance with the degree of error.[4] Again in 1536
Melanchthon delivered an opinion with Luther's approval on how to
treat Anabaptists to Philip of Hesse. Philip disliked executing the
Anabaptists. He believed that exile was punishment enough. But what
should he do when the exiled Anabaptists returned to Hesse? He inquired of several theological faculties, some of the free cities, and some
of the princes; one of the sternest replies came from Melanchthon.
Luther wrote briefly at the end that the rules Melanchthon laid down
were valid on the whole. But he hoped the Landgrave would show mercy

---

[1] Koehler, *ME*, III, 419.
[2] See below, pp. 156–157.
[3] *CR*, IV, 740.
[4] July 16, 1535, *CR*, II, 889–90.

according to the degree of error. There was little necessity for Luther's added remark unless he wished to express a divergence from Melanchthon's severity. One cannot escape the conviction that the execution of heretics, for blasphemy or whatever other reasons, did not please Luther.[1]

By 1540 it is possible that Luther had returned to the milder position of Philip of Hesse with respect to punishment of Anabaptist heretics. He held more firmly to the distinction between the "heretic only" and the seditious heretic. The latter was to be killed indeed. But for the former banishment was enough.[2] On this occasion he did not define sedition. Nor did he resort to the use of the term blasphemy to bring the majority of the Anabaptists under the judgment of death, as was previously the case. Perhaps he still retained his earlier views on sedition and blasphemy. But his position in 1540 was milder than that of Melanchthon who held that all Anabaptists who did not recant should be killed.

---

[1] *WA*, L, 15.
[2] *Tischreden*, September 2–17, 1540, *EA*, LXI, 91.

CHAPTER V

MELANCHTHON AND THE ANABAPTISTS

Until well into the 1520's the Reformation had consisted primarily of an attack on papal practice and theology plus an earnest appeal to the newly liberated Word as the revelation and power of God to redeem the heart of man. The old order had crumbled under these attacks in the regions of Electoral Saxony and elsewhere in Central Germany. But little had been done to reconstruct a new church order. Luther had rested confidently in the power of the unaided Word to transform the churches. The development of radicalism culminating in the disaster of Frankenhausen in 1525, plus the fact of lapses in public worship, compelled him to take action. He began by urging a general visitation of churches on the Elector to ascertain the nature and degree of ecclesiastical problems which confronted the authorities. This information would provide a basis for the progressive reorganization of the church order along Evangelical lines.[1] The Elector looked with favor on the proposal. Accordingly Electoral Saxony was divided into a number of parts, each to be examined by a body of visitors who would investigate the spiritual and economic conditions within the various parishes throughout the land. Philip Melanchthon was quickly designated as one of the theologians to participate in some of the early visitations.

Philip Melanchthon was born in Bretten on February 16, 1497, the son of the armorer George Schwartzerd. His relatives on the maternal side included the humanist Johann Reuchlin. Reuchlin influenced his education and training in the humanist tradition. It was he who hellenized his family name into Melanchthon, a name which gradually prevailed in common usage. Melanchthon studied with private tutors, matriculated at Heidelberg and Tübingen, and earned his M.A. at the

---

[1] Letters to the Elector, October 31, 1525, and November 30, 1525, De Wette, III, 39 and 51. Among other things Luther was much concerned over the financial conditions in the parishes. The pastors were not receiving proper financial support.

latter institution early in 1514. He stayed on at Tübingen for four years
to lecture in the classics. Finally ecclesiastical conservatism and antipathy to his enthusiastic humanism forced him to find a position
elsewhere. He had already achieved limited fame as a student of
classical letters. Some of the best humanists of the time, including
Erasmus, regarded him highly. From several offers he chose that of the
Saxon Duke Elector to teach Greek at the relatively new university at
Wittenberg. Reuchlin had proposed his name to Frederick and urged
his grand-nephew to accept the offer when it came. His arrival in the
town of Wittenberg aroused no great excitement among the professors
and students of the university. Some of the professors had openly
encouraged the invitation of Peter Mosellanus of Leipzig, a scholar of
greater maturity. Melanchthon's inaugural address and subsequent
lectures dispelled all notions of immaturity. Luther in particular was
enthusiastic about Melanchthon's learning and by his espousal of the
study of the classics as a means of getting around the glosses to the
sources of knowledge, to the Bible as well as to the Greek classics. The
two men, so different in character and temperament, soon became fast
friends.

Melanchthon helped to breathe new life into the university. Students
flocked from all parts of Europe to hear Luther and Melanchthon. He
worked incredibly hard to prepare his lectures and to publish various
books. But Wittenberg also changed Melanchthon. Constant contact
with Luther, in addition to his study of and lectures on the Scriptures,
brought him gradually to the vanguard of the Evangelical movement.
By 1519 he entered the literary battle which was being waged in the
wake of the Leipzig Debate. He produced a series of theses in defense
of justification by faith, including a forthright attack on the doctrine
of transubstantiation. He added more theses the next year in an attack
on the papal church. He countered Emser's attack on Luther in a
pamphlet that achieved a wide circulation. He replied caustically with
a scholarly rebuttal to the tardy judgment of the Leipzig Debate by the
Sorbonne theologians in 1521. In that same year he produced the
clearest, most concise theological statement within the Evangelical
camp, the *Loci communes rerum theologicarum*. Melanchthon's interests
and the exigencies of his times led him far beyond the boundaries of
classical letters.

For the remainder of his life Melanchthon taught at the University
of Wittenberg and sought by every means possible to enhance the
Evangelical cause. He and Luther did not always agree; notably in the

1530's Melanchthon expressed different views on the Lord's Supper, and he could never quite accept what he considered Luther's over-emphasis on the singularity of justification by faith. But he and Luther had too much mutual respect and love to allow themselves to break with each other. Each needed the other, and both realized it. Melanchthon's evangelical activities brought him into constant theological conflict of the bitterest sort. He abhorred such strife. It raged with especial fury after the death of Luther, in the period after the defeat of the Evangelicals in the Schmalkald War. Melanchthon tried to make the best of a bad situation, and was accused of betraying Lutheranism by men like Flacius Illyricus. Melanchthon was wearied by the innumerable controversies. He died in April, 1560. Despite his remarkable contribution as educator and theologian, he was calumnied so successfully by his enemies that generations of churchmen and scholars after him neglected him almost completely.[1]

Melanchthon was by nature a gentle, soft-spoken individual. Luther said of him, in contrast to himself:

I am rough, boisterous, stormy, and altogether warlike. I am born to fight against innumerable monsters and devils. I must remove stumps and stones, cut away thistles, and thorns, and clear the wild forests; but Master Philip comes along softly and gently sowing and watering with joy, according to the gifts which God has abundantly bestowed upon him.[2]

He complemented Luther, the creative spirit, with his scholarly talents. A man irenic by nature was thrust by the events of his time into constant controversy with Romanists, the radicals, and later the self-styled orthodox Lutherans. In the rough and tumble of sixteenth century religious strife Melanchthon distinguished himself by his composure and the relative absence of acrimony in the treatment of his adversaries, except for his encounter with the Anabaptists. Toward them he displayed nothing but the harshest kind of criticism, which bespoke a passionate dislike of the radicals.

Melanchthon was far from being the kind of scholar who worked only in the solitary confines of his study and in the classroom. He was also a practical churchman. As such he participated in a number of the church visitations in Electoral Saxony. While on the second of these, in July and August, 1527, in Thuringia, Melanchthon encountered what was almost certainly Anabaptism.[3]

---

[1] I have relied for most of the factual information on Melanchthon's life on the biography of Clyde Manschreck, *op. cit.*, *passim* in the first four chapters and the introduction.

[2] *Ibid.*, p. 54.

[3] See below, pp. 239–242 for an analysis of the sources of Melanchthon's information on

Conditions in the churches visited were bad. The visitors found that the priests instructed the people poorly where they instructed them at all. Generally they took the new Evangelical teaching to mean easy grace. They preached much about remission of sins, but seldom on penitence. Melanchthon fully believed that the people were in a worse state than they were before the new doctrine came.[1] Ignorance abounded among those with a cure of souls. Several knew nothing beyond the Decalogue, the Creed, and the Pater Noster. One pastor preached the new doctrine in one church and said mass in the Roman fashion in a neighboring church. The people themselves were utterly immoral. Ignorance and immorality abounded in such degree that Melanchthon was reduced to tears of distress, as he reported in a letter to his friend Camerarius.[2] The visitors also discovered Carlstadters in Kahla and Orlamünde. By this name they probably meant to indicate some who erred on the Lord's Supper. But they also found people who had not had their infants baptized. A full report from the visitors in the most crucial area around Jena and Orlamünde is no longer extant.[3] Elector John's orders, which were issued immediately after the Thuringian visitation of July–August, 1527, designated infant baptism and rebaptism as points on which pastors were to be questioned.[4] Apparently the visitors discovered both the rejection of infant baptism and the practice of some kind of adult baptism. Melanchthon began to formulate a rebuttal to the Anabaptist position on baptism a few months after his return from the visitation.[5]

Anabaptism. He was accompanied on this visitation by Hans von der Planitz, Asmus von Haubitz, and Jerome Schurff. They visited regions slightly to the east of those places where Anabaptists were the most conspicuously located later. Emil Sehling, *Die evangelischen Kirchenordnungen des XVI. Jahrhunderts* (6 vols.; Leipzig: Reisland, 1902–1913), I, 35–38.

[1] Report of Melanchthon to the Elector, August 13, 1527, printed in Otto Clemen, *Supplementa Melanchthoniana* (Leipzig: Heinsius Nachfolger, 1926), I, Abt. 6, p. 369.

[2] J. W. Richards, *Philip Melanchthon* (New York: G. P. Putnam, 1898), pp. 160–61.

[3] Sehling, *op. cit.*, I, 35–38, 143–44. C. A. H. Burkhardt, *Geschichte der sächsischen Kirchen-und Schulvisitationen* (Leipzig: Grunow, 1879), pp. 18–21.

[4] Sehling, *op. cit.*, I, 149.

[5] Technically his first writing against the Anabaptists was a sketch of a refutation of their views on infant baptism. It was never published. He defended the baptism of infants on two grounds:
    (1) Baptism in the New Covenant as parallel to circumcision in the Old.
    (2) Christ's promise of the Kingdom to the children that were brought to him.
He refuted four Anabaptist objections to the practice:
    (1) The absence of direct Scriptural command to baptize infants.
    (2) A sacrament was not valid apart from faith in the recipient, and infants did not possess faith.
    (3) Infants were incapable of understanding, and hence of the instruction which should precede baptism.
    (4) The Word did not properly belong to infants since they could not understand it.
The sketch is printed in the *CR*, I, 931–33, under the caption of the editors "Phil. Melanchth. argumentum quod parvulis sit adhibendus baptismus."

By October 23, 1527, Melanchthon had begun work on his first major treatise on Anabaptism.[1] The treatise was essentially completed by January, 1528.[2] It is the most theological of Melanchthon's pamphlets against the Anabaptists, and by far the most dispassionate and calmly reasoned piece of work that he ever wrote on the subject. He did not mar it with the bitter invective that characterized his later works. He wrote it probably at the request of others, and certainly in order to fulfil a sense of obligation to declare himself forthrightly on a problem that was troubling the church.[3]

At the outset he accused the Anabaptists of being so thoroughly preoccupied with matters of outward ceremony and human tradition that they completely neglected the central truths of historic Christendom. By implication he accused them of faulty exegetical principles, if indeed it is fair to say they had any principles of exegesis at all. Melanchthon had declared himself on the major points of Christian doctrine on other occasions:[4] repentance, forgiveness of sins, faith, patience, love, and good works as fruits. These cardinal points of the Christian faith were to be held in the center of one's thinking in any

---

[1] Letter to Baumgartner, October 23, 1527, *CR*, I, 900.

[2] Letter to Baumgartner, January 23, 1528, *CR*, I, 937. By May the manuscript was in the hands of the printer, Setzer, in Hagenau, according to Melanchthon's letter to Nikolaus Gerbel, May 10, 1528, *CR*, I, 973. It was published under the title *Adversus Anabaptistas Philippi Melanthonis Iudicium*. Several other Latin editions appeared. One was printed by Brubachius in Frankfurt, in 1562, together with Brenz's *An Magistratus iure possit occidere Anabaptistas, Ioannis Brentij Sententia*. Another was printed, without date or place given, with Brenz's *Judgment* and also with the Saxon Visitation articles in Latin. Little is known of the Latin original. Apparently no copies of it are extant. (R. Stupperich, ed., *Melanchthons Werke in Auswahl* [6 vols.; Gütersloh: Bertelsmann, 1951–], I, 272.) Stupperich used the 1541 edition, Basel, of Melanchthon's works for his copy of the *Iudicium*. The *Corpus Reformatorum* version is from the same Latin edition. (*CR*, I, 955–73.) The pamphlet was translated into German by Justus Jonas and published in Wittenberg in 1528 under the title *Underricht Philip Melanchthon wider die Lere der Widerteuffer auss dem Latein verdeutschet durch Just. Jonas*. Two additional German editions appeared the same year, one in Marburg and another in Erfurt. (Stupperich, *op. cit.*, p. 972; *CR*, I, 955.) The German version appeared in a 1534 *Sammelband* with Luther's *Von der Widertauffe* and Menius' *Der Widdertauffer Lere* at Wittenberg from the press of Schirlentz. I have used throughout the Wittenberg 1528 German translation of Jonas, checking it with the 1562 Latin edition at crucial points. Stupperich cited my previous use of the Jonas translation without comparison to the Latin as presumably somewhat less than desirable. (R. Stupperich, "Melanchthon und die Täufer," *Kerygma und Dogma*, III [1957], 150, n. 1, referring to J. S. Oyer, "The Writings of Melanchthon against the Anabaptists," *MQR*, XXVI [1952], 259–79.) I had no access to the Latin edition at that time; and subsequent comparison of the two versions discloses that access to a Latin version was not necessary. The changes made by Jonas were minute, and principally in the nature of enlargement for clarification purposes.

[3] Dedicatory letter to Friedrich Pistorius, *ca.* May 10, 1528, *CR*, I, 955; letter to Pistorius, end of October, 1528, *CR*, I, 1006. He enjoyed the task of combating the evils of this sect because he strengthened himself in the faith thereby. Letter to Pistorius, end of October, 1528, *ibid.*

[4] Undoubtedly a reference to at least the *Loci*.

discussion of Christian doctrine and in each examination of the Scriptures. It was precisely at this point that the Anabaptists erred. Rebaptism and community of goods, plus other ideas which Melanchthon only enumerated but did not explain or refute, attained so great a prominence in Anabaptist teaching that the heart of the true Christian faith could not be found at all.[1]

The Anabaptists erred not only in their preoccupation with outward ceremonies to the exclusion of central truths; they also misinterpreted the outward ceremonies. For them the sacrament was a sign and witness before all men of one's profession as a Christian. Melanchthon suggested that they believed such a witness would in itself attract men to faith. A sacrament was more than that to Melanchthon. He agreed that it was a sign, established by God. But it signified God's gracious will toward men, rather than one man's profession of faith before others. The Anabaptists had made a human institution out of that which was instituted by God and which bore therefore a divine character.

Melanchthon followed the ancient statement: *Accedat verbum ad elementum, et fit sacramentum.* The sacrament thus consisted of two parts. First was the sign, or act, which meant the promise of grace. Then came the Word, which bore the promise of God itself. Any act or occurrence which carried within it the possibility of God's blessing or succor was a sacrament. A work of love, or a misfortune, could be a sacrament. Neither the sign, i.e., the act, nor the Word justified. But the observer or recipient of the sign and the Word was justified precisely by the faith which that sign and Word had aroused and strengthened in him. Thus Gideon was not justified by either the fleece or God's Word to him, but rather by the faith in Israel's promised victory which was engendered by the fulfillment of God's promises concerning the fleece. The sign, though it did not justify, was a real aid and support to one's faith. The earnest Christian should look with gratitude upon the many signs, including misfortune, which carried with them the promise of God's grace. Many acts could be interpreted as sacraments. Melanchthon limited the sacraments to two – baptism and the Lord's Supper – on the basis of what he termed common Christian usage.[2] Melanchthon

---

[1] *Underricht*, p. A2r. This is a curious charge because it assumes a thorough knowledge on Melanchthon's part of Anabaptist doctrine, an assumption that is highly questionable. It is noteworthy that he included good works as part of central Christian truth that they failed to teach. No other Lutheran ever accused them of neglecting to teach the necessity for good works; they were accused of erring on the question of works, but never in this sense. Melanchthon did not repeat this charge in his later works. One suspects that he knew better.

[2] *Ibid.*, pp. A2v.–A3v.

buttressed his arguments on the nature of the sacrament and its use by Scripture and by appeal to Augustine. Certainly the sacrament as a sign of justification which was both seen and heard should be a constant reminder to men of God's promise of grace. Its continued efficacy as an assurance of grace did not require repetition. A baptism performed once stood for a lifetime: this by implication against the rebaptizers, who in Melanchthon's logic should have felt compelled to repeat their baptism daily.[1]

Melanchthon turned next to baptism. To him it was a sign, first of repentance, then of forgiveness of sins, and finally of the death of the old Adam. John the Baptist preached and baptized unto repentance. But he also announced the imminence of the Kingdom of Heaven – this was the Word of promise which accompanied the sign. Paul (Titus 3:5) called baptism a bath of regeneration; here was the promise of forgiveness of sins and newness of life. Paul also wrote of baptism in the death of Christ (Rom. 6:3, 4). As such the act stood as a sign of man's death and burial with Christ, which death and burial were in themselves the means by which the power of sin was destroyed. One could only stand in terror and in awe of the event by which God's dreadful wrath against sin was ameliorated. Therefore the act of baptism properly understood, which signified that cruel death and burial of God's Son, should produce in all who observed it a terror at the awful penalty which the wrath of God demanded. But it should also remind men of repentance, and even more of the promise of grace, of forgiveness of sins. As such baptism was to be counted among the weapons used to combat doubt and disbelief. It should strengthen man's faith, as he reflected upon it, as much as any miracle God might perform for him, or as much as Gideon's faith was strengthened by the fleece.

But baptism was a sign of still more – of affliction and trouble. Nature imposed distress and death because of sin. It did so in the case of God's Son. And just as Christ's suffering and death constituted a sacrifice well-pleasing to God, so man's suffering pleased God. Melanchthon stopped short of a martyr theology, in which the death of the Christian became for him a means of redemption. But such suffering served at least as a reminder that men were the children of God whom he loved and helped. Hence baptism as a sign of suffering was really a sign of hope. Christians should be encouraged in their troubles, because God would certainly fulfil his promise of grace to his children.[2]

[1] *Ibid.*, pp. A3r.–A4v.
[2] *Ibid.*, pp. A4v.–B2v.

Melanchthon discoursed briefly on distinctions between the baptism
of John and that of Christ. Both preached the same gospel – repentance
and forgiveness of sins – and John baptized to repentance. The differences lay not so much in what they said, but in their offices. John
preached the gospel and baptized with water. Christ forgave sins and sent
the Holy Spirit.[1] On the surface the inclusion of this brief discussion might
seem to indicate that Melanchthon considered the Anabaptists to be
bearers of erroneous views on the subject – i.e., perhaps they held that
there was a more substantial difference between the baptism of John
and that instituted by Christ. Melanchthon did not charge them with
error at this point, beyond a reiteration of the charge that they taught
that baptism was valid only for a given moment or specific time.[2]
One cannot postulate Anabaptist errors by implication on this point,
however, because it is clear that Melanchthon was giving a routine
systematic explanation of sacraments and baptism in the manner of his
earlier *Loci*. There too he included a discussion, of greater length, on
the distinction between the baptism of John and Christ. If anything,
in 1521 his emphasis on the similarities in the two baptisms was even
greater than in this 1528 treatise. John and Christ both baptized unto
mortification and vivification.[3] Indeed, up to this point in his 1528
treatise he did not move significantly beyond his 1521 *Loci* in any
particular. Nor would the Anabaptists have objected to his treatment
of baptism beyond the insistence that the act as man's commitment to
Christ in discipleship required greater emphasis. They might even have
approved of his mild position on the sacrament.[4] What was new in
1528 was his treatment of infant baptism, a treatment occasioned by
the teaching of those who denied its efficacy and condemned it.[5]

The major section of Melanchthon's treatise was devoted to a discussion of infant baptism. Traditionalism was his first argument for
infant baptism. It was clear that the fathers of the early church accepted and justified the practice. He referred specifically to Origen,
Augustine, Cyprian, and Chrysostom. The first two were of the opinion

---

[1] *Ibid.*, pp. B2v.–B3r.
[2] *Ibid.*, p. B3r.
[3] Charles Hill, *The Loci Communes of Philip Melanchthon* (Boston: Meador, 1944),
pp. 247–49.
[4] Hill traces Melanchthon's milder use of *significat dei opus* to Luther's Treatise on the
Babylonian Captivity of the Church, but Luther used *est* rather than *significat*. One does not
sense any justificatory work in the act itself, as Melanchthon interpreted it. At the very most
the sensible apprehension of the elements strengthened and encouraged one's faith in the
promises of God's grace. *Ibid.*, p. 244, n. 116, and also pp. 238–43.
[5] *Underricht*, p. B3v.

that the practice was accepted by the apostles already. One should never dissent from the fathers without clear Scriptural testimony. Indeed, Melanchthon was shocked and a little angered at the audacity of those who defied this ancient tradition. He called them fanatical spirits, which Jonas translated into the *Schwärmer* of Luther.[1] Here was for Melanchthon a clear principle for exegesis: the Scripture was absolutely authoritative in matters of faith and practice; when conflicts arose over its interpretation, the concensus of the fathers was to be sought and followed. The fact of his reliance on the concensus of the fathers in Scriptural matters must be kept in mind when he insisted on the one hand that Christian practices must find their origin in terms of concrete commands in Scripture,[2] and on the other hand demanded that the Anabaptists produce evidence from Scripture that a particular Christian doctrine or practice was specifically forbidden,[3] i.e., infant baptism. Scripture of Melanchthon was more than the "plain" Scripture to the Anabaptists. For Melanchthon it meant also as the fathers in general interpreted it.

Not only did the fathers advocate infant baptism; Scripture itself supported the practice. Melanchthon relied in the first instance on the argument from the Old Testament practice of circumcision that the promise of grace belonged to infants. God declared himself to be the God of the circumcised; he would not extend grace to the uncircumcised. What was this but the conferring of grace upon all infants who participated in the particular rites which stood as a sign and testimony of God's gracious will toward them. Secondly, the assertion was grounded in Christ's statement that the Kingdom of Heaven belonged to children. The gospel writer recorded Christ as saying: "Suffer little children, and forbid them not, to come unto me: for of such is the kingdom of heaven" (Matt. 19:14). Some argued that Christ declared that the Kingdom of Heaven belonged only to those who became like children, but that he did not mean to include children in the Kingdom. Melanchthon replied that such an interpretation was impossible since Christ commanded that the children be brought directly to him, and then proceeded to lay his hands upon them and bless them. To be outside the grace of God was to be an enemy of God. Christ would not have requested that the infants as enemies of God should be carried to him.

---

[1] *Ibid.*

[2] *Ibid.*, pp. C2r., D2r.

[3] *Ibid.*, p. Cv. See Otto Ritschl, *Dogmengeschichte des Protestantismus* (4 vols.; Leipzig: Hinrichs, 1908), I, 276–79, for a discussion of Melanchthon's traditionalism.

Christ bore a grace toward them. Finally, the Scriptures taught plainly that the children killed by Herod in his mad pursuit of the infant Jesus belonged without doubt to the Kingdom of Heaven. The evangelist quoted the prophet Jeremiah to this effect (Matt. 2:16–18).[1]

What was the principal purpose for infant baptism? Melanchthon replied later that it was to remove the guilt of original sin. What was original sin, and how could it be removed? Melanchthon began with Augustine and proceeded from him to Scripture. Original sin was a certain evil desire, a concupiscence, which led man into sin. This evil desire was a corruption of human nature which derived from the fall of Adam. Some denied that this corruption produced in itself death.[2] But Scripture testified that human nature was corrupt, that this corruption was sin, and that it led to death. These examples in Scripture (Rom. 5:12; Eph. 2:3; Psa. 51:5; Gen. 8:21) testified to man's innate sinfulness, not that he sinned because of the example of others as the Pelagians would have it. Moreover such evil inclination not only led to sin; it was in fact sin already. Philosophers often pondered why the human should sin with such willingness when sin was contrary to reason, when reason at least could be used to inform man what was the good. All men were born with this corruptness of nature. The guilt of it was removed by baptism. The contagion to do evil was itself not removed. But the guilt of original sin was not computed against the individual who was baptized. God counted him as righteous. Hence infants were taken within the grace of God and blessed through the sacrament of baptism, which removed the guilt of original sin.[3]

Against this accumulated evidence Melanchthon challenged the Anabaptists to produce evidence to the contrary. In particular he demanded proof that forgiveness of sins belonged outside the church. He reasoned that infant baptism was not a necessity only if it could be proved that salvation lay outside the church, as well as within it. This was a preposterous idea, and Melanchthon did not feel compelled to examine it very carefully. The church had always believed that salvation lay only within its domain, to use the Lutheran formula: where the Word and sacrament were. Scripture supported this, and no Scripture could be adduced to counter it. Indeed, there was no rational argument, nor any Scripture, to stand against his argument in favor of infant

---

[1] *Underricht*, pp. B3v.–B4v.

[2] Not in this instance a particular reference to Anabaptism. He meant to designate more those of a philosophical orientation, both in Augustine's time and in his own.

[3] *Underricht*, pp. C2r.–C3r.

baptism. This to Melanchthon was no idle boast. It was a firm, heart-felt conviction. Melanchthon simply could not conceive of a really good argument to oppose the assertion that the promise of grace belonged also to infants.[1]

What about the argument that infants could not understand, and therefore they were incapable of having either the Word or faith? Melanchthon refuted this argument weakly; either he did not fully understand it, or else he deliberately evaded it. On the one hand he merely repeated the reasoning that circumcision, commanded for infants under the law, was indication enough that infants were properly made the recipients of a sacrament which bespoke a grace bestowed upon them by God. On the other hand, he challenged the opponents to prove that grace belonged to all, including those outside the church.[2] Melanchthon did not meet the challenge of the argument squarely. The Anabaptists meant that, in a technical sense, it was not proper to speak of infants belonging or not belonging to the Kingdom of God. Adherence to the Kingdom, i.e., salvation to them, was absolutely contingent on a prior repentance and prayer for forgiveness, none of which could possibly occur before an individual reached an age at which he could understand in a minimal way the nature of sin and of God's grace in general, and of his own sin and God's forgiveness of it in particular. Melanchthon did not answer this. Possibly he tried to evade the issue, although this is highly unlikely in view of the fact that he had met the view earlier with the Zwickau Prophets. It is much more likely that he did not catch the full force of the Anabaptist argument in any of the Anabaptism he had so far encountered, either personally or through others. To answer the argument fully would have necessitated a shift to a discussion of justification, which he did not feel compelled to give.

Another objection of the Anabaptists required scant attention. There was no express command in Scripture to baptize infants. Therefore they should not be baptized.[3] Melanchthon agreed; there was no explicit command in Scripture on baptism for infants. But there was a first-rate example, that of circumcision in the Old Testament. The burden of proof in Scripture lay with the antipedobaptists; let them indicate where Scripture forbade the practice. He repeated his line of develop-ment: the promise of grace belonged to children; there was no for-

---

[1] *Ibid.*, pp. B4v.–Cr.
[2] *Ibid.*, p. Cr.
[3] *Ibid.*

giveness of sins outside the Christian church; therefore the outward sign of grace, baptism, should be extended to children. The major premise was invulnerable because it was based on Scripture. He insisted that the Anabaptists must attack the minor premise: no forgiveness of sins outside the Christian church.[1] To deny his syllogism he believed they were forced to teach that forgiveness of sins could be somewhere outside the church, where Word and sacrament were. He accused them therefore of teaching the greatest uncertainty (*affirmant rem incertissimam*). Any major departure from the fathers resulted precisely in the promulgation of uncertainty.[2]

A third charge of Melanchthon against the Anabaptists was that they declared baptism of infants to be of no validity. Melanchthon disposed of this quickly with a reiteration of previous arguments. He insisted that baptism itself was necessary; it could not be dispensed with. It was, true enough, a sign, but it was also necessary for forgiveness of sins.[3]

A summary charge Melanchthon raised against the Anabaptists was that of subjectivism. They declared that baptism was valid only at that moment when the condition of the heart coincided the most completely with the sign, i.e., when the heart began to have faith in the forgiveness of sins. Melanchthon believed that the logical extension of this position was to require baptism each time the heart felt repentance for sins committed. Baptism for such a person would be a daily necessity. The Anabaptists erred in putting a subjective human construction on an act which carried the spirit of the divine. They did not make enough of baptism. It was to them only a testimony of one's faith before men, whereas it was in fact a sign of God's will toward men. It did not require repetition.[4] Although Melanchthon did not write extensively on this point in his 1528 treatise, it was always a major means whereby he could identify an Anabaptist. It enabled him in turn to link them with the subjectivism and spiritualism of the Zwickau Prophets. It stood in the way of his discovery of the intense and often legalistic Biblicism, a Biblicism which is immediately apparent to the student of Anabaptism in Melanchthon's own charge that the Anabaptists denied infant baptism because it was nowhere expressly commanded in Scripture.

Over three-quarters of the 1528 treatise was devoted to a discussion of the question of baptism. Melanchthon devoted a few pages to one

---

[1] *Ibid.*, p. Cv.
[2] *Ibid.*, pp. Cv.–C2r.
[3] *Ibid.*, p. C3v.
[4] *Ibid.*, p. C4r.

other issue: community of goods. To demand that the individual Christian surrender all personal property and share his goods with other Christians was a seditious and fanatical doctrine to Melanchthon. He related the conviction on community of goods to the social unrest of the Peasants' War. He believed that the practice of community of goods, with its factionalism, would tear people from the ecclesiastical order and from the civil order. Both orders would be undermined thereby. He viewed with the greatest apprehension any attempt to break the Corpus Christianum. Because of the example of the Peasants' War he tended to label a radical social idea as in itself seditious and provocative of revolution.[1] He postulated Anabaptist communism as a theory advocated by them for the whole of society, as in Plato's *Republic*.[2]

Melanchthon was most disturbed by an Anabaptist insistence that for the true Christian community of goods was mandatory. He countered by showing that Paul encouraged the Christians at Corinth to give to the poor as they were able (II Cor. 9: particularly 7 and 9). They were not forced to give. Certainly the situation in Corinth was one in which private property was allowed for Christians.[3]

The Anabaptists pointed to Christ's command to the rich young ruler. "If thou wilt be perfect, go and sell that thou hast, and give to the poor" (Matt. 19:21). Melanchthon replied that the command was directed to one person only, precisely because he needed it. His love of worldly goods became a hindrance to his love for God. Hence Christ called him to give up private property, much as he called other men to do other things: to preach, or to teach. Scripture nowhere commanded that all Christians relinquish private property and hold goods in community. There were, in brief, many things within this world which the Christian could do: he might marry, serve as a magistrate, work with his hands, raise children, earn his bread. But all of these things were to be done in the fear of the Lord, and in faith.[4]

The Anabaptists undergirded their argument on community of goods with the example of apostolic practice. The true Christian would follow the pattern of the apostolic church literally. Here again was Anabaptist Biblicism in a legalistic sense. Melanchthon declared that apostolic

---

[1] *Ibid.*, p. Dv.
[2] *Ibid.*, p. D3v. He did not accuse Anabaptists of referring to Plato. It is highly unlikely that they did. Their concern for economic community was restricted to their spiritual communion.
[3] *Ibid.*, p. Dv.
[4] *Ibid.*, pp. D2r.–D2v.

practice did not speak to the question of whether or not private property was forbidden to a Christian. The early believers met and pooled their goods out of economic necessity – to escape having their goods confiscated because they were Christians. They were reduced to poverty and depended upon each other for economic livelihood. Melanchthon was of the opinion that similar necessity might arise in his own time, and that those who wished voluntarily to have community of goods could do so in peace. But he objected to making this historic case of economic necessity an ironclad law for the governance of all Christians. To follow Anabaptist reasoning, thought Melanchthon, all pastors should remain single because Paul did.[1]

In view of Melanchthon's subsequent charges of Anabaptist sedition, charges which appear equally grave, why did he discuss their attitude on community of goods rather than the other ideas? In the first place, it may well be that Melanchthon thought this was the most revolutionary of their ideas. If all true Christians were required to hold goods in common, the disruptive effect on society would be incalculable. Many of the necessary functions within society would not be carried out: the exercise of justice, even perhaps the earning of bread for oneself and one's family. Moreover, one suspects that Melanchthon thought the Saxon lands were particularly vulnerable on this point. He declared that it was often those people who declared themselves followers of the Evangelical cause who would not give to the poor, or even to the pastors and deacons. Melanchthon undoubtedly was referring to experiences he had had on his ecclesiastical visitations. The Christian could of course retain private property. But he should gladly give of his goods to the poor.[2]

Finally, the seriousness of the advocacy of mandatory communism of Christians was such that Melanchthon could be certain its advocates were not of God. He did not say they were diabolical in origin. But he admonished all Christians to earnestly test the spirits; the times were dangerous.[3]

Other fanatical ideas advanced by the Anabaptists, according to Melanchthon's information at this point, were that a Christian could not continue as Christian and occupy any civil office, and that a

---

[1] *Ibid.*, p. D3r.
[2] *Ibid.*, p. D3v.
[3] *Ibid.*, p. D4r.

Christian could not use the sword in the exercise of political authority.[1]
Melanchthon had no further comments on these or other issues.

Melanchthon had not declared himself in his *Iudicium* on the increasingly pertinent question of how to treat the Anabaptists. Electoral
Saxony was troubled enough by secret preachers to call forth a mandate
from the Elector on February 27, 1527, against them. Under threat of
severe punishment for violation, it was ordered that all activities related
to a cure of souls must be handled only by those properly ordained and
established in office. Any type of gathering, such as for baptism or
marriage, must be reported to the magistrates so that it could be
carefully watched.[2] This mandate only threatened death. The imperial
mandate of the next year, issued January 4, 1528, was more specific.
The Anabaptists were deemed worthy of death.[3] Elector John followed
the mandate of Charles with one of his own, dated January 17, 1528.
John was somewhat shocked by the severity of the imperial mandate.
His own did not specify the death penalty, except, as in 1527, by way
of vague threat. The immediate punishment accorded any Anabaptists
who were apprehended was that of imprisonment. The mandate was
couched in terms of prohibiting the preaching of those who were outside the legal ecclesiastical office. It was directed specifically against
the Anabaptists and also against those who erred on the sacrament,
these latter probably followers of Carlstadt.[4] Melanchthon had no
official role to play in the formulation of any of these mandates. But
the question of punishment of Anabaptists had been raised, and
Melanchthon was bound to come to terms with it sometime. He declared himself on the subject in February, 1530, in a letter to Friedrich
Myconius, pastor and superintendent at Gotha.[5]

Myconius wrote for Melanchthon's opinion after six Anabaptists
were executed in Electoral territory at Reinhardsbrunn. Myconius was
disturbed by the fact of execution, probably more so because of the

---

[1] *Ibid.*, p. Dv.

[2] Wappler, *Thüringen*, p. 34.

[3] *Ibid.*, pp. 268–69 for a printing of the mandate itself.

[4] Wappler, *Inquisition und Ketzerprozesse*, p. 8, and pp. 164–65 for a printing of the
mandate itself.

[5] Melanchthon had considered Anabaptists worthy of death in 1527 already, but his
declaration was not as complete as that of 1530. He considered Anabaptists who inveighed
against government, who practiced community of goods, or who deserted spouse or children
worthy of execution. He described their leaders as blasphemers, a term which was destined
to play a precise and significant role in his later condemnations. It is clear that the germ of
the idea of death for blasphemy existed in his mind at this relatively early date. Letter of
Melanchthon to Luther and Bugenhagen, September 16, 1527, *WB*, IV, 249–50.

calm manner in which they faced death.[1] Melanchthon replied that all Anabaptists were to be treated with the utmost severity, no matter how blameless they might appear. All Anabaptists rejected some part of their civil duty; and if they were indulged by the magistracy, they took advantage of leniency to build upon seditious ideas until they actually provoked insurrection. It was necessary for the government to act with severity in order to strike fear into their hearts and thus to bring them to respect the civil order. Melanchthon believed that even if in individual cases the situation did not warrant severity of punishment, the government must use a strong arm because the times were dangerous – i.e., an insurrection similar to the Peasants' Revolt could all too easily reoccur.[2]

In 1527 the Anabaptists were called seditious and blasphemous. In 1528 they were *Schwärmer*. In 1530 Melanchthon called them the angels of the devil. When they first gave themselves over to the devil, they were harmless enough. But he drove them until they could no longer hold their peace. Melanchthon saw by 1530 a long train of developments which began with Nicholas Storch, reached a high point of frenzy in Müntzer, and now was manifest in the Anabaptists. Once he was able to connect the Anabaptists to Storch and Müntzer, Melanchthon was certain that revolution was their ultimate goal irrespective of pious pretension or peaceful bearing.[3] He wrote that the Elector had wanted to kill Storch when he appeared in Wittenberg. Melanchthon helped restrain Frederick, and for this mildness and indecision on his part he was now sorry.[4] He did not wish to repeat his error. Melanchthon further cautioned against receiving the advice of Brenz. Brenz was too mild; he had not yet experienced these fanatical spirits at work.[5]

---

[1] See above, pp. 50-51.

[2] *CR*, II, 17–18. Much of it translated into German by Wappler, *Die Stellung Kursachsens*, pp. 13–14.

[3] *Ibid.*

[4] *Ibid.* See document of January 2, 1522, *CR*, I, 535–38, parts of which give Frederick's views. He declared he had no intention of killing Storch and the other Zwickauers. Melanchthon and Amsdorf urged restraint on Frederick.

[5] Brenz was of the opinion that killing heretics served only to strengthen the devil's hand. All heresy had some appearance of truth, and was based to some degree on Scripture. The killing of heretics always tended to make them appear as persons persecuted for righteousness sake. In the final analysis he did not deny the authority of Mosaic Law (Lev. 24:16) with respect to death for blasphemers. But he held back for tactical reasons. Heresy was not ultimately defeated by executing its advocates, else the hangman would be the most learned teacher on earth; only Scripture could ultimately defeat heresy – all this Brenz got from Luther himself. He was also reminded by Luther of the fact that all too frequently in the history of the church the execution of heretics became persecution of the faithful. Brenz denied that specific Anabaptist doctrines would lead to revolution: rejection of personal property, community of goods, no Christian dare be a magistrate, etc. All of these doctrines

Here was articulated a position, formed from deepest conviction, from which Melanchthon did not waver throughout the remainder of his life. He could see, as Stupperich declares,[1] the similarities of the Anabaptists much more clearly than the differences. He did not try to distinguish among types or kinds of Anabaptists; to him there was no such distinction. He saw all Anabaptists as one group, differing from each other only in degree: degree to which their doctrines had captivated them, degree to which the devil had active control over them. All of them deserved the sternest possible penalty upon apprehension. Later in his life he added reasons to those formulated in 1530 for the death penalty. In two documents of October, 1531, he accused them of destroying the true church both by refusing to respect the office of *ministerium verbi*, which was intolerable blasphemy, and also by withdrawing from the church and forming a sect founded on uncertain doctrine. Their destruction of the ecclesiastical order, symbolized by their withdrawal, Melanchthon considered worthy of the punishment accorded civil revolutionaries. Their attempt to create a pure church, withdrawn from the proper ecclesiastical order, was insufferable hypocrisy, and was reminiscent of the Donatist heresy of Augustine's time. Christ warned men that it was impossible to create a pure church in this world.[2]

Melanchthon not only added reasons for killing Anabaptists; he also added advice for those who interrogated and eventually sentenced Anabaptists on how to classify their prisoners. This advice was the result of the Elector's request to the Wittenberg theologians for some guidance on treating Anabaptists. He was troubled by the new rash of Anabaptist prisoners and by the effects of the execution of the six Anabaptists at Reinhardsbrunn in January, 1530.[3] Melanchthon replied

were demanded in greater or lesser degree by the Catholic counsels of perfection, and monasticism did not become the cause or source of revolution in the Catholic church. If revolutionary ideas were held by Anabaptists, this was mere accident, or chance. Every group had its bad members but that did not mean that the entire group was responsible for the insanity of a few. *Ob ein weltliche Oberkeit mit Götlichem und billichem Rechten mög die Widderteuffer durch Fewer odder Schwerd vom Leben zum Tode richten*, 1528, large parts quoted in Julius Hartmann and Karl Jäger, *Johann Brenz, nach gedruckten und ungedruckten Quellen* (2 vols.; Hamburg: Perthes, 1840–42), I, 300–08.
   [1] Robert Stupperich, "Melanchthon und die Täufer," *Kerygma und Dogma*, III (1957), 154.
   [2] a. Letter to Myconius, October 31, 1531, *CR*, II, 549.
      b. Memorandum to Elector John, October, 1531, *CR*, IV, 738–39. Bretschneider dates the memorandum 1541. I have followed the dating of Wappler, *Die Stellung Kursachsens*, pp. 25–27, for the reasons he cites from both internal and external evidence, and also because the ideas in the memorandum are so similar to those expressed in his letter to Myconius, October 31, 1531: i.e., at least the *ideas* of the memorandum were in his mind by 1531. It is therefore proper to use it as an expression of what Melanchthon thought in 1531.
   [3] Wappler, *Die Stellung Kursachsens*, pp. 25–27.

with a memorandum which bore the approval of Luther. He wrote that the Elector must punish the Anabaptists severely in view of their disobedience to the previous mandate of the Elector, undoubtedly a reference to either the mandate of 1527 or the one of 1528. In violation of the mandate they had usurped the office of preacher of the Word and had held secret meetings. Then Melanchthon proceeded to classify Anabaptists into three groups, according to degree of fanaticism, and to make recommendations for the treatment of each group. The first group consisted of instigators and those who harbored or concealed Anabaptists but particularly those who had recommenced to teach and preach in spite of the mandate. These were to be executed with the sword. The second group was composed of followers, persons led astray, who nevertheless pertinaciously held to any of the following points:

(1) No Christian should hold government office.
(2) Christians should hold goods in common.
(3) No Christian should swear an oath.
(4) The church must be reformed, and all godless people destroyed.
(5) Charging interest on money loaned was wrong.
(6) The established church was not the true church.
(7) The Evangelical preaching and baptism were not truly Christian.

Such persons were also to be executed. The third group was composed of those who had erred through misunderstanding, who might be recalled to the true faith. These were to be taught, and if they made public confession of their error, they were to be received back into fellowship with a stern warning against backsliding. If they would not recant, and if they still did not hold to any of the above-outlined errors in belief, they were to be banished from the land, or given some other punishment lighter than the death sentence.[1] One notices that those who erred on non-seditious articles were to be executed. These were deserving of death because of their blasphemy.

Melanchthon encouraged the Elector to persevere in his determination to exercise the death penalty against Anabaptists. Encouragement was necessary, both because some Evangelicals objected and also because the purpose of the severe punishment seemed not to have been fulfilled. Punishment should produce fear and repentance in the hearts of those punished and in potential malefactors. The six Anabaptists at Reinhardsbrunn went to their deaths with joy, not fear or repentance. Nor did the executions stem the flow of new sheep into the Anabaptist fold. Melanchthon knew this. He wrote that the civil authority was still

---

[1] *Gutachten, CR*, IV, 737–40.

responsible before God to continue the firm exercise of justice in the confidence that it would ultimately bear its rightful fruit.[1] Subsequent declarations on the subject of punishment for Anabaptists did not alter this basic severity of tone and content. As Melanchthon learned of more Anabaptist ideas, he included them among those for which punishment was mandatory. The only note of leniency that crept into his declarations was the admonition to be careful with those who were misled, that they might be properly nurtured in the truth and perhaps they could be rescued.[2] He remained unalterably harsh toward this spawn of Satan.[3]

So much for the formulation of Melanchthon's attitude on the question of punishment. We return to the examination of his post-1528 delineations of Anabaptist error. By 1530 the Anabaptist movement was of sufficient seriousness to command a rebuttal in the Augsburg Confession. In his previous confessional statements, the *Loci*, 1521, and the *Unterricht der Visitatoren*, 1528, Melanchthon had not included their errors.[4] The circumstances of the Augsburg Diet rendered essential some effort on the part of the Evangelicals to show that they were no more friendly toward the Anabaptists than were the Catholics. Specifically, John Eck in his *Four Hundred and Four Articles* refused to distinguish among the Lutherans, Anabaptists, sacramentarians, and Zwinglians. Here was at least implicitly the charge that the initial separation from Rome was parent to all subsequent deviations, no matter how fanatical some of them might be.[5] The Protestants smarted.

---

[1] *Ibid.*

[2] See a. Letter to Prince Johannes of Anhalt, October 22, 1534, *CR*, II, 793.
    b. Letter to Eberhard v. d. Thann, July 16, 1535, *CR*, II, 889–90.
    c. Letter to Bucer, March 15, 1534, *CR*, II, 710–13.
There were other occasions, touched below, on which he declared on the subject.

[3] Stupperich, *Kerygma und Dogma*, III, 150, n. 1, along with multitudinous criticisms, takes me somewhat to task for calling Melanchthon "unusually harsh" (*MQR*, XXVI [1952], 260). Although I agree with Stupperich that there are errors in the article, I insist that this is not one of them. The judgment is based on three observations:
    a. Melanchthon was much more severe and harsh toward the Anabaptists than toward other of his opponents. It is precisely this note of harshness that is missing from the Manschreck biography because the author did not give much consideration to Melanchthon's relation to the Anabaptists.
    b. Melanchthon's attitude is harsher than that of Luther, despite the fact that their differences in temperament would lead us to expect the reverse.
    c. Of the replies received by Philip of Hesse to his request for advice in treating Anabaptists in 1536, Melanchthon's was among the harshest, equalled or outstripped only by that of Rhegius. *TA, Hesse*, pp. 98–128.

[4] In the *Unterricht* Melanchthon did bother to justify infant baptism in the section on baptism, though without specifying the Anabaptists. One might consider Melanchthon's *Iudicium* a supplement to the *Unterricht*, of course.

[5] Manschreck, *op. cit.*, pp. 178, 180.

Melanchthon therefore dealt with the charge already in the Preface, which was addressed to Charles V. The Anabaptists did not come from Luther's doctrines, for their ideas occurred before Luther.[1] They appeared mainly in those times and places where there was an absence of skilful preachers to warn against false doctrine. Indeed, not only did the Anabaptists not derive from the Lutherans; but the Lutherans also had brought about no small lessening of this heresy through the promulgation of true Christian doctrine. Anabaptist ideas would have spread much further had not men's hearts been warmed and strengthened by the Evangelical teaching.[2]

In six articles of the completed Confession the Anabaptists were specifically repudiated or damned for their erroneous teachings. Under Faith the Anabaptists were damned for teaching that the Holy Spirit came to men without any external works, but by one's own work and preparation.[3] In Article Eight, the Church, the "Donatists" who taught that the ministry of impious men was of no effect were repudiated. The church was defined as an assembly of believers, whom one could not distinguish from the sinners because of the latters' hypocrisy. Hence priests could administer sacraments with validity irrespective of their own state of righteousness.[4] Article Nine, on Baptism, repudiated the Anabaptist view that children should not be baptized.[5] Article Twelve rejected the Anabaptists who taught that after one's justification he could not sin again.[6] Article Sixteen damned the Anabaptists for teaching that a Christian could not hold magisterial office, use the sword, swear a civil oath, marry, participate in war, etc.[7] Finally, Article Seventeen repudiated (damned in Melanchthon's May version) the Anabaptists who taught that all men, and even the devil, would eventually enjoy eternal bliss.[8] The scope of the Anabaptist ideas represented here suggests a substantial increase in Melanchthon's knowledge of the group since he wrote his 1528 tract. Particularly in

---

[1] Melanchthon probably had in mind, among others, at least the ancient heresies of the Donatists and Novatians, which heresies he specifically charged the Anabaptists with perpetuating.

[2] Augsburg Confession, Preface of May, 1530, printed in Johann M. Reu, *The Augsburg Confession* (Chicago: Wartburg Publishing House, 1930), p.* 141.

[3] *Ibid.*, pp. *172–*173. The charge did not appear in Melanchthon's May 31 draft.

[4] *Ibid.*, pp. *176–*177, from the May 31 draft of Melanchthon.

[5] *Ibid.*

[6] *Ibid.*, pp. *178–*181, from Melanchthon's May 31 draft.

[7] *Ibid.*, pp. *182–*185. Melanchthon used the word repudiated instead of damned in his May 31 draft.

[8] *Ibid.*, pp. *184–*187.

Article Seventeen one suspects that he had gotten hold of some of Denk's ideas.

Münster in Westphalia, like many cities of Central Germany, was also touched by the Evangelical teaching late in the 1520's. Here the movement was influenced in its early stages by economic and social unrest in the town. The Evangelicals won their converts principally among the lower classes, while the upper classes led by the council tended to adhere to the Catholic faith. In 1531 Bernhard Rothmann began to work in Münster for the Evangelical cause. Backed by the guilds Rothmann and those of like mind won increasing support until most of the churches in the town were preaching the Evangelical doctrine. Early in 1534 the movement took a turn toward Anabaptism, especially as the result of the incursion of fiery prophets from the Lowlands. Jan Matthys and Jan van Leyden, converts to Melchior Hofmann's apocalypticism, led an exodus of persecuted Anabaptists from the Lowlands to the New Jerusalem. By late February, 1534, all citizens who refused adult baptism were expelled. Revolutionary Anabaptism was in control. Community of goods and polygamy were introduced and promoted by van Leyden. Bishop Franz of Waldeck began siege of the town early in 1534. By June, 1535, the bishop's army prevailed. All males were rounded up and punished; the leaders were killed.[1] Europe had a flagrant demonstration of the most radical sort of Anabaptism. It took this manifestation as illustrative of the basic tendencies inherent in all Anabaptism.

Rothmann accepted Münsterite Anabaptism and became one of its ablest spokesmen. In October, 1534, he published *Eyne Restitution odder Eine wedderstellinge rechter vnnde gesunder Christliker leer . . . .* He advocated a return to the practice and doctrine of the apostolic church. Melanchthon took up his pen to answer Rothmann's *Restitution* in his own *Etliche Propositiones wider die Lehr der Widerteuffer gestelt durch Philip Melanchthon.*[2] It must have pained Melanchthon deeply to see his erstwhile friend, who had preached the Evangelical doctrine so effectively, turn to radical Anabaptism.[3]

Melanchthon's pamphlet consisted of twenty-two propositions of

---

[1] C. Krahn, "Muenster Anabaptists," *ME*, III, 777–82.

[2] No place, 1535. A second edition, published the same year at Nürnberg has been printed by Walch, *Luther's sämmtliche Schriften* (St. Louis: Condordia Publishing House, 1890), XX, Col. 1698ff., with the title *Wider das gotteslästerliche und schändliche Buch, so zu Münster im Druck neulich ist ausgegangen, etliche Propositiones gestellt durch Phil. Melanchthon.*

[3] In 1532 Melanchthon had written Rothmann gently remonstrating against Zwingli's doctrine on the Lord's Supper which was being defended in Münster. Letter to Rothmann, December 24, 1532, *CR*, II, 619–20.

various sorts. Some were descriptions of Anabaptist errors; some were concise rebuttals; others were extensions of his previously expressed ideas. He summarized Anabaptist error and refuted it so that everyone would be able to see how abominable and blasphemous the sins of this diabolical sect were.[1]

Melanchthon was concerned in this instance with a considerable extension of the body of Anabaptist error. The Münsterites practiced community of goods; Melanchthon had noted this among other Anabaptists. They also practiced polygamy. He noticed their docetic view of Christ; his flesh did not come from Mary. Each of these errors was in itself sin of the worst sort. But the peculiar Münsterite error derived from their view that the church they were assembling was absolutely pure; it permitted no sinful or hypocritical persons in its midst. They added their apocalypticism and extended their church into a temporal Kingdom of Christ in which only the righteous would rule. In their establishment of their Kingdom of Christ they taught rebellion against the established civil authority, and they even assigned the sword to those who occupied the office of the Word. Melanchthon did not attempt an extended refutation. He believed that the Kingdom of Christ would not appear until after the Judgment Day. He denounced revolution, particularly when it was led by the preachers. He considered it impossible for men to winnow out the wicked from their midst because it was not given to them to read the hearts of men. He could not countenance polygamy, or community of goods. Anabaptist doceticism was blasphemy. The gang deserved punishment as robbers and murderers. He considered the occurrence of this evil a punishment on the world for its own ungodliness.[2]

Later in the year Melanchthon had opportunity to learn of Anabaptism at first hand. He helped examine several Anabaptists who were captured in a raid in Kleineutersdorf, a village two kilometers south of Kahla. For some months the village miller, one Hans Peissker (sometimes called Döring), had been under observation by the rent-collector from the Leuchtenburg, Peter Wolfram. Wolfram suspected him of complicity in things Anabaptist because he and his household refrained from church attendance. His wife attended on occasion, Wolfram thought as a palliative. Moreover, they frequently entertained strangers apart from the other villagers, they spoke against the Word of God and the sacraments, and they conducted strange ceremonies with singing before

[1] *Etliche Propositiones*, p. Av.
[2] *Ibid.*, pp. Av.–A4v.

and after meals at the table. Suspicion increased when the miller refused to stand godfather for the child of a neighbor. Wolfram proposed to watch the Peissker household carefully.[1]

On November 20, 1535, Wolfram discovered a house full of strangers with the miller. The following day he arrested the group, with the exception of Peissker's wife because of her pregnancy and her small children. Some sixteen persons in all were taken, including Peissker and his daughter. Peissker bade his wife farewell and blessed her, calling her to remain steadfast in the faith; they called each other "brother" and "sister." As they were taken through the villages to the Leuchtenburg, they sang the Luther hymn "Nun Bitten Wir den Heiligen Geist," and cried out to the villagers to repent before the approaching day of the Lord. At the fortress Peissker was asked who brought him to this group. He declared that God the Creator of heaven and earth had done so. He decried the fact that he was arrested for religious reasons; had he and his friends indulged in wanton feasting and tippling nothing would have happened. When asked for names of the others he replied: "They are children of God whose flesh is from the ground." Their homes were "in the Hand of God between heaven and earth." Little else beyond meager personal details could be gotten from them at the time, except that they did not believe in the Lutheran sacraments, either Eucharist or baptism. Only one among the group, Heinz Kraut, was literate. Rather than burden the security forces of the Leuchtenburg with so many people, the eleven men were distributed to other prisons: four to Jena, four to Neustadt an der Orla, and three to Kahla, leaving the five women at the Leuchtenburg.[2]

Melanchthon and Cruciger from the university, which had been moved to Jena because of the plague, and Anton Musa, the pastor at Jena, plus several of the Jena councilors were called upon to interrogate the four men imprisoned at Jena. This was the key group because it included Kraut, a leader of sorts,[3] and the miller Peissker. The interrogation required parts of two days, December 1 and 6, 1535. Melanchthon directed most of the questions, and Kraut was the prize witness.[4]

---

[1] Wappler, *Thüringen*, p. 138 and sources p. 395.

[2] *Ibid.*, pp. 139–41, 396–99.

[3] Kraut, a native of Esperstedt near Frankenhausen, fell heir to the leadership of some Thuringian Anabaptists when Alexander was executed in 1533. He had been captured in 1530, but he was released when he recanted. He rejoined the brotherhood, and served as a traveling preacher, visiting the believers as far as Moravia. Neff, *ME*, III, 234.

[4] See the account of the interrogation which was attached to letters from the Jena Council, in *CR*, II, 997–1003. The author is unknown. It is not a report from Melanchthon's own hand, although there are marginal notations in his writing.

The interrogators quickly separated one of the four, Hilarius Petzsch, from the rest because he was new in the faith; he had not even been baptized. Melanchthon was of the opinion that he should be shown mercy because he lived in an area where the gospel was not preached and he needed instruction. Petzsch asked for pardon.[1] Kraut, Peissker, and Jobst Moller remained steadfast, or stubborn, however one wants to look at it. Kraut had been baptized by Alexander, near Frankenhausen. He in turn baptized Moller. Peissker, on the other hand, had been baptized two years prior to his arrest by Melchior Rink. All four declared their complete innocence with respect to Münsterite doctrines; indeed, they knew so little about the Münster Anabaptists that they could declare neither for nor against them.[2]

Melanchthon began the interrogation with the charge of sectarianism. Nowhere in historical Christendom could one find an exact counterpart to this sect. Normally he was much more impressed by similarities than by differences among the radicals of the Reformation. In this instance the peculiar features of Münsterite Anabaptism probably so colored his picture that he could not find an exact replica of the movement in history. This initial charge of sectarianism, a very serious charge in those times, met with an unconvincing counter-charge which revealed something of the character of the three Anabaptists. Kraut declared that the true separatists from the ways of God, the true disciples of the devil, were the practitioners of the established church. Their baptism, their sacraments, and their married lives were abominations in the sight of God. Peissker and Moller concurred.[3]

Melanchthon proceeded to other matters. On the question of the Trinity he could find nothing amiss. It should not surprise us to learn that in Melanchthon's opinion the three men were not much aware of the Christological problem of the two natures. But on the problem of forgiveness of sins, the Anabaptists wished to go beyond the position of Melanchthon. They considered his justification a forensic act. For them forgiveness of sins was a joining, so to speak, of justification and sanctification. It began with awareness of one's sins, an earnest desire for forgiveness. Then followed a righteousness with which one, empowered by faith, sought earnestly to follow Christ and to do the will of God. This entire process was one and the same to Kraut. He in-

---

[1] Melanchthon's report (undesignated recipient) of the interrogation, *CR*, II, 1003. This is a very brief, and not very helpful, report.

[2] *CR*, II, 997–98.

[3] *Ibid.*, p. 998.

cluded it within the category of forgiveness of sins, doing it without
theological explanantion. Whereas Melanchthon would have distinguished at least for purposes of theological conversation, between
justification and the subsequent Christian life as the new man in Christ,
the Anabaptist tended to make them one and the same. Indeed, if there
was no evidence of the new man in Christ living a different kind of life
from what he had lived before, if there was no moral change, then there
could have been no forgiveness of sins.[1]

Kraut, and subsequently the other two, held to their convictions that
the Christian should not swear the civil oath, and that all Christians
should hold goods in common. The motivation for the latter was two-
fold: (1) the apostles did; therefore so should latter-day Christians;
(2) its rationale was that of contributing freely to the brethren in need;
one should do this as a Christian with such liberality and freedom that
in truth he could not call his goods his own.[2]

The interrogation on baptism was longer and more arduous. The
Anabaptists began by declaring that no infant, whether heathen, Turk,
or Christian, would be damned. God would never damn an infant
because of the absence of what they contemptuously called a little
water. What God created was good. They did not deny the power of
original sin to lead to sinful acts, except as such power might apply to
infants. Only when the individual matured, and willed to sin did
original sin have power over him. Here was no description or definition
of original sin. But by implication it appeared to them as an inclination,
inherent in human nature, to sin against God. Only after a man, in his
own understanding and volition, repented of sin and had faith in God,
only then was the performance of baptism valid and a requisite.[3]

But the issue of baptism, properly directed by Melanchthon, led to
another field of conversation: the authority of Scripture. One strongly
suspects that both the direction of the inquiry and the length of time
spent on this issue of baptism were the result of Melanchthon's already
firm conviction that baptism was of paramount importance precisely
because it disclosed the subjectivism and the subsequent spiritualism of
the Anabaptists. The Anabaptists met in Melanchthon a man better
versed in Scripture than they were; this did not often happen to them.
He trapped them on the question of whether or not the guilt of original
sin adheres to infants by quoting Psalm 51:5, " . . . in sin did my mother

[1] *Ibid.*
[2] *Ibid.*, pp. 998–99.
[3] *Ibid.*, p. 999.

conceive me" and sections of Paul's letters. At this the Anabaptists recoiled and declared that no one except themselves properly understood the Scripture. Their authority, higher than Scripture itself, was the divine writing in their hearts. They even intimated that the devil wrote at least parts of the Bible.[1] Or perhaps they meant that the devil misinterpreted parts of the Bible to his own advantage, i.e., through Melanchthon.

This was the turning point in the interrogation as the anonymous court reporter has it. Thereafter most of the other issues, when seriously discussed, became in turn the question of the authority of Scripture versus the authority of the Inner Word or Spirit. Thus a recapitulation on the question of oaths led to the authority problem. So did the discussion on obedience to civil authority. On one occasion Kraut declared that Scripture was limited in that it only showed the way; the Christian must be prepared to go further, i.e., by following the leading of the Spirit. But how much they relied on such extra-Scriptural revelation is not clear. It is significant that they relied on the Spirit precisely at that point where Melanchthon quoted Scripture and required a literalistic interpretation. They were accustomed to read Scripture and interpret it in the same fashion. They began the defense of their doctrines with the usual Anabaptist reliance on Scripture, literally interpreted. Only as they faced in Melanchthon a man more clever and better versed in Scripture than themselves, only then did they retreat to the authority of the Spirit.[2]

A major point of conflict was the question of obedience to magistrates. Melanchthon uncovered in these men a substantial antipathy to the political authority of their regions. The Anabaptists agreed that one must obey the Bible; but the Bible called for obedience to magistrates, *for conscience sake*. Kraut replied that they could not be obedient to an authority which imprisoned them[3] precisely because of their consciences, that denied them the exercise of their faith. In such a condition Kraut declared he felt himself bound to obey no one but God, Romans 13 to the contrary notwithstanding. This was to him true Christian freedom. In this context, then, the Christian could own but one Lord, God himself. The Christian himself could not be a magistrate, but he should not condemn that magistrate who properly punished evil and encouraged

---

[1] *Ibid.*

[2] *Ibid.*, pp. 1000–01.

[3] Kraut declared that he fled one government's jurisdiction because it interfered with his conscience.

the righteous – in short, who really obeyed Paul's injunction in Romans
13.[1] Later, when Kraut was being led to the execution block, he denounced the tendency of most people to make idols. He included as
idolatry the use of the word *Herr* as a term of address, and also the
doffing of the hat as a token of respect. So far his egalitarianism could
be no more than a Biblical literalism rigidly adhered to: only God was
Lord. But then he repeated the social revolutionary jingle of recent
Peasants' War and earlier John Ball fame: When Adam delved and
Eve span, who then was the gentleman? Kraut was sentenced in part
for his participation in the Peasants' War. Kraut cannot be regarded
as a peaceful Anabaptist.[2] One suspects the influence of Müntzer or
Münster; the latter they denied outright, and they were not questioned
on the former.[3]

On the Lord's Supper there was no agreement. Kraut charged the
Lutherans with turning it into idolatry. In a return to the charge of
sectarianism, Melanchthon asked why they preached and assembled
secretly. Why did they eschew preaching in the open, implying there
was something sinister which needed hiding? Kraut denied any intention of being secret. The civil authorities drove them underground
with their persecution of the true Word. He declared himself called of
God to preach, which was infinitely better than being called by the
magistrate for the task. Finally they turned to the question of marriage.
The Anabaptists held that a marriage between believer and non-
believer was no marriage at all. The believer should patiently seek to
win his spouse to the faith. Failing that the marriage was dissolved.[4]
Melanchthon heard later from one of the prisoners at Kahla that Kraut
had left his wife and had taken another.[5] The prisoners criticized the
weddings of the Evangelicals for their feasting and tippling.[6]

The interrogation was not an entirely peaceful affair. The Anabaptists were overbearing in their egalitarian insistence on addressing the
learned theologians as *du*. They accused them of being executioners;
such persons could not possibly be in favor with God. The examiners

---

[1] *CR*, II, 1000–01.

[2] Wappler, *Thüringen*, p. 150, and sources p. 417. Hege, *ME*, III, 728ff. regards the whole
group as nonresistant Anabaptists. A nonresistant Anabaptist who quoted the Ball jingle
in 1535 was certainly begging to be misunderstood. The three steadfast women examined later
at the Leuchtenburg used their argument that only God should be Lord to exclude any
political lord whatsoever. Wappler, *Thüringen*, p. 147.

[3] *Ibid.*, pp. 143 and 400.

[4] *CR*, II, 1001–02.

[5] Letter to Elector John Frederick, January 19, 1536, *CR*, III, 16.

[6] *CR*, II, 1002.

remonstrated and insisted the entire affair was being conducted in a friendly Christian manner. They warned the Anabaptists that their rudeness would be properly dealt with by the magistrates. Whereupon the Anabaptists accused them of washing their hands like Pilate.[1] Melanchthon declared that, despite his patience, they were full of hatred and wrath.[2] He reported to Luther that he had refuted them and thereby exposed their crassness.[3]

Melanchthon was called to help interrogate four of the captured Anabaptists, all women,[4] plus two other men previously captured, all at the Leuchtenburg. This interrogation took place on January 13, 1536, in company with Anton Musa of Jena, the pastor of Kahla, and the bailiff. One of the four women agreed to recant without much discussion. She said that her mother had forced her to become an Anabaptist against her own will,[5] and that she had had her newborn child baptized recently at Halberstadt.[6] Melanchthon dismissed her as completely ignorant and childish.[7] The other three remained steadfast in their opinions despite Melanchthon's attempts to show them their errors from Scripture. They were interrogated on infant baptism, civil authority, marriage, and community of goods.[8]

The two men interrogated were Hans Schleier and Klaus Heiligenstedt, both arrested around April, 1535, as suspected Anabaptists. Schleier had refused to have his children baptized because he objected to the wanton living of his parish priest. If this was not enough to make him an Anabaptist suspect, he was also accused of sympathy for Thomas Müntzer. This latter charge was unjust in view of Schleier's heated dispute with Müntzer, in which the followers of Müntzer almost killed Schleier.[9] Schleier answered all of Melanchthon's questions satisfactorily. Heiligenstedt was not very responsive, not because he was a stubborn Anabaptist, but because he was too ignorant. It is clear from the interrogation that Schleier had been influenced by Anabaptism. But both he and his comrade said they were not Anabaptists.[10] Melanch-

---

[1] *Ibid.*, p. 998.
[2] Melanchthon's report of the interrogation, *ibid.*, p. 1004.
[3] Letter to Luther, December 6, 1535, *ibid.*, p. 1006.
[4] The fifth, Peissker's daughter Margarete, recanted. Wappler, *Thüringen*, pp. 143–44.
[5] Report to Elector John F., January 19, 1536, *CR*, III, 20.
[6] Wappler, *Thüringen*, pp. 146 and 420.
[7] Report to Elector John F., January 19, 1536, *CR*, III, 20.
[8] Letter of Musa to Stephen Roth, Townclerk of Zwickau, January 16, 1536, *CR*, III, 12–14.
[9] Wappler, *Thüringen*, p. 145.
[10] *Ibid.*, pp. 145–46; *CR*, III, 18–20.

thon recommended that Schleier be released, and cautioned the Elector against doing anything with Heiligenstedt since he was really a subject of Duke George.[1]

On the following day Melanchthon helped interrogate the three men at Kahla. He discovered no new ideas. None of these was a leader in any sense. One was new in the Anabaptist faith, and came from a region where the true faith was not preached. He was never rebaptized, and was willing to recant. Another had left his wife and taken a new Anabaptist wife. Melanchthon considered him stubborn, and recommended punishment, both for his Anabaptism and his adultery. The third, also new in the faith, with a pregnant wife and small children, Melanchthon had hopes of persuading. Not that Melanchthon could do it by interrogation; the man remained steadfast. But Melanchthon suggested that the example of others being executed might sway him. Further, he suggested Pastor Johann von Uhlstädt be placed with him in jail to instruct him. Von Uhlstädt had been incarcerated for rape, had proved very amenable to correction, and might be helpful in turning the Anabaptist from his errors.[2]

Melanchthon was profoundly impressed by his contacts with these Anabaptists. He recommended that the stubborn be executed; he meant particularly the three men at Jena. He thought that the example of their execution would so influence the others that they might be willing to acknowledge error and receive instruction.[3] In this he was not wrong.[4] But his alarm was such that he urged the Elector to issue a

---

[1] *CR*, III, 15.

[2] *Ibid.*, pp. 15-16.

[3] *Ibid.*, p. 16.

[4] The three men Kraut, Moller, and Peissker, were heard in court by the jurists from the university on January 25, 1536. Their verdict was death by the sword on the following counts:

    a. They had been rebaptized, despite the Imperial and Electoral Saxon mandates.

    b. They wished to spread their ungodly and revolutionary ideas.

    c. They met secretly, despite the Electoral mandate.

    d. They refused to recant.

    e. Kraut rebaptized others.

    f. Kraut participated in the Battle of Frankenhausen.

(Urteilsspruch der Richter und Schöppen zu Jena, January 26, 1536. Printed in Wappler, *Thüringen*, p. 410.) The sentence was carried out the same day. The three men were courageous as they laid their heads, of their own accord, on the block. Because this kind of courage always made a deep impression on the people, it elicited from Melanchthon a stern warning not to be deceived by a show of faith and courage at their deaths by the Anabaptists. (*CR*, III, 34.) The fourth man at Jena, Petzsch, denied any connection with Anabaptism. He escaped from prison the day before the execution of the other three. Three of the men at Neustadt an der Orla eventually publicly confessed their errors. The fourth, Heinrich Moller, brother to Jobst at Jena, remained steadfast and was executed. (Wappler, *Thüringen*, pp. 151-52.) All of the other prisoners eventually recanted. (Wappler, *Die Stellung Kursachsens*, p. 56.)

mandate against the sect, which mandate would display the infamous, radical teachings of the Anabaptists.[1]

The Elector responded favorably to Melanchthon's suggestion. He asked Melanchthon to draw up such a mandate.[2] Melanchthon drafted a preliminary sketch in February.[3] On April 10, 1536, the mandate appeared. It was followed by Melanchthon's *Verlegung etlicher vnchristlicher Artickel welche die Widerteuffer furgeben*.[4] The *Verlegung* was to be read, together with the mandate, every third Sunday from each pulpit in the Electoral lands.[5]

Elector John's earlier mandates served as models for the mandate of 1536. Their prohibitions were repeated: no one outside the ordained office could preach, nor could anyone house or protect the secret preachers of the Anabaptists. No rebaptism was permitted. The punishment stipulations followed the imperial mandate, to which reference was made, more than the 1527 and 1528 Electoral Saxon predecessors; the death penalty was prescribed.

The mandate listed the prevalent beliefs of the Anabaptists as follows:

(1) Christians could not and should not hold government office.

(2) Christians should serve in no other capacity except as servants of the gospel.

(3) Christians were forbidden to swear oaths.

(4) Christians should practice community of goods; they should not own private property.

(5) An Anabaptist should leave his non-Anabaptist spouse.[6]
These five errors were standard from this time on for Melanchthon's characterization of Anabaptism. He added three errors on the issue of baptism:

(1) Infant baptism was not right.

(2) Infants had no sin; original sin and natural weakness of the flesh were not sin.

(3) That alone was sin which a man of his own free will committed.[7]
From his contacts with Anabaptism, personal or secondary, Melanchthon culled these points as the most dangerous and/or most characteristic of Anabaptism.

[1] *CR*, III, 17.

[2] *Ibid.*

[3] Printed in *CR*, III, 28–34.

[4] Wittenberg, Georg Rhau. A later edition appeared the same year from the press of Wolffgang Meyerpech in Zwickau.

[5] Wappler, *Die Stellung Kursachsens*, p. 56.

[6] Mandate printed in Wappler, *Inquisition und Ketzerprozesse*, Urkunde 19, pp. 181–83.

[7] *Ibid.*

The *Verlegung* reflected the disgust Melanchthon experienced in his encounter with the Anabaptists at Jena and Kahla, plus his anger at Münster. It is the bitterest, most venomous tract he wrote against the sect. He indulged in frequent bursts of bitter invective and name-calling reminiscent of Luther, except that he was not blessed with the genius of Luther at vulgarity.[1] This was not the calm, unruffled analysis and refutation of Anabaptist doctrine of eight years earlier. He knew much more about the sect, and this knowledge was anything but heartening to a dedicated scholar and servant of the church. It reflected moreover his frustration at dealing with men and women whose very errors became the foci of their attraction, not of course as errors, but rather as examples of the utmost piety and holiness. To this end he directed his pamphlet to those simple-minded souls who could learn through it something of the diabolical, hypocritical character of Anabaptist thought and members, and also of the responsibility of magistrates to severely punish the sectarians.[2]

How did Melanchthon know that the piety of the Anabaptists was hypocrisy? Certainly his experience with Storch, and the recent encounters in Thuringia came to his mind. Here were people who professed an outward holiness and a familiar intercourse with the divine, who were anything but holy and divine. But a more revealing example yet was Münster. In this Westphalian center Anabaptist humility and forebearing love were well advertised at first. They spoke of love and nonresistance. But as soon as they assumed control of the city, robbery, murder, and unchastity replaced their holiness. Whenever Anabaptists of any degree or persuasion were given an opportunity to assume social control, they would display their true colors as the devil's workmen. For they regarded their very unchastity and murder, not as gross sin, but as the purest righteousness and holiness. The power of the devil in these folk was so great that the utmost severity was necessary in the treatment of even the apparently pious among them.[3]

The *Verlegung* was well organized. It does not consist of theological discussion of any length. Rather, it is a masterful outline of errors, together with brief refutations, hardly more than suggestions. Melanchthon stated and refuted each of the errors in his core of five

---

[1] Anabaptist teaching was "vol jrthumb vnd blindheit," or "eigne erfunden lere," or "solch gifftig geschmeis." The Anabaptists were "Manichey," "lügenhafftigen geist," "Falschen Propheten," "Wölfe in Schafskleidern," "der grausamen Teufflischen sect." *Verlegung*, pp. A2r.–A3v.

[2] *Ibid.*, pp. A2v.–A3v.

[3] *Ibid.*, pp. A4v.–Br. Melanchthon reflected here, no doubt, on his dealings with Rothmann.

displayed in the mandate, plus infant baptism. He prefaced his remarks, as in 1528, with the charge that the Anabaptists neglected the central body of Christian truth — righteousness, holiness, and love for one's neighbor — in order to haggle over peripheral matters such as outward ceremonies and the social order.[1]

Melanchthon proceeded to set forth and refute six points of Anabaptist teaching.

(1) Christians should not and could not hold an office which required the use of the sword. Melanchthon declared that there were many righteous, sword-wielding magistrates recounted in the Bible, men such as Abraham, Joseph, David, Daniel, and the centurion in Matt. 8. Moreover John the Baptist told the soldiers to be satisfied with their pay, implying that their office as such was without fault (Luke 3). The Anabaptists' basis for this belief was Paul's admonition that Christians were not to avenge themselves. Melanchthon interpreted Paul to mean that outside of the office of the magistracy all vengeance was forbidden. But magistrates were to serve vengeance for God on the evil and were to protect the good. Moreover God commanded the magistracy to care for widows and orphans; therefore punishment of evildoers by the magistracy was also ordained of God.[2]

(2) Christians should profess no other authority than that of servants of the gospel. Melanchthon protested that absolute obedience to political authority was required both on grounds of conscience (Rom. 13:5) and because the civil office was ordained by God.[3]

(3) Christians were forbidden to swear oaths; oath-swearing was sin. Melanchth n felt that the very structure of civil order and government was secured by the swearing of oaths. Without the civil oath, society would disintegrate into anarchy, since people would have no compulsion to obey the God-ordained authorities in society. Paul himself swore (II Cor. 1:23). In Christ's Sermon on the Mount communication on swearing (Matt. 5:33–37) he intended to declare that man should base his oath on God alone, not on any of God's creatures. His "yea, yea" admonition applied only to one's daily conversation. Melanchthon sanctioned idle swearing no more than did the Anabaptists.[4]

(4) Christians must practice community of goods; no one should possess private property. Melanchthon declared that this kind of

---

[1] *Ibid.*, pp. Bv.–B2r.
[2] *Ibid.*, pp. B3v.–B4v.
[3] *Ibid.*, pp. Cr.–v.
[4] *Ibid.*, pp. C2r.–C3r.

doctrine had a strong appeal for the idle rabble who did not like to work anyway. The civil system was ordained by God; and property was the most important part of that system. To own property was not wrong. Kings and princes had to have property of necessity. The Scriptures called some kings and princes blessed; therefore the possession of property must not be wrong.[1]

(5) That marriage was hypocrisy when one partner was a true Christian and the other was not. The true believer should desert his non-believing spouse. Melanchthon used I Cor. 7:10 to show that Paul expected the Christian to remain with his non-Christian spouse.[2]

(6) The Anabaptists held that infant baptism was wrong. They thereby damned a sizable portion of the human race. If people accepted their doctrine, disorder would follow: two distinct groups of people would live in one place, the baptized and the non-baptized. Melanchthon recounted at some length some of the arguments advanced in his 1528 *Iudicium*; he added no new points of significance.[3]

Melanchthon added a final note of warning on the subtlety of the Anabaptists. They moved among the people in several guises, and it was these appearances that were the most attractive to people – more so than their teachings. They appeared to be humble; or they made a show of great brotherly love through having goods in common; and they always displayed great forbearance and courage in court trials and in executions. Melanchthon warned his readers to judge, not by outward appearances which could deceive, but by the truth of God's Word.[4]

One month after the *Verlegung* and the mandate were published, Melanchthon was drawn again into the role of arbiter on the treatment of Anabaptists. Among the Evangelicals Philip of Hesse stood out against the use of the death penalty for heretics.[5] Time and again his patience with the Anabaptists had been sorely tried, and now it sustained another challenge. Thirty Anabaptists had been surprised at worship near Gemünden on the Wohra. Four of these were leaders who had been expelled repeatedly from Hesse: Georg Schnabel, Peter Lose, Hermann Bastian, and Leonhard Fälber. By terms of his 1531 mandate, Philip should execute at least these four. But Philip hesitated, consulted

---

[1] *Ibid.*, pp. C3r.–C4r.
[2] *Ibid.*, p. C4v.
[3] *Ibid.*, pp. D2r.–E2r.
[4] *Ibid.*, pp. E3v.–E4r.
[5] See Letter to John Frederick, then Duke and not Elector, March 7, 1559, *CR*, IX, 757–58, for an example of his leniency of treatment as over against the Saxon Duke. Essentially he held to death for revolutionaries, but no execution for those who erred in matters of faith only.

his lawyers, and finally turned for advice to theologians and magistrates in other territories. He requested advice from Duke Ulrich of Württemberg, Duke Ernst of Lüneburg, the city councils of Strassburg, Ulm, and Augsburg, and the theologians at Wittenberg and those at Marburg. This request went out on May 28, 1536.[1]

Melanchthon drew up the reply for the Wittenbergers entitled: *Ob christliche Fürsten schuldig sind, der Wiedertäufer unchristliche Sect mit leiblicher Strafe und mit dem Schwert zu wehren?*[2] The tract bore the approving signatures of Luther, Bugenhagen, and Cruciger. The entire treatise has a significance as a declaration of Melanchthon's views on the punishment of Anabaptists only in that his views were set in sharper focus, particularly on a few issues at which he had previously only hinted. It is by itself the clearest single declaration of Melanchthon's views on the subject. At this point it will be necessary to discuss only those matters on which Melanchthon gave more light than in his previous declarations.

Melanchthon made a clear distinction between two kinds of Anabaptist doctrines. Some were revolutionary and seditious. Here he repeated the core of five used in his April works. Obviously the death penalty applied to the upholders of these views.[3] But just as civil authority was obligated to execute revolutionaries, so should it also punish blasphemers with the sword. What then was blasphemy to Melanchthon? It was not merely a denial of articles of Christendom's historic creeds. Rarely outside of Münster did he discover that the Anabaptists even spoke to matters touching the creeds.[4] Melanchthon enlarged blasphemy to include false teaching and incorrect order of worship. Within this category he included some of the usual Anabaptist errors on infant baptism, original sin, and special revelations. He added to these several Münsterite views: Christ's flesh did not come from Mary,[5] and

[1] Hege, "Hesse," *ME*, II, 720; Wappler, *Die Stellung Kursachsens*, p. 58; Hochhuth, *op. cit.*, XXVIII, 557–58.

[2] *CR*, III, 195–201. Published also in *WA*, L, 6–15, and under separate cover (Wittenberg: Klug, 1536; Nürnberg: Hergotin, 1536; Wittenberg, 1548) under the title: *Das Weltliche Oberkeitt den Widertaufferen mit leiblicher Straff zu weren schuldig sey / Etlicher Bedenken zu Wittemberg.* Hochhuth, *op. cit.*, XXVIII, 560–65, prints from a handwritten MS which he declares is the most authoritative version of all. His version has material at the beginning and at the end that the other versions do not have, except for the *WA* which apparently used the same source.

[3] *CR*, III, 196.

[4] This calls into question his view of the relationship between Campanus and the Anabaptists. Campanus did deny the Trinity, and erred on the two natures of Christ. It is significant that at the Jena interrogation of Anabaptists Melanchthon began with questions concerning the Trinity and the two natures of Christ. He discovered nothing amiss.

[5] This idea was not confined to Münsterites of course. Menno Simons and some of the Central German Anabaptists held to it also.

there is no forgiveness of sins after death. For these and other un-mentioned views the Anabaptists were determined to establish a new church, a pure one, and thus to separate themselves from even that church whose doctrine was true. Melanchthon protested against their repetition of the ancient Donatist heresy.[1]

Melanchthon based the death penalty for blasphemers on both Mosaic and Roman law. "He who blasphemes the name of the Lord shall be put to death" (Lev. 24:16).[2] In the Justinian Code he discovered a law, coming from both Honorius and Theodosius, which punished rebaptizers with death.[3] It was in this context that he discussed briefly the similarities between the Donatists and the Anabaptists. The Donatists were guilty also of rebaptism, and of separating from a church whose doctrine was beyond reproach, because they wanted a church that was pure. The Anabaptists maintained that they could not endure the established church because of the immoral lives of its priests, so Melanchthon learned.[4] Since the erection of a separatist church was against the will of God, the civil authority was responsible to punish such an attempt with death. Melanchthon proceeded to lay down with clarity the functions of government.

Against those who would have it that political authority was confined to the regulation of the political-social order, Melanchthon argued that indeed its first responsibility was to promote and further the honor and praise of God, whose corollary, equally valid, was to punish blasphemy and idolatry. Civil government did not exist only for the political well-being of its subjects, but primarily for the honor and glory of God. "For rulers are not a terror to good conduct, but to bad.

[1] *CR*, III, 198–200.
[2] *Ibid.*, p. 198.
[3] *Ibid.*, p. 199. Honorius reversed the practice, stemming from Constantine's later days, of allowing heretics – notably the Donatists – to exist unmolested. Constantine had tried persecution, but the sect continued to flourish and he abandoned the effort. In 398 Honorius repealed the legislation (from Julian) allowing Donatists the right of assembly. In 405 he declared them to be heretics, confiscated their places of assembly, excluded them from testamentary rights, and imposed fines on them. (Clyde Pharr, trans. and ed., *The Theodosian Code and Novels* [Princeton: Princeton University Press, 1952], Book XVI, Title VI, p. 464.) Augustine approved of this. In 410 Honorius passed the death sentence for their "criminal audacity in meeting in public." In 413 he and Theodosius: Anyone who baptizes someone the second time, he together with him who induced him to do this shall be condemned to death. (Samuel Scott, trans. and ed., *The Civil Code* [Cincinnati: Central Trust, 1932], XII, 72.) Finally in 415 Honorius threatened with death all those who dared celebrate their religious rites. (William K. Boyd, *The Ecclesiastical Edicts of the Theodosian Code* ["Studies in History, Economics, and Public Law," edited by the political science faculty of Columbia University, Vol. XXIV, Nr. 2 (New York, 1905)], p. 55.) Notice the parallel in increasing severity of punishment to the mandates of Electoral Saxony.
[4] *CR*, III, 198–99.

Would you have no fear of him who is in authority? Then do what is good, and you will receive his approval" (Rom. 13:3). This was Melanchthon's Scriptural basis for the assertion on the function of government.[1] In this connection Melanchthon's interpretation of the parable of the tares is interesting. Melanchthon used it, not to argue against the physical punishment of heretics at all, but to point up the difference between the civil and the ecclesiastical offices. "Let both grow" was addressed to the ecclesiastics; they were never to use bodily punishment in the exercise of their office.[2]

Melanchthon recognized two protests of the Anabaptists, both of which he dismissed. They insisted, on the one hand, that their teaching was not detrimental to the civil order. Melanchthon countered that indeed it was destructive; if everyone adhered to it, the oath as the basis for social order and private property would both be gone. Once Anabaptists gained control they destroyed the civil order.[3] Secondly, one should not employ political power to enforce matters of faith. This of course was a protest raised not only by the Anabaptists, but also by Philip of Hesse. Melanchthon's entire tract was designed to refute this view. He wrote that civil authority did not punish because of the intent of the heart, but because of the promulgation and spread of false teaching. The Anabaptist was not punished for his conviction that a particular doctrine was true when it was actually an error. Punishment came for the public proclamation and spread of the false doctrine, for the distinctive act of blasphemy.[4]

Of all the replies which Philip received, the ones from the Lutherans were the most severe.[5] In this instance he did not follow their counsel. The Anabaptists were retained in prison, but they were not closely guarded, for some of them enlarged the hole through which their food was passed to them to the point where it was possible to escape. They roamed about the countryside and continued their preaching and baptizing, but returned individually to the prison at various times, this for upwards of a year before it was discovered. Philip still employed peaceful measures; he sent theologians from Marburg University to try to convert these prisoners. A final discussion with them, led by Martin

[1] *Ibid.*
[2] *Ibid.*, p. 199. See Roland Bainton, "The Parable of the Tares as the Proof Text for Religious Liberty to the End of the Sixteenth Century," *Church History*, I (1932), 67–99.
[3] *CR*, III, 196–97.
[4] *Ibid.*, p. 197.
[5] Bainton, *Here I Stand*, p. 377. See also Melanchthon letter to Brenz, December 6, 1536, *CR*, III, 201–02, in which he declared that the opinion of the Wittenbergers coincided with that of others.

Bucer on the Evangelical side, was successful in bringing some of them back to the established church, though not without certain stipulations by the Anabaptists. The entire proceedings lasted for more than two years.[1]

The Schnabel-Tasch group in Hesse brought Anabaptism to the attention of Melanchthon in still another connection. A letter from Tasch was discovered among the prisoners in 1538. Tasch wrote of the movement in England and of his desire to visit the brethren there. The Landgrave informed the Saxon Elector, and together they decided the matter was grave enough to warrant a warning to Henry VIII. Melanchthon accordingly was asked to draft a letter to the king explaining the Anabaptist movement to him. After an exchange with Philip's Chancellor Feige, in which the latter made certain alterations, the letter was dispatched to Henry.[2] Henry had been aware of the movement, but the letter apparently added a note of urgency to his subsequent measures against the sect.[3]

In an earlier letter to Henry, Melanchthon had briefly depicted the cultural barbarity of the Anabaptists. Their rejection of the ancients and their general illiteracy constituted a blow to good theology, not to mention good letters.[4] In 1535 Melanchthon did not know of an Anabaptist threat to England. By 1538 he considered the danger to Henry's land very real indeed. He warned Henry of their clandestine character, and of their hypocritically pious appearance. Their doctrines were the usual ones: denial of infant baptism and introduction of rebaptism, community of goods, no Christian in the position of magistrate, no oaths for Christians – in short, all that which tended toward the destruction of civil order. They added their peculiar ideas on illumination of the Word; true exegesis was not enough for them. Melanchthon listed foremost the Anabaptist errors which touched the political order. He added a special note on their disgraceful marriage practices which must have made Henry's ears tingle: they practiced polygamy and permitted divorce without legal process or grounds. Münster was the culmination of this barbaric superstititon. Melanchthon warned Henry of the conditions which gave rise to the sect. The Evangelicals had learned that Anabaptism spread wherever the pure doctrine was not properly preached.[5]

[1] Hege, "Hesse," *ME*, II, 720–24. See above, pp. 72–73.
[2] Hege, "Hesse," *ME*, II, 722.
[3] Irvin Horst, "England," *ME*, II, 216.
[4] Letter to Henry VIII, August, 1535, *CR*, II, 926.
[5] Letter to Henry VIII, September 1, 1538 (first draft), *CR*, III, 577–80.

Melanchthon's contacts with Anabaptists, or judgments concerning them, during the next several decades were very few in number. He together with Luther apparently tried to argue an Anabaptist back into the fold sometime before 1541.[1] In 1551 he wrote a very brief argument for infant baptism, together with a rebuttal of the Anabaptist position, with nothing new in either instance.[2] Finally in 1557 he again took up his pen in behalf of orthodoxy.[3]

The occasion for the declaration against Anabaptism was the discussion between Catholics and Protestants at Worms. The Augsburg Peace of 1555 was not intended as a final solution to the religious problem of Germany. By 1557 both sides agreed to meet at Worms to discuss their points of disagreement in doctrine and practice. The Catholics had the advantage in that the Protestants were split. The genesiolutherans were more concerned about condemning heresy within the Protestant camp than with serious discussions with the Catholics. Discussion opened on September 11, and on the first of October the stricter Lutherans left Worms in protest. Subsequent discussion between the Protestants who remained and the Catholics were completely unsuccessful in repairing the breach. By the end of November both parties were willing to disband and leave the unsolved problems for the next Diet. It was in this context that Melanchthon, together with five other Lutherans,[4] composed the *Prozess*, a set of instructions on how to recognize the Anabaptists from their doctrine and how to treat them.[5]

The pamphlet brought nothing new in the matter of punishment; both the seditious and the blasphemous were to be killed.[6] But Melanchthon laid out the procedure to be followed in interrogating such

[1] Wappler, *Thüringen*, pp. 154–55 and 468.
[2] *De baptismo infantum: et an recipiendi sint Anabaptistae? CR*, VII, 885–86.
[3] *Prozess wie es soll gehalten werden mit den Widertäuffern* (Wormbs: Gebrüder Köpflein, 1557). Printed in G. Bossert, *Quellen zur Geschichte der Wiedertäufer* (Württemberg) (Leipzig: Heinsius Nachfolger, 1930), I, 161–67. Melanchthon was the first of six to sign it. His previous characterizations of Anabaptism so predominate in the booklet that it is only reasonable to call it essentially his work.
[4] Brenz, Pistorius, Andreä, Karg, and Rungius.
[5] G. Kawerau, *Realencyklopädie für protestantische Theologie und Kirche*, ed. Hauck, XXI (3d ed.; Leipzig: Hinrichs, 1908), 492–96. Christian Hege thinks that the *Prozess* was related to the Pfeddersheim *Gespräch* of 1557 between Reformed and Anabaptists. The content of the *Prozess* is much more similar to Melanchthon's previous pamphlets against the Anabaptists than it is to the mandate of Elector Otto Heinrich which was issued after the debate. C. Hege, *Die Täufer in der Kurpfalz* (Frankfurt am Main: Hermann Minjon, 1908), p. 93, n. 2.
[6] In a memo of 1559, *De officiis Magistratus, CR*, IX, 1002–04, which is Melanchthon's final statement on the subject of Anabaptism, Melanchthon retained this position. He speaks more specifically to the execution of Servetus – and his kind, such an Campanus – at Geneva. Melanchthon believed that antitrinitarians should be put to death. But in this instance he made an appeal to a new source of authority: natural law.

persons with much more care and exactitude than he had previously done. He cautioned against haste – the interrogators should take several weeks to instruct the prisoner, and if he would not recant, they should give him two or three years to think it over on the grounds that he was irrational. Melanchthon could speak from the experience of the courts and bailiffs of both Saxony and Hesse on this point. Patience in treatment of these persons was not infrequently rewarded with success.[1]

The seditious errors listed were the same as those in the 1536 mandate, except that Melanchthon added their prohibition of suits at law. Four new errors were added to Melanchthon's list of blasphemous teachings. He thereby covered a broader segment of the Reformation radicals, and included ideas which could well have come to Melanchthon from others of the theologians assembled at Worms. The additional errors were:

(1) In and since Christ there was and had been no original sin.

(2) Rejection of the Trinity.

(3) Man was justified through rebaptism, suffering, his works, and special revelations.

(4) A reborn Christian could not sin; whatever he did was no longer sin for him.

These erroneous teachings, together with the usual points on baptism and special revelations, were damned by the ecclesiastics.[2]

There were two concluding notes in the treatise worthy of mention. The document singled out the Hutterites with their community of goods for special condemnation. A final word was issued to rulers to beware lest their territories should become especial recruiting grounds for Anabaptism on account of the absence of the true doctrine. Melanchthon believed, as he wrote to Henry VIII, that the prevalence of the heresy was directly proportional to the quality and amount of true Christian doctrine otherwise promulgated in a given terriroty.[3]

---

[1] Bossert, *op. cit.*, I, 162–66.

[2] *Ibid.*, p. 163.

[3] *Ibid.*, p. 167. See the Hutterite rebuttal of the *Prozess*, W. Wiswedel and R. Friedmann, "The Anabaptists Answer Melanchthon," *MQR*, XXIX (1955), 212–31.

CHAPTER VI

MENIUS AND THE ANABAPTISTS

Among the Reformers attached in spirit to the Wittenberg circle Justus Menius stands as the leading polemicist against the Anabaptists. Menius knew whereof he wrote. He had more contacts with the Anabaptists than did any of the Lutheran opponents of the radicals in Central Germany.[1] His position as superintendent at Eisenach after 1529 brought him into the heart of West Thuringian Anabaptist territory. He knew Rink, though how well it is impossible to determine.

Menius was born Jodocus Menig in 1499 in Fulda. Of his parentage little is known except that they were poor. His early precocity destined him for an academic career. He attended the school at Fulda where humanist Crotus Rubianus was a teacher. In 1514 he matriculated at Erfurt, where he earned the B.A. in 1515 and the M.A. in 1516. Here he joined the humanist circle led by Mutianus Rufus, which circle participated with enthusiasm in the current struggle between Reuchlin and the Cologne theologians. Menius' anti-scholastic appetite was whetted. By the spring of 1519 he moved to the University of Wittenberg, chiefly to study with Melanchthon. The two soon became fast friends; Menius even lived with Melanchthon in Wittenberg. He also became personally acquainted with Luther. By 1523 he was a humanist-theologian with a passion for the Evangelical doctrine. As such he sought and obtained a pastorate, the first one at Mühlberg between Erfurt and Gotha. Proximity to the humanist band at Erfurt, now led by Eoban Hessus, and to Mutianus at Gotha, was pleasant enough. But Menius did not receive enough income from his village vicarage, especially since he had married. Consequently he laid down his charge and removed to Erfurt where he expected to live off his income as

---

[1] In 1530 he declared he knew of at least 30 cases, *Der Widdertauffer Lere vnd Geheimnis*, p. F4r.; and by 1544 the number had grown to approximately 100, *Von dem Geist der Widerteuffer*, p. H4r.

private tutor to sons of nobles. He entered an Erfurt much disturbed
by riots which were the result of over-zealous Reformation partisans
and from the social unrest of the peasants. The town council turned to
him to fill the pastorate of the St. Thomas Church. His Erfurt days
were troubled. The chief opposition to Menius came from a growing
body of Catholic-minded people whose position was strengthened by
the excesses which followed in the wake of Reformation teaching. By
1528 Menius' position was untenable. Luther advised him to leave, and
his good friend Myconius promised him help in moving. So Menius left
Erfurt during Lent, 1528, and repaired to Gotha where Myconius gave
him material assistance. Again he resigned himself to life as a tutor,
though he kept a sharp eye out for a prospective pastorate. Melanchthon took both Menius and Myconius, along with others, on the
church visitation in West Thuringia from mid-October of that year
to January of 1529. Then late in 1529 he accompanied Melanchthon
and Luther to the Marburg Colloquy as an observer. After his return
he was appointed superintendent at Eisenach. This post he retained
until one year before his death in 1558. Although he succeeded
Myconius as superintendent at Gotha after the latter's death in 1546,
and although he spent some years after 1542 in Mühlhausen in an
effort to introduce and confirm the Evangelical teaching there, his
greatest effort was expended in the exercise of his office in and around
Eisenach. His influence beyond the city limits was great, so that he
can be called with justice the Reformer of Thuringia.[1] The closing
years of his life were marred by the bitterness of conflict with Amsdorf
and Flacius Illyricus. He was grievously slandered, and finally left his
Gotha and Eisenach posts for Leipzig in January, 1557. He died in
Leipzig on August 11, 1558.[2]

Menius accepted the Reformation teaching with enthusiasm. For
years on end God's truth had slumbered beneath the oppressive arm
of Rome. In recent years, wrote Menius in 1530, God in his infinite
mercy allowed the light to break forth in all its power and splendor.
But just as the gospel appeared with freshness and vigor, so also Satan
returned to the fray in various forms with renewed energy. Menius
accepted fully Luther's interpretation of the papacy as antichrist. It
was pre-eminently an institution which exalted itself above God, yet
sat in the very temple of God himself pretending to be God (II Thes.

[1] So Gustav L. Schmidt, *Justus Menius*. For this brief biographical sketch I have used
Schmidt, Vol. I, Books I and II, *passim*.
[2] *Ibid.*, Vol. II, principally in Book IV.

2:4). The raging of Rome against Luther was one manifestation of the devil at work. Satan appeared also in the Turks who threatened to wreak imminent destruction on Christian Europe. The Turks were a gang of godless murderers. A third manifestation of Satan could be found in the viperous gangs of slanderers of God's truth who appeared in the wake of the Evangelical teaching. Menius believed this final manifestation to be the worst one. Murder was bad enough, of course; but the dissemination of false doctrine was infinitely worse. Here souls were murdered rather than bodies. Moreover it required no theological mind to discern Satan in the Turks; but the false teachers displayed the craftiness of their master by their artistry in dissimulation. Their appearance was one of Christian sanctity and holiness. They did their poisonous work in the name of Christ himself.[1] This third manifestation was of course Anabaptism. Menius considered the terms Anabaptist and devil to be synonymous.[2]

The appearance of antichrist, the freeing of the gospel, and the renewal of Satan's attacks spelled the end-times to Menius. He was confirmed in his conviction by mysterious portents in the heavens. From Denmark to Italy, from Hungary to France, all Europe recognized and wondered at the strange movements of the stars. Few there were who could divine their meaning. Menius was convinced that the unusual movements meant the end was approaching. He praised the Lord for releasing the gospel light to bring people from their darkness before the impending Judgment Day.[3]

Menius wrote his first book against the Anabaptists in 1530 in order to reveal the truth about their pious fraud. It was entitled "The Doctrine and Secret of the Anabaptists refuted from Holy Scripture." He intended his work to serve as an aid in recognizing and rejecting error in doctrine.[4] There were other immediate reasons for the work. A group of Anabaptists who had been previously apprehended and released upon recantation were again captured near the monastery Reinhardsbrunn south of Gotha. Six of the nine would not recant a second time and were consequently executed in January, 1530. Some people thought the penalty too severe for individuals who were not guilty of crimes against society, Anabaptists who were not political

---

[1] Justus Menius, *Der Widdertauffer Lere vnd Geheimnis/ aus heiliger Schrifft widderlegt* (Wittemberg: N. Schirlentz, 1530), pp. B2v.–B3r.; Cr.–Cv.; C4r.–C4v.
[2] *Ibid.*, p. A6r.
[3] *Ibid.*, pp. Br.–B3v.
[4] *Ibid.*, p. Dr.

rebels.[1] Menius felt compelled to justify the act. His line of argument was not directed so much toward a clarification of magisterial responsibility in instances where erroneous doctrine was accepted and taught. Rather he concentrated on describing Anabaptist errors and refuting them. A parallel motive was that of proving that the Anabaptists were the devil's angels. Menius pursued these purposes in a style characterized by such prolixity that Melanchthon for one feared that the book would not be purchased and read.[2] Menius dedicated the book to Landgrave Philip of Hesse presumably because the latter did not share the Saxons' conviction that execution of Anabaptists was necessary for the well-being of the church and society.

The most serious error of the Anabaptists was soteriological. They challenged the doctrine of salvation by faith alone with their insistence that one's own works played a decisive role in salvation. One must obey the law, and one must also experience personally the intense suffering of Christ in order to obtain salvation.[3] Menius did not expand and clarify his configuration of Anabaptist doctrine. He set himself rather to the delineation of the true doctrine of salvation.

Men have everywhere and always agreed that salvation belongs to him who is righteous and pious. Both Scripture and reason testify to this. Man's problem is therefore how to become righteous and pious. And here men have never achieved agreement. They have always sought to devise their own methods. The law was therefore given by God as a measure for man to use in reckoning his righteousness, by which it is clear to everyone that no matter how righteous and good a man may appear to be from his conduct before men, his innermost motives cannot measure up to the demands of the law. Menius believed that pure reason by itself is forced to admit that the standard of righteousness portrayed in the law is the highest possible. Both revelation and reason therefore testify to the effectiveness and general excellence of the law as a standard. But reason must also confess the inability of any man to fulfil the requirements of the law. The law above all does not teach us how to fulfil its demands. Another kind of source must be found. God sent his Son, Jesus Christ, to meet this

---

[1] See above, pp. 50–51. Also Christian Hege, "Kolb, Andreas," *ME*, III, 214–15, and Schmidt, *op. cit.*, I, 148–49. Originally Myconius was to have helped in the work. For unexplained reasons he did not. At least the book appeared as the work of Menius alone. See Luther's letter to Menius and Myconius, February, 1530, *WB*, V, 244. Also Melanchthon letter to Myconius, February, 1530, *CR*, II, 17.

[2] Schmidt, *op. cit.*, I, 150.

[3] Menius, *Der Widdertauffer*, pp. H3r.–H4r.

extremity of man. Christ took upon himself the sins of man and by his sinless life and death enabled man to stand righteous before God. The Holy Spirit comes to the believer to bring the release from guilt and punishment and to give assurance of eternal life. Faith is, so to speak, both necessity and limitation. The gracious work of Christ is valid for him who has faith, but it is not valid for the unbeliever. Menius did not develop further the meaning and conditions of faith.[1]

Menius' principal dissatisfaction with Anabaptist soteriology derived from their union of faith and works as necessary for salvation. He was stung by their accusations that the Lutheran faith was dead because it did not issue in good fruit. He heard the charge from Rink in 1525 when the latter was a Müntzerite. Menius interpreted Rink to mean that the Lutherans believed salvation to be a forensic act unrelated to man's experience of Christ. One had only to confess ritually that he had faith and God was forced to save him, irrespective of the true condition of the heart with respect to faith or its absence.[2] Menius considered faith and works to be mutually exclusive, because naturally antagonistic, as means of salvation. He did not mean that one should never do good works. But to rely even to the slightest degree on one's own works as a means of salvation was to buy or earn that which God intended to be given freely. The Anabaptist argument on the necessity for suffering was only another facet of the same argument: man's attempt to earn salvation by his own power. Menius did not deny the fact of their suffering. But it was wrong to relate that suffering to salvation, especially because it was unnecessary. The Anabaptists suffered because of their improper, indeed diabolical, behavior; it was just and righteous to cause them to suffer.[3]

If it was wrong to consider good works as part and parcel of salvation, what place should they occupy in the life of the Christian? Menius did not answer this question directly in his 1530 book. He did devote a number of pages to a description and characterization of Anabaptist works. They put on the most effective possible display of holiness and Christian love. They greeted each other, and strangers, in the name of God's peace. They were diligent in visiting strangers with whom they read Scripture and prayed. They practiced Christian love in their sharing of material goods with one another, up to the point of community of goods. Their teaching emphasized an abstinence from evil for

---

[1] *Ibid.*, pp. H4v.–J4r.
[2] *Ibid.*, p. H4r.
[3] *Ibid.*, pp. Kv.–K3r.

the Christian. A strong concept of the equality of all men before God permeated their doctrine. Menius did not deny the fact of a righteous appearance in the lives of these Anabaptists. But it was only appearance, and as such sheer hypocrisy. He was irate at the construction the Anabaptists put on the relation of faith and works; they judged a man's faith by the presence or absence of spiritual works in his life. They reversed the true perspective. One's works were to be judged by the truth or falsity of his doctrine, of his religious ideas which touched salvation. Since the Anabaptists erred so grievously in doctrine, their works could be accounted in no wise as the product of a true faith. They were rather the result of a calculated attempt to mislead and blind the common people with respect to true Christian doctrine. Menius was especially irked that these devils urged their hearers to stay away from the Evangelical church. The strategy of the devil could be plainly seen here. Satan was not foolish enough to try to improve the moral condition of the world; he was trying to keep people from hearing the truth.[1]

How then was salvation mediated to man? Menius believed that God's grace was extended through both the ministry of the Word and the administration of the sacraments. All the salvation promised to man in the gospels is given him both in the spoken word and in baptism and the Lord's Supper. The Anabaptists were such an abomination to Menius because they denied this. They restricted the application of baptism to those who claimed to have understood and believed the gospel, i.e., to adult believers. Although Menius believed the Anabaptists made baptism the cardinal issue in this catalogue of doctrinal deviations, he refused to give it first place because of its natural subordination to the doctrine of *sola fide;* it was only a segment of the salvation process.[2] But if he did not give the issue first place, he devoted more pages to the refutation of their rejection of infant baptism than to any other issue.

Menius spoke to four successive arguments of the Anabaptists on baptism. In the first place they declared that Scripture nowhere commanded the baptism of infants. They were not willing to build on a tradition. A tradition of centuries was false if it could not be substantiated by Scripture. Moreover, what the Scriptures did not command was absolutely forbidden by God. Menius protested vigorously this twisting of exegetical principles. Scripture nowhere com-

---

[1] *Ibid.*, pp. Dv.–D2r.; E3v.–F2v.
[2] *Ibid.*, pp. K4v.–L2r.

manded specifically adult baptism. Circumcision was not commanded with the New Covenant, yet it was also not forbidden. God nowhere forbad baptism of infants.[1]

The Anabaptists derived their argument from a literalistic rendition of the Great Commission. Christ commissioned the disciples to a ministry of teaching and baptism: "Go ye therefore, and teach all nations, baptizing them in the name of the Father, of the Son, and of the Holy Ghost" (Matt. 28:19). The injunction to teach preceded the command to baptize; it was necessary to observe the correct sequence in the process. Since infants could never understand instruction they should not be baptized. Menius laid the origin of this kind of literalism to Carlstadt. He considered it fantastic, and as usual diabolical. Applied to the events of the Last Supper, it would mean that only after the disciples had eaten the bread, as Christ first commanded, did Christ get around to declaring: "This is my Body." As there was no bread to point to by that time, he had to point to himself. Or, the baptismal formula in the name of the Father, Son, and Holy Spirit would by such literalism imply a subordination of Son to Father and Holy Spirit to both. Menius grew sarcastic.[2]

Menius failed to discuss thoroughly the differences between his and the Anabaptists' concept of the act of baptism itself. He postulated it as one of several media by which the grace of God is given to man. To him this was a fact which did not require proof; he was certain no one could deny it. The Holy Spirit worked "through and under" this medium of grace, and man could with justification build his faith upon it.[3]

He disagreed with the Anabaptist interpretation of Matthew 28:19. Whereas they emphasized the sequence of events, he emphasized the extension of both Word and act to *all* people. No one could deny that "all" must necessarily include infants. If the Anabaptists could insist that the Lutherans did not have the Spirit properly to understand the Scripture,[4] Menius could call his interpretation of Scripture that of the Lord himself.[5] Neither side could conceive of differences of interpretation being honest.

Another disagreement that was not faced squarely by either side was the relation between Old and New Testaments. Both Menius and

---

[1] *Ibid.*, pp. L2v.–L3r.
[2] *Ibid.*, pp. L4r.–Mv.
[3] *Ibid.*, p. M3v.
[4] Jena trial of Anabaptists under Melanchthon, see above, p. 165.
[5] Menius, *Der Widdertauffer*, p. M4v.

the Anabaptists made a distinction between the two, and both precisely on the issue of outward ceremonies. Menius considered New Testament sacraments of infinitely greater value than the Old Testament ceremonies because of the atoning work of Christ. The New Testament sacrament bore a greater degree of God's grace. But there was no change in the recipients of the ceremonies; in both Old and New Testaments the act was designated for all people. The Anabaptists perceived a change in method of God's dispensing his grace. Whereas it was necessary for man's salvation, so to speak, in the Old Testament to perform certain acts, under the New Testament grace was given freely on the basis of individual faith apart from any ceremony. The abandonment of the ceremony for the dispensation of grace they considered a move in the right direction.[1]

Menius closed the first section with an insistence on the absolute necessity of the act itself for the soul's salvation. It would not do to argue that water itself saved no one. Salvation was bound to the Word which accompanied the water. Christ did bind the Word to the water, and there could be no point in rejecting the physical act on grounds of reason. The things of God were not comprehensible to reason.[2]

In the second place the Anabaptists argued from Mark 16:16 that the performance of baptism was contingent on the existence of faith in the candidate. "He that believeth and is baptized shall be saved." Menius objected most emphatically to the subjective construction of the Anabaptists. He admitted that the Mark passage, in contrast to the one in Matthew, spoke to the question of reception of baptism rather than to its administration. But the Anabaptists erred in ascribing too little to the act of baptism, and in making it a sign of the wrong thing. They considered it a sign of one's outward walk before men as a Christian. Menius asserted that it was a sign and assurance to one's conscience that God's promise of salvation was true. But it was more than a mere sign. Not only did God promise salvation; he conferred it in the act of baptism itself. Thus baptism as sign did not belong to a personal experience of faith, but to God's Word and objective dispensation of grace. Faith had indeed a relation to baptism. But it was the result of baptism, not a prerequisite for baptism.[3]

Menius mustered several arguments to refute the Anabaptists' contention that faith must necessarily precede baptism. In the first

---

[1] *Ibid.*, pp. N2r.–N2v.
[2] *Ibid.*, pp. N3r.–N4v.
[3] *Ibid.*, pp. O3r.–Pv.

place he raised the question of the immediate, not ultimate, origin of
faith. The Anabaptists admitted faith derived from a preaching of the
Word. But they stopped there. Menius believed that faith came also
from the sacraments which God instituted precisely to strengthen and
give substance to man's faith. And to men of old God gave his Word
and faith through other media: dreams, faces, or voices of angels.[1]
Secondly, since faith was ultimately a gift of God, it could be bestowed
as well on infants as on adults. It was foolish to argue that faith was
contingent on reason and therefore not dispensed to infants. Menius
used Luther's argument that reason and faith were diametrically
opposed to each other, but his heart was not in this argument. It
meant of course that the infant, without reason, was a better recipient
of a faith-bestowing baptism than was the adult who possessed reason.[2]

A final argument to refute the Anabaptist belief that faith must
precede baptism came from Christ's pronouncement that the Kingdom
of Heaven belonged to children. The disciples did not want Christ
to be pestered with children, but Christ rebuked them and blessed
the children. Rink had argued that Christ meant that the Kingdom
belonged to people who could become like children in humility and
annihilation of self. Insofar as Christ's words applied to children
directly, they meant that children were included in the Kingdom
despite the absence of infant baptism. Strangely enough Menius did
not counter this with the argument from circumcision: these had been
circumcized presumably, and circumcision under the Old Covenant
was similar to baptism under the New Covenant. Menius resorted
rather to logic in a defensive maneuver. If children did not have faith
as the Anabaptists said, this was tantamount to saying that the
Kingdom belonged to unbelievers. Ridiculous! Fantastic! [3]

The third major argument centered around the issue of original sin.
The Anabaptists put the problem in this manner: it was harmful to
baptize infants for the purpose of removing sin or its guilt because
infants had no sin. They argued that Christ's death removed all guilt
of original sin. Only those evil acts or thoughts which a man committed of his own will could be considered sin. One must understand
the difference between good and evil before he can will to do either.
A child or infant manifestly did not have such understanding.[4]

---

[1] *Ibid.*, pp. P3r.–P3v.
[2] *Ibid.*, p. Qr.
[3] *Ibid.*, pp. Qv.–Q2v.
[4] *Ibid.*, pp. Q3v.–Q4r.

Menius argued that original sin was taken on by man at birth, when man became a human being subject to the frailties and blemishes of human nature. It was a kind of poison which welled up within oneself; it did not come from the outside. It was an instinct. Christ indeed removed it by his vicarious death. But each person must receive that removal individually from Christ, i.e., in baptism. To argue that the death of Christ removed sin from humans without the application of baptism would mean that all people, adult and child alike, within Christendom or in heathen lands, would be without sin. Menius considered such an argument too absurd to be worthy of serious consideration. The removal of original sin was accomplished in the sacrament of baptism. He who later in life really believed that the grace of God had been extended to him in baptism for the removal of sin, to him that forgiveness became a reality. Menius did not say so, but the implication was that for him who did not believe in the efficacy of his baptism as an infant, his sins remained to the damnation of his soul. Thus Menius related the faith of the individual to his own baptism at a point after that baptism had taken place.[1]

Of all of Menius' arguments this was his weakest. He did not understand the Anabaptists' argument on original sin, though he complained, and justly so, that they were not clear enough in their teaching to enable him to grasp firmly their notions on the doctrine of orginal sin. The Anabaptists did not argue that baptism, or even faith itself, removed all sin or all tendency to sin. Indeed, the inclination to do evil remained with the Christian throughout his entire life; it was part of his human nature. The Anabaptist would have asked why, if the validity of baptism was contingent on its acceptance by the person baptized, must the act be performed on the infant who could no more accept it at the time than could an adult Turk who was uninstructed? And why was it necessary to receive the forgiveness earned by Christ personally through a particular act? Such an act constituted a kind of recrucifixion of Christ. Menius argued the necessity for the performance of an act in which forgiveness of sin was mediated on the grounds that otherwise that forgiveness earned by Christ's death would apply to Turks and heathen and Jews. This made the existence of Christendom of no value at all. Forgiveness of sins could occur only within Christendom. Menius begged the question: if Christ died for the sins of all men, how could an act performed by only a segment of mankind determine the validity of that sacrificial

---

[1] *Ibid.*, pp. R3r.–Sv.

death for the forgiveness of sins. Menius replied that Christendom had the Word and sacraments, and without these there was no forgiveness of sins, only damnation.[1]

Against the Anabaptist use of Christ's blessing the children signifying the absence of sin in them, Menius reverted again to the argument from Christendom. Christ intended the blessing of children, and their inclusion in Heaven, only for those born within Christendom. Within Christendom itself, Christ came to heal the sick, not those who were whole. Since the children were brought to Christ the master healer, it was obvious that these brought were sick. Such Christ could heal. Menius meant of course that forgiveness of sins could not apply to the child who had not been brought to Christ in the act of baptism.[2]

The final major argument was that of apostolic practice and tradition. The Anabaptists declared that neither Christ nor the apostles after him had ever baptized infants, and they added John the Baptist to the antipedobaptists for good measure. They meant that since the founders of Christianity did not baptize infants, it was wrong to do so. Menius countered with the demand for Scriptural evidence that Christ and his disciples had not baptized infants. This could never be produced. Surely among the three thousand baptized at Pentecost some were children (Acts 2:41). But even if Christ and the apostles had never baptized infants, it did not follow necessarily that no one else should do so. Christ commanded his followers to teach and baptize everyone, and this included children.[3]

The Anabaptists cited the incident in which Paul rebaptized twelve men of Ephesus whose initial baptism had been that of John the Baptist to show that teaching must precede baptism (Acts 19:1–7). The citation embarrassed Menius for other reasons. He felt more compelled to prove this was not a case of bonafide rebaptism than to prove that teaching need not precede baptism. He declared that since the church fathers did not agree in their interpretation of the passage they could not be heeded at all since what was required at this point was the clearest possible grounds for the issue of baptism. Such grounds could be found in Christ's command to baptize everyone. Menius' private interpretation of the passage was centered around the idea that the twelve were baptized, not on John's teaching, but on his person into a kind of *Bund*. John was famous, and justly so, for

[1] *Ibid.*, pp. S2r.–S2v.
[2] *Ibid.*, pp. R2r.–R2v.
[3] *Ibid.*, pp. S3r.–S3v.

his piety and austerity. These twelve represented, in short, a monasticism of which baptism was the sign. But this was error and no baptism at all. Hence Paul baptized them; he did not rebaptize them. If the twelve had been baptized on John's teaching, Paul would not have found it necessary to baptize them.[1]

A subsidiary argument that the Anabaptists used was that since Christ was not baptized until he was thirty years old, no one should receive the rite until adulthood. Menius was surprisingly mild and concise with this foolish argument. Scripture was not to be handled this way. The Anabaptists made of Christ only an example to be followed with ridiculous detail. Technically they must insist that baptism be performed only at the age of thirty, not twenty-nine or thirty-one.[2]

Having disposed of the Anabaptist rejection of one sacrament in a most detailed fashion, Menius did not consider it necessary to dwell at length on the other sacrament. The third major error of the Anabaptists was found in their attitude toward the sacrament of the altar. Briefly, how did they regard the act?

It was not a sacrament given by God to bestow salvation and the assurance thereof. It was a sign of love, faithfulness, and brotherly unity. As they assembled for the celebration of the bread and cup, their leader preached on brotherly love and mutual aid in material things and in spiritual counsel. They read together the twelfth chapter of Romans and heard exhortations on the general theme of life within the Christian brotherhood. As they ate the bread and drank the wine, they spoke of themselves as the true body of the Lord. Just as many grains made one loaf, so many members made one Body. Before the celebration proper, they exercised their power of excommunication where it was necessary. The communion service became the occasion for an examination of the membership. He who had done anything amiss against the group was required to repent before being allowed at the Lord's Table. They were particularly careful to insist that one who had recanted be reinstated only upon repentance of error.[3]

A second meaning of communion for the Anabaptists was suffering. To drink the cup of the Lord meant to suffer. Whenever discovery and capture threatened them, they celebrated communion as a means of

[1] *Ibid.*, pp. S3v.–Tv.
[2] *Ibid.*, p. T2r.
[3] *Ibid.*, pp. T3v.–T4r.

strengthening each other in the faith before the expected ordeal. As the grape or grain must be crushed before it could become wine or bread, so must the Christian endure physical suffering with Christ in order to come to Christ and salvation. Here was the germ of a martyr theology. Menius' Anabaptist informants apparently did not carry it that far. But their emphasis on suffering within the process of salvation bore overtones of Müntzer's spiritualist soteriology.[1]

Menius considered the emphasis on fellowship in the sacrament a scandalous distortion of its true meaning. It was like a gang of robbers or murderers strengthening each other in their camaraderie as they saw their end approaching. This was blasphemy. He considered the doctrine of the real presence so well established in the writings of others that it did not require an exposition in his work.[2] He contented himself rather with a refutation of some of the Anabaptist arguments against it.

The Anabaptists cited a row of silly rationalistic arguments as to why the real body of Christ could not be in the Lord's Supper. They argued against the ubiquity of Christ. They complained that one could not see or feel the body of Christ, and therefore it was not really present. They even declared that the real presence was impossible because if it were true, Christ would have been completely consumed long before; there would be none of Christ left to eat. All of this Menius styled useless twaddle derived from human reason. Against the Word of God: "This is my Body," it could not possibly stand.[3]

The most trenchant Anabaptist argument derived from their interpretation of John 6:63: "It is the spirit that quickeneth; the flesh profiteth nothing; the words that I speak unto you, they are spirit, and they are life." Immediately after Christ had so deeply offended the Jews with the crassest materialistic interpretation of eating his flesh, he called it a spiritual process, a spiritual eating. Moreover, said the Anabaptists, in the doctrine of the real presence the body of Christ is considered to be physical, as well as spiritual. The physical body of Christ could not be ubiquitous. They considered that Christ's presence in Heaven, at God's right hand, ruled out the existence of a physical-spiritual body of Christ on earth under any circumstances. Menius answered in the first place by accusing the Anabaptists of relying on human reason rather than the omnipotence of God. With God all

[1] *Ibid.*, pp. T4r.–T4v.
[2] *Ibid.*, pp. T4v.–Vr.
[3] *Ibid.*, pp. Vr.–Vv.

things were possible. Secondly, the passage from John 6 was directed entirely to the question of reception of the sacrament, not to its nature and composition. The reception of the sacrament was spiritual indeed. But the nature of it was not exclusively spiritual. The Anabaptists did not place sufficient reliance on the power of the Word which was bound to the sacrament.[1]

A fourth major error of the Anabaptists according to Menius was their denial of the divinity of Christ. He gave no detailed outline of the charge. One is suspicious of its accuracy because insofar as the Central German Anabaptists deviated from orthodox Christology, they erred in the opposite direction; they were docetic.[2] Menius derived their denial of Christ's divinity from their denial of the real presence in the sacrament. Their argument was that since God was omnipotent he could have achieved salvation for mankind through means different from that of sending his divine Son to suffer and to die. Such suffering and death were entirely unnecessary for an omnipotent God. Menius did not devote much effort or space to a refutation of this error because he considered it so far removed from historic Christian thought as to require no rebuttal.[3]

To their fifth major error Menius likewise devoted little space. The Anabaptists were universalists. They believed that ultimately all the damned, including the devil himself, would be saved. Their Scriptural exegesis for this point was strained to say the least. Christ, in speaking of the Judgment, consigned the unrighteous to everlasting fire along with the devil and his angels (Matt. 25:41). In effect this meant a shift in responsibility for their salvation from himself to God, for the everlasting fire to which Christ referred was God himself. Those whom Christ had made righteous by his vicarious death would accompany Christ into eternal bliss. The others would be placed in the hands of the Father who, being omnipotent, could very well help them to salvation. Indeed, his omnipotence was such that it was impossible for him not to succeed in saving everyone assigned to his care. Menius did not consider the error worthy of serious refutation. It was too bad.[4]

The Anabaptists erred not only in Christian doctrine, but also with respect to the civil order. Menius considered the former much more

---

[1] *Ibid.*, pp. V2v.–V4v.
[2] See above, p. 89.
[3] Menius, *Der Widdertauffer*, pp. Xv.–X2v.
[4] *Ibid.*, pp. X4r.–Yr.

important than the latter, since the soul's salvation is of greater moment than purely temporal affairs. He treated Anabaptist errors on the civil order with much less detail than those which touched the salvation process. What were their errors?

In the first place they refused to distinguish between problems of salvation and matters of social and political behavior. They imposed a unity on eternal and temporal concerns where no unity in fact existed, and they claimed to derive this unity from Scripture. For example, an Anabaptist preacher was reported to have remarked that wherever the people did not abandon tippling and frivolity and immodesty in dress, there certainly the true gospel was not preached. Menius touched here the Anabaptist insistence on the unity of faith and life. But he persisted in regarding it as a mixture of the religious order with the civil order. He insisted that in salvation the Christian stood absolutely free from the civil order. Just as it was wrong to relate one's salvation to the civil order, so was it wrong to change the civil order in the name of religion. Scripture made a distinction between the two orders. The Christian reading Scripture must make the same distinction.[1]

Under civil order Menius included government, courts of law, the oath, private property, marriage, and domestic discipline. All of these were ordained by Christ. To reject one or more was to be guilty of rebellion, and therefore subject to the penalties for rebellion. Menius did not make his charges specific except for the last three. The Anabaptists rejected private property and insisted on holding all material things in common. Indeed, they went so far as to deny themselves the right to "own" a wife. Some even took the next step, so Menius heard, and held wives in common. He had more direct evidence for the charge of abandoning wives. Rink had done this. Some of the Anabaptists also abandoned their children. The Anabaptists sinned not only against God, but also against the civil order.[2]

Anabaptist raging against the civil order had earlier been directed largely against the princes, all of whom the Anabaptists considered godless. God would extirpate the godless princes; and the Anabaptists were to keep their tinder boxes ready to help the Lord. By 1530 the Anabaptists had changed their propaganda tune. Their new line was that the righteous would assemble to await the personal return of Christ, who would rule the world with the righteous. For this purpose

[1] *Ibid.*, pp. Y2r.–Y4v.
[2] *Ibid.*, pp. Y4r., Zr., Z3v.–ar.

they had gone so far as to collect regal insignia somewhere in Swabia: a sceptre, a crown, and jewels.[1] Menius undoubtedly had in mind the group around Augustin Bader near Ulm.[2]

Menius did not attempt in 1530 to give a detailed defense of the Christian foundations for civil order. Paul in Romans laid the basis for the state in God's ordinance. Even if Scripture did not require Christian obedience to the state, common sense would. Within the province of the state's responsibilities the law court served a necessary function. So did the oath. The oath could be justified on patriarchal and apostolic practice. Abraham utilized the oath. So did Paul. God himself swore on his own name. Menius did not condone frivolous swearing. He spoke of the oath of obedience or allegiance by which society was bound together. The entire civil order in all its aspects was necessary for the preservation of public tranquility. As such it had the sanction and blessing of God.[3]

Throughout the entire book Menius displayed a harshness of tone and language that indicated a blinding hatred of the Anabaptists. This attitude is most apparent in his repeated references to the diabolical origin of the sect. Menius dealt earnestly with the devil, that great archenemy of both God and man. He believed fervently in the reality of the devil's presence in his numerous angels among the sons of men. Through his emissaries in human flesh Satan sought to achieve his nefarious ends: the complete annihilation of God's Truth, and the disruption of the social order. In dealing with Anabaptists the question of diabolical origin did not appear to him as question so much as fact. One repeated the fact endlessly by way of punctuating and under-lining the grossness of Anabaptist error. This does not mean that he made no effort to prove their diabolical origin. But the proof itself needed no earnest effort; nor was it bound by the ordinary rules of common sense or logic. Thus he could declare on the one hand that the Anabaptists were devils because of their error in Christian doctrine; and on the other hand he could say their doctrine was diabolical because of the nature of its teachers.[4] What did he mean?

Menius laid down a three-point formula for ascertaining the truth or falsity, or the satanic origin, of doctrine, and he proceeded to apply it to the Anabaptists. One must first of all compare the doctrine to the

---

[1] *Ibid.*, pp. br.–v.

[2] Christian Hege, "Bader, Augustin," *ME*, I, 209–10.

[3] Menius, *Der Widdertauffer*, pp. Zr.–Z3r.

[4] This kind of approach occurs frequently in Menius. The best single example of it is found in his treatment of the article on the Lord's Supper, *ibid.*, pp. M2r. and M4r.

Word.[1] Menius assumed blandly, as did his sixteenth-century contemporaries, that this kind of comparison could be made without encountering any major obstacles; there could be no honest differences of interpretation. When one compared Anabaptist doctrine with the Word the only conclusion possible, in view of the enormous discrepancy, was that their doctrine was the product of Satan's fertile mind. Menius had spelled out the differences between Anabaptist doctrine and the Word point by point at some length.[2] He summarized this work by declaring that no idea of theirs, not even a single word or letter of it, agreed with Scripture. All of their doctrine was the coarsest kind of blasphemy and falsehood. Its propagators were in the same category as the Turks as disseminators of their father's lies.[3]

Secondly, any new teaching must be accompanied by miracles. Menius considered church tradition a safeguard against the incursion of frivolous and diabolical ideas. God always prepared his people for new revelation by visiting its messengers with miracle-working powers.[4] Did the Anabaptists accompany their new doctrines with miracles? No. Not only did God fail to approve their doctrine by withholding the power of miracles; he also condemned them by actively working against them. In what manner? God used the state to punish them.[5] This was particularly vindictive of Menius. For while he considered the punishment of Anabaptists by the state an act of God, he also constantly urged the state to fulfil its God-ordained function of death to heretics and devils. Indeed, his 1530 work had the ostensible purpose of furnishing rulers with the means for detection of Anabaptists, and more particularly of urging the reluctant Philip of Hesse to a more vigorous exercise of his function as punisher of Anabaptists.[6]

Finally, one needed to inquire as to the office and call of the person teaching new doctrine. "How shall they preach, except they be sent?" (Rom. 10:15)[7] Who sent the Anabaptists? Menius was sensitive on this point. It is here that his declaration that Anabaptist doctrine was diabolical because of the nature of its teachers takes on meaning. He elevated Anabaptist error on the call to the rank of a doctrinal error, though it did not fit naturally into his organizational scheme. He

[1] *Ibid.*, pp. ar.–v.
[2] For one example, *ibid.*, pp. J4r.–v.
[3] *Ibid.*, p. a2r.
[4] *Ibid.*, p. av.
[5] *Ibid.*, pp. a2r.–bv.
[6] See dedication to Philip, *ibid.*, pp. A4v.–A6v.
[7] *Ibid.*, p. av.

interpreted the Anabaptists as teaching that no one except the Anabaptist, sealed with the sign of the *Bund,* could be considered a teacher or preacher of the gospel. How then did the Anabaptist teachers go about their work? Clandestinely, always under cover. One could ascertain their diabolical origin, quite apart from what they taught, from the manner of their teaching.[1]

Anabaptists rarely revealed their doctrine. Menius declared that of approximately thirty Anabaptists he had met only two who would talk about their religious ideas.[2] What kind of gospel was that? It was contrary to the nature of God's Word that upon being heard and believed it should then remain silent. The Word always tended to break out openly and freely; it sought always to move outward to other persons.[3]

The Anabaptists had an overpowering sense of mission. They sought constantly to spread their doctrine wherever they could despite government prohibitions. Menius did not deny that they tried to spread their ideas. But the secretive manner in which they did so was contrary to the manner in which the true gospel of Christ worked. Menius complained that it was not right that men left wives and families and occupations to proclaim secretly their religious ideas.[4] The true gospel was always proclaimed through men who had received their call to office from the church or from those Christians in the church who happened also to be princes. Such men preached the gospel openly for all to hear. Satan knew human nature well; men always thirsted most for forbidden knowledge. Hence it was fitting that his emissaries operate clandestinely. And because they did so, they were obviously his emissaries.[5]

Apparently Menius did not believe that God would allow the gospel to fall upon times so hard that everywhere in the world its true proclaimers would be hounded by government and persecuted.[6] It seems obvious that the Anabaptists did believe this. Menius never faced squarely the persecution of true Christians in his treatment of

[1] *Ibid.,* pp. bv.–b3v.; F3v.–F4r.
[2] *Ibid.,* p. F4r.
[3] *Ibid.,* p. G2r.
[4] *Ibid.,* pp. bv.–b3r. Here at the end of the pamphlet he included material suggested to him by Luther on the question of call. See Luther to Menius, April 12, 1530, *WB,* V, 274. Rink had even left his calling as pastor.
[5] Menius, *Der Widdertauffer,* pp. F4v.–Gr.
[6] Menius' boast of how open and free his own preaching was (*ibid.,* pp. G3r.–v.) sounds hollow in the light of his insistence that the government kill the leaders of the opposition to him (*ibid.,* pp. b3r.–v.).

Anabaptists because he obviously thought they were not true Christians. In their steadfastness before the executioner's ax Menius saw only stubbornness, and this convinced him again of their diabolical origin.[1] It is difficult to say whether doctrine or manner of teaching was more persuasive in bringing Menius to the conclusion that the Anabaptists were devils. He never wavered in his conviction, nor did he consider the Anabaptists capable of shaking off the dominance of their master. "For he has so driven this gang until he has brought them to a completely unchristian, godless character, and has made them so stubborn and obdurate in it that there appears to be no possibility of improvement or repentance." [2]

Menius again answered the call to literary activity against the Anabaptists in 1538, in a book entitled "How Every Christian Should Properly Conduct Himself with Respect to all Kinds of Doctrine, Good and Bad, in Accordance with God's Command." [3] In this instance his major interest was different from that of 1530. He wrote to justify the execution of the two Anabaptists caught outside the wall at Eisenach conversing with Fritz Erbe through his cell window. The common people in the border region of Electoral Saxony and Hesse prized Anabaptist doctrine all the more because of the martyr spirit of its adherents. The people were skeptical of force in religious matters because Philip of Hesse was lenient. The sterner punishment of the Saxons called for justification.[4] Menius wrote the pamphlet and preached on the subject of proper punishment for heretics.[5]

Obviously the peasantry was giving Menius trouble on the question of Anabaptism. They would not report the secret activities of the heretics, but shielded them. Menius found it difficult to get at these fugitives from justice. So he laid down at the outset the responsibilities of all Christians with respect to doctrine. Every Christian must believe God's Truth with all his heart, confess it before men, and follow it in conduct. Likewise the Christian was responsible to recognize error, reject it with his whole heart, and condemn it openly. Menius laid it down more sharply that each Christian must recognize and

---

[1] *Ibid.*, pp. G3v.–G4v.

[2] "Also hat er [the devil] mit dieser Rotten auch vmb gangen/ bis er sie jnn ein gantz vnd gar vnchristlich vnd gottlos wesen bracht/ vnd also darinnen verstocket vnd verhertet hat/ das da keiner besserung noch widderkerung jmer mehr zu hoffen scheinet." *Ibid.*, p. X2r.

[3] *Wie ein iglicher Christ gegen allerley Lere/ gut vnd böse/ nach Gottes Befelh/ sich gebürlich halten sol.* Wittemberg (Nickel Schirlentz), 1538.

[4] See above, pp. 69–70.

[5] Schmidt, *op. cit.*, I, 180.

confess the truth of those who teach and practice God's Word, and contrariwise recognize and publicly damn error in others. Menius meant that error must be exposed in order to help him who erred, to protect the simple, and to see that error was punished. His own work was published out of his sense of responsibility in this respect.[1] According to his own testimony he did not enter the literary lists against Anabaptism because he enjoyed it. His entire dealing with the sect he found odious.[2]

Menius made a sharp distinction between the religious and the civil offices, and between both of these and the position of the layman-subject. All Christians were responsible to help spread the gospel and build the church. But only a few were called to preach and administer the sacraments. The office was ordained by God, whether it was the office of preacher or of magistrate, or of subject. In every type of office the Christian was to help establish truth and fight error. But he was responsible to remain within the limits of his office.[3]

Menius laid down the specific responsibilities of the spiritual office. One must teach and preach the truth: salvation through Christ. One must give over the children of God to their Father. One must also commit the children of Satan to their master. All Christians must accept and regard the minister's classification of people as if it were the work of God himself. Here was the rub. The people would not accept Menius' verdict of heresy serious enough to warrant death in the case of the two Anabaptists caught with Erbe. Menius believed further that God would punish, both eternally and temporally, those whom his ministers delivered to the devil. The punishment of course was not in any way the responsibility of the spiritual office. But the appeal to the civil office for punishment was.[4]

What then were the duties of the civil office? First, the magistrate, as any Christian, must believe the truth. As we shall see Menius did not believe that all magistrates did heed the truth, or that force must be used to make them recognize and adhere to it. Secondly, he must handle temporal, civil affairs. Menius did not spell out the nature of these affairs. He laid it down that the magistrate must abstain from matters of faith, from meddling in the duties of the spiritual office, except where public confession of religious error was involved. Then

---

[1] *Wie ein iglicher Christ*, pp. B3v.–Cr.
[2] *Ibid.*, p. B2v.
[3] *Ibid.*, pp. Cr.–C2r.
[4] *Ibid.*, pp. C3v.–Dr.

the matter was no longer purely spiritual. It involved indeed the welfare and tranquility of the social order.[1]

Menius meant of course that the ruler was responsible for punishing heretics. He was to regard his subjects as a father regarded his children, with respect to seeing that the true faith was promulgated and error was suppressed. False teaching, and especially secret false teaching, must be punished earnestly. Menius raised here the punishment theory that Melanchthon had propounded in 1530.[2] The distinction between unbelief or erroneous belief and blasphemy was insisted upon. No punishment should be meted out to those who were guilty of mere false belief. But when they proclaimed it to others, then they were guilty of blasphemy. Blasphemy threatened the existence of social unity. Menius, along with his sixteenth-century contemporaries, could not of course conceive of religious pluralism in society. Indeed, he was convinced that murder and revolution would break out wherever religious unity was broken.[3] What did he mean?

Essentially he could see no worthwhile distinction between the two tables of the Mosaic Law. To separate the first five commandments from the second five on the grounds that one group touched man's relation to God and the other group man's relations to his fellow man was not very useful. We may infer that some in Menius' circle of opponents did make this distinction by way of criticism. They apparently said that all sins against God, such as blasphemy, were to be left to God's punishment in eternity. Menius believed that a sin against the first table of the Law ultimately developed into a sin against the second table. Why? In what way? One must turn again to Menius' view of the devil. It was the devil who drove men to blaspheme against God. But the devil was both liar and murderer. Hence, if the devil possessed a human spirit, driving him to blasphemy, it could only be a matter of time until murder, revolution, adultery, theft, and a host of sins against society would ensue. In this sense blasphemy was deemed an offense against society as well as one against God. Menius believed, too, that blasphemy was a social sin because it induced others to similar error.[4]

---

[1] *Ibid.*, pp. Dv.–D2r.

[2] See above, pp. 154–56.

[3] *Wie ein iglicher Christ*, pp. D2v.–D4r.

[4] *Ibid.*, pp. D4r.–E2v. Menius argued also that since murder or theft or adultery clearly meant the perpetrator did not love God – i.e., a sin against the second table always involved a sin against the first table – the reverse must also be true. A sin against the first table was a sin against the second. Menius held this conviction earnestly, but it is impossible to avoid the conclusion that he was trying to scare magistrates like Philip of Hesse into severe

The magistrate was therefore responsible to punish blasphemers: to forestall revolution and murder and to protect the common mind against polution. Menius postulated a form of religious freedom: in a Christian society everyone must be free to know the truth. But this required to his way of thinking the forcible suppression of error. It was the duty of the spiritual office to define both truth and error.[1] He urged caution in proceeding against heretics. They must be given a chance to repent; some were misled through their own ignorance and required only some decent instruction. But the magistrate must ultimately insist that the common folk do not heed the clandestine preachers and that they do hear the ordained pastors.[2]

Menius raised finally the question of how Evangelicals ought to conduct themselves in Catholic territories. The Evangelical pastor was to preach the true Word, and to testify to the government of its error. If the government would not tolerate true preaching, then the Evangelical was to flee. If he could not escape, he must under no circumstances agree to preach papal lies. He must suffer unjust punishment if it became necessary. Ultimately one must obey God rather than man. There is no suggestion in Menius of the right of revolution, of resort to force to bring in the true religion. The Evangelical layman in Catholic lands was also to be a witness for the truth. He too should flee to Evangelical territories rather than accept papal untruth.[3] Menius considered papal persecution of Anabaptists inadequate because the eradication of error was followed by more error in doctrine.[4] It should be noted that Menius' advice closely paralleled Anabaptist conviction and practice. Menius did not discuss this fact because he seems not to have recognized it. He would have denied the similarity on the grounds that the Evangelicals handled truth while the Anabaptists dispensed error. There was no substantial territory in Europe where Anabaptist doctrine was tolerated, to which they could flee.

Menius did not devote space to an enumeration or analysis of Anabaptist errors. His treatment of them was summary. As Satan's emissaries they hypocritically put on a pious, religious appearance to deceive the simple.[5] Their martyr spirit was part of the same

punishment of Anabaptists in order to prevent revolution. He did not mention Münster however.

[1] *Ibid.*, pp. E4r., C3v.–C4r.
[2] *Ibid.*, p. E3r.
[3] *Ibid.*, pp. E4v., Fv.–F3v.
[4] *Ibid.*, p. E3v.
[5] *Ibid.*, pp. Br.–B2r.

hypocrisy; it was completely misdirected. They were martyrs to the devil, not to Christ.[1]

After the death of Luther's implacable Saxon foe, Duke George, in 1539, Ducal Saxony turned toward Protestantism. In the course of time Menius and Eberhard von der Thann were called to a church visitation in the region around Mühlhausen. They conducted the visitation in September, 1541. Then in September, 1542, Menius began a period of service as pastor and superintendent in Mühlhausen proper. For two years he labored to bring the Evangelical teaching and church practice to fruition. He had to contend with extensive opposition from Catholics, some of whom attempted to disturb the course of the Evangelical services by boisterous singing outside the churches. One of the leading burgermeisters served as the focal point for opposition.[2] But he also encountered Anabaptists again. Some of those who objected most strenuously to Catholic practices and tactics, particularly after the disastrous Schmalkald War, turned to Anabaptism.[3] So Menius addressed himself again to the task of literary exposé and refutation in order to help establish the Word on a firmer footing in Mühlhausen. The book bore the title, "Concerning the Spirit of the Anabaptists."[4]

In his word of dedication to the city council of Mühlhausen Menius broached a touchy point brusquely. Both Catholics and Evangelicals blamed the advent of the Anabaptist plague on each other. Menius appraised the issue from the touchstone of the gospel. The Anabaptist movement developed in this region because of the absence of the gospel, because the gospel was not truly preached. This was not a matter of proof or disproof; it was an incontrovertible fact. Of course the Catholics were responsible for Anabaptism! In 1544 at Mühlhausen he was not disturbed by the recollection that Anabaptism existed in Protestant lands as well. Menius lamented the previous absence of the gospel. He conceded that humans tended to err; but to fall and then to refuse to accept the truth was serious sin indeed.[5] The reader of Menius marvels not so much at his intense conviction in the truth of his position, which is to be expected. One is astounded rather at the ease with which Menius unraveled the complexities of the devil's machi-

---

[1] *Ibid.*, pp. B3r., E4r.

[2] Schmidt, *op. cit.*, I, 288–90.

[3] *Ibid.*, pp. 298, 302.

[4] *Von dem Geist der Widerteuffer*. Wittemberg (Nickel Schirlentz), 1544. This polemic, like his two previous ones, was provided with a foreword by Luther.

[5] *Ibid.*, pp. A5r.–B2v.

nations, and at his presumption that he always spoke the mind of God and that his opponents spoke the mind of the devil. He saw everything as black or white; the grays never seem to have clouded his horizon.

In 1544 Menius repeated much of what he had given in greater detail in 1530. We need not be concerned therefore with a minute account of the work. General characteristics should be noted, and differences in fact and emphasis from his earlier work should be shown.

Menius was even more certain than before that Müntzer was the founder of Anabaptism. Perhaps this assurance developed from fresh information acquired in his contacts with the Anabaptists in Mühl-hausen. He did not attempt any proof of the relation as such. He made very few specific references to Anabaptists as sources for his deline-ation. He referred to Rink on one occasion, but generally, if he listed an Anabaptist source at all, it was either Müntzer or Münster. In Müntzer Menius perceived one who despised and rejected Scripture, baptism, and the Lord's Supper – in short, Word and sacrament – in favor of the Spirit. Thereby the devil slipped in and wildly tore Müntzer to his death, and drove the later Anabaptists to the same end. Anabaptist martyrs were martyrs to the devil.[1]

The pattern followed by Menius was that of brief statement of error, a longer excursus on the shameful manner of Satan's working, and a still longer refutation. Within this scheme Menius paid little attention to a clarification of Anabaptist error; the reader must find that clarification implicitly in Menius' rebuttal. Menius undoubtedly intended the book for an audience that already had some acquaintance with Anabaptist ideas. But this means that one cannot profitably mine the 1544 book for Anabaptist doctrine; it is too thin in Anabap-tist ideas. It is difficult to escape the conclusion that for Menius the pattern of Anabaptist error had jelled into a fixed pattern. His view of Müntzer as originator is too clear; his picture of Anabaptism is too diabolically black; his delineation of the truth of the Evangelical position is too pure and white. Here we have to deal with a myth, although one that is by no means without basis in historical fact. The only enlivening element within an otherwise static picture is Menius' anger.

Menius devoted relatively more space to a defense against Anabap-tist attacks on the Evangelicals. Here he introduced new elements into an older fundamental charge. The Anabaptists had long main-

---

[1] *Ibid.*, pp. Br.–v., B4r.–v.

tained that the true Christian could not attend the Evangelicals' services. Menius gave a fuller exposition of the charge in 1544.

1. The churches of the Evangelicals are idol temples. God dwells in no temple made by human hand.

2. The Evangelicals do not conduct a truly Christian worship service, nor teach true Christian doctrine.

3. The Evangelical preachers are themselves sinful in conduct.

4. The common people who hear Evangelical preaching do not show moral improvement.[1]

Menius refuted these rather nasty charges with a lengthy defense of Evangelical doctrine and practice. Pictures remained in their church buildings, but he denied that they were worshipped. Common sense told him that Christians should have a fixed place for worship, but God inhabited that building because of the worshipers who gathered, not for the sake of the building itself.[2] He insisted their preaching was the Word of God, not human distortions of it. Moreover, in their worship the true sacraments were dispensed, and God was praised and supplicated. Their teaching likewise was pure Scripture, from the Mosaic Law through Paul. They admonished obedience to God and king. They counseled the performance of good works.[3]

The third charge was amplified in rebuttal. Apparently the Anabaptists believed that true Christian preachers should imitate the apostles in a peripatetic ministry and in rejecting a fixed salary. Menius defended the fixed location of preachers on the grounds that the wandering apostle required miracle-working powers as a sign of his call. The apostles ordained servants of the Word to stay in one location. Common sense tells one that the study of Scripture, prior to preaching it, is a full-time task. The minister must be paid to do it carefully.[4] Menius did not deny that some of the Evangelical preachers were sinners; all men are sinners. Those who were open sinners he refused to defend. But they could not be dismissed from office. One must distinguish between the person and the office. It was sin to stay away from true preaching because of the person of the preacher.[5]

The final charge of no fruit in the lives of the hearers was sheer blasphemy. Even if there were no fruits, it was wrong to judge doctrine by ethics. But there were fruits. Menius expatiated at length on the

---

[1] *Ibid.*, p. C2r.
[2] *Ibid.*, pp. C2v., Dr.-v.
[3] *Ibid.*, pp. D2v.–E2v.
[4] *Ibid.*, pp. E3v.–F4r.
[5] *Ibid.*, pp. F4v.–G2r.

good results of the Evangelical teaching in moral improvement. He ended by repeating his charge of hypocrisy in the conduct of the Anabaptists.[1]

Menius moved from defense to attack. But his section on doctrinal error of Anabaptism was shorter than in 1530; the basic delineation of that error had been brought to light long before. This time he dealt with use of Scripture, doctrine of salvation, baptism, and Lord's Supper. On the use of Scripture he was clearer in putting the Anabaptists, and Rink in particular, into a completely spiritualist category. They rejected Scripture as authority.[2] In soteriology he added nothing new, except perhaps a sharper focus on the problem: Christ was not Redeemer but example to the Anabaptists.[3] In baptism there was no new argument.[4] To the Lord's Supper question Menius devoted much more space. But there was little new in it except his attempt to turn the Anabaptist emphasis on the celebration as preparation for suffering into a sacrifice of Christ on the altar, a recrucifixion of the Saviour. This construction did not logically derive from their ideas as Menius gave them. One may safely assume from the vehemence of the Anabaptist rejection of the Lord's Supper as a medium of grace that they turned it into a sacrifice entirely unwittingly if they did so at all.[5] Menius repeated, with no elaboration, his earlier charge that the Anabaptists denied the divinity of Christ, but he added to it the docetic view of the Münsterites. The Anabaptists denied both the divinity and humanity of Christ.[6]

In Anabaptist sins against the social order Menius again added little that was new. They abandoned wives and children to do their nefarious preaching. They denounced courts of law and civil oaths. They rejected private property. Menius learned from Dorpius [7] that the Münster Anabaptists practiced polygamy. Some took any woman they wanted

[1] *Ibid.*, pp. G2v.–G3v., Hr.
[2] *Ibid.*, pp. Jv.–J2r.
[3] *Ibid.*, pp. J3r.–v.
[4] In 1530 he had spoken sarcastically about the Anabaptists' lack of cleverness in exegesis. He referred to Rink's argument that the Kingdom of Heaven belongs to persons *like* children (Mark 10:14–15). (*Der Widdertauffer*, p. Q2r.) By 1544 he had accepted this exegesis, but of course not the end to which Rink had turned it. The fact that all people must be like children in order to enter heaven argued for those rites which touched children, namely *infant* baptism. (*Von dem Geist*, p. L2v.) See above, p. 187.
[5] *Von dem Geist*, pp. N3r.–v.
[6] *Ibid.*, p. J2v.
[7] Probably Heinrich Dorpius, *Warhafftige Historie/ wie das Evangelium zu Münster erstlich angefangen/ vnnd die Widertäuffer verstöret/ wider auffgehöret hat* (Strassburg: Kraft Müller, 1536).

to wife.[1] He added one new charge. The Anabaptists rejected all government except the rulership of their own preachers. In his refutation he did not touch this point directly. He refuted their prohibition of a Christian in political office. One suspects that Menius, like Eberhard von der Thann, considered the two points synonymous.[2] Menius depicted Anabaptist attitudes toward the civil order in the harshest possible terms.

He [the Anabaptist Spirit] attempts . . . to pervert everything in this human life, which God has everywhere placed under His order, not only into a dissolute, wild, animalistic and disorderly condition, but also into a truly hellish, diabolical, pernicious and damnable ruin. [He wants] to make a temporal hell out of the world, and nothing less than an incarnate devil out of man.[3]

Menius ended the book with a brief recapitulation of his 1538 arguments on death for blasphemers. He remonstrated against an appeal to the parable of the tares (Matt. 13:24–30). Christ meant this parable for apostles and preachers only – for the spiritual office. The civil office could and must punish heretics.[4]

Throughout the 1540's and into the next decade a group of so-called Anabaptists developed a large following in the region between Gotha and Mühlhausen. These called themselves Blood Brothers.[5] Their most important leader was Klaus Ludwig, a native of Tüngeda northwest of Gotha. Klaus Ludwig rose above the limitations of his peasant birth. Among other things, he taught himself to read. He was the possessor of a strong will which he combined with a not inconsiderable native ability to become a man of importance to the local peasantry. On one occasion he publicly criticized the local pastor who had condemned the Anabaptists. Klaus Ludwig, before a considerable following, defended the radicals in a speech held in the graveyard after church services. By all appearances he was an adherent of Anabaptism, and the similarity was strengthened when he refused to have his infant baptized.[6] His following grew, aided no doubt by

[1] *Von dem Geist*, pp. Q4v.–Rr.

[2] *Ibid.*, pp. R3r., S2r.–S3v. See above, pp. 92–93, for Eberhard.

[3] "Also vnterstehet er . . . zuuerkeren/ vnd aus menschlichem Leben/ welchs Gott allenthalb/ in gewisse seine Ordnung gefasset/ nicht allein ein wüste/ wilde/ viehisch/ vnd vnordigs wesen/ Sondern vielmehr ein recht hellische/ teufflische verterbliche vnd verdampte zerstörung/ aus der welt ein leibliche Helle/ vnd aus dem Menschen nicht anders denn rechte leibhafftige Teuffel zu machen." *Ibid.*, p. Q4r.

[4] *Ibid.*, pp. T3v.–T4r.

[5] Menius, *Von den Blutfreunden aus der Widertauff* (Erfurt: Gerasius Sthürmer, 1551), p. Er.

[6] Letter from Hans Georg and Reinhard of Wangenheim to Elector John Frederick, December 12, 1543, printed in Wappler, *Thüringen*, p. 473.

the relative absence of policing activities during the Schmalkald War. One of the converts who rose to the stature of a leader was Georg Schuchard. Schuchard was arrested and imprisoned in 1551 at the Kreuzburg, whereupon the Blood Brothers reacted with vigor. They sent letters to some sixty communities, demanding both the release of Schuchard and new adherents from the populace at large. They threatened violence to those communities that refused to comply. At this juncture others of the Anabaptists were apprehended, and the whole story spilled out. Likewise the picture of the Blood Brothers' religious views became clearer.[1]

The most distinctive doctrine of the Blood Brothers was what they called *Christerie*. It was their peculiar form of the communion service. The highest expression of fellowship they believed was sexual intercourse. For those who had been forgiven by Christ, who belonged to the true body of Christ, it was wrong to restrict one's sexual activities to one mate. Each man was expected to have sexual intercourse with each woman in the group. Klaus Ludwig generally opened the service with a sermon, and then issued the order to multiply. Children born of such unions were born without sin, and required no baptism. Men were considered bread and women were the wine. One elderly man was refused membership in the group because he was considered physically unable to take his cup.[2]

The basic religious root for this form of adultery was their belief that a person could not sin after he was once forgiven by Christ. Whatever he did thereafter was done, they believed, by impulse from the Holy Spirit. Christ's redemptive activity made the individual who accepted it perfect. The service was their only sacrament; one member [3] styled it the true baptism, but for others it was a kind of Lord's Supper – viz., the terminology. Otherwise no attention was given to the sacraments by the group. They did not practice baptism in any form, although they allowed their infants to be baptized in order to avoid conflict with the authorities.[4] They threatened force as a means of settling disputes, especially when they could not gain their ends by argument.[5]

---

[1] From the hearing of Hans Kindervater, August 27, 1551, printed in Wappler, *Thüringen*, pp. 481–86.

[2] Hearing of Kindervater, *ibid.*; hearing of Georg Jacob, February 10, 1552, printed in Wappler, *Thüringen*, pp. 490–94; Hochhuth, *op. cit.*, XXIX (1859), 182–84; Schmidt, *op. cit.*, II, 129.

[3] Georg Jacob.

[4] Kindervater testimony, Wappler, *Thüringen*, pp. 481–86.

[5] Schmidt, *op. cit.*, II, 129.

What then was their relation to Anabaptism? In the common and official minds they were generally considered identical. The Blood Brothers themselves denied any connection. Kindervater declared that they practiced no adult or believers' baptism. They also permitted infant baptism, though they did not encourage it.[1] Klaus Ludwig also reported their rejection of a second baptism.[2] On at least two occasions Anabaptists attended meetings of the group and refused subsequent dealings with them because of basic religious disagreements.[3] Even Menius did not press the relationship, and seemed to accept Klaus Ludwig's complete denial of it.[4] Although there were wild and boisterous elements in the Thuringian Anabaptist movement, this one cannot be considered a part of it. It comes up for consideration because of Menius' treatment of the group.

Schuchard was subsequently burned to death, for adultery and not for religious views – i.e., blasphemy. Decapitation would have been his sentence had he recanted, but he refused.[5] In the course of the official correspondence on the case Johann Friedrich the Mittlere advised Menius as superintendent at Gotha to gather the pastors in his district for a report on the Blood Brothers, to warn them of the group's activities so that they in turn might warn their parishioners.[6] It was in this connection that Menius published his book, "Concerning the Blood Brothers of the Anabaptists."[7] He addressed it to the Christian Diet of Thuringia.[8] Menius was provoked that foreigners, particularly the people in France, tended to condemn the Lutheran cause on the grounds that it spawned Anabaptism. Menius asserted the complete independence of the Evangelicals from these devils. Such wicked slander was indeed the work of Satan.[9]

---

[1] Kindervater testimony, Wappler, *Thüringen*, pp. 481–86.

[2] *Ibid.*, pp. 182–84.

[3] Sebastian Thiele, pastor at Tutterode (Dudenrode), who had been removed as pastor at Niederdorla because of his rejection of infant baptism and association with Anabaptists, wrote a letter to Klaus Ludwig after an association with the Blood Brothers in an effort to refute Ludwig's doctrine and practice. (Printed in *TA, Hesse*, p. 324; see also Wappler, *Thüringen*, p. 167.) Ludwig Spon, a leader of the North Thuringian Anabaptists, met with the Blood Brothers one time and refused further contacts. (Georg Jacob hearing, Wappler, *Thüringen*, p. 492.)

[4] See below, p. 208.

[5] Letter of J. Friedrich der Mittlere to his father, erstwhile Elector John Frederick, August 20, 1551, printed in Schmidt, *op. cit.*, II, 132–34.

[6] Schmidt, *op. cit.*, II, 132–33.

[7] *Von den Blutfreunden aus der Widertauff* (Erfurt: Gerasius Sthürmer, 1551).

[8] Christliche Landstenden von Düringen," *ibid.*, p. a2r. I assume this is the group of pastors under superintendent Menius, whom Johann Friedrich der Mittlere had urged Menius to convene.

[9] *Ibid.*, pp. a2r.–A2v.

Menius began the pamphlet with a recapitulation of Anabaptist error. They tried to destroy both the religious and the social order. He enlarged his usual body of ideas with a greater emphasis on the problem of domestic morality. The influence of the Blood Brothers was clear at this point. He spoke with more assurance and detail than formerly on the manner in which they exchanged mates in sexual union. So far Menius did not distinguish between the two groups, or at most he considered the Blood Brothers a branch of its Anabaptist parent.[1]

The point at which a divergence from the parent was detected was, not in sexual ethics, but in the Blood Brothers' diplomatic and skillful use of recantation and of full acceptance of Lutheran doctrine in order to escape punishment. In this respect they even outdid Menius' previous Anabaptists at deception and hypocrisy. Menius entertained no more doubts than formerly that the devil was behind it all. But one observes a recognition of differences among Anabaptists dawning in Menius' mind.[2]

Menius was called upon to examine three of the Blood Brothers; probably Klaus Ludwig and Hans Kindervater were two of them, although Menius himself did not report their names.[3] One, unnamed, professed to be in full accord with Lutheran doctrine. Only after his release he returned to tell Menius that he believed Christ by his death removed the capacity to sin in man.[4] The second, Klaus Ludwig, was not an Anabaptist; Menius accepted his denial in good faith, although he considered Ludwig's errors as abominable as those of the Anabaptists.[5] Kindervater, the third, gave a clearer statement of their view of sin. After one is born of God, all his desires and inclinations are not sinful lusts but stimulations from the Holy Spirit. He who fulfils these desires is a true child of God and is blessed by the Holy Spirit. Rebirth as a child of God was the act of reception of the Spirit which accompanied one's faith in the redeeming work of Christ. He believed that Christ's vicarious death removed all sin, and tendency to sin, so that his body was pure and without spot or blemish. Kindervater claimed to have derived these ideas from his own reading of Scripture, which he quoted profusely.[6] In his summary of their errors Menius added one: they relied on physical force to achieve their ends. Before, when they

---

[1] *Ibid.*, pp. Br.–B3r.
[2] *Ibid.*, pp. B3r.–v.
[3] Schmidt, *op. cit.*, II, 128, 129.
[4] Menius, *Von den Blutfreunden*, pp. B4v.–Cv.
[5] *Ibid.*, p. C2r.
[6] *Ibid.*, pp. D2r.–D4v.

were called Anabaptists, they went weaponless. Later they carried pikes, swords, and tinder-boxes with them. They invited the Evangelicals to discuss further in an open field, a thinly-veiled threat of force.[1]

Menius' rebuttal need not detain us here. He brought nothing new to light, either by way of clarification of the Blood Brothers' views or of his own theology. He decided that this was the worst of all the sects.[2] Menius concluded with philosophical observations on why the Lord allowed the faithful to be plagued by this gang. He thought it was to test the faithful, punish the unbelievers – mainly Catholics – and remind the world of the imminent Judgment Day.[3]

After the Schmalkald War ended in disaster for the Protestants, the Emperor called for unity of doctrine. At his command John Agricola, Julius von Pflug, and Michael Helding drew up a confession which Charles published in May, 1548. This was the Augsburg Interim. It was designed as a compromise, but it was more Catholic than Protestant in character. Agreement was to be secured in essentials with the government deciding on the non-essentials, the adiaphora. It permitted the cup in the sacrament, it allowed marriage of priests, and it permitted the retention of confiscated ecclesiastical property. But it demanded the seven sacraments, recognition of the pope as the interpreter of Scripture, transubstantiation, return to the rule of bishops, plus other Catholic practices and ideas which Protestants could hardly stomach.[4] On the one hand the Pope and some Catholic princes denounced the Interim for its Protestant tone. On the other hand the Protestant princes in Central and North Germany, including the imprisoned John Frederick and Philip of Hesse, refused to accept it. Menius, together with other superintendents and pastors in Ernestine lands, was called to Weimar at the end of July, 1548, by the Dukes to examine and deliver a judgment on the Interim. Menius wrote the report for the group. It was filled with adverse criticism. None of the theologians in the Ernestine territories would accept the Interim.[5]

One Interim led to another, especially in the Electoral lands of Maurice who was caught in a delicate fence-straddling operation after his betrayal of the Protestant cause in the previous war. The unity

---

[1] *Ibid.*, pp. E1r.–E2r.
[2] *Ibid.*, p. G3r.
[3] *Ibid.*, pp. J3v.–J4r.
[4] Manschreck, *op. cit.*, p. 280.
[5] Schmidt, *op. cit.*, II, 34, 58–59.

of Lutheranism was shattered, after the death of the master, because
of the attempts by Lutheran theologians to meet the blustering threats
of Charles with various degrees of compromise. Some wanted to compromise, or at least discuss; others would have none of either. Melanchthon
returned to Wittenberg to help salvage the university despite its control
by him whom many Protestants regarded as arch-traitor, Elector
Maurice. As the leading Lutheran theologian Melanchthon was called
upon to formulate confessions which might satisfy Charles and still
retain the essence of the Evangelical doctrine. In his willingness to give
in on the adiaphora he excited the enmity of some of the stricter
Lutherans taking shelter in Magdeburg, notably Flacius and Amsdorf.
The former particularly unleashed a scandalous volume of slander and
lies against the milder-mannered Wittenberger.[1] Because Menius did
not join in the attack on Melanchthon, and because his own attempts
at providing the Ernestine Dukes with answers to Charles were considered as jeopardizing Lutheran doctrine, he was also slandered by
Flacius. He was accused of teaching works-righteousness.[2] Obviously
Flacius had not read Menius against the Anabaptists, or against Osian-
der. Menius was stung by the attack, and in a series of writings attempted to reply to the charge. He demanded evidence: where had
he ever departed from the principle of justification by faith alone?
But his explanation of justification was not as purely Lutheran as
it had been in his refutation of Anabaptist error. Man is saved by
faith alone; yet not without the gift of the Holy Spirit which begins
in man the new life in Christ. And the new life in Christ cannot be
separated from good works; it means nothing without good works.[3]
The observer may well wonder where he got the strong emphasis on
the necessity for good works accompanying the faith experience in
man. In view of the frequency of the Anabaptist charge of absence
of works in Lutherans, and in view of Menius' frequent encounters
with them, it is logical to assume that he derived some of his conviction
on the importance of good works from his running battle with the
Anabaptists. Menius did not consider his later statements a departure
from *sola fide* doctrine. But to the more severely orthodox Lutheran
mind it was the opening wedge of compromise on the most cherished
of Lutheran doctrines. Menius ended his days worn out with the
disappointment of bitter controversy.

---

[1] Manschreck, *op. cit.*, pp. 288–92.
[2] Schmidt, *op. cit.*, II, 256–58.
[3] *Ibid.*, pp. 265–66.

CHAPTER VII

THEOLOGICAL CONFLICT
BETWEEN LUTHERANS AND ANABAPTISTS

The discussion up to this point has centered around the attitudes and arguments of the three Lutheran Reformers against the Anabaptists, together with an analysis of the Anabaptist movement in Central Germany derived from sources generally independent of the writings of the three. We now turn our attention to a closer examination of the conflict in religious ideas that was the occasion both for the Anabaptist separation from the Lutherans in Central Germany and for the Lutheran polemics. First there are several preliminary matters that require discussion.

In a technical sense one should reject the term theology in speaking of the conflict in ideas between Lutherans and Anabaptists. It is something of a misnomer. The Anabaptists were not theologically-minded. They did not often use the traditional theological categories in religious discussion. They preached the Bible and ethics to each other. Whenever they encountered the established Protestants they were forced to use theological concepts. In so doing they displayed an ineptitude that betrayed their background.[1]

Why did the Anabaptists not have a theology? Most of them of course were simple peasants or artisans whose lack of education ruled out the possibility of a theological orientation. Those who were capable of developing a theology did not have the leisure to do so. They were compelled to abandon any protracted scholarly pursuit, if they had entertained notions of such, both because of their fugitive existence and also because of the evangelistic fervor which drove them out to lives of wandering apostleship. These reasons in themselves might be

---

[1] See the Jena interrogation conducted by Melanchthon in December, 1535, above, pp. 163–67. There are two notable exceptions to this in Central Germany: the Marburg examination of Rink in 1528, and the 1538 discussion between Schnabel, Tasch, *et al.* and Bucer at Marburg.

sufficient to explain the absence of theological formulations by the Anabaptists. But one suspects there is a much deeper, more important reason for this absence. The burning concern of the radicals was for another kind of religious expression. At least one student of the movement has been led thereby to characterize it as non-Protestant.[1] Whereas the Protestants were driven to theology to explain their departure from Catholic sacramentalism, the Anabaptists relied on Biblical quotations, naively regarded as self-evident, to express their deviation from Protestantism toward a more "existential" [2] Christianity. Theology was the most convenient, and indeed the only, means for explaining the differences between *sola fide* and salvation via the sacraments. It was less convenient as a tool for clarifying a body of religious thought which was preoccupied far more with the problem of obedience to Scriptural imperatives and commands in fulfilment of a Christian walk than with the problem of sin. This does not mean that the Anabaptists were unconcerned with sin. But if Lutheranism had as its heart the search for a merciful God in view of the overwhelming burden of human sin which alienated man from God, Anabaptism developed around the central idea of a righteous walk with the Lord after the experiences of repentance and rebirth. And sanctification, as the Anabaptists conceived of it, was not merely a matter for speculative thought. It was pre-eminently a matter of obedience to simple Scriptural commands. No theology was necessary to clarify these; only the will to carry them out was lacking in men. Indeed, theology might become a means for explaining away the directness and force of the commands themselves.

A second consideration results from the absence of religious discussions or debates between Lutherans and Anabaptists. In Switzerland and southern Germany there were numerous discussions between Reformed and Anabaptist. The *Gespräch* was an accepted means of decision-making in religious matters.[3] The nearest approach to the conversations staged in the South was the examination-discussion of Rink in the presence of the Marburg theologians in 1528. Rink had the freedom to present his own doctrines for discussion after first disposing of a preliminary set drawn up by a hostile pastor. It is possible that he enjoyed even greater freedom in his previous conver-

---

[1] Robert Friedmann, "Anabaptism and Protestantism," *MQR*, XXIV (1950), 12–24.

[2] The phrase is Friedmann's, *ibid.*, p. 19.

[3] See the dissertation of John H. Yoder, *Täufertum und Reformation in der Schweiz. Die Gespräche zwischen Täufern und Reformatoren, 1523–1538* (Karlsruhe: Menn. Geschichtsverein, 1962).

sation with Landgrave Philip, but there is no satisfactory record of the course or content of this discussion. Melanchthon's examination of the three Anabaptists at Jena in 1535 is an example of the more typical pattern for Central Germany. Here the Anabaptists were interrogated on points which Melanchthon considered central to the Christian faith or outstanding deviations from Lutheranism. The reader does not get the heart of the Anabaptist point of view under such circumstances. A fuller exchange between Lutheran and Anabaptist, in the absence of bonafide religious discussions, runs the risk of utilizing a frame of reference that ill befits the historical situation. Both sides tended to talk past each other in their polemics. The historian must uncover the underlying issues which may not ever reach the printed page or public declaration. One brief example will suffice here. There was very little clear dispute on the problem of soteriology between Lutherans and Anabaptists. But the kinds of accusations leveled by both sides resolve themselves in the last analysis in soteriology. Baptism was the major question and it was discussed *ad nauseam*. Obviously there was much more at stake than merely the issue of baptism itself, although that issue was by no means unimportant.

A third preliminary consideration is that of similarities between Lutherans and Anabaptists. In concentrating on the area of conflict between Lutherans and Anabaptists it must be borne in mind that there were also areas of agreement. The tone of most of the documents of the time is much more suggestive of conflict than of agreement. But this should not blind us to the existence of real agreement, and indeed dependence at least of the Anabaptists on Luther. Both sides were opposed bitterly to Catholicism. Although the points of departure for such opposition might well have been different – the Anabaptists might begin with a more Erasmian critique rather than with the profound theological critique of Luther – the Anabaptists would have in all probability supported the Lutheran arguments wholeheartedly. Both sides could agree on the call to repentance as the central concern in life. Both could insist that repentance itself is a work of God, not of man. Both could accept the significance of the Holy Spirit. Both could rely on the Bible as authoritative in matters of faith.[1] There were other points of agreement. The Anabaptists could generally accept the Lutheran theological formulations on God, Christ, and the Trinity, and the fall of man.[2] The lack of theological orientation among

---

[1] Heinold Fast, "The Dependence of the First Anabaptists on Luther, Erasmus, and Zwingli," *MQR*, XXX (1956), 104–19.

[2] Friedmann, "Anabaptism and Protestantism," *MQR*, XXIV (1950), 13.

the Anabaptists, and the absence of bonafide discussions with the Lutherans to clarify differences and similarities of belief, does not mean that the Anabaptists rejected all Lutheran religious formulations. It is the purpose of this chapter to discuss disagreements and their underlying causes. Where did the Anabaptists depart from Lutheran Protestantism?

One notices upon examining Lutheran and Anabaptist declarations against each other two charges which are distinguished by the frequency of their occurrence. The essential objection of the Lutherans was the excessive subjectivism of the Anabaptists. This charge is found repeatedly in Lutheran discussions of Anabaptist error on baptism. It constitutes the primary significance of the baptism issue in Lutheran polemics: the Anabaptists reduced faith to a personal experience only, upon which they made the performance of the baptismal act contingent.[1] The principal Anabaptist charge was that Lutheran faith produced no fruit; the moral condition of Luther's adherents was as bad, or even worse, as it was under the Romanists.[2] Both of these accusations fall within the scope of soteriology. A discussion of the theological conflict must consequently begin with the problem of salvation.

Lutherans and Anabaptists could agree on the essentially sinful nature of man. Sin entered the world through the willful disobedience of Adam in Eden. Yet Adam was not alone in his shame. Each human repeats the sin of Adam: he resists the will and Word of God, preferring to rely on his own righteousness, to rely upon himself in every particular. Man wants to act like and to be God.[3] Lutheran and Anabaptist alike regarded sin with earnestness. Both agreed on the absolute necessity for repentance before man could be considered righteous in the eyes of God. Christ was the absolute key to repentance. But they were not of one mind on the work of Christ. How is Christ's work mediated to man, and how does man apprehend that work? These were questions on which Lutherans and Anabaptists did not see alike.

---

[1] Samples of the charge:
Luther, *Von der Widertauff*, pp. B2r.–v.; Melanchthon, *Underricht*, p. C4r.; Menius, *Der Widdertauffer*, pp. Q3r.–Pv.

[2] The charge is repeated endlessly, but nowhere is it elaborated. For several examples: Adam Angersbach testimony, printed in Wappler, *Thüringen*, p. 328; Hans Hut in his trial, *ibid.*, p. 26; Max Baumgart testimony at Sorga, 1533, printed in Franz, *TA, Hesse*, pp. 64–69.

[3] Julius Köstlin, *Luthers Theologie in ihrer geschichtlichen Entwicklung und ihren inneren Zusammenhange* (2 vols.; Stuttgart: Steinkopf, 1863), II, 362 ff. for Luther; Jan Kiwiet, "The Theology of Hans Denck," *MQR*, XXXII (1958), 10–11, for Denk; Franz, *TA, Hesse*, p. 8, for Rink.

To both parties Christ was the Son of God, the Word Incarnate.[1] To Luther [2] he was pre-eminently Redeemer. The essential work of Christ was his suffering, death, and resurrection, by which Christ took upon himself the punishment and guilt for the sins of all men and thereby delivered man from the power of death, Satan, and hell.[3] Without question the Anabaptists, too, regarded Christ as Redeemer. But he was more than Redeemer; he was also Example. His activities and his words became orders to be obeyed. The gospel was not only the good news of salvation. It was also a series of directives for the well-intentioned Christian on how to live, how to follow Christ the Example.[4] Of the Lutheran critics Menius sensed this emphasis the most keenly. He turned it into a contradiction and rejection of Christ as Redeemer. This was hardly what the Anabaptists intended. They were much too concerned with problems of rebirth to reject the idea of the saving work of Christ.[5] But the distinction was nonetheless a real one; the Lutherans and Anabaptists did not regard Christ in person and work in the same manner.

The nature of Christ's work aside, a far greater divergence of view can be found in the mediation of Christ's work and man's apprehension of it. Luther believed that the saving grace of God was mediated through the Word and the sacraments. The Word as a medium of grace was primarily the spoken Word. The power of God could be released through the private reading of Scripture, but it was released most fully in the preaching of Scripture. Of the two media Luther put the greater emphasis on the Word. Theoretically one did not absolutely require the sacraments in order to be saved, if one heard the Word. But Christ in person and work was indeed revealed and administered in the water and on the altar.

---

[1] We need not be concerned with the Lutheran attempts to pin Christological heresy on Anabaptism here. The charges were too flimsy, except in the case of Hofmann doceticism. But this latter was not universally accepted by Central German Anabaptists, certainly not in the first generation of the movement. The Anabaptists had no essential quarrel with Lutherans on the question of the two natures.

[2] For most of this chapter the theology of Luther will be formative for the Lutheran position. Notations will be made in those places in Lutheran-Anabaptist disagreements where Melanchthon or Menius held views significantly different from those of Luther.

[3] Köstlin, op. cit. (1863), II, 402–18.

[4] Johannes Kühn, Toleranz und Offenbarung (Leipzig: Meiner, 1923), pp. 230–31.

[5] Menius, Von dem Geist, pp. J3r.–J4v. The Anabaptists believed that the work of Christ was not valid for him who failed to follow Christ as Example, but that is not the same thing as saying that one is saved only by following the example of Christ in one's own work, which is Menius' point. He turned a both–and proposition into an either–or one. Bucer accused Denk of rejecting the redemptive work of Christ in favor of Christ who saves by teaching us how to live. Getrewe Warnung der Prediger des Evangelij zü Strassburg... (Strassburg, 1527), p. A2v.

Now this grace of God in Christ was received by man only through faith. Faith to Luther was a kind of receptacle or sack in which all of Christ was received by man. Christ came to dwell in man. There was the mysterious, invisible element here. Faith was also a trust that God's grace and Christ himself belonged personally to the individual. Each man had to believe for himself God's promises of mercy. No one could ultimately be saved by the faith of someone else. But faith was above all the product of God's work in man; it was pre-eminently a gift of God. It was precisely through the Word and sacraments that God distributed faith, so to speak, to man. The Word and sacraments engendered faith in their recipients.[1]

In contrast to the Lutherans the Anabaptists restricted the mediation of God's grace to the Word alone. There is no indication that they insisted the Word operated more exclusively orally as over against the private reading of Scripture. But since the majority of them were illiterate, in point of fact the Word for them became the oral Word. They adamantly rejected the idea of God's grace coming to man via physical, external media. The sacraments to them had an entirely different purpose and meaning. It was this rejection of the sacraments as agencies of God's grace that provoked the Lutherans.[2] Melanchthon in particular considered their reduction of the God-ordained media into instruments of human response a degradation so severe that it could only be considered blasphemy.[3]

God's grace to the Anabaptists was received by man through faith. Since they did not define faith it is difficult to say exactly what they meant it to be. It was a gift from God; that much is clear. Rink was quite insistent that the entire work of salvation including the development of faith in man was the work of God.[4] It came moreover via the hearing of the Word. It was implanted by the Holy Spirit.[5] But its most striking characteristic, by way of distinction from the Lutheran view, was its intensely personal nature. Luther's experience of finding a gracious God, of receiving faith, was intensely personal too. But to

---

[1] Köstlin, *op. cit.* (1863), II, 493–96, 434–44. Karl Brinkel, *Die Lehre Luthers von der fides infantium bei der Kindertaufe* (Berlin: Evangelische Verlagsanstalt, 1958), p. 41 for ideas on *fides aliena*.

[2] I have used Menius' characterization of the Anabaptist attitude toward the Word in this instance. *Der Widdertauffer*, pp. P3r.–v.

[3] *Ob christliche Fürsten...*, 1536, *CR*, III, 198. Luther thought the Anabaptists were in effect denying the omnipotence and even the existence of God by their rejection of the sacraments. Sermon on I Cor. 15:35–38, *EA*, XIX, 114.

[4] Hearing, 1528, *TA*, *Hesse*, pp. 4, 6.

[5] See below for a fuller discussion of the Anabaptist view of the place of the Holy Spirit.

the Anabaptists the Lutheran faith, as it was dogmatized, removed the warm, personal element and made it external and overly formal. They insisted on making religion internal. Salvation was characterized by an awakening of the Spirit with all its emotional overtones. Lutherans, decrying this as subjectivism, insisted that the more important aspect of faith was its divine character rather than the human response to it. They accused the Anabaptists of turning faith into a human institution entirely.[1]

Finally, the Anabaptists maintained that only after man's experience of faith were the sacraments to be administered. As such of course they had no sacramental character. Baptism in particular was valid and necessary only after a conversion experience, after the reception of faith. It was to be performed as a seal of one's experience of repentance and regeneration. They could have gotten the germ of their idea on the relation of faith to the sacraments from Luther himself.[2] For certainly Luther made the validity of the sacrament contingent on faith in the recipient. The problem of the relation of faith to the sacrament was at once more apparent in baptism than in the Eucharist; for here, with the retention of the practice of baptism of infants, the recipient's possession of faith could be more easily called into question. Luther was convinced that Scripture would have infants in the Kingdom of Heaven, and that therefore baptism of infants was legitimate and necessary. But could an infant have faith? Luther believed that faith was bestowed on even infants via baptism. The faith of the congregation, and more particularly the faith of the godparent who brought the infant to baptism, implored God to bestow faith upon the child. This *fides aliena* did not substitute for an absence of faith in the infant. God gave the infant a faith of its own, which justified entirely without the aid of the faith of another.[3]

Luther was beset by the Bohemian Brethren and the Anabaptists. The former baptized infants in view of their future faith, and thereby excluded faith from the ceremony itself. To them Luther declared faith was necessary before and during the baptismal ceremony. The Anabaptists said infants showed no evidence of faith during or after baptism; hence the necessary contingency of faith and sacrament did not exist. To them Luther replied that faith as a gift of God was

---

[1] So one can infer from the charges of Raidt and the responses of Rink in the 1528 Marburg hearing. See also Kühn, *op. cit.*, pp. 233-34.

[2] See Fast, *op. cit.*, p. 107, quoting Luther in the Babylonian Captivity, *WA*, VI, 532f. Or Koehler, "Luther, Martin," *ME*, III, 417.

[3] Brinkel, *op. cit.*, pp. 46-48.

not to be confused with human perceptions about faith. He chided them for resorting to human reason; the infant possessed no ability to understand, and therefore was not capable of receiving faith. Faith was not contingent upon understanding or reason. Indeed, faith and reason were antithetical. God created faith in men as an entirely new thing, contrary to reason. Faith could be given more readily to infants than to adults because they were unencumbered by reason. Luther considered reason as part of human nature which was damaged and ultimately damned by sin.[1]

Not only did Scripture testify to the inclusion of infants in the Kingdom, and therefore in the rite of baptism; tradition also spoke with authority to the Lutheran theologians. It was inconceivable that God would have permitted the church to practice infant baptism for centuries unabated if he did not in fact confer his grace in the act. They discovered the practice in the apostles' time, and found it confirmed by the church fathers.[2] The more radical Anabaptists on the other hand were unmoved by appeals to tradition. In their enthusiasm for a return to the pure Scripture, they rejected all practices that were not specifically prescribed in the New Testament.[3]

Appeals to Scripture and to tradition notwithstanding, Luther's marriage of faith and the sacrament, particularly his delineation of infant faith, was not entirely satisfactory. The primacy of faith as a means of salvation, and the fullness of faith as a confident trust in God's loving mercy, suffered when it was described as adhering more naturally to the infant than to the adult, and when the water of baptism itself was magically turned into a vehicle for God's grace. "Luther's formulation is theologically unsatisfying." [4] No one could imagine that Luther wanted to demean faith of some of its importance. In his struggles with the radicals on all sides he was forced into declarations and solutions that were quite beyond his intention.

All men have sinned and are deserving of death and damnation. Christ took upon himself the sins of mankind. How does man come to stand righteous before God? Luther held that faith in the saving work of Christ justified man before God. His emphasis lay on the fact that it was only faith that justified. Man's sins were forgiven, he was considered righteous by God, and he experienced a new birth so that

---

[1] *Ibid.*

[2] *Ibid.* Luther, *Von der Widertauff*, pp. Dr.–Er.; Melanchthon, *Underricht*, p. B3v. Also Otto Ritschl, *op. cit.*, I, 276 ff. for a discussion of Melanchthon's traditionalism.

[3] In Menius, *Der Widdertauffer*, pp. L2v., reporting on Rink.

[4] Koehler, *ME*, III, 417.

he became a new, righteous, pious individual: all of this through faith alone.[1] But faith was not so singular a means of salvation for the Anabaptists. The Lutheran solution was too formalistic, too much of a solitary forensic act for them. More was demanded of man than faith alone. God required obedience – if not perfect obedience, which was impossible for humans, at least a strenuous, determined effort to obey. They had none of the antipathy of Luther toward works; indeed, works were necessary to salvation. It was on this point that they leveled their most trenchant critique against Lutheran theology.[2]

In his concept of the Word Luther distinguished sharply between law and gospel. The former was essentially command, the latter promise or gift. Law was necessary in order to frighten man and prepare him for the grace promised in the gospel. After justification law was still necessary to maintain in man a deep feeling of repentance.[3] But law was not necessary as command. The Christian was not bound to obey a set of precepts. Luther eschewed legalism in this sense in the strongest terms. He was particularly vehement against human efforts to fulfil the law as a method of placating God and becoming righteous because of his own bitter experience in seeking a merciful God within traditional Catholic monasticism. And he always was apprehensive about the exercise of good works lest man tend to regard them as a means to his salvation. It is in this sense that his remarks against good works are to be interpreted. On one occasion he even declared that we must guard against good works more than against sin.[4] He meant good works as precepts from the law which man tried to obey in order to gain his own salvation. Because man in pride always sought to earn salvation on his own terms, by his own means, good works needed to be handled with the greatest of care. Luther's utterances on the subject were often very negative.

Luther did not mean that the new man in Christ was to perform no good works.[5] But his declarations on the necessity of works, and the nature of those that ought to be performed, are not numerous. The greatest good work of all was to believe in Christ,[6] which only serves to emphasize his reliance on the absolute primacy of faith in

---

[1] Köstlin, op. cit. (1863), II, 444–61.
[2] See p. 214, n. 2, above.
[3] Köstlin, op. cit. (1863), II, 493–503.
[4] From the Sermon on the Mass, quoted ibid., I, 314.
[5] He complained in 1520 that people took his emphasis on faith to mean that he rejected all good works. "Von den guten Werken," 1520, WA, VI, 205.
[6] Ibid.

the problem of the relation between faith and works. What good works the Christian did perform were in reality the work of God in him, and issued from faith in Christ. Such works centered primarily around the idea of loving one's neighbor. In the name of love good works were to be performed.[1] If God's grace was such that man was absolutely free from the requirement of works in order to stand in righteousness before God, he was still not free from a responsibility of service to his neighbor. But he did works not out of a sense of necessity, but because of his nature as a believer, because he had been made good, so to speak, by Christ. A good man did good works, without compulsion, in the natural course of his life as a creature loved of God and loving others because of God's love for him. On one occasion Luther declared that a Christian who performed no works in love was in reality no true believer.[2]

The humanist backgrounds of Melanchthon and Menius made them less reticent to ascribe a relatively higher position to works than Luther did. Melanchthon in particular, as an erstwhile follower of Erasmus, could be expected to look for and appreciate the ethical renewal in justification. Erasmus laid the greatest importance on the new righteousness of the justified person. Early in his Wittenberg career Melanchthon declared that Pauline doctrine served essentially to define the ethical conduct of man. He too emphasized the new creation in salvation, in which righteousness had been restored. And the new creature must of necessity do good works. Melanchthon retained a dividing line between justification and good works, but he did not underestimate good works.[3] Menius likewise was too much a humanist to bear the antipathy to works that Luther had. He admitted that works and faith operated at cross-purposes in the process of justification. But that did not rule them out as a necessary part of the Christian life.[4] His bone of contention with Anabaptists on the subject was that they built salvation entirely on works, and they evaluated doctrine by the presence or absence of good works. Menius declared the reverse to be true: the goodness of works was to be evaluated by the doctrine which produced them.[5]

[1] Köstlin, op. cit. (1863), II, 480.
[2] Luther, "A Treatise on Christian Liberty," trans. by W. A. Lambert, printed in *Three Treatises* (Philadelphia: Muhlenberg Press, 1947), pp. 268, 271, 272, 275, 278. Köstlin, op. cit. (1863), II, 458–59.
[3] Robert Stupperich, *Der Humanismus und die Wiedervereinigung der Konfessionen* (Leipzig: Heinsius Nachfolger, 1936), pp. 9–10, 20–22.
[4] Menius, *Der Widdertauffer*, pp. Kv.–K3r.
[5] *Ibid.*

How did the Anabaptists regard works and the relation of works to faith? On the importance, indeed the absolute necessity, of works in the Christian life the Anabaptists of Central Germany spoke with rare unanimity. They did not always emphasize the same activities as works, but most of them included separation from the world, the sharing of material goods with the brother, and suffering for the sake of the gospel. They insisted the new man in Christ must abstain from drunkenness, vice, and all forms of evil. He should share his abundance with the less fortunate brother. He should be prepared for inevitable suffering. He should visit the sick. He must also be ready to do the work of evangelism. Many Anabaptists insisted also that the commands of love, under which the Christian lived, included the rejection of force in treating anyone because force was itself evil.[1] Now this discipleship, this following of Christ by the new creature, had a distinct relation to salvation, so that one could not say it was unnecessary for salvation. The question of faith versus works in soteriology was not viewed as a sharp either-or proposition by the Anabaptists. That was no true faith, they insisted, which did not issue in the fruit of good works, in holiness of life. The Christian must live a noticeably different life from the non-Christian, else he did not have true faith. Anabaptists differed on the degree to which works were necessary for salvation. Some thought they were of little value; others almost insisted on their primacy. Unanimously they held that faith and obedience to the commands of Christ could not be separated in the salvation process.[2]

But was obedience to the commands of Christ really possible? Not completely, in the sense that the Christian became perfect.[3] Most of the Anabaptists retained a healthy respect for the presence of sin in the Christian's life. It made the ban necessary. But there was an incredible confidence, by way of contrast to Luther,[4] that holiness of life was possible. It was not a matter for debate: could Christ be obeyed or not? They did not posit the conceivability of obedience. It was an assumption with them that what Christ said and commanded could be understood and fulfilled by man.[5] The emphasis with them lay always on the question of the desire or will to obey, not on the

---

[1] See above, pp. 89–92. Menius, *Der Widdertauffer*, p. Dv. Kühn, *op. cit.*, pp. 230–31.

[2] See above, p. 83.

[3] There were of course some radicals who declared that after they were baptized whatever they did was no longer sin. See above, p. 84.

[4] Köstlin, *op. cit.* (1863), II, 461–91. On the question of life and conduct in the condition of grace Luther was quite negative; he was keenly conscious of the continuing tendency to sin on the part of the Christian.

[5] Kühn, *op. cit.*, pp. 235–36.

question of capability. It was at this point that they criticized the Lutherans. What was the substance and meaning of that critique?

Essentially Lutheran faith was erroneous because it was unfruitful. Those who adhered to its tenets continued to live in sin. There was no effort to unify faith and the new life in Christ, and this could only mean that the faith was false. The Anabaptists generally addressed themselves to this theme with the charge of no fruit. Sometimes the charge was altered slightly in configuration, if not in meaning: Lutheran faith was dead. It was a forensic act, stripped of that lively presence of the Spirit so necessary for the subsequent new creation in Christ. This could not mean that the accusers were looking for an exuberance of Spirit; they were looking for good works. For they claimed to have detected the absence of Spirit by the absence of fruit.[1]

How justifiable was the Anabaptist charge? It is evident from various sources that the spiritual condition of the churches in Lutheran lands was bad; all hands admitted it.[2] Undoubtedly some of the less

---

[1] See Rink's charge, above, pp. 85–86. Menius understood the accusation in this light. *Der Widdertauffer*, p. H4r. One of the more detailed charges: "So habe er bis daher wenig guts gesehen, das von der Lutherische pfaffen predigen komme, dan alles ergernus, freiheit, buberei, und sei böser und erger dan underm bapstum, und woe Gottes wort, die warheit und der heilig geist rechtschaffen gelert, da breng es frucht, stehen die leut von sunde ab, bessern sich. Darumb konne er nit erkennen, das Gottes wort warhaftig durch sie gelert, dan sie, die prediger, selbst furen offentlich ein sundlichs, ergerlichs leben. So sage Christus: An fruchten soll man sie erkennen die falschen lerer, dan ein schleen dorn brenge kein wein dreubel etc. [Matt. 7:16.] Darumb glaub er nit, das sie den heiligen geist haben, dan der heilige geist wank nit wie sie, sei auch nit geizig, etc, wie itzt under den Lutherischen befunden als wol als underm bapstum gewesen etc. Und woe nun der heilige geist nit wone und leer, do moge auch nit die warheit gelert und erkent werden. So hab er nun Melchior Rincken erkent an der leer und leben, das er nit anders erkennen habe konnen, das er die warheit gelert;... Daruff [teaching of Rink] habe er sich uf gut begeben und von Gottes schwuren, fressen, saufen und andere sunde abgezogen, und eines solche gute gewiessens sei die taufe ein bundtnuss mit Christo und den menschen, die ein gude leben anfangen und von sunde abstehen wollen...." Testimony of Adam Angersbach, 1531, printed in Wappler, *Thüringen*, pp. 328–29.
[2] Melanchthon reporting on his first visitation in Thuringia in the summer of 1527 was deeply distressed at the spiritual condition of the people and at the incompetence of pastors in their cure of souls. Melanchthon report to Elector John, August 13, 1527, Clemen, *Supplementa Melanchthoniana*, I, Abt. 6, p. 369; also letter to Camerarius, August 11 or 12, 1527, *ibid.*, p. 368. Ambrosius Blaurer reported similar conditions, and blamed the Evangelicals, himself included, for them: "Wir selber tragen einen grossen Teil der Schuld. Man will bei uns so wenig von wahrhaftiger Busse hören, dass unsere Lehre selbst dadurch verdächtig werden muss. Arbeit und Leben wird mir zuwider, wenn ich den Zustand vieler wenig evangelischen Städte betrachte, in welchen kaum irgend eine Spur ächter Bekehrung sich aufweisen lässt. Aus der Christlichen Freiheit wird durch eine gottlose Auslegung die Freiheit, Sünde zu üben, gemacht. Alles preist die Gnade des Heilands. Es ist behaglich, umsonst gerechtfertigt, erlöst, beseligt zu werden. Aber da ist keiner, der gegen die Abtötung des Fleisches, gegen Kreuz und Leiden und gegen christliche Ergebung sich nicht mit Händen und Füssen sträubt." Printed by K. Rembert, *op. cit.*, p. 554, n. 1.

competent priests, caught off guard by the change of faith, took to preaching easy grace, a popular distortion of Luther. The Anabaptists tended to judge Lutheran doctrine by its nearest geographical manifestation, and not by what went on in Wittenberg or by what Luther himself said. Menius vigorously protested that they condemned all Evangelicals because of the sins of some, and especially because of the existence of iniquitous priests. They overlooked the pious among the Evangelicals and took notice of the flamboyant sinners only.[1] From the visitation reports it appears likely that they did not have to look hard for the kind of rogues to which Menius referred. But if there was basis for the charge, even an abundance of incriminating material, it is also clear that they did not know or try to understand the Lutheran interest in good works. At least they gave no evidence of such knowledge. They seized upon a valid issue for discussion purposes and exaggerated it with respect to bonafide Lutheran doctrine.

One of the undiscussed differences of opinion, still within the faithworks problem was the kind of works which might qualify as good. One can observe that when Luther and the Anabaptists talked about works they were not always talking about the same thing. Neither Luther nor Melanchthon – nor the Anabaptists either, for that matter – saw the problem as one in which the nature of good works was a matter for dispute. Menius did see it, and commented appropriately.[2] But a few conjectures as to Luther's reactions had he seen the issue clearly are in order here.

Luther's comments on works reveal a preoccupation with those practices in Catholicism by which the Christian earned merit in the sight of God: monasticism in general, celibacy, fastings, observation of feast days, and the like. It was this kind of work that he found so injurious to the reality of faith-righteousness. He directed his vehemence against anything that smacked of legalism as a means of obtaining grace.[3] Needless to say the Anabaptists would have rejected these practices on the same grounds.[4] But much of what they insisted upon, by way of following the example and commands of Christ, he would have labeled at least silly if not worse. For example, the question of alcohol. Luther was certainly no prude when it came to drinking.[5]

---

[1] *Von dem Geist*, pp. Gv.–Hr.

[2] *Der Widdertauffer*, pp. Yr.–Y4v.

[3] Köstlin, *op. cit.* (1863), I, 154, 171, 314 for examples.

[4] See Wiswedel and Friedmann, "The Anabaptists Answer Melanchthon," *MQR*, XXIX, 220–21. See also Rink, Tract on Baptism, *Sammelband*.

[5] He advised those who had difficulty with scruples about drinking to drink the more richly in Christ. Köstlin, *op. cit.* (1863), II, 479.

The Anabaptists were not total abstainers,[1] but their injunctions against tippling would have impressed Luther as being on the prudish side, not that Luther endorsed drunkenness. Or their remonstrances on the matter of dress would have sounded foreign to his ears.[2] At the very least, such conduct could not have impressed him as the natural fruit of the Spirit in the new creature. At the most it might well have sounded like a new legalism, a renewed effort of the devil to encumber the freedom of the gospel with the pitfalls of works-righteousness. Their injunction against the use of the sword by the Christian he would certainly have considered wrong. Because Christ did not use the sword it did not follow that the sword was forbidden to all Christians. Discipleship in this instance was limited by office. The Christian should not use the sword in self-defense, or for the gospel. But Christ was not a magistrate. The civil magistrate, as Christian, not only could but should use the sword in the exercise of his office.

But Anabaptist restriction of the sword to the non-Christian was more than mildly erroneous. It was seditious. What Luther did see of Anabaptist fruits, what they considered as good works,[3] he saw generally as a threat to the civil order. By 1530 he could find this view most clearly expressed in Menius' book to which he had written the foreword.[4] Because of the absence of previous comment, it is safe to say that he looked for it, and expected it, in Anabaptism because of the example of Müntzer. Müntzer displayed a subjectivism in the sacraments, and then turned revolutionary. So would the Anabaptists. Münster could have been no surprise to Luther. There is no full-bodied discussion of Anabaptist error on works within the context of soteriology in Luther's writings because Luther always considered their "works" as sedition. Such an analysis served to bring the Anabaptist menace under the watchful eye of the civil authorities, although it would be wrong to suggest that his analysis was deliberately invented to serve this end. Luther had genuine fears of a renewed Peasants' Revolt.

It is astounding that neither Luther nor Melanchthon saw very clearly the faith-works issue as a matter of conflict with the Anabaptists. In a few instances Luther spoke of Anabaptist attempts to appear holy through a repetition of Catholic piety: dress in rags, or at least

---

[1] H. S. Bender, "Alcohol," *ME*, I, 36–40.

[2] Menius, *Der Widdertauffer*, p. Y3v.

[3] The best examples: Exegesis of the 82nd Psalm, 1530, *WA*, XXXI, 208. *Vorrede* to Menius' *Der Widdertauffer*, pp. A2r.–A5r.

[4] *Ibid.*, pp. Y2r.–Y4v.

very simply, deny themselves private property, and forsake family and home to lead the life of a wandering preacher. He called these activities their type of works, the absence of which among the Lutherans they considered proof of the Lutheran faith being a false faith.[1] But the appearance of holiness was only appearance, and as such it was hypocrisy.[2] Quite apart from the type of work which the Anabaptists actually performed, they were incapable of avoiding hypocrisy in their good works because their faith was deficient.[3] Luther would have certainly subscribed to Menius' formulation that all works were to be evaluated by the doctrine which produced them; doctrine was never to be called into question by the presence or absence of works.[4] Melanchthon never declared himself on the topic except in his last major work, written in collaboration with other leaders of the Reformation.[5] Whether or not he saw the issue at all is questionable. One cannot avoid the observation that he would have been more sympathetic to the Anabaptist view had he known it. Menius did see the issue.[6] Luther and Melanchthon were much too preoccupied with their characterizations of Anabaptism as overly subjective, which led in turn to spiritualism and, following the Müntzer pattern, to revolution. They did not follow the Anabaptists' view of baptism through to their insistence on obedience to the commands of Christ. As such their view of the radicals remained partial and warped.

The Lutherans preached a faith so weak that it could produce no fruit, which was surely a caricature of the true faith – so ran the Anabaptist accusation. For their part the Lutherans found Anabaptist faith insufferably subjective and personal. But the Lutheran charge ran deeper. Not only did the Anabaptists turn faith as a work of God into a purely human experience; they also infused the work of God in the heart of man with a Spirit so lively that it soared beyond control. The issue of subjectivism carried through logically enough to excessive spiritualism. For Luther and Melanchthon the examples of Müntzer and the Zwickau Prophets, particularly the latter, were

---

[1] Exegesis of Matt. 5, 6, and 7, 1532, *EA*, XLIII, 317–21; Exegesis of John 6, 7, 8, 1530–32, *EA*, XLVII, 313; Exegesis of John 7, 1530–32, *EA*, XLVIII, 105. See also the items reported in n. 3, p. 224. Luther's brief mention in his 1528 pamphlet of the topic of works-righteousness in the act of rebaptism is too insubstantial to permit serious consideration of it. See above, p. 121.

[2] Especially the first item cited in n. 1.

[3] See his formulation in "Von den guten Werken," 1520, *WA*, VI, 217.

[4] Menius, *Der Widdertauffer*, p. E4v.

[5] *Prozess wie es soll gehalten werden*, discussed above, pp. 177–78.

[6] See above, pp. 183–84.

indisputable at this point. It is safe to say that Luther always looked for and expected spiritualism in the Anabaptists. On one occasion he characterized the movement with remarks based on a report of the "Prophet" and his followers sent to him by the Abbot of Fulda.[1] It is significant that from all the Anabaptists for whom information was potentially available to him in Central Germany he should select as typical the most extravagently spiritualistic people. The incident tells us more about Luther's view than it does about the Anabaptists themselves. Melanchthon declared in 1528 that they seldom cited Scripture: they relied on their personal opinions for authority.[2] Later, in a letter to Bucer, he described them as being wildly possessed of the Spirit.[3] This charge requires a more thorough examination. We must begin with the place of the Spirit in salvation for both Luther and the Anabaptists.[4]

Luther believed in a vigorous activity on the part of the Spirit as it was bound to the Word. No one could understand the Word unless the Spirit brought it to him. The power of the Word to convict of sin, to bring the promise of grace, to implant faith was above all the power of the Spirit in the Word. Luther's higher regard for the oral Word as opposed to the private reading of Scripture can be laid in part to his belief that the Spirit breathed more effectively in the former.[5] He insisted that each person must experience the Spirit himself in order to gain the assurance that the Word was beyond doubt the Word of God himself.[6] Luther declared himself on numerous occasions, particularly in the early years of the Reformation, on the necessity for, and vitality of, the Spirit.[7] Above all, the ability to recognize the incarnation, the making visible of the invisible God, was the product of

---

[1] *Tischreden*, no date, *EA*, LXI, 82–83.

[2] Dedication letter to Pistorius, 1528, *CR*, I, 955.

[3] Letter to Bucer, March 15, 1534, *CR*, II, 710–13.

[4] Menius' opinion on the question of spiritualism is not so clear. The most extreme case that came to his attention was Rink's statement that all Scripture was false, meaning that the Spirit was absent. But this attitude is in complete contradiction to Rink's practice. It is an isolated instance which does not at all fit the man who appears in the sources after 1528. It is therefore fair to assume that Menius got the statement from Rink in his Müntzer days around 1525. See above, p. 87, n. 6. Menius does not display Anabaptists as markedly spiritualistic. Only in 1544 does he characterize them as relying on the Spirit as authority above Scripture. (*Von dem Geist*, pp. Jv.–J2r.) In 1530 he had insisted that they restricted the revelation of God to man to the spoken Word, to preaching. Here at least was no spiritualism. (*Der Widdertauffer*, p. P3r.)

[5] Karl G. Steck, "Luther und die Schwärmer," *Theologische Studien*, Heft 44 (Zollikon-Zurich: Evangelischer Verlag, 1955), p. 16.

[6] *Ibid.*, pp. 12–13; Köstlin, *op. cit.* (1863), II, 493–96; W. Wiswedel, "Bible: Inner and Outer Word," *ME*, I, 324.

[7] Steck, *op. cit.*, pp. 10–21.

a miracle worked by the Spirit. The Spirit had the task of clarifying the gospel, of revealing the secrets of Christ.[1]

The Anabaptists clearly thought Luther did not emphasize the Spirit enough, or else he did not have it at all. It is quite evident that they had not read his stronger statements on the subject. They always sought to make religion internal, to strip it of its formal character. They spiritualized in the sense that they restricted faith to the heart of man.[2] One must assume that they considered it the task of the Holy Spirit to lead men to conviction of sin and repentance. They obviously believed that the Spirit gave them the power, in the new life, to live in obedience to Christ.[3] The Spirit was assigned the additional task of calling and holding together the congregation.[4] All these things the Spirit did. But the work most frequently mentioned in the records was of another type. The Spirit spoke to the individual with an authority that paralleled and even went beyond the authority of Scripture. The Spirit revealed God to man in a most personal, individual manner.

There is a sense in which this revelatory work of the Spirit went no further for the Anabaptists than it did for Luther. Heinz Kraut's statements that the Spirit wrote the truth of God in the heart of man might well have been similar to the kind of assurance to the believer that Luther expected from the Spirit.[5] But there were those Anabaptists in Central Germany who relied on dreams and visions in a manner reminiscent of the Zwickau Prophets.[6] It was this function of the Spirit which Luther and Melanchthon especially expected from the Anabaptists and then in turn condemned. The logic of the position,

[1] Erich Seeberg, "Der Gegensatz zwischen Zwingli, Schwenckfeld, und Luther," *Reinhold-Seeberg Festschrift*, ed. W. Koepp (Leipzig: Scholl, 1929), I, 66–69.

[2] Kühn, *op. cit.*, p. 227. It is very difficult to ascertain the role of the Spirit in the religious thought of the Anabaptists in Central Germany because they discussed aspects of the Spirit and his work so seldom. This relative absence of material is significant when one considers how much present scholarship tends to consider the Anabaptists as spiritualists. See Heyer, *Der Kirchenbegriff der Schwärmer.*

[3] The only direct example of this that I could find was that of Hans Römer. After the act of baptism as Römer embraced the new member he pronounced the blessing of the Holy Spirit on him. Immediately he issued a series of charges on how the new man, now living in the power of the Spirit, was to live morally. Wappler, *Thüringen*, pp. 38–41. The oft-repeated charge of the Anabaptists that the Lutheran faith was devoid of Spirit was always turned to the question of post-conversion ethical behavior.

[4] Letter of Elders of Moravia to Mathes [Hasenhan], 1538, printed in *TA, Hesse*, p. 180.

[5] See above, p. 165. Also E. Seeberg, *op. cit.*, I, 66–69.

[6] Three Anabaptists caught with Erbe, 1539, printed in Wappler, *Die Stellung*, pp. 203–04; Jacob Storger, hearing in 1537, printed in Wappler, *Thüringen*, p. 429; the "Prophet," 1533, *ibid.*, pp. 83–85; Hans Römer, *ibid.*, pp. 38–41. All of these cases are in themselves somewhat exceptional. One finds this reliance on dreams missing in most of Central German Anabaptism. But it is found here in sufficient quantity to give a spiritualistic coloration to the movement as a whole.

in relation to the denial of grace in the sacrament, underscores the Lutheran expectancy. This is most clearly seen in the Augsburg Confession where Melanchthon specifically condemned the Anabaptist doctrine that the Spirit came to man apart from external activities, i.e., the oral Word and the sacraments.[1] We have to consider therefore primarily the question of authority with respect to the Spirit. What was the highest authority for the Anabaptists?

Most historians who picture the Anabaptist movement as spiritualist have completely neglected their literalistic interpretation of Scripture.[2] Their literalism is everywhere apparent, but nowhere quite so clearly as in the argument on baptism. Here their major bastion was their slavish adherence to the prescribed sequence of events in Mark 16:16: "He that believeth and is baptized shall be saved." [3] Faith must of necessity precede baptism. Christ himself fixed the sequence. Any change in that sequence was human trifling at the least and the work of the devil at the most. In the exercise of their literalism the Anabaptists stooped to the use of ludicrous arguments. Christ was baptized at the age of thirty; therefore his followers should at least be baptized only in adulthood.[4] The Anabaptists carried their literalistic exegesis into other regions. They turned the gospel into a handbook of ethics. They held the view that the admonitions in the Sermon on the Mount could be obeyed in the present world.[5] In those areas where they exercised a strict discipline, this literalism developed into outright legalism.[6] But in baptism particularly their subjectivism was the more galling to the Lutherans because they defended their view with a literalistic reliance on the authority most treasured by their opponents. In this instance the Lutherans felt compelled to go beyond the authority of Scripture. They took refuge in tradition. Melanchthon was the most detailed in his reliance on tradition, and the clearest in

---

[1] Reu, *op. cit.*, pp. *172–*173. Also *CR*, XXVI, 276.

[2] Heyer is a notable exception. See *op. cit.*, p. 33. Heyer's work has much useful material. It is marred by his adamancy on the question of the relation of the Anabaptists to the Spiritualists. His proof of his thesis that the Spiritualists and Anabaptists differed in their views on the nature of the church because of eschatological differences is not convincing. His work is limited in its application to Central German Anabaptism because:

  1. the attitude toward the church was not central in Anabaptist thought in this region;

  2. not all, or even the major part, of Anabaptism here placed a great deal of emphasis on eschatology. It was certainly peripheral to Rink's thought, for instance.

[3] Menius has them emphasizing the same point – i.e., sequence of events adhered to literally – in their interpretation of Matt. 28:19: "Go ye therefore, and teach all nations, baptizing them...." Menius, *Der Widdertauffer*, pp. L4r.–Mv.

[4] *Ibid.*, p. T2r.

[5] Kühn, *op. cit.*, pp. 230–31. See above, pp. 89–98.

[6] Heyer, *op. cit.*, p. 33.

relating the authority of Scripture to the authority of tradition. Already in 1522 he had been impressed with the fact that Augustine had been disturbed by the issue of infant baptism.[1] Scripture was pre-eminent to Melanchthon, but it was Scripture as the fathers had interpreted it.[2] Tradition as authority meant nothing to the Anabaptists when it was set against Scripture. They held the radical view that every traditional ceremony of the church must be abolished if it was not specifically commanded in Scripture.

What role did the Spirit play as authority for the Anabaptists? They insisted that the Spirit be present in the Word.[3] But it is significant that they resorted to the authority of the Spirit at that point when they were overcome by arguments from the authority which they recognized as the highest authority, namely Scripture.[4] If they forced the Lutherans to fall back on tradition, the Lutherans forced them to fall back on Spirit. In both cases the maneuver appears to be a defensive one. Neither side recognized what is obvious to a twentieth-century mind: the Scriptures taken as a whole are not without contradiction; nor are their meanings always transparently clear. Differences in interpretation can be held by men of honest intention.[5]

Why did Luther and Melanchthon fail to see the literalism of the Anabaptists? The question is a natural one, and it is not easily answered. Other Reformers did see literalism in Anabaptism, and they condemned it as excessive. Bullinger, following Zwingli, at first criticized them for being spiritualists. When his personal experience with them taught him otherwise, he accused them of a stifling literalism.[6] Andreas Althamer, a Lutheran pastor in the Principality of Ansbach, observed their tendency toward literalism and condemned it.[7] This is all the more astonishing in view of the fact that Althamer's

---

[1] Melanchthon to Spalatin, January 1, 1522, CR, I, 533–34.

[2] See above, pp. 147–48.

[3] See above, p. 87.

[4] So the 1535 Jena interrogation by Melanchthon, above, p. 165.

[5] Another difference in attitude toward Scripture is found in the problem of the relation of Old and New Testaments. The Lutherans tended to see the New Testament as more intense than the Old. The Anabaptists considered that the New Testament for all practical purposes superceded the Old.

[6] Heinold Fast, "Heinrich Bullinger und die Täufer" (MS dissertation at Heidelberg, 1957), p. 253. Bullinger leveled the charge of spiritualism in 1530 in his *Von dem vnuerschampten Fraefel/ ergerlichem Verwyrren/ vnnd vnwahrhafftem Leeren/ der selbsgesandten Widertoeuffern/* ... (Zurich: Froschouer, 1530), pp. 9–13. By 1532 he was accusing the Anabaptists of literalism. See Heinold Fast and John H. Yoder, "How To Deal with Anabaptists: An Unpublished Letter of Heinrich Bullinger," *MQR*, XXXIII (April, 1959), 83–95.

[7] Andreas Althamer, *Ein kurtze Unterricht den Pfarrherrn und Predigern...* (no publisher, 1528), pp. A3v.–A4v.

picture of Anabaptism was dominated by the figure of Hans Denk. Menius himself saw their literalism.[1] The only answer to this question that is even partially satisfactory is that Luther and Melanchthon were so preoccupied with their picture of the *Schwärmer*, with whom they had had personal contact, that they could not see the Anabaptists in anything but the same light. Müntzer and the Zwickau Prophets were spiritualists. They had been quite fluent in Scripture, though they did not put the literalist twist to exegesis that the Anabaptists did. Luther and Melanchthon expected spiritualism and revolution from Anabaptism because the *Schwärmer* had excelled in these arts. Luther never had sufficient contact with Anabaptists to induce him to question the transfer of his picture of the *Schwärmer* to the Anabaptists. Melanchthon had indeed met Anabaptists. But the picture was too firmly fixed to permit change by impressions from his infrequent meetings with Anabaptists.

To the Anabaptists then the Spirit played a vital role as authority. God in his Spirit spoke through the Scriptures in a manner which made them authoritative, as well as highly personal. Sometimes the Spirit spoke outside the Scriptures. But most of Central Germany's Anabaptists relied heavily on a literalistic rendition of Scripture as a restraint on the exuberance of the Spirit. Authority was more Scripture than Spirit, though it was hardly an either-or issue for them.

Although the Lutheran charges centered on the problem of authority, the problem of spiritualism carries logically into other issues. These should be examined briefly. First it should be noted that spiritualism is a relative matter. Christians have always believed in the existence and work of the Holy Spirit. The Lutheran charge of spiritualism in Anabaptism meant of course that the Anabaptists attributed a larger role to the Spirit than did the Lutherans.[2] Within the problem of soteriology, particularly if this included ethics as it did for the Anabaptists, the latter were more spiritualistic than the Lutherans.

---

[1] *Der Widdertauffer*, pp. L4r.–Mv., O3r.–Pv., T2r. Menius' failure to pronounce the Anabaptists spiritualists in 1530 can probably be laid to his realization of their counterbalancing Scriptural literalism. He even criticized the Anabaptists for failing to acknowledge the validity of dreams, visions, and the proclamations of angels as means of the dispensing of God's grace and revelation. But the criticism is curious in view of his subsequent brief statement that they relied on dreams as more authoritative than Scripture. (*Ibid.*, pp. P3v.–P4v.) By 1544 he was prepared to forget their literalism in favor of condemnation as spiritualists. See above, p. 226, n. 4.

[2] Luther was inclined to draw the lines of definition rather tightly on at least one occasion. In 1532 he declared that the denial of grace in baptism constitutes spiritualism. *Eine Andere Predigt am Sonntage Trinitatis, EA*, XII, 440. This is a reworked form of the sermon preached on Trinity Sunday, 1526, printed in *WA*, XX, 413 ff.

The Anabaptists were spiritualizers of the Lord's Supper in comparison to the Lutherans. On baptism they were more subjective, beyond question. But they can hardly be termed spiritualists on this issue. Their demand that the Spirit be present in the act was no greater than that of Luther. Their fundamental reason for the performance of the ordinance, apart from the subjective desire to symbolize the previous experience of repentance and new birth, was far more because Scripture commanded its execution |than because the Spirit impelled them to it. Finally, on at least one issue, Luther was more a spiritualist than the Anabaptists. The Anabaptists persisted in the conviction that it was possible to gather a body of true believers into the true church. Luther insisted that the true church remain invisible.[1]

The Lutheran charge of spiritualism was exaggerated. There was undeniably spiritualism present in Thuringian Anabaptism, certainly more of it than among the Hutterites for example.[2] But that spiritualism had a counterbalancing and restraining Scriptural literalism. There was not the excessiveness that the Lutherans pictured. The Anabaptists appeared as spiritualists to Lutherans partly because they were forced to find authority for their deviation from the Lutheran Reform. That they resorted to an appeal to Spirit, after Scripture, should not surprise us in view of the fact that Luther did the same when challenged for the source of his authority by the Catholics.[3] Perhaps it is fair to say that Anabaptist spiritualism appeared more dangerous because it was not governed by tradition. This would be particularly alarming to Luther. His own appeal to Spirit against

[1] Herman Preus, *The Communion of Saints* (Minneapolis: Augsburg Publishing House, 1948), pp. 84–85. See Franklin Littell, "The Anabaptist Concept of the Church," *The Recovery of the Anabaptist Vision*, G. F. Hershberger, ed., p. 122, n. 14. Also Littell, "Spiritualizers, Anabaptists, and the Church," *MQR*, XXIX (1955), 34–43. The point can be easily run into the ground. After all the Anabaptists did rely on the Spirit to help them determine who belonged to the true church. And an argument can be made for Luther's visible church – where the Word was truly preached – as an objective fact, though this was never the true church to Luther. The true church could only be discerned by faith, and faith is a trust in things invisible. The outward organization which bore the name church always remained for Luther a human institution and not therefore the true church. He could speak, as did the Anabaptists, of the church as a fellowship of believers. But as such it was invisible to human perception. The true church has certain signs – true preaching of the Word, and administration of the true sacraments – but these do not in themselves make the true church. They do not touch the nature of the church. Preus, *op. cit.*, pp. 86–89, 95–97.

[2] See the Letter of the Elders of Moravia to Mathes [Hasenhan], 1538, printed in *TA, Hesse*, pp. 180ff. Hans Bott, though probably a deviant from Rink's ideas, was clearly too spiritualistic for the Moravian Anabaptists. The relative disinterest in church discipline in Thuringian Anabaptism makes one suspicious on this point.

[3] In Worms he relied on the revelation of God *to him* – through the Word, but via the Spirit in a personal manner. Steck, *op. cit.*, p. 13. He insisted that a bonafide doctor of the Scriptures could be created only by the Spirit. Fast, *op. cit., MQR*, XXX, 106.

the claims of Rome did not lead him away from church tradition so radically as did that of the Anabaptists.

A third major issue dividing the Lutherans and Anabaptists was the question of office, or call to preach. The Anabaptists felt compelled to go out on a preaching ministry in regions under Lutheran influence. They did so because of what they considered inadequacies in Lutheran faith. The issue of call to them was related to their view of the inseparability of faith and ethics. Because Luther's faith quenched the Spirit and produced no fruit, the true believers were forbidden to hear Lutheran preaching, and were constrained to proclaim the truth to others. The Anabaptists' accusation could be more specific on occasion. The Evangelicals did not preach Christian truth; they could not because they were themselves sinners. Moreover, their hearers produced no evidence of having had a vital encounter with Christian truth, in that they demonstrated no moral improvement.[1] The Lutherans naturally responded energetically to this caustic charge.

The Lutherans replied by charging the Anabaptists with suppressing the truth in their prohibition of attendance at Lutheran services. In itself that was bad enough. But the Anabaptists had the audacity to proclaim their gospel to whoever would listen. This they did covertly in order to avoid detection and eventual punishment. Both Luther and Menius considered the clandestine character of Anabaptist activity sufficient proof of their diabolical intent.[2] They gave no heed to the question of office. God had ordained the existence of various church offices in order to provide a defense against the repeated incursions of diabolical teachings in the church. The call to fill an office came primarily from men, from the church or the civil community. Whenever God's people failed to respond to his will and direction, God raised a prophet or apostle outside the ordained offices. But the special call from God was always attested by miracle-working powers, so that people could acknowledge the bearer of God's message. Luther and Menius were shocked at the anarchy that would ensue if everyone who felt himself called could preach whatever he liked.[3]

[1] The most detailed configuration of charges is found in Menius, *Von dem Geist*, p. C2r. See also hearing of Köhler and Scheffer, 1537, printed in Wappler, *Die Stellung Kursachsens*, p. 197.
[2] Luther, "Brief an Eberhard von der Thann, von den Schleichern und Winkelpredigern," 1532, *WA*, Vol. XXX, Part 3, pp. 518, 522. See above, pp. 128–29. Menius, *Der Widdertauffer*, pp. F4v.–Gr. See above, pp. 194–97. Menius had had his attention called to this problem by Luther after the latter had read the first draft of his 1530 book. Menius apparently extended his discussion of the problem as a result of Luther's recommendation (Menius, *Der Widdertauffer*, pp. av.–b3r.). Letter of Luther to Menius, April 12, 1530, *WB*, V, 274.
[3] Luther, Letter to Eberhard v. d. Thann, *WA*, XXX, Part 3, 521–27; Menius; *Der Widdertauffer*, pp. ar.–v.; Menius, *Von dem Geist*, pp. E4r.–F4r.

In defense of their practice the Anabaptists argued first the necessity for preaching the true gospel. Beyond that they cited the example of Christ and the apostles, who carried out a peripatetic ministry. In their passion for literalism they insisted that the true Christian follow this divine example.[1] They also claimed on occasion the right to rise and speak because they had a message from the Lord. The pastors installed by the magistrates erred grievously in suppressing the prophetic Word brought by the Anabaptists.[2] Most of the time they did not exercise their prophetic prerogative in public. Realistically, to have done so would have resulted in their capture. So they confined their activities to the remote villages and forests.

Without question Anabaptist tactics were intensely irritating. To charge the Lutherans with promulgating error was annoying enough. But when after repeatedly evading discussion, or suffering defeat in discussion,[3] they sneaked to the lonely byways to spread their ideas among the simple peasantry, this was exasperating beyond measure. One must observe again that they did not know the real Lutheran preaching, from all appearances at any rate. They heard and condemned what was likely a cheap substitute. They caught the Lutheran church in its formative days before it could muster a fixed organization. Their unrestrained and provocative character with respect to usurpation of the ordained office earned for them, along with the earlier Zwickau Prophets, Carlstadt, and Müntzer, Luther's appellation *Schwärmer*.[4]

On the other hand the Lutheran critique was less than fair. After having declared two years earlier that Anabaptists were deserving of death and should be hunted out,[5] Luther could not have been serious when he suggested in 1532 that they should always seek out the pastor of a region and request permission to preach. If permission were denied them, they should shake the dust from their feet, in good apostolic tradition, and depart.[6] Menius' assertions that the Christian must suffer unjustly and subsequently flee the land rather than accept and preach error sounded highly academic.[7] It should be noted that

[1] Menius, *Von dem Geist*, p. E3v.
[2] Luther declared that they referred to I Cor. 14:30: "If anything be revealed to another that sitteth by, let the first hold his peace." Letter to Eberhard, *WA*, XXX, Part 3, 521–27; W. Koehler, "Luther, Martin," *ME*, III, 418.
[3] Menius, *Der Widdertauffer*, p. F4r.
[4] Heyer, *op. cit.*, p. 3.
[5] Exegesis of the 82nd Psalm, 1530, see above, pp. 126ff.
[6] Luther, Letter to Eberhard v. d. Thann, *WA*, XXX, Part 3, 518–19.
[7] Menius, *Wie ein iglicher Christ*, pp. E4v., Fv.–F3v.

he kept within the relative safety of Electoral Saxony, and ventured into Ducal Saxony only after the demise of hostile Duke George. The Anabaptists had no place to which they could escape. They preached secretly because they were driven underground; their only alternative was to refrain from any exercise of their religion, to act as Luther's "heretic only." They could not have accepted the restraint of silence and remained in any sense true to their consciences. It is difficult to believe that Luther would have acted any differently under the same circumstances. Luther had chafed at the institutionalism of Rome, which restricted the free work of the Spirit. He declared that a doctor of the Holy Scriptures could be created only by the Spirit, in heaven.[1] How similar was the argument of the Anabaptists. Menius' advice to the Evangelical pastor or layman living in Catholic territory on how to conduct himself sounded very similar to Anabaptist conviction and practice.[2] The Lutherans denied the Anabaptists the right of appeal to the same Spirit they appealed to because Anabaptist doctrine was erroneous. Menius asserted the Lutherans required no attestation of miracles because they taught what the apostles had taught.[3] In view of the Anabaptists' conviction that their teaching was distinctly the restitution of apostolic purity, Menius was evading the issue.

The Lutheran-Anabaptist conflict centered in soteriology, and was waged from there on spiritualism and office. But there were other issues on which each side declared itself in opposition to the other. Obviously there was disagreement on the meaning and purpose of the Lord's Supper. The argument never figured as decisive in the records, because of its similarity to that on baptism. Baptism was argued so exhaustively that there was little more to say beyond a statement of basic positions on the question of the Lord's Supper. Luther undoubtedly considered his pamphlets against the sacramentarians sufficient to cover the Anabaptists also. Christology was a source of Lutheran expressions of disagreement. But the topic was peripheral to the central conflict largely because there was so little tangible material to provoke controversy. With a few exceptions of a minor nature the two groups regarded the Christological problems in much the same manner. There were other issues however which, though not discussed much, or at all, by either side, were nonetheless issues

---

[1] Quoted in Fast, *op. cit.*, *MQR*, XXX, 106.
[2] See above, p. 200.
[3] Menius, *Von dem Geist*, pp. Fv.–F2v.

on which real differences of opinion existed. A brief examination of several of these is in order here.

Anabaptist emphasis on the post-conversion conduct of the Christian led them to erect a church radically different from the Lutheran church. They tried to create a church of believers only. In so doing they rejected both the concept of the Corpus Christianum and Luther's view of the true church remaining invisible. The attempt was nothing short of revolutionary. It is all the more amazing, therefore, that the Lutherans did not seriously raise this issue as an important source of conflict. The Zurich Reformers discerned the conflict at a relatively early stage.[1] The Lutherans saw it only dimly.[2] Why?

The Anabaptists geographically nearest the Lutheran leaders did not practice an extraordinarily strong congregational life, in comparison to those of South Germany, Switzerland, and later Holland. Persecution and their early evangelical impulse prevented their settling into an established congregational life with fixed roots.[3] Still, the Anabaptist view of the church was different from that of the Lutherans. A more important reason must be found. Religious pronouncements of the Anabaptists in the realm of ethics were regarded by the Lutherans as politics, and seditious politics at that. The entire emphasis of the Lutherans was focused therefore on the menace to the state, not to the church. They did not see very clearly the logical extension of Anabaptist ethics into the creation of a radically different type of church because they were preoccupied with their fear of revolution. Their identification of Anabaptism with Müntzer set the pattern.

There is one aspect of this conflict that has been little emphasized by historians. The Anabaptists were willing to die rather than surrender their duty to evangelize. They made the most determined efforts to call people from sinful society. The Lutheran sense of mission was quite different. It was indeed not so much mission as pastoral care.

---

[1] John S. Oyer, "The Reformers Oppose the Anabaptist Theology," op. cit., pp. 203–05.

[2] From Luther's numerous off-the-cuff remarks on Anabaptism I could discover only two which touch the question of Anabaptist error on the church: WT, V, 19; and Sermon on Matt. 13:24–30, 1546, EA (2d ed.), XX, 541.

Melanchthon commented very briefly on five occasions: Memorandum to Elector John, October, 1531, CR, IV, 738–39; Letter to Myconius, October 31, 1531, CR, II, 549; Etliche Propositiones, 1535, p. Av.; Interrogation of Ana. at Jena, 1535, CR, II, 998; Das Weltliche, CR, III, 198–200.

Menius had to deal with Anabaptist accusations against the Evangelical church. (Von dem Geist, pp. C2r.–G3v.) But he did not write specifically of Anabaptist ethical ideas leading to a new, pure church of believers.

[3] See above, pp. 101–06.

The Anabaptists erred in thinking that the Lutheran pastors considered their entire flock as good Christians, or even as serious candidates for heaven. To be sure baptism did some good. But Luther and Melanchthon in particular took a very dim view of the spiritual condition of the people in Lutheran lands. Luther was as much concerned as the Anabaptists that the Word be proclaimed in order to release its power to bring repentance. The Anabaptists and the Lutherans did not differ in their analyses of the spiritual condition of the people.

Anabaptist emphasis on the post-conversion conduct of the Christian led them in the second instance to reject the sword. They said that no Christian could therefore be a magistrate. Luther believed in nonresistance for the Christian with respect to his own person, and he rejected force as a means of spreading the gospel because the Word did not need human force. But Luther could not conceive of applying the gospel as a rule for all of society.[1]

On the issues of the place of the state in society, and the individual's responsibility to the state, there was wide disagreement between Lutheran and Anabaptist. The Lutherans aired the issues frequently.[2] These need not be repeated here. But the validity of the Lutheran charge, with respect to known Anabaptist views, must be considered briefly.

The most serious charge of the Reformers was that the Anabaptist doctrine was directed against the continued existence of civil authority.[3] Part of the accusation stemmed from the Anabaptist conviction that the true Christian could in no wise occupy an office of civil authority. They rejected Christian participation in government for a number of reasons,[4] chief of which was the necessity for the use of force by the magistrate. Certainly this did not mean for them that government

---

[1] George Forell, *Faith Active in Love* (New York: American Press, 1954), p. 149.

[2] The fullest charges for each of the men discussed in this study are found in:

Luther, "An Exposition of the Eighty-Second Psalm," 1530, translated and printed in *Works of Martin Luther, op. cit.*, IV, 285–310.

Melanchthon, *Wiedertäufermandat für Kursachsen*, 1536, in Wappler, *Inquisition und Ketzerprozesse*, pp. 181–83. Melanchthon repeated this basic core of accusations on several occasions subsequent to the publication of the mandate.

Menius, *Der Widdertauffer*, pp. Y2r.–ar.

[3] So Eberhard v. d. Thann anent Rink, see above, pp. 92–93. Also Menius, *Von dem Geist*, pp. R3r., S2r.–S4r. Menius accused the Anabaptists of teaching that the Christian could admit no civil authority beyond that of his own preacher-minister. His refutation of the point, however, is a defense of the right of the Christian to hold political office, which the Anabaptists did in fact challenge. The denial of the use of the sword for the Christian was the basis for the Anabaptist belief that no Christian might hold civil office.

[4] Hans J. Hillerbrand, "The Anabaptist View of the State," *MQR*, XXXII (1958), especially 95–97. Also Wiswedel and Friedmann, "The Anabaptists Answer Melanchthon," *MQR*, XXIX, 213–14.

should not exist; there would always be enough men, essentially non-Christians from their point of view, who would be willing and eager to occupy positions of political authority.[1] That the Reformers turned the rejection of civil office for Christians into a threat, premeditated or unconscious, against the existence of any civil authority can only tell us of the Reformers' failure to understand the Anabaptists on this point. They were radical beyond a question. They were socially irresponsible in that they had virtually no interest at all in problems of social control; their interest in society was of a different nature – evangelistic. But they were not social revolutionaries in the ordinary sense of the phrase, or as the Reformers portrayed them.

It was not only Anabaptist rejection of the civil office for the Christian that led to accusation of sedition by the Reformers. Their rejection of the civil oath, of participation in warfare, their interest in economic sharing to the point of community of goods, and their abandonment of family in the interests of evangelism likewise constituted a serious threat to the civil order. Here again the Reformers refused to recognize Anabaptist views as deriving from Scripture, interpreted correctly or incorrectly. The Anabaptists were trying to bring into existence an order of Christ that was sharply separated from conventional society. Their complete rejection of the Corpus Christianum solution of the problem of church and society [2] became the basis for the Reformers' alarm and for their accusations of sedition. The Reformers were thoroughly justified in sensing in Anabaptist doctrine a threat to the Corpus Christianum. They turned that threat into sedition by persisting in regarding the movement, quite naturally, against the background of the Peasants' Revolt in general and the activities of the spiritualist Müntzer in particular. They probably found enough isolated instances of recurrent Peasants' Revolt sentiment in Central German Anabaptism to confirm their view.[3]

A final issue for consideration is that of eschatology. Here was no open conflict between the Anabaptists and the Reformers, but it has been considered a question on which differences of opinion or at least emphasis led to different ends. Heyer suggests that the Anabaptist eschatology played a decisive role in their view of the church, their attempt to gather the believers or the elect together in expectation

[1] Hillerbrand, op. cit., p. 98.
[2] Robert Friedmann, "The Doctrine of the Two Worlds," Recovery of the Anabaptist Vision, pp. 105–18. This is an excellent study of the Anabaptists' idea of the Kingdom of God as opposed to a world society dominated by Satan.
[3] See above, pp. 165–66, and pp. 95–98.

and anticipation of a cataclysmic end to world history.[1] Central
German Anabaptism had its prophets and teachers who interpreted
Biblical passages in order to prepare the believers for the rapid
approach of the Lord. They took their interpretations further, and
tried to induce the non-committed to join the Anabaptist brotherhood
because of that imminent return, and in order to avoid the punishments
in it.[2]

Whatever the detail and emphasis of the Anabaptist view on the
end times, it could not have been very decisive in formulating a different approach to the church from that of the Lutherans, because the
Lutherans had much the same expectancy of the imminent violent
return of the Lord. Luther rushed the publication of his German
translation of the book of Daniel to appear before the rest of the Old
Testament, so that everyone might read and comprehend the prophecy
in Daniel before the end of the world.[3] Melanchthon did not anticipate
an end quite so soon. He reckoned on the return of the Lord in a
little over four hundred and fifty years. But he was as anxious to
decipher the prophetic mysteries in Scripture in a detailed prognosti-
cation as was Luther, or the Anabaptists for that matter.[4] Menius
also lived in the expectancy of an immediate return of the Lord,
attended with violence. He relied in part on astrological calculations.[5]
The political turmoil of the sixteenth century was in part responsible
for the widespread preoccupation of religious minds with eschatology.[6]
In this respect the Anabaptists were no more fanatical than the Reformers. Historians, however, have tended to examine their more
radical eschatological views with scrupulous zeal and to overlook the
equally fantastic views of the Reformers.[7]

[1] Heyer, op. cit., p. 41. Heyer finds the concept particularly useful because it enables him
to base the difference on church view between Anabaptists and *unparteiische* Spiritualists on
differences in eschatology. His subsequent quotations from Schwenckfeld and Franck (pp.
44–47) reveal the Spiritualists' rejection of the visible church for purely spiritualist reasons
more convincingly than they show a rejection for eschatological reasons.

[2] See above, pp. 100–01.

[3] Leroy Froom, *The Prophetic Faith of Our Fathers* (4 vols.; Washington, D.C.: Review
and Herald, 1948), II, 266–83. Forell points out that it was Luther's confident expectancy
of an immediate end of the world that resulted in his relative neglect in matters of social
ethics. He believed there was little necessity for repairing the social structure since this world
would pass away in a short time anyway. Forell, op. cit., pp. 162–63.

[4] Froom, op. cit., II, 285–91. One must remember also the astounding superstition of
Melanchthon, and his predilection for divining the mysteries of the stars and comets. See
Manschreck, op. cit., pp. 102–12.

[5] See above, p. 181.

[6] See the pessimistic comments of several sixteenth century writers on the political chaos
in Europe signaling the end of the world, especially those of Conrad Heresbach, printed in
Rembert, op. cit., pp. 361 ff.

[7] Gerhard Neumann, "Eschatologische und chiliastische Gedanken in der Reformationszeit, besonders bei den Täufern," *Die Welt als Geschichte*, XIX (1959), 58–66.

CHAPTER VIII

EVALUATION OF THE LUTHERAN WRITINGS
AGAINST THE ANABAPTISTS

Within the examination of Lutheran writings against the Anabaptists
there remains the problem of evaluation. What were the sources of
information on Anabaptism used by Luther, Melanchthon, and
Menius? What precisely does their Anabaptism consist of? Whom
do they regard as typical Anabaptists? How does their picture of the
movement compare with that derived from other sources, from the
Anabaptists themselves? These are questions which require our
attention at this point.

We begin with the problem of sources of information. For Menius
the question is easily answered. He wrote his books on the basis of
personal encounters with Anabaptists of Central Germany. He could
have referred to pamphlets published by or against the Anabaptists.
He might have relied on reports from persons he knew and trusted
within his circle of acquaintances in Central Germany. But his
authority in both of his major works was his personal encounter
with Anabaptists in pursuit of his spiritual office.[1]

For Melanchthon the question is much more difficult to answer.
As early as October, 1527, he had enough information about the
Anabaptists to begin writing against them. From what sources?

In all probability his earliest useful source of information was
knowledge of the movement in Central Germany. Since the summer
of 1526 the Anabaptists evangelized in northern Franconia, and since
December, 1526, their presence was known to public officials. In
February, 1527, Duke John issued a mandate against the Anabaptists
in his Coburg region. Melanchthon carried on a correspondence of sorts

---

[1] Menius, *Der Widdertauffer*, p. F4r.; Menius, *Von dem Geist*, p. H4r. It is not without
significance that in both instances when he cited the approximate number of Anabaptists he
knew – thirty in 1530 and one hundred in 1544 – he did so to prove that the Anabaptists were
devils because secretive; he complained that from all of these persons he could pry scarcely
any information at all.

with Balthasar Düring, preacher at Coburg, in which on one occasion early in 1527 Melanchthon remarked about the unrest that prevailed in the church there.[1] It is reasonable to suppose that he had reference to those who were later to be called Anabaptists. During his first church visitation in Thuringia, in midsummer of 1527, he discovered what he termed Carlstadters who caused disturbances.[2] His later statement about Anabaptists whom he had seen return to their senses [3] may well have been a reference to some of these Carlstadters with whom he had disputed, some of whom in fact did leave their errors.[4] What he meant by Carlstadters is not altogether clear. He probably had reference to those who accepted Carlstadt's view of the Eucharist. But he also specified some who had refused to have their children baptized.[5] At no point did he specify those who caused the disturbances as Anabaptists. The term first appeared from his pen in October, 1527, when he reported to Camerarius that he intended to write against the Anabaptists.[6] By December, 1527, he had learned of Anabaptists in Erfurt and near Gotha.[7] Central Germany, then, was a source of information; but one dare not overstate the case in view of Melanchthon's statement early in 1528 that "these regions" were tranquil enough with respect to Anabaptism in comparison to other parts of Germany.[8] "These regions" most likely referred to Electoral Saxony. But what were the other parts of Germany to which he made reference?

Nürnberg immediately suggests itself by virtue of Melanchthon's frequent correspondence with two of its citizens on the problem of Anabaptism. Hieronymous Baumgärtner lived there. And Friedrich Pistorius, Abbot of St. Giles monastery, to whom Melanchthon dedicated his 1528 work against the Anabaptists, was also a resident of Nürnberg. Both received several letters from Melanchthon on the subject during Melanchthon's earliest preoccupation with the radicals.[9]

---

[1] Letter to Düring, March 12, 1527, CR, I, 861.

[2] Letter to Camerarius, August 11 or 12, 1527, CR, I, 881.

[3] Letter to Pistorius, October 12, 1528, CR, I, 1001.

[4] Visitation report to Elector John, August 13, 1527, Clemen, *Supplementa Melanchthoniana*, I, Abt. 6, 369.

[5] *Ibid.*, p. 370.

[6] Letter to Camerarius, October 23, 1527, CR, I, 919-21.

[7] Letter to Spalatin, December 18, 1527, CR, I, 913-14.

[8] Letter to Camerarius, January 23, 1528, CR, I, 951-52.

[9] To Baumgärtner: October 23, 1527, CR, I, 900-01; January 23, 1528, CR, I, 936-37. To Pistorius: Dedication of 1528 tract, May 10, 1528, CR, I, 955; October 12, 1528, CR, I, 1001; and of October, 1528, CR, I, 1006.

Moreover Melanchthon himself was in Nürnberg before June of 1526.[1] It is likely that he at least heard of Hans Denk. But he did not allow much of Denkian Anabaptism to influence his picture of the movement in his first pamphlet. In his correspondence with the Nürnbergers he warned them of the danger of the sect,[2] and he appeared if anything to be writing on the subject at the request of the Nürnbergers,[3] to give them information. It is not likely that he learned much from Nürnberg.

Melanchthon could have heard of Anabaptism from another center of the movement, Strassburg. He corresponded with both Bucer and the jurist, Nicholas Gerbel, in Strassburg. He wrote to inform the latter of his 1528 work being printed in neighboring Hagenau.[4] It does not appear from this letter that Gerbel provided him with information.[5] Nothing can be found from Bucer to Melanchthon in these early years either.

Melanchthon did hear of something in Steyr, Austria, from a citizen of that city studying at Wittenberg-Jena. From Wolfgang Callistus he learned of what he called Manicheans and Arians.[6] In view of the known activities of Anabaptists in Steyr, particularly the followers of Hans Hut, these were almost certainly Anabaptists. His brief description of their activities corresponded exactly with his later accounts of Anabaptists.

Melanchthon could have used any of a large number of pamphlets written by persons closer to the movement than he was as a source of information for his pamphlet. Zwingli in Zurich, Oecolampadius in Basel, Bader in Landau, Bucer in Strassburg, Link in Nürnberg, Rhegius in Augsburg, and Schmid in Switzerland, all of these men had seen substantial works against the Anabaptists through the press before Melanchthon wrote his first book.[7] Or Hubmaier, Denk,

---

[1] Manschreck, *op. cit.*, p. 134.

[2] Letter to Baumgärtner, October 23, 1527, *CR*, I, 900–01.

[3] Letter to Pistorius, end of October, 1528, *CR*, I, 1006.

[4] Letter to Gerbel, May 10, 1528, *CR*, I, 973–74.

[5] A letter of Gerbel to Luther, August 29, 1527, *WB*, IV, 240, did mention that Anabaptism existed in Strassburg.

[6] Letter to Luther and Bugenhagen, September 16, 1527, *WB*, IV, 249–50.

[7] Zwingli's major works up to this point were: *Von dem Touf, vom Wiedertouf und von der Kindertouf*, May 27, 1525, *Huldreich Zwinglis sämtliche Werke* (ed. by Egli, Finsler, Koehler) (Leipzig: M. Heinsius Nachfolger, 1914), IV, 188–337; *Antwort über Balthasar Hubmaiers Taufbüchlein*, November 5, 1525, *ZW*, IV, 577–647; *In Catabaptistarum Strophas Elenchus*, July, 1527, *ZW*, VI, 1–196.

Oecolampadius, *Ein Gesprech etlicher Predicanten zu Basel, gehalten mit etlichen Bekennern des Widertouffs* (Basel: Curio, 1525); *Vnderrichtung von dem Widertauff/ von der Oberkeit/ vnd von dem Eyd/ auff Carlins N. Widertauffers Artickel. Antwort auff Balthasar Hübmaiers Büch-

242   EVALUATION OF LUTHERAN WRITINGS

Dachser, Langenmantel, and perhaps Freisleben from the Anabaptist side could have been consulted via their printed works.[1] Melanchthon did not rely on any of these. In the polemics there was far too much incriminating material unused in his 1528 work; Melanchthon surely would have availed himself of the opportunity to utilize the accusations, if not the rebuttals, of the other writers. He appears not to have read any of the Anabaptist tracts, again judging from the absence of identity of information.

Information on Anabaptism for the early period of Melanchthon's literary activity against them came largely from Central Germany, with the probability of some from other regions in Germany and Austria. Melanchthon did not attempt to make clear the sources of his information prior to publication of his first work. For his subsequent writings his potential sources of information were too great to come under consideration here. He likely learned more during his Thuringian church visitation late in 1528.[2] He most certainly read Menius. He met and interrogated Anabaptists at Jena in 1535. But above all, his works of the mid-1530's rely on information about that most notorious of Anabaptist centers, Münster.

What sources of information did Luther use in his first tract against

lein wider der Predicanten Gespräch zu Basel/ von dem Kindertauff/ ... (Basel: Cratander, 1527).

Bader, Brüderliche Warnung für dem newen Abgöttischen Orden der Widertäuffer/ darinn von nachfolgenden Artickeln gehandelt würt... (no publisher, 1527).

Bucer, Getrewe Warnung der Prediger des Euangelij zū Strassburg/ vber die Artickel/ so Jacob Kautz Prediger zū Wormbs/ kürtzlich hat lassen aussgohn... (Strassburg, 1527).

[Link], Grundtliche Vnterrichtung/ eins erbern Rats der Statt Nürmberg/ Welcher Gestalt/ jre Pfarrher vn Prediger in den Stetten vn auff dem Land/ das Volck/ wider etliche verfürische Lere der Widertauffer/ ... (Nürmberg: Gutknecht [1527]).

Rhegius, Wider den Newen Taufforden/ Notwendige Warnung an alle Christglaubigen ... (Augsburg, 1527).

Schmid, Ein christliche Ermanung zu warer Hoffnung in Gott vnd Warnung vor dem abtrülligen Widertouff... (Zurich: Froschauer, 1527).

[1] Any of a number of writings of Hubmaier and Denk could have been used. See W. O. Lewis and G. D. Davidson, The Writings of Balthasar Hubmaier, trans. by Davidson, 3 vols. (MS, 1939, at William Jewell College, Liberty, Mo.; microfilm at University of Chicago and Goshen College). See also Walter Fellmann, Hans Denck Schriften, Quellen zur Geschichte der Täufer, Bd. VI, 2. Teil (Gütersloh: Bertelsmann, 1956).

[Jakob Dachser], Ein Göttlich vnnd gründtlich Offenbarung: von den warhafftigen Widertauffern: mit Götlicher Warheit angezaigt ([Augsburg: P. Ulhart], 1527).

Eitelhans Langenmantel, Dies ist ain Anzayg: einem meynem, etwann vertrauten Gesellen über seine hartte Widerpart, des Sacrament und anders betreffend (Nürnberg, 1526); Ain kurtzer Begriff von den Alten und Newen Papisten auch von den rechten und wahren Christen ([?], 1526); Ain kurzer Anzayg, wie doctor M. Luther ain Zayt hör hatt etliche Schrifften lassen ausgeen vom Sacrament, die doch straks wider einander ([?], 1527).

Stoffel Eleutherobion [von Freisleben], Vom warhafftigen Tauff Joannis/ Christi vnd der Aposteln... ([Worms: Schöffer], 1528).

[2] Letter to Christian Beyer, December (?), 1528, CR, I, 1012.

Melanchthon's later works against the Anabaptists also. On the occasion when Melanchthon interrogated the Anabaptists at Jena he wrote a terse report to Luther.[1] Rhegius among others kept him informed on Münster.[2] Although snatches of information reached Luther from a wide circle of friends and acquaintances, some of it no better than rumor in character,[3] it is reasonable to suppose that Menius and Melanchthon constituted his principal sources of information anent Anabaptism in the years after 1528.

Menius knew them personally. Melanchthon had more than a nodding acquaintance with their ideas, knew a few of them personally, but used secondhand information for the most part. Luther relied on secondhand information exclusively. What did the three do with these sources? Which Anabaptists come to the front as typical in their accounts? What kind of "Anabaptism" emerged in their picture of the movement?

Menius illustrated a number of his accusations in his 1530 work. He called largely on Rink as a disciple of Müntzer, and secondly on the master himself.[4] He cited the Reinhardsbrunn group several times as disciples of Müntzer.[5] He referred to Römer, Hans Denk, and the gang around Augustin Bader.[6] By 1544 he did not illustrate his points with descriptions of Anabaptist activities. He merely made passing reference to certain Anabaptists, assuming that his readers were well enough acquainted with the contemporary literature on the sect so as to require no explanation on his part. Thomas Müntzer and the Münsterites were his overwhelming favorites.[7]

In Melanchthon's writings there are no references to specific Anabaptists. His information concerning the Anabaptist ingress into Erfurt

---

[1] Letter to Luther, December 6, 1535, *CR*, II, 1005–06.

[2] Luther wrote the foreword to Rhegius' *Widderlegung der Münsterischen newen Valentinianer vnd Donatisten...* (Wittenberg: Georg Rhaw, 1535).

[3] See: a. Letter to Johannes, Prince of Anhalt, October 20, 1534, *WB*, VII, 111–12. Luther referred here to information from an unidentified Master Franciscus.

b. *Tischreden*, undated, *EA*, LXI, 82–83, when Luther referred to a letter from the Abbot of Fulda concerning the "Prophet" and his group.

c. *Tischreden*, August 14, 1538, *EA*, LXI, 89–90. Here Luther received some information from a woman of Freiburg, the wife of Burgermeister Wolf Lose.

[4] Three of his five references to Rink were to his statements or activities around 1525, although all three would have been confirmed by the post-1528 Rink also. See Menius, Der *Widdertauffer*, pp. E2v., H4r., L2v., Q2r., ar. for Rink; and pp. Fv., G4r.–v., H4r. for Müntzer.

[5] *Ibid.*, pp. G4r.–v., K3r., Vv.

[6] *Ibid.*, pp. ar., E2r., bv.

[7] He referred to Rink on only one occasion and I suspect this to be the 1525 disciple of Müntzer. See above, p. 202.

in December, 1527, must have had Römer at its center, but this is only a surmise.[1] There is a faint possibility that be connected the Steyr, Austria movement with that in Thuringia in 1527, both of which owed much to Hans Hut.[2] There is no indication whatsoever that Melanchthon knew of Hut however. For Melanchthon one figure of importance did loom as Anabaptist, namely the anti-trinitarian Johannes Campanus.[3]

Luther referred briefly on a few occasions to specific Anabaptists or groups of Anabaptists. He knew Melchior Hofmann, but not as an Anabaptist.[4] He heard of the "Prophet" and his gang.[5] His other bits of information concerned the same type of Anabaptist, the wild, irrational crackpot.[6]

So much for the post-1525 figures. The pre-1525 "Anabaptists" were known much better, and referred to more frequently, by Melanchthon and Luther. Anabaptism was exemplified best of all by the first "Anabaptists," the *Schwärmer*: the Zwickau Prophets, Carlstadt, and Müntzer. This identification of Anabaptists with *Schwärmer* is encountered repeatedly in the writings of all three of the Lutherans. It is seen the most clearly in their consideration of the question of the origins of the movement.

Menius did not know much about Carlstadt and the Zwickau

---

[1] Letter of Melanchthon to Spalatin, December 18, 1527, *CR*, I, 913–14.

[2] Letter of Melanchthon to Luther and Bugenhagen, September 16, 1527, *WB*, IV, 249–50.

[3] Letter of Melanchthon to Myconius, January, 1530, *CR*, II, 13. Campanus was born in the Lowlands, received a humanist education, studied theology at Cologne and was expelled for attacking the educational system there. By 1528 he was studying in Wittenberg, after he had embraced Reformation views while living in the Jülich region. He thought his understanding of Scripture was a unique revelation of the Spirit to him. He considered himself called to mediate between Luther and Zwingli at Marburg, but he was not permitted to speak. His concept of the Lord's Supper differed from both Luther's and Zwingli's. After his departure from Wittenberg his views on the Trinity became known. When he returned in 1530 the Elector imprisoned him for anti-trinitarianism. Melanchthon disputed with him in jail. Melanchthon considered further discussions with him useless. He spent the remainder of his life wandering about Germany and the Lowlands, including a 20-year imprisonment in Jülich. He died around 1575. He disclosed his peculiar views in a number of writings from *ca.* 1530 on. He considered Christ a created being, the first-born son of God. The Holy Spirit was not a personality in itself. It was a moral power existing in man. Melanchthon was particularly struck by his views on Spirit as over against literal Scripture. (Brecher, "Campanus," *ADB*, III [1876], 729–31; Rembert, *op. cit.*, pp. 160–214, 242–64.) Melanchthon thought Campanus should be punished not only for sedition, but also for blasphemy. (Otto Ritschl, *op. cit.*, I, 283.) It was as a spiritualist and as a rejector of grace in the sacrament that Melanchthon related him to the Anabaptists. Melanchthon's interest in questioning the Jena Anabaptists on the Trinity probably stemmed from his conviction that the Anabaptists shared Campanus' view on the subject.

[4] See above, p. 244.

[5] *Tischreden, EA*, LXI, 83–83.

[6] *Tischreden, EA*, LXI, 89–90. Letter to Johannes, Prince of Anhalt, October, 1534. *WB*, VIII, 111–12.

Prophets. To him the leading figure of early Anabaptism was Thomas Müntzer. Müntzer planted the Anabaptist sect in Central Germany. His spirit lived in them after his death in 1525.[1] One suspects that Menius made this connection on two grounds: (1) the lineal descent, so to speak, of leadership from Müntzer to his follower Rink; (2) the similarity in doctrine, as Menius saw it. In both Müntzer and the Anabaptists he found a fundamental spiritualism which despised and rejected Scripture, and a rejection of baptism and the Lord's Supper as sacraments.[2]

Melanchthon did not ascribe so much to Müntzer as did Menius or Luther. This does not mean that he did not regard Müntzer as an Anabaptist. Rather, he had had more personal experience with the Prophets and Carlstadt. He encountered the trail of Carlstadt's teachings in people he examined on his first Thuringian church visitation, in the region of Carlstadt's Orlamünde parish. He was incensed at the mischief the man had done.[3] But more important than Müntzer and even Carlstadt were the Zwickau Prophets in Melanchthon's view of Anabaptist origins. The entire movement began with Storch and his followers. Melanchthon even considered Zwingli a disciple of Storch.[4] He found similarity of error – rejection of sacraments and sedition – in both the *Schwärmer* and the Anabaptists.[5]

In Luther the greatest emphasis falls on Müntzer and secondarily on Carlstadt. This reflected his own experience. Anabaptists in his mind had the spirit of Müntzer.[6] They followed in the footsteps of Carlstadt.[7] They were all part of a huge coterie of leftists who began with the

---

[1] Menius, *Von dem Geist*, p. B4r. In 1530 he did not feel compelled to prove, or even explicitly suggest, the connection between Müntzer and the Anabaptists. By his attitude toward Müntzer, it is immediately evident that he regarded him without any question as an Anabaptist.

[2] *Ibid.*, pp. Br.–v.

[3] Letter to Camerarius, August 11 or 12, 1527, *CR*, I, 881; letter to Camerarius, January 23, 1528, *CR*, I, 951–52.

[4] Letter to Myconius, February, 1530, *CR*, II, 17–18.

[5] In his letter to Henry VIII, August, 1538, Melanchthon gave Belgium as the place of Anabaptist origins. From there the movement spread to Friesland and Westphalia. (*CR*, III, 577–80.) I do not take this suggestion very seriously. Melanchthon was making the point that Anabaptists did not appear where true doctrine was preached; it would not do to attribute their origins to Storch or Müntzer in Central Germany where Lutheran doctrine was preached. Feige, Chancellor to Philip of Hesse, rejected Melanchthon's explanation of origins by refusing to include the Belgian origin of Anabaptism in his revision of Melanchthon's letter. (*TA, Hesse*, pp. 162–65.) In a report to Philip he declared that Anabaptism existed everywhere, unfortunately, and even more in Evangelical than in papal lands. It was not correct to write that Anabaptism existed only where the truth was preached. (Max Lenz, *Der Briefwechsel Landgraf Philipps mit Bucer*, I, 320, n. 3.)

[6] Letter to Johann Hess, January 27, 1528, *WB*, IV, 371–72.

[7] Letter to Wenzel Link, May 12, 1528, *WB*, IV, 457.

Prophets and continued with Müntzer; the group included Zwingli, too, despite his vehement protests to the contrary.[1]

Apart from specific references to the earlier *Schwärmer*, the reader of the three Lutherans against Anabaptism discovers the absolute identity of Anabaptist with *Schwärmer* in doctrine. The errors of the Anabaptists, especially to Luther and Melanchthon, were precisely the errors of the *Schwärmer*: subjectivity in religion running to excessive spiritualism, and sedition. All of them were recognizable by their symbol, their rejection of infant baptism. The Lutherans appear never seriously to have questioned the continuity of *Schwärmerei* in Anabaptism.[2]

There is one other Anabaptist manifestation that the Lutheran writers belabored in their picture of the sect: Münster. For all of them it stood as the example par excellence of Anabaptism's final stage of development. All Anabaptists would develop the debauchery and violence of the Münsterites if they had the opportunity to operate unhindered by civil authority. The degree of alarm which the three possessed with respect to Anabaptism derived from a genuine fear of just that kind of excess.[3]

Anabaptism to these Lutherans meant first the *Schwärmer*, then persons and groups like Römer, Rink as a disciple of Müntzer, Augustin Bader, Campanus, the Reinhardsbrunn group, the "Prophet," capped finally by the Münsterites. To this motley crew they added Zwingli. Where are the Rink of the 1528 hearing and later imprisonment, Alexander, Fritz Erbe, or any of the peaceful sort that one finds so frequently in the court records? The Anabaptists themselves protested the Lutherans' characterizations of them.[4] Melanchthon apparently was aware of some such protests.[5] Melanchthon at least admitted that other types did exist. But no useful purpose could be served in making distinctions among types of Anabaptists. Differences could be viewed

---

[1] Foreword to Menius' *Von dem Geist*, p. A2v.

[2] See John S. Oyer, "The Reformers Oppose the Anabaptists," *op. cit.*, pp. 210–13.

[3] For examples see Menius, *Von dem Geist*, p. J2r.; Melanchthon, *Verlegung*, p. A4v.; Luther, *Vorrede* to Rhegius' *Widderlegung der Münsterischen*, pp. A2r.–A4v.

[4] Schnabel, "Verantwortung," in *TA, Hesse*, pp. 165–80. Schnabel directed this against the Visitation order of the state church. Wappler, *Die Stellung Kursachsens*, p. 70.

One Anabaptist objected specifically to Melanchthon's *Verlegung*, declaring that there was not one true word in it. Wappler, *Inquisition und Ketzerprozesse*, p. 78.

Wiswedel and Friedmann, "The Anabaptists Answer Melanchthon," *MQR*, XXIX (1955), 212–31. This was a protest to the *Prozess* of 1557.

[5] Melanchthon, *Das Weltliche Oberkeitt*, *CR*, III, 196. Clearly none of the items cited in n. 4, this page could have caused Melanchthon to make allowance for Anabaptist protest, since all of them were aired or published after 1536. Melanchthon must have had still another protest in mind.

as differences in degree only. The devil had torn all of them, some more and some less; but they all served the same master.[1]

Here was a completely disordered picture, with *Schwärmer* and spiritualists predominating. The confusion is understandable in view of the Anabaptists' own relative uncertainty as to who belonged to their church.[2] One is left with the unmistakable impression, however, that the Lutheran gallery of Anabaptist rogues was the product of deliberate choice.

The refusal to distinguish among different groups of Anabaptists brought inaccuracies and contradictions into the Lutheran accounts. Here we have to deal not only with the inadequacies of the Lutheran understanding, some of which has already been pointed out: their exaggeration of spiritualism and failure to see literalism, and their failure to see the earnestness of Anabaptist ethics in their exaggeration of the "seditious" ideas of the radicals.[3] We have to deal rather with certain contradictions which resulted in a distorted and thus inaccurate picture of Anabaptists from their pens. Here are a few examples. Luther depicted Anabaptism as believing that the act of baptism was both necessary and useless for the soul's salvation. He believed they taught both nonresistance and also the Christian duty of raising the sword to extirpate the godless.[4] Menius had the Anabaptists denying the redemptive character of Christ's death, and at the same time denying the validity of the baptism of infants because infants were not capable of faith in Christ as Redeemer.[5] They denied the divinity of Christ and also his human nature.[6] As contradictions these could be explained on various grounds: lack of information, misinformation, or contradictions inherent in the Anabaptists themselves. The most important reason, however, was their refusal to distinguish among types of Anabaptists on the grounds that they were all tarred with the same brush. Indeed, it was impossible to know their doctrines well, precisely because they were good craftsmen in the exercise of their satanic master's art of dissimulation. Their one purpose was to subvert; therefore they argued both sides of a question at once if they could

---

[1] Melanchthon, *Wider das gotteslästerliche und schändliche Buch so zu Münster im Druck newlich ist ausgangen, etliche Propositiones, gestellt durch Phil. Melanchthon* (Nürnberg [?], 1535), printed in Walch, *Luther's sämmtliche Schriften* (1890), XX, Col. 1699. This is a second edition of his *Etliche Propositiones*.

[2] See above, pp. 101–06. See also Littell, *The Anabaptist View of the Church* (1st ed.), p. 49.

[3] See above, chap. vii.

3 See above, pp. 123–24, 127–28, 131–32.

[5] Menius, *Von dem Geist*, pp. J3v., K3r.

[6] *Ibid.*, p. J2v.

gain adherents thereby. One questioned only the effectiveness of their technique.

We come now to a fuller assessment of the Lutheran picture of Anabaptism as diabolical. The Anabaptists were Satan's minions in a vast cosmic struggle. The Lutherans could detect the demonic character of their opponents by their doctrine and also by their secrecy in spreading their ideas. They preferred darkness to light. The configuration of the charge by Luther and Menius has already been given.[1] Melanchthon held unquestionably much the same view. He had no difficulty discerning the diabolical nature of the Anabaptists.[2] What concerns us here is more the effect of this identification on the Lutherans' attitude toward the radicals, and subsequently the effect on their descriptions of the group.

The importance of the Anabaptists' diabolical origin for the Lutheran picture of the movement can scarcely be exaggerated. It meant on the one hand that the Lutherans could never view the Anabaptists as an earnest, sincere religious people. There was no pure religious motivation in them. Their religious appearances were only a sham. Their major purpose in life was to subvert the truth.

Luther was the kind of man who might have been able to appreciate their religious earnestness. Melanchthon even more so. There is something pathetic about Melanchthon's misunderstanding. He had the capability in mind and personality to understand very well indeed the aspirations of the best in Anabaptism. He was scholar enough to be able to make careful distinctions. With a minimum of effort he could have discovered the peaceful, God-fearing type of Anabaptist whom twentieth-century researchers find in abundance in the records. He could well have sympathized with their desire to live morally pure lives; he was distressed at the absence of ethical living among the Evangelicals. He had the personality to sympathize with their patience and steadfastness; but this he found to be a stubbornness characteristic, not of saints, but of devils. Because they were devils he could not imagine peaceful Anabaptists, except as some were forced to the peace of the forests and the isolated villages for refuge. Anabaptists differed in degree only, not in kind. They were all the spawn of their satanic master.

On the other hand Anabaptists as devils meant that the Lutherans

---

[1] See above, pp. 133–35, 194–97.
[2] Melanchthon, *Verlegung*, p. A4v. See Manschreck, *op. cit.*, pp. 106 ff. for Melanchthon's attitude on the devil.

did not feel constrained to inquire overly much concerning Anabaptist doctrines to fill out an absolutely accurate picture of the faith of the radicals. As a consequence that picture became fixed and unyielding. It could be added to; Melanchthon compiled a formidable catalogue of Anabaptist errors in the course of his polemical activity. But one added only more error in the sense of incrimination. To do even this was useless,[1] except as it served as a means for identifying Anabaptists by the unwary. Melanchthon's pictures of the group in the mid-1530's and in 1557 and Menius' picture of 1544 are stereotyped. The purpose for writing was essentially propagandistic: (1) to advertise to the unsuspecting the danger of the sect's ideas; (2) to persuade the interested that the group was heretical and diabolical; (3) to give due warning to magistrates who refused to kill the radicals that such tolerance in itself constituted a fall from the gospel and from grace.[2]

Two additional factors in the Lutheran distortion should be mentioned. Both were of great importance in formulating the basic attitudes of the Lutherans toward the radicals. One was the alarm at the rapid success of the Anabaptists among the lower classes, an alarm that grew into a deep-seated fear in the hearts of the Lutherans. For Luther himself this fear was much more a fear of revolution than one of dissolution of the Lutheran church.[3] Most of Melanchthon's brief references to Anabaptist error with respect to the rejection of the *ministerium verbi* can be seen in the light of his apprehension of the consequences of Anabaptist propaganda to the Lutheran church; he feared dissolution, or at least irreparable damage, more than Luther did. But he too was alarmed primarily at the potential threat to civil authority that he found in Anabaptist doctrine.[4] Menius feared both consequences about equally, it appears. His polemics emphasized the danger to the civil order more than that to the religious order because

---

[1] Erich Meissner, "Rechtssprechung über die Wiedertäufer und die antitäuferische Publizistik (MS dissertation at Göttingen, 1921), p. 91, rightly points out that Menius reduced the total number of errors listed in 1544 from those of 1530.

[2] *Ibid.*, p. 87 for the final idea. Meissner's treatment is generally excellent. Because he pointed his treatment to the juridical problems, he tended to overemphasize a kind of cold, calculated desire on the part of the Lutherans to find any means available to give them legal sanction to do what they wanted to do, namely kill the Anabaptists. He misses the genuineness of their anger at theological error and to a lesser extent their fear of Anabaptist success.

[3] Oyer, *op. cit.*, pp. 212–13 for summary views.

[4] *Ibid.*, pp. 214–15. Also above, p. 235, n. 2. See also Letter to Myconius, February, 1530, *CR*, II, 18, in which Melanchthon declares that Brenz was too mild in his opinion on how to handle Anabaptists; Brenz had had no experience with the fanatics and therefore did not know what damage they could do to the church.

those writings were designed primarily to convince the magistrates that stern measures were necessary.

The second factor is that of anger. This requires little comment. The Lutheran writings, particularly those from 1530 on, were written in the heat of anger. The Anabaptists would have tried the patience of a saint. But it is impossible to avoid calling into question the accuracy of the Lutheran reports on the grounds of the anger with which they were composed.

On the question of accuracy of the Lutheran writings there can be no doubt whatsoever. They were based too frequently on insufficient primary association with the radicals. They persist in thoroughly mixing the most diverse kinds of Anabaptists so-called. They reveal a want of understanding of the real Anabaptist position on various issues. They are indelibly colored with the view of Anabaptism as a literal outgrowth of Satan's kingdom. They were written for a propagandistic rather than a descriptive purpose. They were conceived in fear and anger. They are grossly inaccurate.

Inaccuracy does not mean complete uselessness as primary source material. The polemics can be used as a means of finding some of the fundamental differences of opinion between Lutherans and Anabaptists. They are by no means trustworthy by themselves for this purpose. Menius at least can be mined for some interesting material on Central German Anabaptism, material not found elsewhere. His information in general must be used with caution, preferably against the background of known views derived from Anabaptist sources. Where the latter is impossible his delineation of Anabaptist ideas must be judged by whether or not it conforms to general Anabaptist thought and practice. Obviously the polemics are useful as a means of determining what the three Lutherans thought the dangers of Anabaptism to be. But the usefulness of these materials, for an accurate knowledge of Anabaptist thought and practice, is very limited.

BIBLIOGRAPHY

I. BIBLIOGRAPHICAL AIDS

Bender, Harold S. "The Historiography of the Anabaptists," *MQR*, XXXI (1957), 88–104.

Catalogus der Werken over de Doopsgezinden en Hunne Geschiedenis aanwezig in de Bibliotheek der Vereenigde Doopsgezinde Gemeente te Amsterdam. Edited by J. G. Boekenoogen. Amsterdam: J. H. de Bussy, 1919.

Hege, Christian. "Mennonitische Literatur in zeitlicher Reihenfolge." Unpublished catalogue, typewritten in Fellbach, Germany, a copy of which is in the Mennonite Historical Library at Goshen College, Goshen, Indiana. 1949.

Koehler, Walter. "Das Täufertum in der neueren kirchenhistorischen Forschung," *ARG*, XXXVII (1940), 93–107; *ibid.*, XXXVIII (1941), 349–64; *ibid.*, XL (1943), 246–70; *ibid.*, XLI (1948), 164–86.

Krahn, Cornelius. "Historiography of the Mennonites in the Netherlands," *MQR*, XVIII (1944), 195–224.

Pauck, Wilhelm. "The Historiography of the German Reformation during the Past Twenty Years," *Church History*, X (1940), 305–40.

Schottenloher, Karl. *Bibliographie zur deutschen Geschichte im Zeitalter der Glaubensspaltung, 1517–1585*. 6 vols. Leipzig: Karl W. Hiersemann, 1933–1940.

Teufel, Eberhard. "Täufertum und Quäkertum im Lichte der neueren Forschung," *Theologische Rundschau*, XIII (1941), 21–57, 103–27, 183–97; *ibid.*, XIV (1942), 27–52, 124–54; *ibid.*, XV (1943), 56–80.

Williams, George H. "Studies in the Radical Reformation: A Bibliographical Survey, I and II," *Church History*, XXVII (1958), 46–69, 124–60.

II. REFERENCE WORKS

Allgemeine Deutsche Biographie. Edited by von Liliencron and Wegele for the Historische Commission bei der Königliche Akademie der Wissenschaften. 56 vols. Leipzig: Verlag von Duncker und Humblot, 1875–1912.

Benzing, Jacob. *Buchdruckerlexikon des 16. Jahrhunderts*. Frankfurt am Main: V. Klostermann [1952].

The Mennonite Encyclopedia. Edited by Harold S. Bender and C. Henry Smith. 4 vols. Scottdale, Pa.: Herald Press, 1955–1959.

Mennonitisches Lexikon. Edited by Christian Hege and Christian Neff. 3 vols. Frankfurt am Main and Weierhof: Selbstverlag der Herausgeber, 1913—.

Realencyklopädie für protestantische Theologie und Kirche. Edited by Albert Hauck. 3d ed. rev. 24 vols. Leipzig: J. C. Hinrichs, 1896–1913.

The New Schaff-Herzog Encyclopedia of Religious Knowledge. Edited by Samuel
M. Jackson. 12 vols. New York and London: Funk and Wagnalls, 1908–1912.

III. SOURCE MATERIALS

A. Luther

*D. Martin Luthers sowol in deutscher als lateinischer Sprache verfertigte und aus
der letztern in die erstere übersetzte sämtliche Schriften.* Edited by Johann Georg
Walch. 24 vols. Halle: J. J. Gebauer, 1739–1753.
Luthers sämmtliche Schriften, Vol. XX. Edited by Johann Georg Walch. St. Louis,
Mo.: Concordia Publishing House, 1890.
Dr. Martin Luther's sämmtliche Werke. Edited by J. G. Plockmann and J. K.
Irmischer. 67 vols. Erlangen: Heyder und Zimmer, 1826 ff.
Dr. Martin Luther's Briefe, Sendschreiben, und Bedenken. Edited by Wilhelm M.
de Wette. 6 vols. Berlin: G. Reimer, 1825–1856.
D. Martin Luther's Werke. Kritische Gesamtausgabe. Edited by J. K. F. Knaake,
G. Kawerau, *et al.* 57 vols. Weimar: H. Böhlau, 1883–1914.
*D. Martin Luther's Briefwechsel, D. Martin Luther's Werke, kritische Gesamtaus-
gabe.* Edited by Konrad Burdach *et al.* 11 vols. Weimar: H. Böhlau, 1930 ff.
Tischreden, D. Martin Luther's Werke, kritische Gesamtausgabe. Edited by Karl
Drescher. 6 vols. Weimar: H. Böhlau, 1912 ff.
Luther's Correspondence and Other Contemporary Letters. Translated and edited
by Preserved Smith and Charles Jacobs. 2 vols. Philadelphia: The Lutheran
Publication Society, 1918.
*Conversations with Luther. Selections from Recently Published Sources of the Table
Talk.* Translated and edited by Preserved Smith and Herbert Gallinger.
Boston: The Pilgrim Press [1915].
Works of Martin Luther. Edited by Adolph Spaeth and H. E. Jacobs *et al.* 6 vols.
Philadelphia: A. J. Holman, 1915–1932.
Luther, Martin. *Von der Widertauffe an zwen Pfarrherrn, ein Brief.* Wittemberg:
Georg Wachter, 1528.

B. Melanchthon

Philippi Melanthonis Opera. Corpus Reformatorum, Vols. I to XXVIII. Edited
by Carl G. Bretschneider and Bindseil. Halle: C. A. Schwetschke et Filium,
1834–1860.
Melanchthons Briefwechsel, Supplementa Melanchthoniana, Vol. I, Abt. 6. Edited
by Otto Clemen. Leipzig: Heinsius Nachfolger, 1926.
Melanchthons Werke in Auswahl. Edited by Robert Stupperich. 6 vols. (I, II, 1,
II, 2, and VI published to date). Gütersloh: C. Bertelsmann Verlag, 1951—.
The Loci Communes of Philip Melanchthon. Translated and edited by Charles L.
Hill. Boston: Meador Publishing Co., 1944.
Melanchthon, Philip. *Underricht Philip Melanchthon wider die Lere der Wider-
teuffer auss dem latein verdeutschet durch Just. Jonas.* Wittemberg, 1528.
—— *Etliche propositiones wider die Lehr der Widerteuffer, gestelt durch Philip Me-
lanchthon.* No publisher, 1535.
—— *Das weltliche Oberkeitt den Widertaufferen mit leiblicher Straff zu weren schuldig
sey/ Etlicher Bedenken zu Wittemberg.* Wittemberg: Joseph Klug, 1536.
—— *Verlegung etlicher unchristlicher Artickel welche die Wiedertäufer vorgeben.*
Wittenberg: Georg Rhaw [1536].
The Augsburg Confession. A Collection of Sources with an Historical Introduction.
Edited by Johann M. Reu. Chicago: Wartburg Publishing House, 1930.

Camerarius, Joachim. *De Philippi Melanchthonis ortv, totius vitae cvrricvlo et morte.* ... Leipzig, n.d.

C. Menius

Menius, Justus. *Der Widdertauffer Lere vnd Geheimnis aus heiliger Schrifft widderlegt/* .... Wittemberg: Nickel Schirlentz, 1530.
— *Wie ein iglicher Christ gegen allerley Lere, gut und böse, nach Gottes Befelh, sich gebürlich halten sol.* Wittemberg: Nickel Schirlentz, 1538.
— *Von dem Geist der Widerteuffer, mit Vorrede Luthers.* Wittemberg: Nickel Schirlentz, 1544.
— *Von den Blutfreunden aus der Widertauff.* Erfurt: Gerasius Sthürmer, 1551.

D. Other Sixteenth Century Writings

Bader, Johannes. *Brüderliche Warnung für dem newen Abgöttischen Orden der Widertäuffer/* .... No publisher, 1527.
Bucer, Martin. *Getrewe Warnung der Prediger des Euangelij zü Strassburg/ vber die Artickel/ so Jacob Kautz Prediger zü Wormbs/ kürtzlich hat lassen aussgohn/* .... Strassburg, 1527.
[Link, Wenzel]. *Grundtliche Vnterrichtung/eins erbern Rats der Statt Nürmberg/* ... *wider etliche verfürische Lere der Widertauffer/* .... Nürmberg: Jobst Gutknecht [1527].
Oecolampadius, Johannes. *Vnderrichtung von dem Widertauff/ von der Oberkeit/ vnd von dem Eyd/ auff Carlins N. Widertauffers Artickel* .... Basel: Andreas Cratander, 1527.
— *Ein Gesprech etlicher Predicanten zu Basel, gehalten mit etlichen Bekennern des Widertouffs.* Basel: Valentin Curio, 1525.
Rhegius, Urbanus. *Wider den Newen Taufforden/ Notwendige Warnung an alle Christglaubigen.* Augsburg: [Heinr. Steiner], 1527.
Schmid, Conrad. *Ein christliche Ermanung zu warer Hoffnung in Gott vnd Warnung vor dem abtrülligen Widertouff, der da abwyset von Gott, an die christlichen Amplüt zu Grünigen.* Zurich: Froschauer, 1527.
Huldreich Zwinglis sämtliche Werke. Edited by E. Egli, G. Finsler, and W. Koehler. 10 vols. Vols. LXXXVIII–XCVII of *Corpus Reformatorum.* Leipzig: Heinsius Nachfolger, 1905–1929.
Zwingli, Huldreich. "Refutation of the Tricks of the Catabaptists," translated by Henry Preble and George Gilmore and printed by Samuel M. Jackson in *Selected Works of Huldreich Zwingli.* Philadelphia: University of Pennsylvania Press, 1901.
Hans Denck Schriften. Vol. XXIV of *Quellen und Forschungen zur Reformationsgeschichte.* 1. Teil, Bibliographie, edited by Georg Baring. Gütersloh: C. Bertelsmann, 1955.
Hans Denck Schriften. Vol. XXIV of *Quellen und Forschungen zur Reformationsgeschichte.* 2. Teil, Religiöse Schriften, edited by Walter Fellmann. Gütersloh: C. Bertelsmann, 1956.
[von Freisleben], Stoffel Eleutherobion. *Vom warhafftigen Tauff Joannis/ Christi vnd der Aposteln* .... [Worms: Peter Schöffer], 1528.
"The Writings of Balthasar Hubmaier." Typewritten MS translated by G. D. Davidson and collected by W. O. Lewis. 3 vols. William Jewel College, Liberty, Mo., 1939.
[Dacher, Jakob]. *Ein göttlich vnd grundlich Offenbarung: von den warhafftigen Wiederteufferen; mit göttlichen Warheit angezeigt.* No publisher, 1527.
Langenmantel, Eitelhans. *Ain kurzer Anzayg, wie doctor M. Luther ain Zayt hör*

*hatt etliche Schrifften lassen ausgeen vom Sacrament, die doch straks wider ein-
ander.* No publisher, 1527.

E. Collections

Briefwechsel Landgraf Philipps des Grossmüthigen von Hessen mit Bucer. Edited
by Max Lenz. 3 vols. Leipzig: S. Hirzel, 1880–1891.
Quellen zur Geschichte der Wiedertäufer. Vol. I, edited by Gustav Bossert, Herzog-
tum Württemberg. Leipzig: M. Heinsius Nachfolger, 1930.
Spiritual and Anabaptist Writers. Vol. XXV of *Library of Christian Classics.*
Edited by George Williams and Angel Mergal. Philadelphia: The Westminster
Press, 1957.
Thomas Müntzers Briefwechsel. Edited by Heinrich Boehmer and Paul Kirn.
Leipzig and Berlin: B. G. Teubner, 1931.
Urkundliche Quellen zur hessischen Reformationsgeschichte, Vol. IV. Edited by
G. Franz *et al.* Marburg: N. G. Elwert'sche Verlagshandlung, 1951.
Wappler, Paul. *Die Stellung Kursachsens und des Landgrafen Philipp von Hessen
zur Täuferbewegung.* Münster i. W.: Aschendorffschen Buchhandlung, 1910.
— *Die Täuferbewegung in Thüringen von 1526–1584.* Jena: Gustav Fischer, 1913.

IV. SPECIAL STUDIES

Bainton, Roland H. "The Development and Consistency of Luther's Attitude to
Religious Liberty," *Harvard Theological Review,* XXII (1929), 107–49.
— "The Parable of the Tares as the Proof Text for Religious Liberty to the End
of the Sixteenth Century," *Church History,* I (1932), 67–99.
— *Here I Stand, A Life of Martin Luther.* New York and Nashville: Abingdon
Press, 1950.
Barge, Hermann. *Andreas Bodenstein von Karlstadt.* 2 vols. Leipzig: F. Brand-
stetter, 1905.
— *Frühprotestantisches Gemeindechristentum in Wittenberg und Orlamünde.*
Leipzig: M. Heinsius Nachfolger, 1909.
Bender, Harold S. "The Anabaptist Vision," *MQR,* XVIII (1944), 67–88.
— "The Anabaptist Theology of Discipleship," *MQR,* XXIV (1950), 25–32.
— *Conrad Grebel, ca. 1498–1526.* Goshen, Ind.: Mennonite Historical Society,
1950.
— "The Zwickau Prophets, Thomas Müntzer, and the Anabaptists," *MQR,*
XXVII (1953), 3–16.
Berbig, Georg. "Die Wiedertäufer im Amt Königsberg i. Fr. i. J. 1527/28,"
Deutsche Zeitschrift für Kirchenrecht, XIII (1903), 291–353.
— "Die Wiedertäuferei im Ortslande zu Franken, im Zusammenhang mit dem
Bauernkrieg," *Deutsche Zeitschrift für Kirchenrecht,* XXII (1912), 378–403.
Boehmer, Heinrich. "Thomas Müntzer und das jüngste Deutschland," *Ge-
sammelte Aufsätze.* Gotha: Perthes, 1927. Pp. 187–222.
Bornkamm, Heinrich. "Äusserer und innerer Mensch bei Luther und den
Spiritualisten," *Imago Dei. Beiträge zur theologischen Anthropologie Gustav
Krüger zum siebzigsten Geburtstag.* Edited by Heinrich Bornkamm. Giessen:
A. Töpelmann, 1932. Pp. 85–109.
— *Luthers Geistige Welt.* Gütersloh: C. Bertelsmann, 1953.
Brandt, Otto. *Thomas Müntzer, sein Leben und seine Schriften.* Jena: E. Die-
derichs, 1933.
Brinkel, Karl. *Die Lehre Luthers von der fides infantium bei der Kindertaufe.* Vol.
VII of *Theologische Arbeiten,* edited by Hans Urner. Berlin: Evangelische
Verlagsanstalt, 1958.

Burkhardt, C. A. H. *Geschichte der sächsischen Kirchen- und Schulvisitationen, 1524 bis 1545.* Leipzig: Grunow, 1879.

Clauss, R. D. "Kleine Beiträge zur Geschichte der Wiedertäufer in Franken," *Zeitschrift für bayrische Kirchengeschichte*, XV (1940), 105ff.; *ibid.*, XVI (1941), 165ff.

Clemen, Otto. "Zur Geschichte des 'Wiedertäufers' Melchior Rink," *Monatshefte der Comenius-Gesellschaft*, IX (1900), 113–16.

Eberlein, Karl. "Auf dem Wege zu einer neuen Wertung Müntzers," *Mühlhäuser Geschichtsblätter*, XXVII (1926–1927), 210–13.

Ellinger, Georg. *Philipp Melanchthon. Ein Lebensbild.* Berlin: R. Gaertner, 1902.

Fast, Heinold. "The Dependence of the First Anabaptists on Luther, Erasmus, and Zwingli," *MQR*, XXX (1956), 104–19.

— "Heinrich Bullinger und die Täufer." Unpublished Doctor's dissertation, Theologische Fakultät, University of Heidelberg, 1957.

Fast, Heinold, and Yoder, John H. "How To Deal with Anabaptists: An Unpublished Letter of Heinrich Bullinger," *MQR*, XXXIII (1959), 83–95.

Forell, George W. *Faith Active in Love. An Investigation of the Principles Underlying Luther's Social Ethics.* New York: The American Press, 1954.

Friedmann, Robert. "Über Thomas Müntzer (Sammelreferat)," *Mitteilungen des Österreichischen Instituts für Geschichtsforschung*, XLVII (1933), 90–97.

— "The Schleitheim Confession and Other Doctrinal Writings of the Swiss Brethren in a Hitherto Unknown Edition," *MQR*, XVI (1942), 82–98.

— "Anabaptism and Protestantism," *MQR*, XXIV (1950), 12–24.

— "A Critical Discussion of Meihuizen's Study of 'Spiritual Trends'," *MQR*, XXVIII (1954), 148–54.

— "Thomas Müntzer's Relation to Anabaptism," *MQR*, XXXI (1957), 75–86.

— "The Doctrine of the Two Worlds," *The Recovery of the Anabaptist Vision. A Sixtieth Anniversary Tribute to Harold S. Bender.* Edited by Guy F. Hershberger. Scottdale, Pa.: Herald Press, 1957. Pp. 105–18.

Froom, Leroy E. *The Prophetic Faith of Our Fathers.* Vol. II of 4 vols., Pre-Reformation and Reformation, Restoration, and Second Departure. Washington, D.C.: Review and Herald, 1948.

Hartmann, Julius, and Jäger, Karl. *Johann Brenz, nach gedruckten und ungedruckten Quellen.* 2 vols. Hamburg: F. Perthes, 1840–1842.

Hege, Christian. *Die Täufer in der Kurpfalz.* Frankfurt am Main: Hermann Minjon, 1908.

— "The Early Anabaptists in Hesse," *MQR*, V (1931), 157–78.

Herrlinger. *Die Theologie Melanchthons in ihrer geschichtlichen Entwicklung.* Gotha: Perthes, 1879.

Heyer, Fritz. *Der Kirchenbegriff der Schwärmer.* Jahrgang 56 of *Schriften des Vereins für Reformationsgeschichte.* Leipzig: Heinsius Nachfolger, 1939.

Hillerbrand, Hans J. "The Anabaptist View of the State," *MQR*, XXXII (1958), 83–110.

Hinrichs, Carl. *Luther und Müntzer. Ihre Auseinandersetzung über Obrigkeit und Widerstandsrecht.* Vol. XXIX of *Arbeiten zur Kirchengeschichte*, edited by Aland, Eltester, and Rückert. Berlin: W. de Gruyter, 1952.

Hochhuth, Karl W. H. "Mittheilungen aus den protestantischen Secten-Geschichte in der hessischen Kirche: Landgraf Philipp und die Wiedertäufer," *Zeitschrift für die historische Theologie*, XXVIII (1858), 538–644; *ibid.*, XXIX (1859), 167–234.

Holl, Karl. "Luther und die Schwärmer," chapter vii of *Gesammelte Aufsätze zur Kirchengeschichte.* Tübingen: J. C. B. Mohr-Paul Siebeck, 1923.

Jacobs, Eduard. "Die Wiedertäufer am Harz," *Zeitschrift des Harz-Vereins für Geschichte und Altertumskunde*, XXXII (1899), 423–536.
Jordan. "Wiedertäufer in Mühlhausen," *Mühlhäuser Geschichtsblätter*, XV (1915), 35–50.
Keller, Ludwig. "Der sog. Anabaptismus am Harz im 16. Jahrhundert," *Monatshefte der Comenius-Gesellschaft*, IX (1900), 182–85.
Kiwiet, Jan J. "The Life of Hans Denck," *MQR*, XXXI (1957), 227–59.
— "The Theology of Hans Denck," *MQR*, XXXII (1958), 3–27.
Klassen, Herbert C. "Some Aspects of the Teachings of Hans Hut (*ca.* 1490–1527)." Unpublished Master's dissertation, Department of History, University of British Columbia, 1958.
Köstlin, Julius. *Luthers Theologie in ihrer geschichtlichen Entwicklung und ihrem inneren Zusammenhange*. Stuttgart: J. F. Steinkopf, 1863.
Krahn, Cornelius. *Menno Simons, 1496–1561*. Karlsruhe: H. Schneider, 1936.
Kretschmer, Konrad. *Historische Geographie von Mitteleuropa*. Munich and Berlin: R. Oldenbourg, 1904.
Kühn, Johannes. *Toleranz und Offenbarung*. Leipzig: Felix Meiner, 1923.
Linden, Friedrich O. zur. *Melchior Hofmann, ein Prophet der Wiedertäufer*. Haarlem: De Erven F. Bohn, 1885.
Littell, Franklin H. *The Anabaptist View of the Church*. Vol. VIII of *Studies in Church History*, edited by W. Pauck and J. H. Nichols. [Berne, Ind.]: American Society of Church History, 1952. 2d rev. ed.; Boston: Star King Press, 1958.
— "Spiritualizers, Anabaptists and the Church," *MQR*, XXIX (1955), 34–43.
— "The Anabaptist Concept of the Church," *The Recovery of the Anabaptist Vision*. Edited by Guy F. Hershberger. Scottdale, Pa.: Herald Press, 1957. Pp. 119–34.
Lohmann, Annemarie. *Zur geistlichen Entwicklung Thomas Müntzers*. Leipzig: B. G. Teubner, 1931.
Mackinnon, James. *Luther and the Reformation*. London and New York: Longmans, Green and Co., 1925–1930.
Manschreck, Clyde L. *Melanchthon. The Quiet Reformer*. New York and Nashville: Abingdon Press, 1958.
Maurer, Wilhelm. "Neue Veröffentlichungen zur Täufergeschichte," *Hessisches Jahrbuch für Landesgeschichte*, II (1952), 176–82.
— "Luther und die Schwärmer," *Schriften des Theologischen Konvents Augsburgischen Bekenntnisses*. Edited by Fr. Hübner. Berlin-Spandau: Lutherisches Verlagshaus, 1952. Heft 6, pp. 7–37.
— "Gestalten aus der hessischen Täufergeschichte," *Pastoralblatt für Kurhessen-Waldeck*, Jahrgang 55 (1953), Nr. 1 (February), pp. 10–12; *ibid.*, Nr. 2 (April), pp. 5–8.
Meissner, Erich. "Die Rechtssprechung über die Wiedertäufer und die antitäuferische Publizistik." Unpublished Doctor's dissertation, Juristische Fakultät, University of Göttingen, 1921.
Meihuizen, H. W. "Spiritualistic Tendencies and Movements among the Dutch Mennonites of the 16th and 17th Centuries," *MQR*, XXVII (1953), 259–304.
Müller, Karl. *Luther und Karlstadt*. Tübingen: J. C. B. Mohr, 1907.
Müller, Nikolaus. *Die Wittenberger Bewegung, 1521 und 1522*. Leipzig: Heinsius Nachfolger, 1911.
Neumann, Gerhard J. "Eschatologische und chiliastische Gedanken in der Reformationszeit, besonders bei den Täufern," *Die Welt als Geschichte*, XIX (1959), 58–66.

Oyer, John S. "The Writings of Melanchthon against the Anabaptists," *MQR*, XXVI (1952), 259–79.

— "The Writings of Luther against the Anabaptists," *MQR*, XXVII (1953), 100–10.

— "The Reformers Oppose the Anabaptist Theology," *The Recovery of the Anabaptist Vision*. Edited by Guy F. Hershberger. Scottdale, Pa.: Herald Press, 1957. Pp. 202–18.

Preus, Herman A. *The Communion of Saints*. Minneapolis, Minn.: Augsburg Publishing House, 1948.

Rembert, Karl. *Die Wiedertäufer im Herzogtum Jülich*. Berlin: Gaertner, 1899.

Richard, James W. *Philip Melanchthon, the Protestant Preceptor of Germany, 1497–1560*. New York and London: G. P. Putnam, 1898.

Rietschel, Ernest. *Das Problem der unsichtbar-sichtbaren Kirche bei Luther, mit einem Anhang: "Die Kirche bei Melanchthon," Schriften des Vereins für Reformationsgeschichte*, Jahrgang 50. Leipzig: M. Heinsius Nachfolger, 1932.

Ritschl, Albrecht. "Witzels Abkehr vom Luthertum," *Zeitschrift für Kirchengeschichte*, II (1878), 386–417.

Ritschl, Otto. *Dogmengeschichte des Protestantismus*. 4 vols. Leipzig: J. C.Hinrichs, 1908–1927.

Rödel, Friedrich. "Die anarchischen Tendenzen bei den Wiedertäufern des Reformationszeitalters dargestellt auf Grund ihrer Obrigkeitsanschauung." Unpublished Doctor's dissertation, Philosophische Fakultät, University of Erlangen, 1950.

Rogge, Joachim. *Der Beitrag des Predigers Jakob Strauss zur frühen Reformationsgeschichte*. Vol. VI of *Theologische Arbeiten*, edited by Hans Urner. Berlin: Evangelische Verlagsanstalt, 1957.

Schaff, Harold H. "The Anabaptists, the Reformers, and Civil Government," *Church History*, I (1932), 27–46.

Schlüter, Otto and Oskar August, hrbg. *Atlas des Saale- und mittleren Elbegebietes*. 1. Teil. 2. Auflage. Leipzig: Verlag Enzyklopädie, 1959.

Schmidt, Gustav Lebrecht. *Justus Menius, der Reformator Thüringens*. 2 vols. Gotha: Perthes, 1867.

Schwiebert, Ernest G. *Luther and His Times*. St. Louis: Concordia Publishing House, 1950.

Seeberg, Erich. "Der Gegensatz zwischen Zwingli, Schwenckfeld, und Luther," *Reinhold-Seeberg Festschrift*, I, 43–80. Edited by Wilhelm Koepp. Leipzig: Deichert, D. Werner Scholl, 1929.

Sehling, Emil. *Die evangelischen Kirchenordnungen des XVI. Jahrhunderts*. 6 vols. Leipzig: O. R. Reisland, and Tübingen: J. C. B. Mohr-Paul Siebeck, 1902—.

Smith, Preserved. *The Life and Letters of Martin Luther*. Boston and New York: Houghton Mifflin Co., 1911.

Steck, Karl Gerhard. "Luther und die Schwärmer," *Theologische Studien*, Heft 44. Edited by Karl Barth. Zollikon-Zurich: Evangelischer Verlag, 1955.

Stupperich, Robert. *Der Humanismus und die Wiedervereinigung der Konfessionen*. Jahrgang 53 of *Schriften des Vereins für Reformationsgeschichte*. Leipzig: M. Heinsius Nachfolger, 1936.

— "Melanchthon und die Täufer," *Kerygma und Dogma*, III (1957), 150–69.

Wappler, Paul. *Inquisition und Ketzerprozesse in Zwickau zur Reformationszeit*. Leipzig: M. Heinsius Nachfolger, 1908.

— *Thomas Münzer in Zwickau und die Zwickauer Propheten*. Zwickau: R. Zückler, 1908.

Wiswedel, Wilhelm. "War Thomas Müntzer wirklich 'der Urheber der grossen Taufbewegung'?" *Mühlhäuser Geschichtsblätter*, XXX (1929–1930), 268–73.

—*Bilder und Führergestalten aus dem Täufertum*. 3 vols. Kassel: J. G. Oncken, 1928–1952.

Wiswedel, Wilhelm, and Friedmann, Robert. "The Anabaptists Answer Melanchthon: The Handbuechlein of 1558," *MQR*, XXIX (1955), 212–31.

Yoder, John H. *Täufertum und Reformation in der Schweiz. Die Gespräche zwischen Täufern und Reformatoren, 1523–1538*. Karlsruhe: Menn. Geschichtsverein, 1962.

Zschäbitz, Gerhard. *Zur mitteldeutschen Wiedertäuferbewegung nach dem grossen Bauernkrieg*. Berlin: Rütten und Loenig, 1958.

INDEX

Adiaphora, 209
Adultery, 12, 58, 103n, 168, 193, 206-08
*Adversus Anabaptistas Philippi Melan-
thonis Iudicium,* 144-54
Alexander, 45n, 47, 65, 71, 85, 97, 105,
163, 248
Allstedt, 16-18, 108
Althamer, Andreas, 229
Amsdorf, Nicolas, 13f, 33, 180, 210
Anabaptist (Anabaptism)
Definition, 5
Ana. reaction to name, 81
Central German
Origins, 41, 106-13
Relation to Müntzer, 106-10, 246-
49
Relation to Denk, 111
Relation to Strauss, 112
Pre-Reformation groups, 113
Relation to Lutherans, 207, 212
Relation to others, 247n
Reasons for appearance, 176, 201,
207, 247n
Geographical configuration, 46
Sources about, 42-45
Groups
Franconian, 47-50
Römer, 50
Reinhardsbrunn, 50f
Sorga, 51f, 65
Rink, 52-64
Berka, 65
Moravia, 66
Erbe, 68-71
Harz, 71f
Hesse, 72f
Kraut, 162-67
Fringe groups
"Prophet," 67
Krug, 68
"Blood Brothers," 74, 205-09
Size of movement, 74 and n
Doctrines

Use of theology, 75, 211f
Salvation, 75-77, 83f, 163f, 214-25
Baptism, 78-83, 84f, 107-09, 164
Spirit and Spiritualism, 85-89,
109f, 165, 226-31
Ethics, 89-98, 109f, 164-66, 219-
25, 235-37
Christology, 98f, 137, 163
Lord's Supper, 45, 99f, 110, 166
Eschatology, 109, 110f, 237f
Brotherhood, 101-06
Relation to Evangelicals
Attacks on Ev., 89-91, 167, 174,
184, 203, 214, 222f, 232
Luther's critique of, 116-39
Melanchthon's critique of, 147-78
Menius' critique of, 179-210
Ana. influence on Ev., 74
Angersbach, Adam, 89, 103
Antichrist, 100, 180
Apocalypticism, 10, 48, 50, 85, 100 and n,
181, 193
Ascherham, Gabriel, 66
Augsburg, 48, 158, 173, 177, 209
Augsburg Confession (Melanchthon), 159f
Augustine of Hippo, 22, 146f
On baptism, 14, 38, 229
On war, 91
Augustinian Order, 14, 23, 28, 39, 129
Aurachsmüller, 84
Austria, 47f, 98, 241f

Bader, Augustin, 194, 245, 248
Bader, Johannes, 54f, 79, 241
Baptism (and rebaptism) (See also Origi-
nal Sin)
Importance of issue, 81-83, 184, 213
Infant baptism, 10-11, 21, 28, 56, 80-
82, 107, 119-22, 147-51, 159, 164,
169, 172f, 176, 184, 217f
Believers' baptism (adult), 11, 81, 107f,
120, 123, 184, 189f
As a sacrament, 11, 29, 78, 124, 146

JOHN STANLEY OYER
1925-1998

THE MENNONITE QUARTERLY REVIEW announced the death of John Stanley Oyer of Goshen, Indiana on May 4, 1998. Oyer was best-known internationally as the editor of MQR (1966-74 and 1977-92) and as a scholar of sixteenth-century Anabaptism.

Born on January 5, 1925, the son of Noah and Siddie Oyer, John grew up in Goshen, Indiana where his father served for a period of time as dean of Goshen College.

When, in 1951, after finishing his undergraduate degree at Goshen College, Oyer embarked on a master's program in history at Harvard, he brought to his studies fresh memories of European cities smoldering in ashes and a keen awareness of the fragility of human civilization, which profoundly shaped his historical studies and his teaching. In his University of Chicago doctoral dissertation, for example, later published as *Lutheran Reformers Against the Anabaptists* (Nijhoff, 1964), Oyer recognized in the angry Lutheran polemics against the Anabaptists a deeper concern to preserve order in a society seemingly on the verge of chaos. And in his careful studies of Anabaptist martyrdom, he painstakingly sought to interpret the worldview, not only of the heroic martyr, but of the executioner and the Anabaptist recanter as well.

In the fall of 1955 Oyer began teaching in the Goshen College history department, a vocation that would continue for the next 38 years, interrupted only by several sabbatical leaves spent doing research in Europe.

During his 25-year tenure as editor of MQR, Oyer broadened the journal's inter-disciplinary scope and moved it beyond the self-affirming tone characteristic of the "Bender school" by opening its pages to a new generation of scholars, even though their findings were occasionally critical of traditional Mennonite historiography.

Later in life, he collaborated with Robert Kreider in writing *The Mirror of the Martyrs* (Good Books, 1990). The book highlighted his efforts, along with Kreider, to purchase 23 of the original copper plates etched by Dutch artist Jan Luyken to illustrate the 1685 edition of the *Martyrs' Mirror*. The plates eventually became the centerpiece of a traveling exhibit on Anabaptist martyrdom aimed at a popular audience.